Studies in International
Environmental Economics

Studies in International Environmental Economics

Edited by

INGO WALTER
New York University

A WILEY-INTERSCIENCE PUBLICATION

JOHN WILEY & SONS, New York • London • Sydney • Toronto

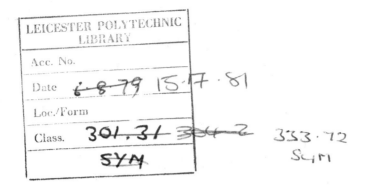
Library of Congress Cataloging in Publication Data:

Symposium on International Economic Dimensions of
    Environmental Management, New York, 1975.
    Studies in international environmental economics.

    "A Wiley-Interscience publication."
    Includes bibliographical references.
    1. Pollution—Economic aspects—Congresses.   2. En-
vironmental policy—Congresses.   3. International
economic relations—Congresses.   I. Walter, Ingo.
II. Title.

HC79.P55S95   1975   301.31   75-38614
ISBN 0-471-91927-6

Printed in the United States

10 9 8 7 6 5 4 3 2 1

Symposium on International Economic Dimensions of Environmental Management

PARTICIPANTS

Jaleel Ahmad

Associate Professor of Economics, Sir George Williams University, and Consultant, UNCTAD Secretariat, Geneva

Jean-Philippe Barde

Economist, Environment and Industry Division, Environment Directorate, Organization for Economic Cooperation and Development, Paris

William J. Baumol

Professor of Economics, New York University and Princeton University

Al Brueckmann

Economic Division, Office of Planning and Evaluation, United States Environmental Protection Agency

Ruben Brown

Executive Director, Council on the Environment of New York City

John A. Butlin

Lecturer in Economics, University of Manchester and Visiting Professor of Economics, University of British Columbia

Samprit Chatterjee

Professor of Statistics, Graduate School of Business Administration, New York University

Toby Clark

Senior Economist, Council on Environmental Quality, Washington, D.C.

Ralph C. d'Arge

Professor of Economics, University of Wyoming, and Consultant, Mathematica, Inc., Princeton, N.J.

William R. Dill

Professor of Management and Dean, Graduate School of Business Administration, New York University

Jacob S. Dreyer	Assistant Professor of Economics, New York University
Guy Erb	Economist, Overseas Development Council, Washington, D.C.
Don Fink	Economics Division, Office of Planning and Evaluation, United States Environmental Protection Agency
Thomas N. Gladwin	Faculty Member, Centre d'etudes Industrielles, Geneva
H. Peter Gray	Professor of Economics, Douglass College, Rutgers University
Maria H. Grimes	Analyst, Environmental Policy Division, The Library of Congress, Washington, D.C.
Herbert G. Grubel	Professor of Economics, Simon Fraser University and Visiting Research Fellow, Nuffield College, Oxford University
Stanley P. Johnson	Head, Prevention of Pollution and Nuisances Division, Commission of the European Communities, Brussels
Donald J. Kahn	Senior Adviser, Environmental Conservation, Exxon Corporation
Howard S. MacAyeal	Director, Corporate Planning, Eaton Corporation
Judith Marquand	Senior Economic Advisor, Department of Environment, United Kingdom
Craig Mathews	President, Environmental Law Institute, Washington, D.C.
Tracy Murray	Associate Professor of Economics and International Business, Graduate School of Business Administration, New York University
John H. Mutti	Assistant Professor of Economics, University of Wyoming
Greg Ondich	Assistant Director, International Technology Division, United States Environmental Protection Agency
Toby Page	Economist, Resources for the Future, Inc.
David W. Pearce	Director, Public Sector Economic Research Centre, University of Leicester
Charles Pearson	Associate Professor of Economics, School for Advanced International Studies, The Johns Hopkins University

Rüdiger Pethig

Center for Mathematical Studies in Economics and Management Science, Northwestern University, and University of Mannheim

Michel Potier

Head, Environment and Industry Division, Environment Directorate, Organization for Economic Cooperation and Development, Paris

J. David Richardson

Assistant Professor of Economics, University of Wisconsin

Lawrence Rosenberg

Program Manager, Advanced Productivity Research and Technology Division, National Science Foundation

Larry E. Ruff

Program Officer, Resources and the Environment, The Ford Foundation

Anthony Scott

Professor of Economics, University of British Columbia

Edwin B. Shykind

Director, Environmental Affairs Division, Bureau of Domestic Commerce, United States Department of Commerce

Horst Siebert

Professor of International Economics, University of Mannheim

Robert E. Stein

Director, North American Office, International Institute for Environment and Development, Washington, D.C.

Jan Tumlir

Director of Research, General Agreement on Tariffs and Trade, Geneva

Ingo Walter

Professor of Economics and Finance, and Associate Dean, Graduate School of Business Administration, New York University

Jeremy J. Warford

Economic Adviser, Utilities Department, International Bank for Reconstruction and Development

John G. Welles

Vice President, Institutional Planning and Development, Colorado School of Mines

Preface

As nations go about the business of protecting the environment in different ways, according to different time schedules, employing different policy instruments, international economic relations are certain to be affected. At the same time, international economic pressures may influence plans for achieving national environmental targets. There are, in addition, direct effects of pollution in one nation on others, or on the world as a whole, to which the analytical tools of the economist can usefully be applied. Such problems of environmental management in an economically interdependent community of nations form the focus of the studies contained in this volume.

The book follows my *International Economics of Pollution* (New York, Halstead-Wiley; and London, Macmillan, 1975), which attempts to delineate the dimensions of the problem in an integrated way. The studies presented here probe each of these dimensions in considerable depth, and present both new conceptual insights and new empirical findings. They are the product of an international symposium held in New York City on April 17–18, 1975, under the joint auspices of the International Institute of Management of the Science Center Berlin and the Graduate School of Business Administration of New York University, with financial support from The Ford Foundation.

The volume centers around ten thematic papers that were commissioned about a year in advance. Some of the authors are established contributors to the field. Others are young scholars beginning their professional careers with research in this area. Still others are distinguished international economists who were asked to apply the tools of their trade to the problem of environment. Added to this mixture were ten formal discussants, most of whom are actively involved in public and corporate policies concerning the environment, assigned the task of contributing a practical side to the deliberations. Around this core group of authors and discussants, an equal number of symposium participants, representing equally variegated backgrounds, debated the issues in open forum.

The symposium design proved to be a success, and the results are reproduced here as faithfully as possible. However, all of the contributions have been edited and revised, and the sequencing has been changed where this appeared to make sense for purposes of publication. Inevitably, the authors differ in the way they treat their subject matter, and this comes through quite clearly in the book.

While it has been my pleasant task to organize the symposium and draw together the various contributions in this volume, credit for the substance of the work belongs entirely to the individual authors. The financial support of The Ford Foundation made the symposium possible and is gratefully acknowledged. The International Institute of Management of the Science Center Berlin and the Graduate School of Business Administration of New York University as co-sponsors of the symposium provided logistical support and physical facilities. Tracy Murray helped run the conference, while Sonia Maltezou, Demitrios Cacnis, and Sezai Demiral served as rapporteurs. Finally, Marion Epps worked hard to make the symposium a success and to prepare this volume for publication.

INGO WALTER

New York, New York
January 1976

Contents

Studies in International
Environmental Economics

On International Issues in Environmental Management

William J. Baumol

I am delighted to have been given the opportunity to introduce this distinguished group of studies focusing on a topic of such critical importance for the future welfare of society.

A great deal has of course been written in recent years on the topic of environmental protection, much of it ill considered, some of it seeking to wish the problem away, some of it tinged with hysteria. It is a subject on which reliable data are not always easy to acquire, and in which the evidence often does not mean what it seems to at first.

READING THE EVIDENCE

An example should serve to bring out the point. I myself had earlier cited the declining oxygen content of the lower Baltic as evidence of man's inhumanity to nature. Figures from 1900 to the present from samples taken at a point about midway between Stockholm and Helsinki showed a steady decline in dissolved oxygen, up to the point where by 1970 the oxygen had virtually disappeared—so that the body of water was on its way to becoming a "stagnant sea." The attribution seemed pursuasive until a comparison with the corresponding figures for the Bay of Bothnia, where pollution from paper mills was a far more serious problem, showed no sign of a parallel trend.

Further investigation revealed that the oceanographer's best evidence suggests that the oxygen content of the lower Baltic in the area originally considered probably depends, more than anything else, upon rainfall in Norway and the runoff from Norwegian rivers into the waters between Denmark and Germany, and from there into the central Baltic. The evidence indicated also that, at least from the beginning of the century, there had been a secular decline in rainfall and river runoff in the area. So much for the pollution explanation.

But could it perhaps have been man's damage to climatic conditions which caused the decline in rainfall, after all? We cannot reject that possibility, but there is independent evidence suggesting that in fact rainfall in the region had been increasing in the second half of the 1800s, and that just before the middle of the nineteenth century things might have been nearly as bad as they are now in terms of rainfall. *Mea culpa.* I too was guilty of a hasty reading of the evidence.

I do not, of course, mean to conclude that there is no environmental problem in the Baltic Sea. On the contrary, our fairly painstaking review of the available time-series does suggest that there are a number of areas in which problems are serious and pressing. But that makes it all the more necessary that analysis be careful and objective, that the data be gathered and evaluated with caution, and that policy be designed accordingly. In short, what the subject area calls for is the attention of careful and dedicated scholars.

NATIONAL AND TRANSNATIONAL POLICY ISSUES

The international side of our environmental problems is not, of course, a field totally separated either in analysis or in factual substance from the domestic field. Pollutants that are harmful in the one will be damaging in the other. Remedial costs that are substantial in the first area are not likely to be negligible in the second. Policy measures that are efficient and effective in the first arena are likely to offer similar advantages in the other. What, then, is it that makes *international* environmental management a subject to which it is appropriate to devote an entire volume such as this?

This is no idle question, for a specification of this distinction can serve to provide the appropriate agenda for research in the field.

In my view, the reasons that make international environmental management a special subject fall under two general headings, the two having little in common either analytically or in their influence on policy. The first arises out of the circumstance that *domestic* environmental measures must be designed under the shadow of the fact that the economy of the nation that undertakes them is part of the economy of the world. The second derives from the common environment which is shared by all the inhabitants of the globe, so that activities that damage the environment of one nation are likely to have adverse effects upon that of another. The first issue, then, is a matter of national policy as it is influenced by feedback from other economies. The second is an environmental matter that is truly international.

To be more specific, the basic problem that constitutes the first of our two dimensions is that no businessman or politician is likely to ignore the international competitive consequences of any measure advocated for the protection of the environment within his country. All such measures increase monetary costs to some degree, even if they do so to a smaller extent than sometimes has been feared. Higher costs inhibit one's ability to compete, and this in turn is likely to give rise to opposition to such measures on the part of the affected industries, or to cause them to be watered down considerably.

It would seem, on the surface, that the only interesting questions involve an evaluation of the magnitude of the effects of national pollution control on the balance of payments, employment, and national income measured in conventional terms. But this may not be the end of the story. We know from international trade theory that a reduction in the price of an exported commodity may sometimes have results quite different from those expected by a layman. It may improve the balance of payments rather than causing it to deteriorate. It may increase employment and real per capita income. Where these things happen, strict environment rules may become a double blessing for the nation that adopts them. It may protect its environment and simultaneously give it an edge in terms of its international economic relations. Once more, the widow's cruse may be the apt analogy.

An interesting question in this area is whether such a widow's cruse case is in fact a likely possibility, and to whom and under what circumstances it is likely to apply. In any event, estimates of the pertinent magnitudes will remain very much to the point, both in this case and in cases that are more in line with common anticipations.

It is noteworthy that analysis of this first of our two broad problems of international environmental management falls largely into the conventional patterns of international economics. The theory of international trade and the empirical evidence of international finance are both likely to apply to this subject, virtually intact, as the following studies show.

Things are quite different in the second of our broad subject areas—the area of transnational environmental damage. Here too, however, there is a great deal of overlap with another portion of economic analysis, the general subject of environmental economics. For, given the opportunity to apply it, the broad type of policy program that is likely to work well in serving the interests of the citizens of a particular nation is very likely to be a promising prescription for the inhabitants of other lands as well. The relative advantages of direct environmental controls and effluent charges are no different in any one country than they are for the world as a whole.

The distinguishing problem in which environmental damage traverses international boundaries, then, does not lie in the mix of programs that would work best if they could be adopted and enforced. The essential distinguishing feature, rather, lies in the difficulty in achieving any sort of effective international agreement and in seeing that it is carried out faithfully by all parties to that agreement.

ALTERNATIVE APPROACHES

There are several ways in which this general subject area might be approached. One can, for example, explore the range of policies that may plausibly be expected to recommend themselves to a group of nations with variegated political systems and divergent economic interests, who are united only in their determination to pressure their own sovereignty. One could then examine whether such measures—if any can, indeed, be devised—are likely to suffer from some incidental and undesirable side effects.

I must confess, however, that I am not terribly sanguine about the prospects for such an approach to policy. I have really very little confidence in the likelihood of workable agreement among a substantial number of countries to design an effective program to protect those natural resources that have, unfortunately for the world's inhabitants, been classified as their common property. Certainly the uninspiring performances in the series of meetings on the protection of the oceans that have recently taken place offer little basis for optimism on this score. I recognize that such a view will not recommend itself to those who devote their time and effort to the achievement of international agreements. But one does not have to go so far as to join me in my pessimism. One need merely concede that the probability of failure to achieve agreement is not negligible, and the desirability of considering some alternative line of approach to policy for the control of transnational environmental damage becomes manifest.

Such an alternative approach must, by definition, be one that does not depend on international agreement, at least not on the part of all of the nations concerned. Ideally, it should be made up of a set of *unilateral* measures which, even if they are not capable of yielding results for which one can make any claim of optimality, do at least demonstrably move matters in the right direction. Such an autarchic approach to international environmental protection will admittedly not bring with it all that might be hoped, but it seems hard to believe that one cannot design some such measures which are far better than nothing.

An example is easy to produce. One of the most publicized problems of the international environment is that of oil spills by tankers. The shorelines of several of the leading petroleum-importing nations are particularly vulnerable to damage from this source. Any or all of these oil-importing countries can, if they wish, adopt regulations requiring any tankers landing at its ports to submit evidence documenting where the ships' tanks have been cleaned, accounting for the disposal of their cargo, and requiring them to use the oil-cleaning facilities provided at the ports at which they discharge their cargo.[1] They can also require that these ships meet a variety of safety standards in order to reduce the danger of accidental spills. In that way the pollution of the sea by oil would certainly not be eliminated altogether— indeed we know that zero pollution goals are neither attainable, nor particularly desirable. Yet the effect could be presumed to go in the right direction. Moreover, the larger the number of nations that adopted such regulations, the more desirable the result might be.

CONCLUSION

A volume composed of independent papers by a number of highly qualified contributers will not, of course, follow a set of agenda suggested post hoc, such as those that are implicit in the preceeding remarks. Undoubtedly, in what follows my comments will be contradicted by valuable discussions and observations which fall outside the areas I have suggested as prime regions of concern for environmental management. The area is sufficiently large and sufficiently demanding to permit no simple circumscription of the topics that urgently require attention. Yet I am sure that the dimensions that have been raised will recur many times for, clearly, they are important components of the overall issue even if they are not as exclusive as I may seem to have been suggesting.

N O T E

1. An estimate provided to the Ocean Affairs Board of the National Academy of Sciences in May 1973 suggests that almost 1.4 million tons of oil are discharged into the sea every year during routine ship operations. That accounts for about 80% of the total, with accidents accounting for the remaining 350,000 tons. See Noel Mostert, *Supership* (New York: Alfred A. Knopf, 1974), p. 45.

PART *One*

THE COMPETITIVE DIMENSION

Some Effects of Environmental Controls on International Trade: The Heckscher–Ohlin Model

Herbert G. Grubel

The increased public concern over the quality of the environment that has developed during the last half of the 1960s has attracted much attention from politicians, engineers, and economists. The stock of knowledge about the economic aspects of pollution is impressive, and it may be fair to say that all of the major theoretical and practical issues have now been sorted out. What remains are problems of measurement both in general and for specific projects, and, as in all fields of economics, the continuous need to refine and extend theoretical models by relaxing assumptions and making them more realistic. The economists whose writings are cited in the bibliographic references in this paper have done an outstanding job in applying conventional economic theory to the particular problems of pollution control, for the most part blending superbly theory with policy concerns and available, but often sparse, empirical information.

In the present chapter an attempt is made to analyze some interesting aspects of pollution control programs in the most widely used pure-theory model of international trade, the Heckscher–Ohlin model, whose properties are known extremely well. An important barrier to the use of this model for a full general equilibrium analysis is due to the fact that environmental quality should be treated logically as a third good, the output of which competes with the production of the conventional goods X and Y. As Walter (1974) has shown, it is possible to find the general equilibrium solution in such a three-good model, but most of the interesting theorems about terms of trade, efficiency of different policies, and trade effects cannot be handled within this analytical framework. To overcome the limitations inherent in the three-good model in the present chapter the analysis is made partial in the sense that we assume that the size of a country's expenditures on pollution control are given. Thereafter, however, the analysis is of a general equilibrium nature, and a special effort is made to analyze how the foreign trade repercussions of pollution control should enter into the choice of a welfare-maximizing level of environmental quality and, implicitly, into the determination of expenditures on pollution control.

The chapter is divided into three main parts. The first deals with the case of the small country. It examines the proposition that it is more efficient to eliminate production and consumption pollution directly rather than through restrictions of international trade, drawing on theorems developed by Bhagwati (1971) and Johnson (1965). In the same part we also present a taxonomy of biases in trade that is based on Johnson's work on economic growth and trade (1958). Part two uses the geometric version of the two-country model developed by Meade (1952) to examine likely terms of trade effects of pollution control measures on the output of one good initiated first only by one country and then by both countries. We consider the possibility that pollution control measures can reverse patterns of comparative advantage. In the third part of the chapter we relax the assumption that production pollution has no spillover effects into other countries. We show that the efficient solution under these conditions requires treatment of the world as one country and of production facilities in each country as a separate factory. We then analyze the case in which tastes for environmental quality differ between countries. Under these conditions the country desiring the higher level of environmental quality can use international trade restrictions to induce shifts in productive patterns abroad and achieve the desired pollution level even though the rest of the world does not implement environmental controls. To keep the analysis simple, in the last two parts of the chapter we consider only pollution due to production.

SMALL COUNTRY, NO SPILLOVER EFFECTS

In Fig. 2-1 we show a small country's production possibility frontier $X_0 Y_0$ which has been derived in a manner familiar from the construction of the Heckscher–Ohlin model by assuming the existence of given production functions and stocks of labor and capital. With international trade possible at the world price ratio $W_0 W_0'$ the country is in equilibrium, producing at point P_0 and consuming at point C_0. The assumed conditions imply that Y is the export and X is the import good. The level of welfare in equilibrium is depicted by the indifference curve tangent to the world price line at C_0.

The main purpose of our analysis is to consider the implications for national welfare and the pattern of trade resulting from the institution of controls on pollution associated first with the production, and second, with the consumption of good Y. The simplest way to introduce production pollution controls into the analysis is to assume that a thorough evaluation of the costs and benefits of pollution control among scientists, engineers, economists, including international trade economists, and the general public has led to the conclusion that the achievement of desired ambient levels of environmental quality requires producers of good Y to install certain, specified equipment for the reduction of pollutive emissions. The construction and installation of this equipment requires the expenditure of capital and labor which has the primary effect of shrinking the country's production possibility frontier in terms of goods X and Y from its initial $X_0 Y_0$ to $X_0 Y_1$. As can be seen from Fig. 2-1, the two frontiers have in common a segment $X_0 P_2$. This common segment arises from the assumption that up to an output of OY^* of good Y the assimilative capacity of the country's environment is sufficiently great to permit maintenance of the desired level of environmental quality without the installation of pollution control equipment.

It would be of some analytical interest to specify rigorously the determinants of the extent of the induced shrinkage of the production possibility frontier and the effects that it has on factor prices. For this purpose we could use the analytical tools developed for the Heckscher–Ohlin model in the context of economic growth and technical change, except that the initiating process involves the equivalent of a shrinkage of factor supplies and the reversion of technological process. It may also be possible analyze the implications of the existence of linear and nonlinear pollution abatement cost functions. Such questions are tangential to the main theme of this chapter and require the development of different tools of analysis than are needed here. Therefore we shall not pursue this area of enquiry further.

Before we begin our main analysis we have to discuss the meaning of the indifference map in the presence and absence of pollution. A logically com-

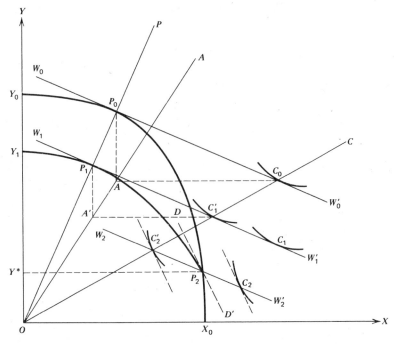

Figure 2-1   Small-country good Y production externality.

plete model of international trade in the presence of pollution should have
three goods, X, Y, and Z, where Z is the quality of the environment. In this
model we would specify interdependent production functions and a welfare
function encompassing the three goods. Walter (1974) has produced such a
model and derived some interesting results. However, as is well known, the
extension of the Heckscher–Ohlin model into cases of more than two factors and goods is very difficult and results in ambiguous answers to the
most interesting questions about trade and welfare. For this reason we
consider here only the two-commodity model, but it forces us to make the
assumption specified above that the determination about the precise amount
of pollution reduction is outside the model. In terms of the indifference map
this assumption has the important and unambiguous meaning that, in the
new equilibrium after the installation of the pollution control equipment, the
community indifference curve tangent to the world price line $W_1 W_1'$ at point
C_1' represents a higher level of welfare than that associated with C_0. The
reason for this conclusion is that, although at C_0 the country consumes more
of X and Y than at C_1', in the former position the level of welfare derived
from this bundle of goods is diminished by the disutility derived from the

pollution created by the production of good Y. At point C_1' the lower welfare attributable to the reduced consumption of X and Y is more than compensated for by the benefits from a less polluted environment, making consumption point C_1' superior to C_0. Otherwise society would not have chosen to adopt the pollution abatement program. In the further analysis it is important to remember, therefore, that we cannot interpret the indifference map in the conventional way. But as we shall see this fact does not prevent us from demonstrating one important policy principle and deriving a taxonomy of trade effects.

Figure 2-1 and the underlying model can also be derived in a different manner, which may provide additional insights for some readers but can be skipped by others without loss of continuity by moving to the beginning of the next paragraph. Consider that one small country uses all its capital and labor to produce the normal goods X and Y and environmental quality, good Z, employing a linearly homogeneous production function. As is well known from international trade models involving three goods, under this assumption the production frontier is a three-dimensional hypersurface, and the given relative goods prices are represented as a three-dimensional plane along which trade takes place and leads to the attainment of the highest hypersurface representing the welfare function in which all these goods appear as arguments. Let us now envision such a country in trade equilibrium and consider making two cuts along the X-Y plane. The first cut is made at the point where Z is zero and in the X-Y plane reveals the production frontier $X_0 Y_0$. The second cut is made at the equilibrium output of Z, at which we find in the X-Y plane the frontier $X_0 Y_1$, the world trade ratio $W_1 W_1'$, and the indifference map C_1. These last relationships represent the two-dimensional projection of the full three-dimensional equilibrium conditions at which the positive production of Z requires the use of some capital and labor that, therefore, is not available for the production of X or Y and causes the shrinkage of the frontier in the X-Y plane from $X_0 Y_0$ to $X_0 Y_1$.

The model just specified now permits us to show the validity of the principle presented by Johnson (1965) and generalized by Bhagwati (1971) that the first-best method for dealing with an externality is to eliminate it directly, leaving international trade unrestricted, rather than introducing a new distortion of economic efficiency through the restriction of trade. Thus, the country could achieve the same level of environmental quality as was attained under free trade at point of consumption C_1' and production P_1 by granting an export subsidy on good Y or imposing an import duty on good X such that the domestic relative price is established at DD'. At this domestic price producers are induced to move to production point P_2, at which the low output of good Y, even in the absence of pollution abatement equipment, results in the maintenance of the desired quality of the environment. The point of consumption under these conditions would be on the world price ratio W_2W_2' going through P_2, such as C_2, where the domestic price ratio DD' is tangent to the indifference curve. Depending on tastes, the new consumption could also be one such as C_2', where good Y is an import rather than an export good as it is at point C_2.

The establishment of a given level of environmental quality through interference with free trade must lead to a lower level of consumption opportunity loans for goods X and Y than does the establishment of the same level of environmental quality through legislation requiring the removal of pollutants from the production process directly, maintaining at the same time free trade (see Fig. 2-1). This conclusion holds generally for all desired levels of environmental quality so that it is independent of our foregoing assumption about the superiority of welfare at point C_0 over C_1. The validity of this proposition can be seen by considering that we could have argued alternatively that point P_2 was chosen such that C_2 was superior to C_0. As long as this point P_2 is to the right of P_0 the particular standard of environmental quality chosen must also be attainable by free trade and the installation of pollution abatement equipment that causes a shrinkage of the production frontier and leads to a point such as C_1 superior to C_2. Generally, the lower the standard of environmental quality demanded, the closer is P_2 to P_0 and the smaller is the loss of welfare due to the installation of pollution control equipment.

Our model of Fig. 2-1 can be used to develop a taxonomy of the effects of pollution abatement on international trade as a proportion of total output, which is logically analogous to that developed by Johnson (1958) for the analysis of the effect of growth on trade. Considering consumption alone, if the community's tastes are such that under free trade the two points of consumption before and after the pollution control program are along the ray OC such as C_0 and C_1', then the consumption effect of environmental control on trade is neutral. If the two points are such as C_0 and C_1, then the effect is pro-trade biased because at the lower level of income, proportionately less of the export good is consumed domestically and, therefore, is available to exchange in the international market for good X, which in turn is consumed in proportionately greater quantity than was initially the case. It is possible that the public has such a preference for good X that at the lower availability of the goods it consumes a greater absolute amount than it does at the higher level. Under these conditions the consumption point would be on W_1W_1' but to the right of a line from C_0 to the X-axis (not shown), and the effect would be ultra-pro-trade biased. By analogy, consumption could be on W_1W_1' but to the left of the ray OC. If the absolute amount of Y consumed is less than at C_0, the consumption effect has been termed antitrade biased, if it is more than at C_0 it is known as ultra-antitrade biased. An analogous classification of production effects on trade can be specified, though we will not do so here.

Instead, we now turn to a taxonomy of the combined effects of consumption and production. For this purpose consider the ray OA which goes through the corners of the pre- and post-pollution control trade triangles P_0AC_0 and $P_1A'C_1'$, respectively. These triangles result from the fact that both production at P_0 and P_1 and consumption at C_0 and C_1' independently imply neutrality, leaving the relative quantities of X and Y traded unchanged and resulting in an overall neutral effect on trade. Now consider that production remains unchanged at P_1 but tastes are such that consumption is to the right of C_1'. Under these conditions the overall trade effect of the pollution control program is pro-trade biased, and the corner of the trade triangle is to the right of the ray OA. In general, of course, the production frontier and consumption tastes could occur in any combination of effects. If the corner of the new trade triangle is to the left of the ray OP it is the condition known as ultra-anti-trade biased. Between OA and OP it is known as anti-trade biased. By analogy, location of the trade triangle corner between OA and OC reflects pro-trade bias and to the right of OC ultra-pro-trade bias.

We can use the preceding analysis to speculate about the likely trade effect of pollution control programs if we know something about the relative capital intensity of the production process for goods X and Y and of the antipollution capital goods themselves, and if we know the income elasticity of demand for the two goods. Thus, as Heller (1973) shows, in the Cobb–Douglass production function case underlying the Heckscher–Ohlin model the production effect is neutral if the pollution control equipment requires capital and labor in the same ratio as the country's overall ratio of capital to labor. On the other hand, if the pollution control equipment requires capital and labor in the same proportion as good Y, then the production effect is anti-trade biased because the production frontier is shifted inward such that at the unchanged world price in equilibrium only the output of good Y is reduced and that of X remains unchanged. If the demand for good Y is relatively more income elastic than the demand for good X, then the lower income in terms of goods X and Y (caused by diversion of resources into pollution control investment) causes a proportionately greater reduction in demand for good Y and X, and the consumption effect is also anti-trade biased. Presumably engineers can provide us with information about the capital–labor intensity of pollution control equipment relative to the factor proportions used in the industry required to install it. Similarly, data should be available about the income elasticity of demand for traded goods. Consequently, it should be possible to engage in some speculation about the likely direction of the trade bias for individual small countries resulting from the installation of the pollution control equipment.

The preceding analysis can be modified readily for the case where good Y is a small country's import rather than export good. The qualitative results of the analysis are the same as above, and we need not go through it again. Instead, we turn briefly to the case where the environmental pollution is associated with consumption of good X rather than production of good Y and demonstrate again that free trade and a consumption tax is superior to a tariff. For this purpose consider Fig. 2-2, which is basically the same as Fig. 2-1, with the country's production frontier given by XY and the initial consumption at C_0 reached through production at P_0 and trade along the world price $W_0 W_0'$. Now consider that the consumption of good X, such as alcohol, imposes a welfare cost on society that can be reduced to collectively desired levels only through lower consumption of the good. Suppose, given the costs and benefits of attaining the desired level of environmental quality, society decides that consumption of environmentally damaging good X needs to be reduced from X_0 to X_1 and that this change increases overall welfare. Thus, assume that point C_1 in Fig. 2-2 is considered to be superior to point C_0. Point C_1 is reached by imposing a tariff on imports of good X which raises its relative price to $D_0 D_0' = D_1 D_1'$ and induces production to move to point P_1. Trade at the unchanged world price $W_1 W_1'$ permits consumption to take place at C_1. The alternative method of reducing consumption of good X from X_0 to X_1 is to retain free trade and keep production at P_0 but to impose an excise tax on consumption at a rate greater than the tariff rate in order to establish the domestic consumer price $D_2 D_2'$. At this price, point C_2, which is attainable through trade and has consumers in equilibrium, is reached. As can readily be seen from Fig. 2-2, at point C_2 the consumption of X is at the desired level OX_1 (as at C_1) and the externalities have been reduced to the desired level. However, the free trade and excise tax solution results in a higher level of welfare than the tariff solution because the former permits an additional consumption of $C_1 C_2$ units of good Y.

The preceding analysis can readily be changed to the case in which the export good Y produces a negative consumption externality. Under these conditions it is necessary to subsidize the consumption of good X in order to obtain a reduction of the free-trade consumption level of Y and move to a point to the right of C_0 on $W_0 W_0'$. Analogous reasoning can be employed to show the proper policies required when consumption of either good X or Y yields a positive externality. The principle that free trade combined with a tax or subsidy on consumption is superior to interference with free trade in order to attain the given level of consumption still holds true.

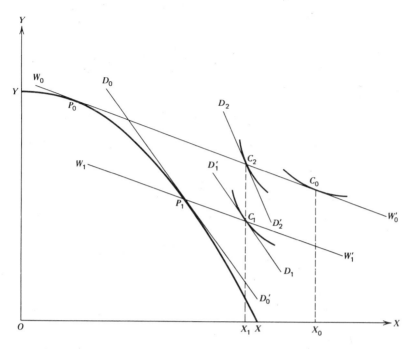

Figure 2-2 Small-country good X consumption externality.

The preceding analysis has some interesting implications for the fears voiced by many politicians and environmentalists that the demand for higher pollution abatement standards would lead simply to an "export" of polluting industries from the high income to the developing countries because the former would find it cheaper to encourage polluting industries to move abroad rather than to require them to install pollution abatement equipment. According to our analysis, such explicit export of polluting industries is not in the welfare-maximizing interest of industrial countries, and the fears of politicians and environmentalists appear to be misplaced. On the other hand, in spite of these conclusions it remains true that pollution control programs in industrial countries are likely to shift patterns of comparative advantage and may involve the relative decline and growth of polluting industries in developed and developing countries, respectively. Such shifts however, are a matter of economic efficiency and are the coincidental effects of pollution control programs. They are not part of a deliberate attempt to export polluting industries.

LARGE COUNTRY, NO SPILLOVER OF EXTERNALITIES

A large country that initiates a program to reduce production-related pollution faces the problem that the policies adopted may change its terms of
trade with the rest of the world, which in turn may increase or lower the
cost of attaining a given level of environmental quality from what it would
have been if the terms of trade had remained constant. We now turn to the
analysis of the likely terms of trade effects of pollution control programs
undertaken first in Country B alone and then in both countries A and B.
Throughout the present section of this paper we assume that the environmental quality in one country is independent of the levels of production in
the other country. This assumption is relaxed in the following section.

In Figure 2-3, we present the trade offer curves OA and OB of Countries
A and B, whose derivation is well known from Meade's (1952) pioneering
work. We recall that good X is Country A's import and Country B's export
good and that the opposite holds true for good Y. Initial equilibrium is at

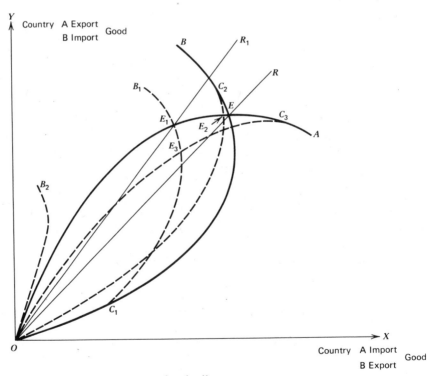

Figure 2-3 Large-country terms of trade effects.

point E and the terms of trade is represented by the slope of the line OR. A steepening of the terms of trade line to, say, OR_1 implies an increase in the welfare of Country B since at the new international price it can obtain more units of its import good Y for the export of a given quantity of good X. By analogy, this same terms of trade change from OR to OR_1 lowers the welfare of Country A.

Now consider that Country B imposes a pollution control program on the production of its export good X. As a result, its production frontier shrinks in an analogous manner to that shown in Fig. 2-1 and the offer curve changes to OC_1B_1. The two offer curves have in common the segment OC_1 because at the level of trade and pattern of production implied by a point along this segment Country B produces so little of good X that the assimilative capacity of the environment permits the maintenance of the desired environmental quality without the installation of pollution control equipment. As can readily be seen from Fig. 2-3, under the assumed conditions Country B can expect an improvement in its terms of trade, which implies a lowering of the social cost of pollution control from what it would be if the terms of trade remained unchanged. In a proper welfare calculus, this terms-of-trade benefit would be considered in the determination of the desired level of environmental quality, as we had argued in the first section of this chapter. We assume that this level is known and that it determines the extent of the inward shift of the offer curve shown in Fig. 2-3.

Now we turn to the case where good Y production causes environmental pollution, whereas good X production does not. Under these conditions Country B's initiation of a pollution control program leads to the offer curve BC_2O that has the segment BC_2 in common with the original curve, because in this range Country B's output of good Y is so small that the resultant pollution is assimilated without damage by the environment. However, if good Y production requires any pollution control equipment at the initial trade pattern at point E, then it must be true that point C_2 is above OA as shown, and the pollution control program leads to an improvement of Country B's terms of trade at a point of equilibrium such as E_2 in Fig. 2-3. As can be seen from Fig. 2-3, this improvement in the terms of trade would tend to be smaller than the one enjoyed under the assumption that the export good is the polluting one. We may consider this result to be the "normal" one, because it seems reasonable to assume that the higher level of output of the export good X considered here causes the cost of pollution control per unit of output to be higher than it would be in the case when the low-output, import-competing good Y is the polluting one. However, we cannot rule out, on logical grounds, the possibility that pollution control of a country's import good leads to a greater improvement in the terms of trade than does pollution control of the export good since nothing is known a priori about the relative factor intensity of pollution control equipment for industry X or Y. Generally, we can interpret the preceding analysis as yielding the important result that international trade makes it possible for a large country to share with the rest of the world its costs of pollution control generated entirely within its own borders, assuming no retaliation or equivalent pollution control program in the rest of the world.

Let us now turn to the analysis of the case in which both countries A and B are of roughly equal size and initiate controls of the pollution caused by the production of good X, good Y production being pollution free. We recall that in this case the offer curve of Country B is B_1C_1O. For Country A, for which X is the import good, the offer curve looks like AC_3O in Fig. 2-3 with the common part of the initial and new offer curves at the upper end for the reasons discussed above. As we can see in Fig. 2-3, under the "normal" conditions analyzed above, the inward shift of Country B's offer curve is proportionately greater than that of Country A, resulting in trade equilibrium at point E_3 and an improvement in Country B's terms of trade. It is easy to work out, and we shall not do so here, that if good Y production alone causes pollution, the presumption is that the terms of trade moves in favor of Country A. We may conclude from this analysis generally that in the framework of the Heckscher–Ohlin model there is a presumption that a pollution control program instituted by both countries on one of the two traded goods will improve the terms of trade of the country exporting this particular good. Competition leads to the result that a country that has a relatively high level of output of the polluting good, and therefore has to incur heavier cost of pollution abatement than the rest of the world, is sharing some of this cost with its trading partners through an induced favorable shift in its terms of trade. At the same time, the rest of the world suffers a corresponding decrease in its welfare due to the deteriorated terms of trade.

An interesting case for analysis in the model just developed arises when pollution control measures lead to the reversal of comparative advantage. Thus, consider that good X causes production pollution while good Y does not, and that, as an extreme, Country A imposes no pollution controls, while Country B imposes them with such an intensity that its offer curve shrinks by a very large amount and lies entirely to the left of A's offer curve, as does OB_2 in Fig. 2-3. Under these conditions profitable opportunities for trade arise from a switch in trade patterns with Country B exporting Y and importing X, and Country A reversing its trade pattern analogously. Trade equilibrium in the new situation could be shown in Fig. 2-3 by redrawing each offer curve as a mirror image of itself with a 45° line from the origin serving as the mirror surface. Also, the labeling along the axis would have to be altered to reflect the new pattern of specialization.

We do not show the new equilibrium in Fig. 2-3 in order to keep the diagram simple and because the new terms of trade are of no particular analytical interest. In considering the welfare implications of the postulated changes we should remember the basic feature of our model that the intensity of the pollution control measures is assumed by Country B in the full knowledge of all of the costs and environmental benefits so that by assumption the new point of equilibrium reached after the reversal of comparative advantage is considered to be superior to the initial point in the presence of pollution. On the other hand, the model implies a loss of welfare of the country that does not adopt pollution control measures.

The results just obtained may occur in the real world if densely populated and highly industrialized countries need to incur heavy expenses in removing air pollutants from such industries as steel in order to reach a publicly desired purity of the environment; whereas in developing countries with low population density the environment can absorb the pollution accompanying conventional steel production methods without a significant lowering of the quality of the environment. Under these conditions, steel may become an import rather than an export commodity of highly industrialized countries. This finding is consistent with the conclusion derived by Siebert (1974b, p. 505) that there is the tendency that "the country richly endowed with the environment will export the commodity with a high pollution content."

LARGE COUNTRIES, POLLUTION SPILLOVER

There are some types of pollution that are created by production activities in one country and affect the welfare of people living in others. Examples of this type of pollution are DDT residues that are picked up by winds, are deposited, and enter the food chain in all parts of the world, or air and water contamination crossing international boundaries with wind and water currents. In this case we encounter two problems of particular analytical interest. First, how can the world's environment be brought to a desired level of purity in the most efficient way, and second, what can one country do if the rest of the world is not cooperating in the attainment of a joint, efficient approach to pollution control? We now discuss briefly and at a theoretical level these two problems in turn, referring interested readers to the detailed and more practical discussions published by the OECD (1974).

Let us consider a world consisting of two countries A and B with trade patterns as in the case analyzed in Fig. 2-3, assuming that only the production of good X results in pollution that transcends the borders of the two countries. The efficient solution for the attainment of a desired level of environmental quality is straightforward in principle. The two countries should be treated as if they were only one, and collectively a target level for environmental quality should be selected on the basis of technical information and aesthetic judgments about the economic costs and benefits. We again take as given, for our purposes of analysis, this target level for pollution control, though in fact, of course, its determination in the case involving the population of two countries is far more difficult that it is when people from only one country are involved. Not only are there all the usual difficulties of uncertainties about the levels and incidence of costs and benefits, there are the added problems that the people in the two countries on average may have different tastes and incomes and, as we shall discuss in more detail below, that the benefits from pollution control in one country spill over into the other. However, the solution to these problems is a matter of political bargaining, and economic analysis has little to contribute to our understanding of how the solution is reached. For this reason we now assume that a political process has determined the desired level of global environmental purity and that it is to be attained at least cost to the world as a whole.

Under these conditions the allocation of responsibility for the installation of pollution control equipment is the same as in the domestic case in which there are different production units generating the pollution. Taking into consideration the assimilative capacity of the environment of each production facility, its level of output, and factor costs, engineers can develop a functional relationship between the value of expenditures on pollution control equipment and the marginal reduction of pollution, as is shown in Fig. 2-4 as the functions CC' for Country A and PP' for Country B. The functions will first be considered to be applicable to the initial level of output in both countries, and, therefore, we show the function for Country B to be much further away from the origin than that for Country A, on the grounds that Country B is specialized in the production of good X and exports it to Country A, although there is no technical necessity that this condition must hold. The efficient solution is found by pushing expenditures on pollution control in each country to the point where the marginal reduction in global pollution is equal in both countries and the total reduction in pollution gives the desired level of global environmental quality. In Fig. 2-4 we indicate such an efficient solution which requires Country A to spend OE_A^* on control in order to eliminate OE_A^*BC of pollution. Country B needs to spend OE_B^* and eliminates OE_B^*NP pollution. The sum of pollution reduction $OE_A^*BC + OE_B^*NP$ brings the world the desired level of environmental quality. The marginal cost of pollution per unit of expenditures on control is equal in both countries, $OA = OM$, and, therefore, the program is efficient in the sense that a different allocation of control expenditures between the two countries could achieve the same level of pollution reduction only at higher total expenditures.

The preceding analysis is partial because, as noted earlier, there are general equilibrium and terms-of-trade repercussions from the use of resources in pollution control. The consequent shrinking of the production frontiers and offer curves are deemed likely to lead to an improvement in Country B's terms of trade and different levels and mixes of output in both countries. These changes in output levels and mixes cannot be established theoretically without the introduction of much special information about production and pollution control functions and tastes. However, it is clear that in the new equilibrium, output levels of good X in both countries should be different from the initial ones that gave rise to the functional relationships between expenditures on pollution control and reduction of pollution shown in Fig. 2-4. Therefore the initiation of the control program is likely to cause shifts in these functions. For our purposes of analysis we can disregard this problem and simply assume that the functions shown in Fig. 2-4 are those in the new global equilibrium after the initiation of the control program. This assumption hides may interesting and possibly important aspects of the process of adjustment and social choice, but it allows us to make the central point that an efficient solution requires international cooperation and the allocation of costs such that in equilibrium marginal expenditures on pollution control in both countries result in equal reductions of global pollution, as is shown in Fig. 2-4.

Let us now turn to the case in which international agreement on a joint and efficient program of global pollution control cannot be reached. Such a failure to reach agreement can easily arise if, for example, absolute levels of per capita incomes between countries differ widely and if the high income countries wish to consume a higher quality environment than the poorer countries at the same cost. The lack of demand for environmental quality

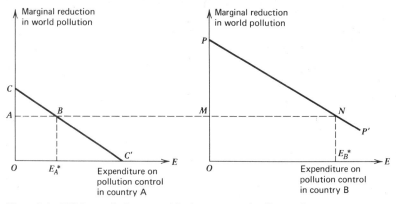

Figure 2-4   Efficient pollution control in the presence of spillover effects.

by the poorer countries may be genuine in the sense that even if there were
no international spillover effects they would prefer to use their resources to
produce conventional goods rather than a higher quality environment, much
like the presently high income countries have done in the past. However,
there is no way in which the true nature of this demand pattern can be
tested because of the public-goods nature of the environment for the world
as a whole postulated here. Thus, in any negotiations between rich and poor
countries, both have an incentive to hide their true preferences, hoping that
the other group of countries is willing to make pollution control expenditures that yield benefit to themselves for which they do not have to pay because allegedly they consider them to be worthless. It may not be unreasonable to assume that the poorer countries would have stronger incentives than the rich countries to play this kind of game. This "free rider"
problem is well known from the theory of public finance, and according to
principles developed by Coase (1966), the efficient solution involves the
creation of an administrative unit with tax and expenditure authority over
all producers of pollution and all beneficiaries of the control programs,
which thus, in effect, internalize all the externalities. In the case of international pollution spillovers the optimal solution, therefore, would be the creation of an international agency with authority to order and the capability of
forcing every country to contribute its share of the cost involved in attaining
a collectively chosen level of environmental quality for the world as a
whole. The assignment of costs carried out efficiently under these conditions would lead to the same solution as the international agreement
assumed to have been attained voluntarily, as shown in our analysis in connection with Fig. 2-4.

Let us now assume that, in the two-country world postulated above,
international agreement for the efficient attainment of global environmental
quality has not been reached. To simplify the argument assume that
Country A wishes to attain the same level of pollution reduction as it did
under the case of cooperation analyzed above so that the area under the
pollution reduction functions in Fig. 2-4 $OE_A^*BC + OE_B^*NP$ is needed to
achieve the target. Country B is assumed to refuse to make any pollution
control expenditures whatever. Under these conditions Country A can push
its control expenditures to the level OE_2 at which pollution emission from
its plants is absolutely zero. However, as can be seen from Fig. 2-4, the
total area under the CC' function is so small that the total reduction of
global pollution is insufficient to reach the level of environmental quality
desired by Country A. If it wishes to move closer to this level it can adopt
policies that lead to a shift of production of X away from Country B to its
own territory. Such policies are import quotas or tariffs, which for reasons

familiar from international trade theory raise the relative price of X in Country A, induce increased output, reduce import demand, and cause a reduction of output of X in Country B. In terms of Fig. 2-4, the result of these changes in the location of production of good X is that the schedule CC' is shifted upward and PP' is shifted downward. The total amount of pollution produced in Country B decreases even without the installation of control equipment simply because output of the polluting good is reduced. In Country A the increased production of good X is not accompanied by pollution because the control measures prevent it completely. Consequently, there is a net reduction in global pollution through the imposition of an import tariff on good X by Country A.

Generally, under the assumed conditions the level of global environmental quality attained by Country A is an increasing function of the tariff, except under the condition that the cost of attaining zero pollution on the output of good X may be so large as to cause a shrinking of Country A's production frontier by so much that trade would be profitable only by a reversal of comparative advantage. We are describing here a case analytically equivalent to the one presented in the context of Fig. 2-3, when the offer curve OB_2 failed to intersect with the offer curve OA. In this case Country A would become an exporter of good X, and in order to obtain further reduction in the output of good X in Country B it would have to subsidize the export of good X.

In the real world it is likely that under the conditions of unilateral attempts to clean up the global environment postulated here Country A finds the cost of attaining the desired level of environmental quality very high, since it is forced to shoulder all of the burden without any cooperation from Country B, even though favorable changes in its terms of trade lower the cost somewhat. For this reason we would expect Country A to compromise and lower its target for environmental quality from the one it would have pursued under a cooperative solution.

We should briefly note here that the preceding arguments could be carried out under the assumption that Country A's export good Y is the cause of pollution, retaining the other features of the model, in particular Country B's unwillingness to incur pollution control costs. Under these conditions Country A, producing the larger share of the world's output of good Y, is more likely to be able to attain the desired level of global environmental quality by unilateral pollution control measures. If it does not succeed, it has to have recourse to an export subsidy on good Y that induces Country B to lower its domestic output of the polluting good in a manner analytically equivalent to the one developed above in the case in which the production of import good X was assumed to be accompanied by pollution.

CONCLUSIONS

The analytical framework of the traditional Heckscher–Ohlin model of international trade and specialization yields some useful insights about the effects of pollution controls on international trade and welfare. In the case of the small country faced with fixed terms of trade, we have seen that the direct elimination of pollution reduces welfare less than do trade restrictions imposed to achieve the same goal. Therefore, it tends not to be in the interest of countries to "export" pollution through the direct discouragement of polluting industries. Instead, they face incentives to set environmental standards and let the laws of comparative advantage determine the location of industries.

In the large-country model we showed that countries applying production pollution control measures unilaterally can expect to benefit from an improvement in their terms of trade, which in effect permits them to share the cost of the pollution abatement with, and imposes a cost on, the rest of the world. When both countries adopt pollution controls the terms of trade are likely to move in favor of the country whose export good is associated with production pollution. Under some extreme conditions pollution control programs can lead to a reversal in the pattern of comparative advantage.

When pollution spills over into other countries, an efficient solution requires expenditures on environmental control in every country up to the point where the marginal outflow yields equal returns in terms of reduced global pollution. If such an efficient solution cannot be reached because of the free-rider problem or genuinely differing tastes among countries for environmental quality, then the country desiring the greater reduction in pollution can install environmental control equipment in its own factories and use restrictions on international trade to shift production of the polluting good away from the rest of the world and into its own territory. The use of such policies can lead to a reversal of comparative advantage and require the use of an export subsidy.

ACKNOWLEDGMENT

I am grateful for the useful comments made on an earlier draft of this chapter by Ingo Walter and Tracy Murray, and by a number of participants at the Symposium.

REFERENCES

d'Arge, R. C., "International Trade and Domestic Environmental Control: Some Empirical Estimates," in *Managing the Environment: International Cooperation for Pollution Control,* A. V. Kneese et al., Eds., New York: Praeger, 1971.

d'Arge, R. C., and A. V. Kneese, "Environmental Quality and International Trade," *International Organization, 26,* 1972.

d'Arge, R. C., "Trade-Environmental Controls, and the Developing Economies," *Problems of Environmental Economics,* Paris: OECD, 1972.

Baumol, W. J., "Environmental Protection, International Spillovers and Trade," *Wicksell Lectures 1971,* Stockholm: Almquist and Wicksell, 1971.

Bhagwati, J., "The Generalized Theory of Distortions and Welfare," in Bhagwati et al., Eds., *Trade, Balance of Payments and Growth,* Amsterdam: North-Holland, 1971.

Coase, R., "The Problem of Social Cost," *Journal of Law and Economics,* October 1966.

GATT, *Industrial Pollution Control and International Trade,* GATT Studies in International Trade, No. 1, Geneva, 1971.

Heller, H. R., *International Trade,* Englewood Cliffs: Prentice-Hall, 1973.

Johnson, H. G., *International Trade and Economic Growth,* London: Allen and Unwin, 1958.

Johnson, H. G., "Optimal Trade Intervention in the Presence of Domestic Distortions," in *Trade Growth and the Balance of Payments,* R. Baldwin, Ed., Amsterdam: North-Holland, 1965.

Magee, S. and W. F. Ford, "Environmental Pollution, the Terms of Trade and the Balance of the United States," *Kyklos, 25,* 1972.

Meade, J., *A Geometry of International Trade,* London: Allen and Unwin, 1952.

OECD, *Transfrontier Pollution,* Paris: OECD, 1975.

Scott, A. D., "The Economics of International Transmission of Pollution," in *Problems of Environmental Economics,* Paris: OECD 1972.

Siebert, H., "Trade and Environment," in *The International Division of Labor: Problems and Perspectives,* H. Giersch, Ed., Tuebingen: J.C.B. Mohr, 1974a.

Siebert, H., "Environmental Protection and International Specialization," *Weltwirtschaftliches Archiv, 110,* 3, 1974b.

Walter, I., "Environmental Control and the Patterns of International Trade and Investment. An Emerging Policy Issue," *Banca Nazionale del Lavoro Quarterly Review, 100,* March 1972.

Walter, I., "Environmental Management and the International Economic Order," in C. Fred Bergsten, Ed., *The Future of the International Order: An Agenda for Research,* Lexington, Mass: D.C. Heath 1973.

Walter, I., "The Pollution Content of American Trade," *Western Economic Journal, 11,* 1973.

Walter, I., "International Trade and Resource Diversion: The Case of Environmental Management," *Weltwirtschaftliches Archiv, 110,* 3, 1974.

Environmental Control, Economic Structure, and International Trade

Horst Siebert

The relevance of environmental problems and environmental quality management for international trade depends on the type of environmental problem given. The following cases have to be distinguished: (1) pollution of international environmental goods such as the increasing carbon dioxide concentration in the atmosphere or of spatially limited international environmental systems such as the Baltic Sea; (2) transfrontier pollution where two countries are linked to each other via some environmental system (e.g., upstream–downstream relations in river systems); and (3) pollution of national environmental goods where pollutants are emitted into a national environmental system and are not diffused to another country.

Solutions to these problems will differ in terms of the required institutional arrangements, feasibility, and economic impact on international trade. In this chapter we concentrate on the relevance of national environmental goods for international trade.

The interrelation of environmental control and international trade is summarized in Fig. 3-1. Three different "systems" are distinguished.

The technological–economic system can be categorized into technological, economic, and environmental subsystems; it determines the level of environmental quality resulting from economic activities. Gross emissions are a function of (1) production (and consumption) technology, (2) the pollution technology describing emissions as by-products per unit of output (or consumption), and (3) economic structure. Pollution abatement is influenced by technologies designed to prevent the occurrence of pollution or to abate pollutants after they have entered environmental media, and by the adaptability of production technology and sectoral and spatial structure to changes in the valuation of environmental quality and environmental policy. The gross emissions and pollutants that are reduced define net pollution, and net pollution influences environmental quality via intricate environmental interdependencies.

Environmental disruption represents a situation in which consumers demand a better environmental quality than polluters are willing to provide by their behavior.[1] Observe that the demand for environmental quality by consumers can be interpreted in terms of the supply of assimilative services tolerated by consumers, and that the supply of environmental quality, on the other hand, is equivalent to the effective demand of polluters for assimilative services. Consequently, environmental disruption represents a situation in which polluters demand a larger quantity of assimilative services than consumers are willing to tolerate.

Environmental disruption can be explained by the competing uses of the environment, that is, for consumption purposes and as a receptacle of wastes, with pollution-reducing ambient levels of environmental quality. Competing uses of the free public good are the reason for the existence of externalities and the divergence of private and social costs (Siebert, 1973a). There is no automatic or market mechanism that ensures consistency of the decisions of "consumers" and "polluters." The resulting suboptimal allocation of resources (including environmental resources) can only be improved if collectively determined environmental policy succeeds in changing the public good character of the environment (with respect to at least one of its roles) by levying an effluent charge or introducing emissions norms or other policy instruments.

Because of the character of the environment as a public consumption good, private individuals cannot determine the supply of assimilative services so that either the supply of assimilative services (immission norms)—or the effective (tolerable) demand for assimilative services

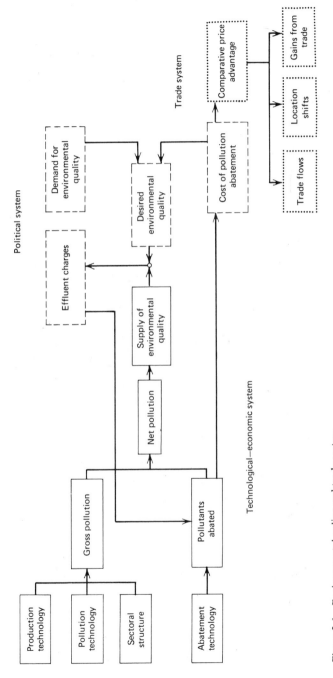

Figure 3-1 Environmental policy and trade system.

(emission norms)—or the price of the assimilative services have to be set politically. In Fig. 3-1, the *political system* is shown as comparing the valuation of alternative environmental qualities with the costs of reaching these situations. Abatement costs are an "input" to the *political system* whereas environmental policy instruments represent an "input" to the *technological system*.

For the present study the *trade system* is relevant. It is linked to the technological–economic and political systems via the costs of pollution abatement. The latter determines comparative price advantages, which in turn influence trade flows, international location patterns, and the distribution of gains from trade.[2] The following problems arise: (1) To what extent does environmental policy affect comparative price advantages betweeen countries? (2) What are the effects of changes in comparative prices on international trade flows, balance of payments situations, exchange rates, and terms of trade? (3) Will comparative cost and price changes between countries also affect the international flow of production factors such as capital and, therefore, influence the location of firms? (4) What will be the gains from trade if economic welfare is also defined with respect to environmental quality? Problems (1), (2), and (4) will be studied in this chapter.

One of the basic hypotheses for trade is that a country exports a commodity if it has a comparative price advantage in that commodity. Let P_i denote commodity prices in Country I and P_i^+ prices in Country II. Then for trade to take place in a two-country world, domestic price ratios before trade have to differ:

$$\frac{p_1}{p_2} \gtrless \frac{p_1^+}{p_2^+} \tag{1}$$

The following model specifies the demand and supply to assimilative services and describes a situation of ecological equilibrium. The model determines the effects of environmental scarcity on comparative price advantages.

THE DEMAND FOR ASSIMILATIVE SERVICES

The demand for assimilative services is determined by consumption, production and pollution technology, economic structure, technical possibilities to abate pollutants, as well as costs of polluting the environment expressed in terms of effluent charges (or maintaining emission norms). In the following it is assumed that consumption activities do not generate pollutants.

Assume a two-commodity economy in which for reasons of simplicity only resource R is used. The production functions are given by

$$Q_i = F_i(R_i) \qquad \text{with } F'_i > 0, F''_i < 0, \text{ and } i = 1, 2 \qquad (2)$$

The production of output (Q_i) generates a single pollutant S_i^P as a joint product. The primes $(')$ and $('')$ indicate the first and second derivatives of the function, respectively. Pollutant emission occurs at a constant or increasing rate as output increases.

$$S_i^P = H_i(Q_i) \qquad \text{with } H'_i > 0, \quad H''_i \geq 0; \quad i = 1, 2 \qquad (3)$$

Each sector has a pollution abatement technology

$$S_i^a = F_i^a(R_i^a) \qquad \text{with } F_i^{a'} > 0, \quad F_i^{a''} < 0; \quad i = 1, 2 \qquad (4)$$

S_i^a denotes pollutants abated and R_i^a stands for resources used for pollution abatement in sectors i. Pollutants emitted into environmental media are defined as

$$S_i = S_i^P - S_i^a \qquad (5)$$

Total emissions (S) are

$$S = S_1 + S_2 \qquad (6)$$

Also assume that two types of environmental protection agencies exist being independent from each other. Type A can reduce pollutants ambient in the environmental media and charges a price z^* for a unit of pollutants abated, whereas Type B (representing the political system) charges a price z for emitting pollutants into environmental systems.

The environmental agency of Type A can be thought of as providing abatement services to firms. Type A can be privately organized or be operated by the government. It also may be a "cooperative" of polluters. Finally, it can be interpreted as a cooperative with enforced membership such as in the case of water quality management cooperatives in the Ruhr basin[3] or the *Agence de Bassins* in France. The abatement technology of the agency of Type A is given by

$$S_3^a = F_3^a(R_3^a) \qquad F_3^{a'} > 0, F_3^{a''} < 0 \qquad (7)$$

with S_3^a denoting the quantity of pollutants abated and R_3^a the resources used for pollution abatement.

Pollutants ambient in the environment (T) are defined by total emissions (S), assimilative capacity of the environment $(\overline{T^a})$, and pollutants abated by the environmental pollution agency of Type A (S_3^a) as

$$T = S - S_3^a - \overline{T^a} \qquad (8)$$

T can be interpreted as the net demand by productive activities for assimilative services of the environment. Environment quality U^S is influenced by pollutants ambient in the environment

$$U^S = U(T) \qquad \text{with } U' < 0, \ U'' < 0 \tag{9}$$

that is, environmental quality declines progressively with increasing pollutants. Equation 9 is a technological damage function relating environmental quality in nonmonetary terms of ambient quantities of pollutants. Since T represents the demand for assimilative services of polluters, U^S can be interpreted as the environmental quality that polluters are willing to "supply."

Output and gross emissions are determined if the resources used by firms (sectors) are specified. Firms maximize profit. Costs include costs for resources used in production (r_i) and pollution abatement (r_i^a), charges to be paid to the protection agency of Type B, that is a charge z per unit of emission S_i, and payments z^* made to agency of Type A per unit of pollutants abated. The existence of an agency of Type A presupposes that it is possible to attribute pollutants abated to the different sectors. In the simplest case, we have

$$S_3^a = S_3^{a1} + S_3^{a2}$$

with S_3^{ai} being pollutants abated by agency of Type A and being attributable to sectors i. If firms pay both the effluent charge z to agency B and the price z^* for abatement services to agency A, no incentive exists to use the services of agency of Type A. Consequently, firms must be reimbursed if pollutants are abated by an agency of Type A. In that case, a term zS_3^{ai} "decreases" costs. Under these assumptions, the resource demand of firms if found by maximizing the following Lagrangean expression

$$\begin{aligned}
L_i = \ & p_i Q_i - r_i R_i - r_i^a R_i^a - z S_i - (z^* - z) S_3^{ai} \\
& - \lambda_i^1 [Q_i - F_i(R_i)] \\
& - \lambda_i^2 [S_i^p - H_i(Q_i)] \\
& - \lambda_i^3 [S_i - S_i^p + S_i^a] \\
& - \lambda_i^4 [S_i^a - F_i^a(R_i^a)]
\end{aligned}$$

We obtain

$$r_i = p_i F_i'(R_i) - z H_i'(Q_i) F_i'(R_i) \tag{10}$$

which can be rewritten as

$$R_i = G_i(r_i, p_i, z) \qquad \text{with } G_{ri}' < 0, \ G_{pi}' > 0, \ G_{zi}' < 0 \tag{10a}$$

and[4]

$$r_i^a = z F_i^{a'}(R_i^a) \tag{11}$$

or

$$R_i{}^a = G_i{}^a(r_i, z) \text{ with } G_{ri}^{a'} < 0, G_{zi}^{a'} > 0 \tag{11a}$$

Finally, we have

$$z = z^*,$$

that is, firms are willing to pay a price z for pollution abatement up to the effluent charge z, so that in equilibrium the revenue of the agency of Type A is given by the effluent charge multiplied by the pollutants abated. Costs accrue to the agency of Type A in terms of resources used. The agency maximizes the expression

$$L = zS_3{}^a - r_3{}^a R_3{}^a - \lambda[S_3{}^a - F_3{}^a(R_3{}^a)]$$

This yields[5]

$$r_3{}^a = zF_3^{a'}(R_3{}^a) \tag{12}$$

or

$$R_3{}^a = G_3{}^a(r_3{}^a, z) \quad \text{with } G_{r3}^{a'} < 0, G_{z3}^{a'} > 0 \tag{12a}$$

For a given effluent charge z, and for given resource prices in the different resource uses, eqs. 10a, 11a, and 12a determine resource use. Once the resources used in the different occupations are specified, the supply of private goods Q_i as well as the level of pollution abatement processes in the private sector and by the public authority are given. The demand for assimilative services or its equivalent, the environmental quality supplied U^S, is also determined.

THE SUPPLY OF ASSIMILATIVE SERVICES

The determination of the supply of assimilative services tolerated by consumers of the public good environment or the demand for environmental quality seems to be an unsolved problem. This stems from the fact that we intend to link the demand for the public good environmental to individual preferences, with all of the well-known problems of social welfare fuctions coming to light. The following approaches can be distinguished.[6]

1. Individuals specify their preferences in bargaining solutions. This approach ensures that benefits and costs of environmental policy are taken into consideration when the desired environmental quality is determined. Although this proposal is largely of theoretical interest, its implementation for practical policy seems to raise insurmountable obstacles—such as the spatial delineation of the environmental media, the free-rider problem, and the bargaining positions of polluter and pollutee.

2. Individuals specify their willingness to pay in interviews. In this case the supply of a pure public good is determined by the group with the highest willingness to pay, and the willingness to pay will in turn vary with income so that the supply to the public good is a function of income distribution—a result that is not politically desirable.
3. Individuals specify their willingness to pay in referenda in which the public good to be provided, its costs, and the cost-sharing are indicated. This procedure, being possible in the case of local public goods, ensures that the willingness to pay of a "representative" household will specify the demand for the public good.
4. Alternatively, the effective demand for environmental quality will be determined politically, that is, in a system of representative democracy in which individuals vote for political parties according to their preferences and in which parties attempt to maximize votes.

The solution to these problems is left open here. Instead, the demand for the environment as a public consumption good is regarded as being determined by the demand characteristics of a representative household. Assume L is a variable representing this household's income (or preference). The demand for environmental quality is given by

$$U^D = f(\alpha) \qquad \text{with} \frac{\partial f}{\partial \alpha} > 0 \tag{13}$$

where α is a variable shifting the willingness-to-pay function outward.

EQUILIBRIUM CONDITIONS

Equilibrium of the economy requires that no environmental disruption occurs, that is, that the environmental quality supplied by polluters U is identical to environmental quality demanded by the representative household.

$$U^S = U^D \tag{14}$$

Equilibrium on the commodity market requires that quantities demanded (Q) and quantities supplied (Q) be identical

$$Q_i^D = Q_i \tag{15}$$

with quantities demanded[7] being determined by

$$Q_i^D = D_i \frac{p_1}{p_2} \tag{16}$$

with

$$D_1' = \frac{dQ_1^D}{d(p_1/p_2)} < 0$$

and[8]

$$D_2' = \frac{dQ_2^D}{d(p_1/p_2)} > 0$$

Equilibrium on the factor market requires that the quantity of resources used is equal to the total supply of the resource in the economy (R), that is,

$$\bar{R} = \sum R_i + \sum R_i^a + R_3^a \qquad (17)$$

Finally, it is assumed that the resource price is identical in each of the different uses, so that

$$r_i = r_i^a = r_3^a = r \qquad (18)$$

Otherwise mobility functions would have to explain the use of resources in the different sectors (Siebert, 1974c).

The model contains 24 variables and 24 equations. Combining Eqs. 2–9, 13, and 14 we obtain

$$f(\alpha) = U(\sum_2 H_i[F_i(R_i)] - \sum_3 F_i^a(R_i^a) - \bar{T}_a) \qquad (19)$$

Equation 19 represents environmental "equilibrium," that is, case in which the demand for environmental quality equals environmental quality supplied by the behavior of polluters, with U depending on production activities and pollution technology, abatement of pollution, and assimilative capacity. From Eqs. 2, 15, and 16 we have

$$F_i(R_i) = D_i \frac{p_1}{p_2} \qquad (20)$$

The reduced system containing Eqs. 10a, 11a, 12a, 19, and 20 determines resource use, commodity prices, resource earnings, and the relevant effluent charge. From these solutions, the variables of the larger system can be determined.

The model represents a partial equilibrium approach, since quantities of commodities demanded depend only on relative prices and not on factor earnings. Also, the receipts from the effluent charge z by the environmental protection of Type B are not "recycled" in the model.

Figure 3-2 shows the simplified structure of the model, including commodity markets, resource market, and the environmental system. The

$$
\begin{bmatrix}
G'_{z1} & G'_{r1} & 0 & G'_{p1} & 0 & 0 & 0 & 0 & -1 \\
G'_{z2} & G'_{r2} & G'_{p2} & 0 & 0 & 0 & 0 & -1 & 0 \\
G'^{a}_{z1} & G'^{a}_{r1} & 0 & 0 & 0 & 0 & -1 & 0 & 0 \\
G'^{a}_{z2} & G'^{a}_{r2} & 0 & 0 & 0 & -1 & 0 & 0 & 0 \\
G'^{a}_{z3} & G'^{a}_{r3} & 0 & 0 & -1 & 0 & 0 & 0 & 0 \\
0 & 0 & -D'_1 & D'_1 & 0 & 0 & 0 & 0 & -F'_1 \\
0 & 0 & -D'_2 & D'_2 & 0 & 0 & 0 & -F'_2 & 0 \\
0 & 0 & 0 & 0 & 1 & 1 & 1 & 1 & 1 \\
0 & 0 & 0 & 0 & -U'F'^{a}_3 & -U'F'^{a}_2 & -U'F'^{a}_1 & U'H'_2F'_2 & U'H'_1F'_1
\end{bmatrix}
\cdot
\begin{bmatrix}
dR_1 \\ dR_2 \\ dR_1^{a} \\ dR_2^{a} \\ dR_3^{a} \\ dp_1 \\ dp_2 \\ dr \\ dz
\end{bmatrix}
=
\begin{bmatrix}
0 \\ 0 \\ 0 \\ 0 \\ 0 \\ 0 \\ 0 \\ 0 \\ \dfrac{\partial f}{\partial \alpha}
\end{bmatrix}
d\alpha
\qquad (21)
$$

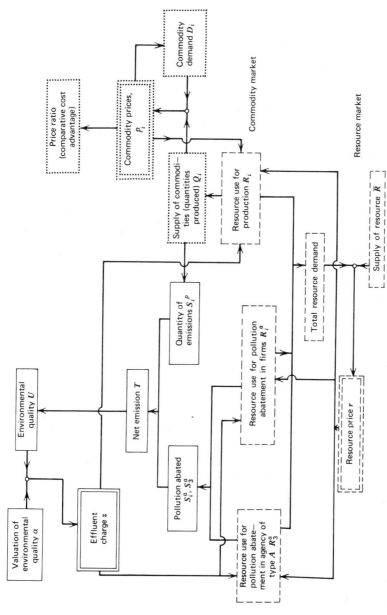

Figure 3-2 Structure of the model.

Environmental system

Price ratio (comparative cost advantage)

Commodity prices, p_i

Commodity demand D_i

Commodity market

Supply of commodities (quantities produced) Q_i

Resource use for production R_i

Resource market

Supply of resource $\bar{R}$

Quantity of emissions S_i^p

Resource use for pollution abatement in firms R_i^a

Total resource demand

Environmental quality U

Net emission T

Pollution abated S_i^a, S_3^a

Resource use for pollution abatement in agency of type A R_3^a

Resource price r

Valuation of environmental quality α

Effluent charge z

central role of prices (commodity prices, resource earnings, and the effluent charge) is indicated. Markets or other institutions for coordinating decisions of independently-operating agents are denoted by a circle.

SOLUTION AND IMPLICATIONS

With the use of total derivatives Eq. 21 determines the effect of a shift in the parameter, expressing such factors as environmental preferences or income on the variables of the system.

Setting initial prices equal to 1, we have for the change in relative commodity price as a function of the parametric shift in the valuation of environmental quality[9]

$$\frac{d(p_1/p_2)}{(\partial f/\partial \alpha)\, d\alpha} = \frac{-F_1' F_2' [A\,(G_{p2}' G_{r1}' - G_{p1}' G_{r2}') - B(G_{p2}' G_{z1}' - G_{p1}' G_{z2}')]}{\Delta} \tag{22}$$

with

$$\Delta = U' \{ (F_1' F_2' G_{p1}' G_{p2}' + D_2' F_1' G_{p1}' - D_1' F_2' G_{p2}')[(F_1^{a'} - F_2^{a'})$$
$$\cdot (G_{r2}^{a'} G_{z1}^{a'} - G_{r1}^{a'} G_{z2}^{a'}) + (F_3^{a'} - F_2^{a'})(G_{r2}^{a'} G_{z3}^{a'} - G_{r3}^{a'} G_{z2}^{a'})$$
$$+ (F_3^{a'} - F_1^{a'})(G_{r1}^{a'} G_{z3}^{a'} - G_{r3}^{a'} G_{z1}^{a'})] - (D_1' F_2' + D_2' F_1')$$
$$\times [A^*(G_{p2}' G_{r1}' - G_{p1}' G_{r2}') - B^*(G_{p2}' G_{z1}' - G_{p1}' G_{z2}')]$$
$$- F_1' F_2' (D_1' H_1' + D_2' H_2')[A\,(G_{p2}' G_{r1}' - G_{p1}' G_{r2}')$$
$$- B(G_{p2}' G_{z1}' - G_{p1}' G_{z2}')] \}$$

where

$$A = \sum_3 G_{zi}^{a'} > 0$$

$$A^* = \sum_3 F_i^{a'} G_{zi}^{a'} > 0$$

$$B = \sum_3 G_{ri}^{a'} < 0$$

$$B^* = \sum_3 F_i^{a'}\, G_{ri}^{a'} < 0$$

Assume Country I has a comparative price advantage in commodity 1, so that $P_1/P_2 < P_1^+/P_2^+$. Let Country I's preference for environmental quality shift upward ($\partial f/\partial \alpha > 0$). Then the comparative price advantage of

Country I will be reduced if the following sufficient[10] conditions hold:

$$-D_1' > D_2' \qquad \text{(i)}$$

$$F_1' < F_2' \qquad \text{(ii)}$$

$$H_1' > H_2' \qquad \text{(iii)}$$

$$F_1^{a'} < F_2^{a'} \qquad \text{(iv)}$$

$$F_1^{a'}, F_2^{a'} > F_3^{a'} \qquad \text{(v)}$$

$$\frac{G_{p2}'}{G_{z2}'} < \frac{G_{p1}'}{G_{z1}'} \qquad \text{(vi)} \qquad\qquad (23)$$

$$\frac{G_{p2}'}{G_{r2}'} < \frac{G_{p1}'}{G_{r1}'} \qquad \text{(vii)}$$

$$\frac{G_{z1}^{a'}}{G_{r1}^{a'}} > \frac{G_{z2}^{a'}}{G_{r2}^{a'}} \qquad \text{(viii)}$$

$$\frac{G_{z3}^{a'}}{G_{r3}^{a'}} > \frac{G_{z2}^{a'}}{G_{r2}^{a'}}, \frac{G_{z1}^{a'}}{G_{r1}^{a'}} \qquad \text{(ix)}$$

Equation 23 (i) indicates that commodity 2 is only a relatively weak substitute. Sector 1 should be less productive (ii), be relatively pollution-intensive (iii), and have a less efficient abatement technology (iv). Condition (v) ensures that the comparative disadvantage of sector 1 with respect to its abatement technology is not compensated by a higher productivity in abatement technology of the environmental protection agency of Type A. if contrary to condition (v) the environmental protection agency has the higher productivity, the comparative disadvantage of sector 1 in abating pollutants does not count.

Conditions vi–ix can be easily specified if instead of Eqs. 10a, 11a, and 12a we use Eqs. 10, 11, and 12. Then conditions i–ix can be expressed in terms of conditions i–v only.[11]

Alternatively, conditions vi–ix can be interpreted in terms of demand elasticities for resource R with respect to commodity prices (ζpi), factor prices (ζri), and the effluent charge (ζzi). The elasticities ζri^a and ζzi^a relate to resource-use for abatement purposes.

With commodity prices being set equal to 1 initially, condition vi can be specified as

$$\left| \frac{\zeta_{p2}}{\zeta_{z2}} \right| > \left| \frac{\zeta_{p1}}{\zeta_{z1}} \right| \qquad (23 \text{ vi a})$$

This indicates that the resource demand (for production purposes) of sector 2 is more sensitive[12] to commodity price changes than in sector 1. Also, output is more sensitive to commodity prices in sector 2. This can be explained by the fact that sector 2 has lower environmental costs by increasing production, that is sector 2 has a lower marginal tendency to pollute or has a more productive abatement technology.

Also, the resource demand in sector 1 is more sensitive to changes in the effluent charge than in sector 2. This also implies that output of sector 1 is more sensitive to the effluent charge; that is, sector 1 has a higher marginal tendency to pollute than sector 2. Condition vii can be expressed as

$$\left| \frac{\zeta_{p2}}{\zeta_{r2}} \right| > \left| \frac{\zeta_{p1}}{\zeta_{r1}} \right| \qquad (23 \text{ vii a})$$

In addition to the interpretation given for condition (vi) a the factor demand of sector 1 is more sensitive to changes in the resource price r than in sector 2; that is, sector 1 is less productive than sector 2. Condition (viii) can be expressed as

$$\left| \frac{\zeta^a_{z2}}{\zeta^a_{r2}} \right| > \left| \frac{\zeta^a_{z1}}{\zeta^a_{r1}} \right| \qquad (23 \text{ viii a})$$

Condition (viii) a implies that resource demand (for abatement purposes) of sector 2 is more sensitive to the effluent charge, or that pollutants abated in sector 2 are more sensitive to z. This implies that sector 2 has lower costs of pollution abatement or a higher productivity in the abatement activity. Also, sector 1 is more sensitive to the resource price r which again indicates that sector 1 is less productive in abatement activities. Condition ix can be interpreted similarly. The discussion of these conditions confirms the interpretation of conditions i–v.

We thus have the result that the comparative price advantage (P_1/P_2) of a country is reduced with the introduction of environmental policy; that is, a change in environmental demand (1) if sector 1 has a higher pollution intensity, (2) if it has a less efficient abatement technology, (3) if it is less productive, and (4) if internal demand cannot shift production to sector 2 because of weak distribution possibilities.

Relative prices (and consequently comparative price advantages) depend on the abundance[13] of environmental resources, that is, on such factors as the output level (production technology), pollutants emitted (emission technology), pollutants abated (abatement technology), assimilative capacity of the environment, and the evaluation of environmental quality (α) with

$$\frac{p_1}{p_2} = \phi(Q_i, S_i{}^p, S_i{}^a, T^a, \alpha) \qquad (24)$$

It can be assumed that the factors determining the demand for, and supply of, assimilative services differ between countries, and that consequently environmental scarcities differ between countries. Environmental scarcity (or abundance) is a factor explaining comparative price advantages in international trade.

Differences in these factors require different effluent charges (or emission norms). *Ceteris paribus*, the effluent charge must be higher; the smaller the assimilative capacity of the environment, the higher the demand for assimilative services, and the higher the value attached to the environment for consumption purposes. It would be economically absurd to attempt to harmonize internationally these production and location advantages by imposing identical effluent charges.

The change in comparative price advantage caused by a shift in the valuation of environmental quality by consumers is accompanied by a reallocation of resource R between the different activities. Assume sector 1 is relatively pollution intensive and the other conditions in Eq. 23 hold. Then resource use in sector 1 will decline. This follows from

$$\frac{dR_1}{(\partial f/\partial \alpha)\,d\alpha} = \frac{1}{\Delta}\,D_1'F_2'[B(G_{p2}'G_{z1}' - G_{p1}'G_{z1}') - A(G_{p2}'G_{r1}' - G_{p1}'G_{r2}')] \qquad (25)$$

$$\frac{dR_2}{(\partial f/\partial \alpha)\,d\alpha} = \frac{1}{\Delta}\,D_2'F_1'X \qquad (25a)$$

where X is the bracketed term in Eq. 25.
The effluent charge[14] will rise according to

$$dz = \frac{\partial f}{\partial \alpha} \cdot d\alpha[(D_1'F_2' + D_2'F_1')(G_{p2}'G_{r1}' - G_{p1}'G_{r2}')$$

$$+ B(D_1'F_2'G_{p2}' - D_2'F_1'G_{p1}' - F_1'F_2'G_{p1}'G_{p2}')] \qquad (25b)$$

EFFLUENT CHARGE EQUALIZATION

In the discussion on the problem of harmonizing environmental policy instruments between countries, one has to recognize that some mechanisms exist that will make for an equalization of effluent charges between countries in the very long run.

Assume Country I has a greater net demand for assimilative services as defined by Eq. 8 compared to Country II. Assuming an identical evaluation of environmental quality in the two countries, the lower effluent charge in II will attract factors of production if they are perfectly mobile internationally. Net demand for assimilative services will rise in II and decline in I, and the effluent charges will tend to equalize.

These mechanisms assume that the demand for environmental quality (that is, the tolerable supply of assimilative services) is identical between countries. Now assume that international differences in environmental abundance are due to differences in demand for environmental quality. These differences may be reduced by an international "demonstration effect" with respect to consumption behavior. That is, the political effort of one country to improve environmental quality will stimulate the political demand for environmental control in other countries. Also, if labor were internationally mobile, and if labor mobility is responsive to environmental quality, people will migrate to the area with a better environmental quality, thus increasing the demand for environmental consumption goods in this area (Siebert, 1973b). This leads to a rise in the effluent charge. In the area from which people emigrate, the demand for environmental quality declines and the effluent charge falls. Admittedly, these factors may be more important in the case of interregional trade than in international trade.

ENVIRONMENTAL POLICY AND TRADE FLOWS

We have analyzed the effect of environmental policy on the comparative price advantage of a country in international trade. Although the answer to this problem gives some hints on changes in trade flows, additional hypotheses have to be introduced into the system described in Eq. 21 if trade flows are to be determined. Specifically, the system of equations now has to be formulated for two countries with $(+)$ denoting variables of the foreign country. The equilibrium condition on the commodity markets (Koo, 1974) now is for the world market

$$Q_i^D - Q_i = -(Q_i^{D+} - Q_i^+) \qquad (26)$$

where $Q_i^D - Q_i$ stands for excess demand.
We also have

$$p_i^+ = \frac{1}{w} p_i \qquad (27)$$

with w denoting the exchange rate, and a balance of payment equation

$$B = -p_1(Q_1^D - Q_1) - p_2(Q_2^D - Q_2) \qquad (28)$$

Since this system of equations is not manageable, we discuss a reduced form of the model where (1) the effluent charge is an exogenous variable be-

$$
\begin{bmatrix}
\left(D'_1 - \dfrac{1}{w}D_1^{+\prime}\right) & -\left(D'_1 - \dfrac{1}{w}D_1^+\right) & -F'_1 & +F_1^{+\prime} & 0 & 0 \\[2mm]
\left(D'_2 - \dfrac{1}{w}D_2^{+\prime}\right) & -\left(D'_2 - \dfrac{1}{w}D_2^+\right) & +F'_2 & -F_2^{+\prime} & 0 & 0 \\[2mm]
G'_{p1} & 0 & -1 & 0 & G'_{r1} & 0 \\[2mm]
0 & G'_{p2} & +1 & 0 & G'_{r2} & 0 \\[2mm]
\dfrac{1}{w}G_{p1}^{+\prime} & 0 & 0 & -1 & 0 & G_{r1}^+ \\[2mm]
0 & \dfrac{1}{w}G_{p2}^+ & 0 & +1 & 0 & G_{r2}^+
\end{bmatrix}
\cdot
\begin{bmatrix}
dp_1 \\[2mm] dp_2 \\[2mm] dR_1 \\[2mm] dR_1^+ \\[2mm] dr \\[2mm] dr^+
\end{bmatrix}
=
\begin{bmatrix}
0 \\[2mm] 0 \\[2mm] -G'_{z1}\,dz \\[2mm] -G'_{z2}\,dz \\[2mm] -G_{z1}^{+\prime}\,dz^+ \\[2mm] -G_{z2}^{+\prime}\,dz^+
\end{bmatrix}
\tag{29}
$$

ing determined politically, (2) abatement technologies are not included, and (3) the exchange rate is fixed.[15]

The model determines the effects of changes in effluent charges in the two countries on commodity and resource prices, and resource allocation between sector 1 and sector 2. From

$$d(p_1/p_2) = dp_1 - dp_2 \tag{30}$$

for P_1, $P_2 = 1$ in the initial situation, the terms of trade effect can be calculated.[16] The effect of trade flows can be analyzed from Eq. 28 with

$$dB = - [D_1(p_1/p_2) - F_1(R_1)]dp_1 - p_1 D_1' dp_1 + p_1 D_1' dp_2 + p_1 F_1' dR_1$$
$$- [D_2(p_1/p_2) - F_2(R_2)]dp_2 - p_2 D_2' dp_1 + p_2 D_2' dp_2 - p_2 F_2' dR_1 \tag{31}$$

Substituting the solutions for the variables dp_1, dp_2, and dR_1[17] into Eq. 31, we obtain the balance of payments effect of a rise in the effluent charge. In order to simplify the interpretation, consider the first four expressions— which all relate to Commodity 1—so that these expressions either define the changes in export or import values depending upon whether country exports or imports Commodity 1.

Assume that $dz^+ = 0$ and $dz > 0$ and that instead of Eq. 10a, Eq. 10 is used. Moreover, all positive constants are omitted. Then we have for the change in the trade balance with respect to commodity 1 as a consequence of $dz > 0$

$$dB_1 = \frac{dz}{\Delta'} [H_1' F_1' - H_2' F_2'] \Big\{ [F_2^{+'} - F_1^{+'}]$$
$$\times [F_1^+ F_2' - F_1' F_2^+ + F_2^{+'}(D_1' - D_1^{+'}) + F_1^{+'}(D_2' - D_2^{+'})]$$
$$- [D_1(p_1/p_2) - F_1(R_1)] \Big\langle F_2^+ [F_1 F_2^+ - F_1^+ F_2]$$
$$+ [F_2(D_1' - D_1^{+'}) + F_1(D_2' - D_2^{+'})] \frac{1}{\sum a_i^+} \Big\rangle \Big\} \tag{32}$$

with

$$\Delta' = [F_2^{+'}(D_1' - D_1^{+'}) + F_1^{+'}(D_2' - D_2^{+'})] \frac{1}{\sum a_i} (F_2^+ - F_1^+)$$
$$+ [F_2(D_1' - D_1^{+'}) + F_1(D_2' - D_2^{+'})] \frac{1}{\sum a_i^+} (F_1 - F_2)$$
$$+ [F_1 F_2^+ - F_2 F_1^+]^2 \tag{33}$$

A similar expression is obtained for dz^+. The trade balance effect will depend on the level of effluent charges in the two countries, the pollution intensity of the two sectors, and the production and demand conditions. A sufficient condition for $dB_1 < 0$ is given in the following case:

$$F_1' > F_2' \qquad \text{(i)}$$
$$F_1^{+'} < F_2^{+'} \qquad \text{(ii)}$$
$$-D_1^{+'} < -D_1' \qquad \text{(iii)} \qquad (34)$$
$$D_2' < D_2^{+'} \qquad \text{(iv)}$$
$$H_1' > H_2' \qquad \text{(v)}$$

Conditions i–iv specify that Commodity 1 is exported by Country I. Country I is more productive in Activity 1 and it is more sensitive to price changes Commodity 1, that is, its demand is more elastic and Country II has a relatively inelastic demand for Commodity 1. Also Country II is better able to substitute Commodity 2 in its demand behavior. Condition (v) indicates that Commodity 1 exported by Country I is produced with a high pollution intensity so that environmental policy will hit the export sector of Country I. It should be stressed that (i)–(v) are sufficient for $dB_1 < 0$ and that other data configurations may also ensure that $dB_1 < 0$. Note that the conditions in Eq. 34 can easily be expressed in terms of elasticities.

THE POLLUTE THY NEIGHBOR THESIS

In the case of transfrontier pollution a country pollutes its neighbor by diffusing pollutants via environmental media across national boundaries. In the case of national pollution, environmental management in one country may affect environmental quality in other countries by exporting pollution via trade.

Assume Country I introduces environmental policy. It will lose its comparative price advantage with respect to commodities of a high pollution content. Its import potential will be reduced, and welfare on the commodity account will decline. Welfare, however, also depends on environmental quality. Country I will show a gain on its environmental quality account since emissions are reduced. Incidentally, the usual optimality condition of implementing environmental policy up to the point where the marginal benefit of environmental policy equals its marginal costs implies that Country I will realize a net gain from trade on both accounts since "marginal costs" also must include welfare losses due to the reduction of import potential. Otherwise, environmental policy would not be undertaken.

Consider now Country II, with a less strict (or no) environmental policy. Country II will improve its comparative price advantage by continuing the use of the environment at a very low (zero) price. The output of pollution-intensive commodities will be increased in Country II. Either factors of production will migrate to Country II or the country will increasingly specialize in the production of pollution-intensive commodities. In both cases pollution will rise. Country II will experience a welfare loss on the environmental quality account. Pollution has thus been exported via factor mobility or trade.

The country "importing" pollution via trade can protect itself against the welfare loss on the environmental quality account if it so desires by making its own environment more scarce. Its newly gained production and location advantage is then partly diminished, and the original trade and location shift is partly reduced. Country II can restore the original situation in terms of environmental quality and reduce the improvement in the price advantage completely by choosing an effluent charge such that costs of production are identical to those in Country I. Under the foregoing assumption Country II may choose an effluent charge such that part of the newly gained comparative advantage is retained and part of the imported environmental disruption is accepted. Country II will also have a net gain from trade on both accounts (private goods and environmental quality).

Observe that one country making the environment more scarce does not initiate a "pollute-thy-neighbor" conflict situation with possible cumulative retaliation such as in the case of tariffs or devaluation. This can be ascribed to the fact that a country can gain in environmental quality (and consequently export pollution) only at the opportunity cost of a reduction in output, import potential, and employment. Empirical evidence suggests that abatement costs rise progressively with improvements in environmental quality. The progressively rising economic costs of environmental quality disprove the "pollute-thy-neighbor" policy thesis.

DISTRIBUTION OF THE GAINS FROM TRADE

Let us assume that all countries gain from trade if the definition of "gains from trade" also includes welfare increases from an improved environmental quality. The problem then arises as to how these newly defined gains from trade are distributed between countries.

Distribution of the gains from trade will depend on such factors as the valuation of environmental quality in the two countries, assimilative capacity, and abatement technologies, as well as production and demand conditions. It is especially important to analyze the extent to which the actual unequal distribution of income between countries in the world may be affected by environmental policy, and which international distribution of welfare will be the result of environmental policy in the industrial countries.

INFORMATION REQUIREMENTS

The model presented above indicates the informational requirements to be fulfilled in order to analyze empirically the interrelation of environmental policy and international trade. The informational requirements that are needed for different countries are summarized in Fig. 3-3.

In order to calculate the changes in production costs and in relative costs between commodities one has to know the pollutants to be abated, the pollution content to commodities and the costs of abatement. The quantity of pollutants to be abated is influenced by politically determined immission norms and assimilative capacity.

Costs of abatement include all costs that arise from reaching immission norms or that are incurred in order to avoid effluent charges, that is, costs to avoid emitting pollutants into environmental media, including costs of substitution of inputs, of changes in the product mix, of changes in prevention technologies, costs of abating pollutants after they have entered environmental media, costs of transforming pollutants into less damaging ones, and costs of changing the location of a firm. Overall abatement costs of a sector are the result of optimizing behavior of firms, each of which is choos-

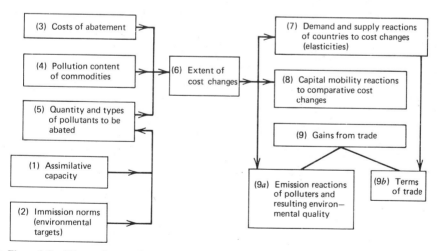

Figure 3-3 Information requirements.

ing between a set of possibilities to reduce pollutants. Empirical information on these different possibilities of firms is seldom available. Moreover, overall abatement costs are available for some sectors only.[18] No information seems to be available on differences in abatement costs from country to country.

For the United States, the pollution content of commodities (with respect to some pollutants) has been calculated by Leontief and Ford (1971), Koo (1974) relying on input–output techniques, and Walter (1973). For the Federal Republic of Germany the SO_2-content of final demand has been estimated following Leontief's approach [Der Rat von Sachverständigen (1974)]. Data are not sufficient to allow an international comparison of the pollution content of commodites.

Assume that cost changes resulting from environmental policy can be determined for different countries. Then the additional information problem arises to specify the effect of cost changes on trade flows. For this one has to know the reactions of demand and supply to these cost changes, possiby in terms of demand and supply elasticities. It should be expected that data in this area are more reliable since they have been estimated for a longer period.

APPENDIX: EMPIRICAL ESTIMATES

Pollution Content in Tons of Emissions

The pollution content of exports and imports has been calculated with input–output models for the United States and Germany [Leontief and

Table 3-1 Pollution Content of Exports and Imports in Tons of Emissions per 1 Million Dollar of Final Demand for Export and Import Substitutes and Change in Pollution Caused by Shifting Resources[a]

	Net exports	Competitive imports	Change in pollution
SO_X	65	101	+36
Particulates	23	32	9
CO	71	94	23
HC	10	9	−1
NO_X	11	10	+1

[a] From Leontief and Ford (1971, Table 3).

Table 3-2   SO$_2$-emissions per One Million German Marks of Final Demand

Private consumption	Private investment	Government consumption	Government investment	Export
98	74	51	63	112

[a] From Der Rat von Sachverständigen (1974, p. 583).

Ford (1971), Koo (1974), and Der Rat von Sachverständigen (1974)]. The studies all related to air pollution.

The pollution content is expressed in terms of tons of emissions per million dollars of exports and imports. Assume a country reduces export sales by one million dollars (1 million German marks) setting free the resources used in the export activities, and increases output of import-substitutes for final demands by one million dollars. According to Leontief and Ford (1971) (Base year: 1963; 90 sector-model) we get the results in Table 3-1. Calculations by Koo (1974) (base year 1963; 64 sector-model; based on Leontief and Ford's direct and indirect emission coefficients) seem to contradict Leontief and Ford considerably:

Consider a situation where the United States decides to reduce both its imports and exports by one million dollars each and increase the domestic output of import-competing industries by one million dollars . . . Then the particulates in the United States air would be increased by 394.53 thousand tons, hydrocarbons by 80.36 thousand tons, and nitrogen oxides by 12.64 thousand tons, while the sulfur oxide and the carbon monoxides in the air could be reduced by 22.96 and 377.92 thousand tons, respective. (Koo, 1974, p. 243/4.)

For the Federal Republic of Germany, [Der Rat von Sachverständigen (1974)], export demand has the highest SO$_2$-content of all components of final demand. This is explained by the fact that the energy sector, primary sectors, and investment goods are the most important inputs to the export sector. No data are available on the pollution content of import substitutes.

Pollution Content in Monetary Terms

Whereas estimates of the pollution content of trade in terms of tons of emissions should be comparable internationally, empirical results in terms of abatement costs are not comparable. This is due to the fact that, (1) the pollution content in physical terms may be calculated by different methods,

(2) that the studies rely on different estimation procedures of emission data, (3) countries show differences in abatement costs, and (4) immission norms to be reached differ between countries.

Examples of this approach are the calculations of price effects by Leontief and Ford (1971) and of control cost loadings by Walter (1973).

ACKNOWLEDGMENT

I appreciate comments to a first draft from Tracy Murray, Ingo Walter, Ralf Gronych, and Rüdiger Pethig.

N O T E S

1. Consumers of the good "environmental quality" may be identical in person to polluters.

2. The trade system also may have a feedback not shown in the chart on the other systems. Trade flows, location pattern and gains from trade determine to what extent trade targets, that is, balance of payments equilibrium and gains from trade, are realized. If trade targets are not realized, this represents additional "costs" of environmental policy if the term cost does not only denote resources used but also includes policy targets forgone.

3. In that case the market for abatement services is substituted by a political voting mechanism in the "Genossenschaften."

4. From Eq. 11, the effluent charge will be $(z = r_i{}^a/F_i{}^{a\,\prime})$ equal to marginal costs of prevention. The same holds true for Eq. 12.

5. Equation (12) is also obtained from

$$L = z^*(S_3^{a1} + S_3^{a2}) - r_3{}^a R_3{}^a$$
$$-\lambda_1[S_3{}^a - F_3{}^a(R_3{}^a)]$$
$$-\lambda_2[S_3{}^a - S_3^{a1} - S_3^{a2}]$$

for $z = z^*$.

6. On the problem of demand for a public good compare f. i. 5, 24, Chapter 7.

7. Quantities demanded may also depend on L, the valuation of environmental quality, of U, the existing environmental quality. Similarly, environmental quality demanded in Eq. 13 may depend the quantities of private commodities available.

8. $D_2{}^\prime < 0$, if products are complimentary. In a two-commodity world with an income constraint we cannot have complementary goods. I owe this comment to Tracy Murray.

9. For d_{p1} we have

$$d_{p1} = -\frac{\partial f}{\partial \alpha} \cdot d\alpha \{A[F_1'F_2'G_{p2}'G_{r1}' + D_2'F_1'G_{r1}' - D_1'F_2'G_{r2}']$$
$$- B[F_1'F_2'G_{p2}'G_{z1}' + D_2'F_1'G_{z1}' - D_1'F_2'G_{z2}'] + G_{r1}'G_{z2}'(D_1'F_2' + D_2'F_1')$$
$$- G_{r2}'G_{z1}'(D_2'F_1' + D_1'F_2')\}$$

and for dp_2

$$dp_2 - \frac{\partial f}{\partial \alpha} \cdot d\alpha \{ A[-F_1'F_2'G_{p1}'G_{r2}' - D_2'F_1'G_{r1}' + D_1'F_2'G_{r2}']$$
$$- B[F_1'F_2'G_{p1}'G_{z2}' + D_2'F_2'G_{z1}' - G_{r1}'G_{z2}'(D_1'F_2' + D_2'F_1') + G_{r2}'G_{z1}'(D_2'F_1' + D_1'F_2')] \}$$

10.   We only have discussed "sufficient" conditions. Possibly one or some conditions in Eq. 23 can be violated and compensated by the other conditions in Eq. 23.

11.   From Eq. 10 we have

$$dR_i = \frac{1}{a_i} dr_i - \frac{F_i'}{a_i} dp_i + \frac{H_i'F_i'}{a_i} dz$$

and from the equivalent equation to Eq. 10 (p. 34)

$$dR_i = G_{ri}'dr_i - G_{pi}'dp_i + G_{zi}'dz,$$

so that

$$G_{ri}' = \frac{1}{a_i}, G_{pi}' = -\frac{F_i'}{a_i} \quad \text{and} \quad G_{zi}' = \frac{H_i'F_i'}{a_i}$$

with

$$a_i = F_i''(p_i - zH_i') - zF_i'^2 H_i''$$

From Eq. 11 and its equivalent formulation we obtain

$$G_{ri}^{a'} = \frac{1}{zF_i^{a''}}, \quad \text{and} \quad G_{zi}^{a'} = -\frac{F_i^{a'}}{zF_i^{a''}}$$

12.   Observe that the argument depends on whether resource demand varies directly or inversely with the relevant variable (commodity price, resource price).

13.   On the concept of environmental scarcity and abundance, compare with Siebert (1975b).

14.   For the resource price we have

$$dr = -\frac{\partial f}{\partial \alpha} \cdot \frac{d\alpha}{\Delta} \{ D_1'F_2' + D_2'F_1' \} (G_{p2}'G_{z1}' - G_{p1}'G_{z2}')$$
$$+ A(D_1'F_2'G_{p2}' - D_2'F_1'G_{p1}' - F_1'F_2'G_{p1}'G_{p2}') \}$$

The first term in the bracket is positive, the second is negative.

15.   Alternatively, if w is flexible, B will be zero.

16.   The solution of Eq. 29 for dp_1 is:

$$dp_1 = \frac{dz}{\Delta'} [G_{z1}'G_{r2}' - G_{z2}'G_{r1}'][- G_{p2}^{+'}G_{r1}^{+'}(F_1F_2^+ - F_2F_1^+) + (F_2U + F_1V) \sum G_{ri}^{+'}]$$

$$\frac{dz^+}{\Delta'} [G_{z1}^{+'}G_{r2}^{+'} + G_{z2}^{+'}G_{r1}^{+'}][-G_{p2}'G_{r1}'(F_1F_2^+ - F_2F_1^+) + (F_2^+U + F_1V) \sum G_{ri}']$$

with $U = (D_1' - D_1^{+'})$ and $V = (D_2' - D_2^{+'})$

The solution of Eq. 29 for dp_2 is:

$$dp_2 = -\frac{dz}{\Delta'}[G'_{z1}G'_{r2} - G'_{z2}G'_{r1}][G^{+'}_{p1}G^{+'}_{r2}(F_1F_2{}^+ - F_2F_1{}^+) - (F_2U + F_1V)\sum G'_{rt}]$$

$$+\frac{dz^+}{\Delta'}[G^+_{z1}G'_{r2} - G^+_{z2}G^+_{r1}][G'_{p1}G'_{r2}(F_1F_2{}^+ - F_2F_1{}^+) - (F_2{}^+U + F_1V)\sum G'_{rt}]$$

17. The solution of Eq. 29 for dR_1 is:

$$dR_1 = \frac{F_2{}^+U + F_1{}^+V}{\Delta'}\{dz[G'_{z1}G'_{r2} - G'_{z2}G'_{r1}][G^+_{p1}G^+_{r2} - G^+_{p2}G^+_{r1}]$$

$$- dz^+[G^{+'}_{z1}G^{+'}_{r2} - G^{+'}_{z2}G^{+'}_{r1}][G_{p1}G_{r2} - G_{p2}G_{r1}]\}$$

18. On cost studies, compare Der Rat von Sachverständigen (1974), Chapter 5.2 with OECD (1972, 1973a, 1973b).

REFERENCES

d'Arge, R. C., "International Trade and Domestic Environmental Control: Some Empirical Estimates," in *Managing the Environment: International Economic Cooperation for Pollution Control*, A. V. Kneese et al., eds., New York: Praeger, 1971.

d'Arge, R. C., and A. V. Kneese, "Environmental Quality and International Trade," *International Organization, 26*, 419–465, 1972.

d'Arge, R. C., G. C. Hufbauer, and I. Walter, "Environmental Quality, Basic Materials Policy, and the International Economy," in *Management, Materials and Environment*, Cambridge, Mass.: MIT Press, 1973.

Baumol, W. J., *Environmental Protection, International Spillover and Trade*, Stockholm: Amqvist and Wiksell, 1971.

Bergstrom, T., and R. P. Goodman, "Private Demands for Public Goods," *American Economic Review, 63*, 280–296, 1973.

Bower, B. B. T., "Studies in Residuals Management in Industry" (Manuscript), *Conference on Economics of the Environment* sponsored by Resources for the Future and the National Bureau of Economic Research, Chicago, November 1972.

Connolly, M., "Public Goods, Externalities and International Relations," *Journal of Political Economy, 78*, 279–290, 1970.

Connolly, M., "Trade in Public Goods, A Diagrammatic Analysis," *Quarterly Journal of Economics 86*, 61–78, 1972.

Council on Environmental Quality, Department of Commerce, and Environmental Protection Agency, *The Economic Impact of Pollution Control*,Washington, D.C.: U.S. Government Printing Office, 1972.

Der Rat von Sachverständigen fur Umweltfragen, *Umweltgutachten 1974* Mainz-Stuttgart, 1974.

Estele, J., "Optimal Pollution Control and Trade in Collective Goods," *Journal of Public Economics, 3*, 203–216, 1974.

General Agreement on Tariffs and Trade, *Industrial Pollution and International Trade*, Geneva: GATT, 1971.

Gerelli, E., "Problèmes économiques internationaux de l'environnement: Commerces internationaux et pollution transfrontière, *Schweizerische Zeitschrift fur Volkswirtschaft und Statistik, 108,* 439–451 1972.

Klotz, B. P., "The Trade Effects of Unilateral Pollution Standards" in OECD, *Problems of Environmental Economics,* Paris, 1972.

Koo, A. Y. C., "Environmental Repercussion and Trade Theory," *Review of Economics and Statistics, 56,* 235–244, 1974.

Leontief, W., and W. F. Ford, "Air Pollution and the Economic Structure: Empirical Results of Input–Output Computations," in *Input–Output-Techniques,* A. Brody and A. P. Carter, Eds., Amsterdam-London: Elsevier, 1971, pp. 9–30.

Majocchi, A., "The Impact of Environmental Measures on International Trade: Some Policy Issues," *Revista Internazionale di Scienze Economiche e Commerciali,* 458–475, 1972.

Magee, S. P., and W. F. Ford, "Environmental Pollution, the Terms of Trade and Balance of Payments of the United States," *Kyklos, 25,* 101–118, 1972.

Malmgren, H. B., "Environmental Management and the International Economy," in *Managing the Environment, International Economic Cooperation for Pollution Control,* J. W. Harned, et al., Eds., New York: Praeger, 1971, pp. 53–70.

OECD, *Survey of Pollution Control Cost Estimates made in Member Countries, Environment Directorate,* (mimeographed) Paris, 1972.

OECD, *Pollution by the Pulp and Paper Industry: Present Situation and Trends,* (mimeographed) Paris, 1973a.

OECD, *Environment Directorate, Analysis of Costs of Pollution Control.* Paris, 1973b.

Pearson, C., and W., Takacs, "International Economic Implications of Environmental Control and Pollution Abatement Programs," in *United States International Economic Policy in an interdependent World: Report of the Williams Commission,* Washington, D.C.: U.S. Government Printing Office, July 1971.

Pethig, R., "Pollution, Welfare, and Environmental Policy in the Theory of Comparative Advantage," *Beitrage zur angewandten Wirtschaftsforschung,* Universität Mannheim, Discussion Paper No. 48/74.

Siebert, H., *Das produzierte Chaos, Ökonomie und Umwelt* (Stuttgart: 1973a).

Siebert, H., "Environment and Regional Growth," *Zeitschrift für Nationalökonomie, 33,* 79–85, 1973.

Siebert, H., "Environmental Protection and International Specialization," *Weltwirtschaftliches Archiv, 110,* 494–508, 1974a.

Siebert, H., "Trade and Environment," in *The International Division of Labor: Problems and Perspectives,* H. Giersch, Ed., Tübingen: J. C. B. Mohr (Paul Siebeck), 1974b.

Siebert, H., "Externalities, Environmental Quality and Allocation," a *Zeitschrift für die Wirttionalökonomie, 34,* 397–402, 1974.

Siebert, H., "Externalities, Environmental Quality and Allocation," a *Zeitschrift für die Wirtschafts- und Sozialwissenschaften,* 1975a, in press.

Siebert, H., "Regional Aspects of Environmental Allocation," *Zeitschrift für die gesamte Staatswissenschaft,* 1975b, in press.

Tietenberg, T. H., "Controlling Pollution by Price and Standard Systems: A General Equilibrium Analysis," *Swedish Journal of Economics, 75,* 193–203, 1973.

Tietenberg, T. H., "Specific Taxes and the Control of Pollution: A General Equilibrium Analysis," *Quarterly Journal of Economics, 87,* 503–522, 1973.

United Nations Conference on Trade and Development, *The Implications of Environmental, Measures of International Trade and Development,* Document TD/130, Santiago, 1972.

Walter, I., *Environmental Control and Consumer Protection: Emerging Forces in Multinational Corporate Operations,* Washington, D.C.: Center for Multinational Studies, Occasional Paper No. 2, 53, 1972.

Walter, I., "The Pollution Content of American Trade," *Western Economic Journal 11,* 61–70, 1973.

Walter, I., "Environmental Management and Optimal Resource-Use: The International Dimension," in *Das Umweltproblem in Ökonomischer Sicht,* H. Giersch, Ed., Tübingen: J. C. B. Mohr (Paul Siebeck), 133–152, 1974a.

Walter, I., "International Trade and Resource Diversion: The Case of Environmental Management," *Weltwirtschaftliches Archiv, 110,* 482–508, 1974b.

Walter, I., "Pollution and Protection: U.S. Environmental Controls as Competitive Distortions," *Weltwirtschaftliches Archiv, 110,* 104–113, 1974c.

Industrial Displacement Through Environmental Controls: The International Competitive Aspects

J. David Richardson and John H. Mutti

One accepted rationale for pollution-control standards is that even with competitive markets, we find industries where externalities exist, and where the social cost of production is greater than the private cost. For the particular case of production–consumption externalities, firms are not forced to take into account the reduction in welfare among unorganized consumers resulting from any pollution they create. By setting pollution-control standards, the government implicitly has assumed itself able to calculate the consumers' valuation of freedom from pollution, and to arrive at a situation where the marginal costs of meeting the standards are equal to the marginal benefits from achieving them. We do not know whether such a benefit–cost framework was used in establishing United States environmental controls. With respect to benefit calculations, we do not know what assumptions were made about the future demand for environmental quality, whether it was assumed to be a superior good, or what rate of growth was assumed for the future. With respect to cost calculations, we do not know what attention was paid to changing technology, or to the displacement of resources in industries adversely affected by changing relative prices. Displacements in output occur to the extent that users turn from pollution-intensive domestic goods to less expensive foreign goods, and factors of production are left unemployed because inputs are immobile and factor prices are inflexible. The lost output and employment, even if only temporary, are social costs of meeting pollution-control standards.

In this paper we explore several methods for analyzing the effect of current environmental controls on relative prices among United States industries, and the consequent change in our international competitive position. In one sense, efforts like this one can be considered necessary first steps in evaluating the costs of meeting pollution-control standards, and, therefore, should have been attempted before current standards in the United States were established.

However, the information generated is of interest both methodologically and in its own right. We approach the impact of United States environmental controls on prices, outputs, and international competitiveness by relying on available estimates of parameters that determine domestic and foreign demands and supplies, and on existing data relating to interindustry linkages. The major significance of our calculated increases in price and reductions in output from imposing controls is to show which industries feel the greatest impact when standards are adopted. We develop these measures not only for the case where the polluter himself must pay for any costs of meeting the standards, but also for cases where such expenditures are subsidized by the government and the revenue is raised by two different tax schemes. The incidence of environmental controls on prices and output from these three cases can be used in turn to determine the displacement of labor and the reduced profitability of capital in impacted industries, both of which represent issues of major political importance to any government.

In the next section of the chapter, we explain the general macroeconomic setting assumed in our analysis, and present the microeconomic framework for determining the relative price and output changes. Our empirical estimates of these changes are reported and discussed briefly in the third section of the chapter. In the fourth section, we speculate on how these estimates might be altered if a less confining set of assumptions were made. The final section summarizes the chapter.

METHODOLOGY AND FRAMEWORK FOR AN ILLUSTRATIVE EMPIRICAL ANALYSIS

Unlike earlier research on the domestic impact of environmental controls, ours is neither aggregate nor partial in its orientation. We adopt a model that allows us to focus on the effects of such controls on major industries, yet one that also allows comprehensive treatment of all industries simultaneously. Thus our work differs from that of Magee and Ford (1971), d'Arge (1971), and d'Arge and Kneese (1972), which focuses on the effects of environmental controls on a country's terms of trade, balance of payments, national income, and other macroeconomic variables. And it also differs from studies like those of the Council on Environmental Quality, the U.S. Department of Commerce, and the EPA (1972), which focus on the effects of environmental controls on particular industries' prices, output, profits, and employment in isolation.

The principal question we ask is: What are the price and output effects of environmental controls by industry, and how do they differ across industries? We narrow the question here and in the following section by devoting special attention to the heightened international competition that such controls induce for a number of industries, and by ignoring several important impacts of the controls. We shall go on to speculate on some analytical and methodological implications of adopting a broader, less restrictive, approach.

Narrowness and restrictiveness seem to be costs that are necessary to make a disaggregated-but-comprehensive approach empirically tractable. For perhaps the most important example, theoretical work has recognized the critical importance of identifying how environmental controls alter both interindustry flows of goods, and the composition of final demand, particularly investment demand. Both points are difficult to allow for empirically, although the former is somewhat less so because of data on the input–output structure of many modern economies. The latter point is often finessed by making dollar estimates of all costs of meeting environmental standards without explicitly considering what sectors will be most affected by the new pattern of demands (e.g., Walter, 1972). That approach is quite understandable. Even the breakdown of current expenditures for pollution abatement by industry is not well established, much less the capital expenditures. Capital flow tables are available with considerable lag and cannot yet be expected to reflect the shift in capital flows required by investment in environmental control equipment.

This limitation in particular suggests that any analysis ignoring changes in technology and industry demand is descriptive only for a relatively short time horizon over which major technological shifts have not occurred yet.

One tractable alternative—allowing for technical change through predicting new input–output coefficients on the basis of past changes (Carter 1970)—seems inappropriate since best-practice technologies in the future may not be closely related to what is indicated by past trends, especially in the case of shocks as fundamental as environmental controls. Therefore in adopting input–output analysis to estimate industry-by-industry price and output changes, we have additional reason to treat the results as applicable in the short run only.

As an illustration of one possible approach to estimating quantitatively the short-run impact of environmental controls on a disaggregated level, we focus first on the effects of such controls on industrial prices. Industrial prices will tend to rise directly because of the increased cost of environmental controls for which the industry is itself responsible, and indirectly since prices rise in supplier industries that are also saddled with environmental controls. Increased prices imply international competitive losses for many industries—losses which depend on how sensitive their business is to a change in the foreign-domestic price ratio. We measure such sensitivity by a weighted average of two demand–price elasticities: (1) the price elasticity of foreign demand for the industry's products (the export elasticity of demand), and (2) the price elasticity of domestic demand for the industry's products.[1] Employing this measure of sensitivity, we are able to estimate the response of industries' output (as well as prices) to the imposition of environmental controls.[2]

A critical, and somewhat novel, element in our calculations is elasticity (2) above, which indicates the responsiveness of demand by domestic residents for domestic output to a change in the foreign–domestic price ratio. This "domestic demand elasticity" is closely related to the more familiar import–demand elasticity: When domestic prices rise relative to foreign prices, imports rise and demand for domestic import-substitutes falls. The import demand elasticity measures the former effect; the domestic demand elasticity measures the latter. But it is impossible to compare the quantitative size of the former effect to the latter without further assumptions about structure. We treat imports and domestic goods in any industry classification i as imperfect substitutes from the perspective of the user, and further assume that each pair of imports and domestic competing goods can be treated independently from all other goods in other industry classifications.[3] Under these assumptions, a plausible representation of the markets for the two goods is:

$$\ln M_d{}^i = \alpha_m + \beta_m \ln Y^i + \xi_m \ln (P_m{}^i/P^i) \qquad (1)$$

$$\ln M_s{}^i = \delta_m + \epsilon_m \ln P_m{}^i - \epsilon_m \ln C_m{}^i \qquad (2)$$

$$\ln D_d{}^i = \alpha + \beta \ln Y^i + \xi \ln (P^i/P_m{}^i) \tag{3}$$

$$\ln D_s{}^i = \delta + \epsilon \ln P^i(1 - E^i) - \epsilon \ln C^i \tag{4}$$

where

$M_d{}^i, M_s{}^i$ = the quantity of imports of i demand by domestic residents and supplied, respectively;

$D_d{}^i, D_s{}^i$ = the quantity of domestic good i demanded by domestic residents and supplied, respectively;

$P_m{}^i, P^i$ = the dollar prices of "foreign i" and "domestic i," respectively;

Y^i = an appropriately defined scale variable;

E^i = an "environmental cost loading" for good i, that is, the percentage of the price of good i made up of the direct costs of environmental control in that industry;[4]

$C_m{}^i, C^i$ = some composite or index of the costs of foreign and domestic production, respectively, costs being defined to exclude the return to entrepreneurial activity.

More precisely, for our purposes, let C^i be defined by

$$\ln C^i = \sum_j a_{ji}^D \ln p^j + \sum_j a_{ji}^M \ln P_m{}^j + \sum_k c_{ki} W_k \tag{5}$$

where

a_{ai}^D, a_{ji}^M = the *value* input–output coefficients for inputs of domestic goods and imported goods, respectively, in domestic production of good i;

$\sum_k c_{ki} W_k$ = the costs of all primary inputs apart from the return to entrepreneurial activity.

The information requirements of such a system clearly are quite large if we hope to analyze each industry of, say, the 83 industry input–output table for the United States. To make the analysis more manageable we made the additional, simplifying assumption that import prices facing the United States are given exogenously. The assumption, which is implied by infinitely price-elastic import supply curves, has been resorted to quite often in empirical international-trade studies (Magee, 1972), and does not seem to conflict too strongly with estimated import supply elasticities (Richardson, 1973). If on the contrary, import prices did rise with the imposition of environmental controls in the United States, then we overstate the decrease in domestic production resulting from increases in environmental costs. We also understate the increase in domestic prices resulting from increases in environmental costs.

Another simplifying assumption we made is that all "income" or "scale" effects can be ignored. For purposes of the illustrative analysis of this and the next section, one methodological defense of the assumption is our aim of evaluating the effects of environmental controls alone, apart from their effects on admittedly real distortions in the economy, such as unemployment. Thus employment and capacity utilization can be assumed to be held constant, even in the short run (say by government policy). A weaker rationale is the comparative ignorance on how income and scale effects differ from industry to industry.[5]

The implication of all these assumptions for the manageability of the equation system 1–5 is striking. The import supply equation drops out because of the exogeneity of import prices; the definition of domestic production costs can be substituted into the domestic supply equation; and the whole system can be expressed succinctly in terms of rates of change of the variables:[6]

$$\frac{dM_d{}^i}{M_d{}^i} = - \xi_m \frac{dP^i}{P^i} \tag{6}$$

$$\frac{dD_d{}^i}{D_d{}^i} = \xi \frac{dP^i}{P^i} \tag{7}$$

$$\frac{dD_s{}^i}{D_s{}^i} = \epsilon \left(\frac{dP^i}{P^i} - E^i \right) - \epsilon \sum_j a_{ji}^D \frac{dP^j}{P^j} \tag{8}$$

Since the focus of this chapter is on the response of domestic prices and output to environmental controls, Eq. 6 has limited interest to us for the moment. Furthermore, since Eqs. 7 and 8 describe only domestic demand and output for use by domestic residents, we must add exports to both equations:

$$\frac{dQ_d{}^i}{Q_d{}^i} = \eta \frac{dP^i}{P^i} \tag{9}$$

$$\frac{dQ_s{}^i}{Q_s{}^i} = \epsilon \left(\frac{dP^i}{P^i} - E^i \right) - \epsilon \sum_j a_{ji}^D \frac{dP^j}{P^j} \tag{10}$$

where

$Q^i = D^i + X^i =$ domestic output sold to domestic residents plus exports (X^i);

$$\eta = \xi \frac{D_d{}^i}{Q_d{}^i} + \xi_x \frac{X_d{}^i}{Q_d{}^i}$$

= the price elasticity of demand facing domestic producers, a weighted average of the price elasticities of domestic and foreign demand, respectively, for the industry's products (ξ, ξ_x), the weights being the domestic and foreign shares of the industry's total business;

and where domestic supply behavior is not assumed to differ between domestic and foreign customers:[7] Thus Eq. 10 differs in no important way from Eq. 8.

There are as many pairs of Eqs. 9 and 10 as there are goods in the economy. If we chose to work with 81 disaggregated industries, as is possible employing the most familiar United States input–output table, and as we do in the following section, the entire 162-equation system could be solved for price–output changes by industry as a function of environmental cost loadings (E_i). The necessary parameters would be the domestic supply and demand elasticities, all domestic input–output coefficients in value terms, and the assumed cost loadings.

We began our analysis by retreating from this most general case in order to tie our study to previous work in the field. Walter (1973), in his study of the effects of environmental controls on United States "international competitiveness" (see note 1), presents both direct and overall environmental cost loadings for most industries producing tradeables in the standard input–output table. In doing so, however, he implicitly assumes that all domestic supply curves are infinitely elastic ($\epsilon = \infty$), since all of the cost loading is passed on to the purchaser in the form of higher prices. Such an assumption is particularly convenient because it further decreases the information necessary to carry out the analysis sketched above. Equations 9 and 10 can be rewritten for the entire economy, using matrix notation, as:[8]

$$\frac{dP}{P} = [I - A^{D'}]^{-1}E \tag{11}$$

$$\frac{dQ}{Q} = [I - A^{D'}]^{-1}E \cdot \eta \tag{12}$$

P, Q, E, and η represent vectors of prices, outputs, cost loadings, and demand–price elasticities; where A^D represents the matrix of domestic-good requirements per unit of output; and where the symbol·stands for scalar multiplication of each row in the left-hand matrix by its corresponding element in the right-hand vector.

The principal difficulty with this scheme for assessing the price-output effects of environmental controls is that values of η, the demand price elasticities facing domestic producers, have not been estimated for most of the industry categories included in the input output table. Buckler and Almon (1972), however, report export price elasticities of demand (ξ_x) for similar categories to those in the standard input–output table,[9] and as is clear from the definition of η following Eq. 10, these constitute a portion of the value of η. Furthermore, by imposing more structure on the model of Eqs. 1–5, we are able to relate the domestic demand price elasticity (ξ) functionally to import demand price elasticities [ξ_m in Eqs. 1 and 6]—that Buckler and Almon (1972) also estimate.

The additional structure we assume in every pair of markets for imports and domestic substitutes is familiar in empirical international economic research (e.g., in Salant and Vacarra, 1960, Baldwin and Kay, 1973): It is that any change in either import prices or domestic prices that increases one by some *dollar* value, decreases the other by the *same* dollar value. Expenditure on the two together remains constant, implying, under our other assumptions as well, that:

$$\xi = \xi_m\left(\frac{P_m{}^iM^i}{P^iD^i}\right) - 1 \tag{13}$$

Thus ξ can be obtained from Buckler's and Almon's estimates of ξ_m. And η, the price elasticity of demand facing domestic producers is a weighted average of ξ and ξ_x (also gleaned from Buckler and Almon).

Estimates of η based on these assumptions are reported in Appendix A. Solution vectors dP/P and dQ/Q for Eqs. 11 and 12 are reported in Section III of this paper. They are based on these estimates of η and, largely, on the environmental cost loadings (E) presented by Walter (1972).[10]

Before uncritically accepting such calculations, we focus again on the question of a relevant time horizon for our analysis. Infinitely elastic domestic supply curves, on which Eqs. 11 and 12 are based, may be appropriate for nearly all industries over some short time span before any price response is made to sales declines. However, when fixed capital accounts for some share of value added, we expect prices to be driven down in competitive markets. Therefore, infinitely elastic supply curves are tenable over longer periods of time only if firms in all industries have a considerable amount of market power. At the same time there is an alternative justification for highly elastic domestic supply curves which assumes a much *longer* time horizon: if firms reattain their long run equilibrium positions when producing with constant-returns-to-scale production functions, prices do not rise in a competitive, partial-equilibrium setting.[11] Evidence from cost and production function studies (e.g., Johnston, 1960, Walters, 1963) indicates this high elasticity may not be too inappropriate for many service and manufacturing industries. However, how long such adjustment takes has not been well determined by economists. Admittedly, complete adjustment does not occur in the very short run.

Additionally, the time horizon relevant to an analysis of the industrial displacement from environmental controls depends on how such controls are imposed. If the controls are phased in gradually over time, then perhaps firms in an industry need not deviate greatly from their long-run desired capital–labor ratio, and correspondingly they do not face as large a loss on resources that are fixed and industry-specific in the short run. In such a case, the assumption of highly elastic domestic supply curves may be appropriate (although if a considerable compliance lag is allowed, predictions into the future based on constant input–output coefficients are less likely to be accurate).[12]

We raise these points about time horizons in order to justify an alternative set of calculations to those for Eqs. 11 and 12. If the controls underlying Walter's (1972) environmental cost loadings must be met in the immediate future, then we should allow for the short run immobility of resources and consequent finite price elasticities of domestic supply. In this case, the calculations we present can serve as a basis for calculating the social loss arising from the idling of resources that occurs when controls are imposed, and the private distributive effects felt by workers and capitalists who lose the rents they formerly collected on industry-specific skills and equipment. When resources are industry-specific in the long run as well as the short run, as is likely in mining and agriculture, using less-than-infinite elasticities is all the more appropriate. Given finite domestic supply elasticities, Eqs. 11 and 12 are inappropriate. Instead, Eqs. 9 and 10 must be rewritten for the entire economy as:[13]

$$\frac{dP}{P} = \left[I - \left(A^{D\prime} \cdot \frac{\epsilon}{\epsilon - \eta} \right) \right]^{-1} E \cdot \frac{\epsilon}{\epsilon - \eta} \tag{14}$$

$$\frac{dQ}{Q} = \left\{ \left[I - \left(A^{D\prime} \cdot \frac{\epsilon}{\epsilon - \eta} \right) \right]^{-1} E \cdot \frac{\epsilon}{\epsilon - \eta} \right\} \cdot \eta \tag{15}$$

where $\epsilon/\epsilon - \eta$ is a vector of these ratios for each industry, and all other notation corresponds to that of Eqs. 11 and 12.

Calculating price–output responses to environmental controls from Eqs. 14 and 15 obviously requires that we know the appropriate short-run supply elasticity for each industry. Most empirical work for manufacturing industries has rejected supply equations in favor of price-determination equations. However, in a simultaneous system where we believe both price and output are endogenously determined, we can derive a structural supply elasticity.[14] Following that procedure in the next section, we have derived manufacturing supply elasticities from price equations estimated by Perry (1973), Eckstein and Wyss (1972), and Goldstein (1972). Agricultural supply elasticities were taken from Tweeten (1969). By casual empiricism, supply elasticities in mining industries appeared to be quite low, but were assumed to be no less than 0.2. Supply elasticities in service industries were assumed to be quite large, even in the short-run. A complete listing of these price elasticities of supply is reported in Appendix A. Quantitative price–output shocks from the imposition of United States environmental controls for the regime summarized by Eqs. 14 and 15 are reported in the following section in the same tables as those for the regime of Eqs. 11 and 12.

Both of the methods we have proposed above for calculating the industrial incidence of environmental controls begin with the vector of environmental cost loadings, E. As has been mentioned, our employment of these cost loadings implicitly assumes that every industry "bears the cost" of its own environmental control, either by absorbing these environmental costs into primary factor incomes and profits, or by passing them through to the final user in higher prices.[15] This method of bearing the cost of controls is sometimes called the "polluter-pays" principle—the firm violating government environmental standards must invest in the necessary pollution abatement process or go out of business. Because some industries may be quite adversely affected by environmental controls financed according to the polluter-pays principle, there is a political temptation either to relax the standards or to subsidize such industries. We shall not consider the first case in detail, since it is implicitly allowed for in the first set of calculations. Instead we shall analyze the case where subsidies are paid to all industries, subsidies sufficient to cover the full cost of environmental controls. At first glance, one might think that there would thus be no tendency for any industrial price to rise, no consequent competitive disadvantage for any industry in export-or import-substitute markets, and no industrial displacement from environmental controls. Such a blissful scenario cannot possibly be descriptive, however, since it neglects the fact that revenues must be raised in some way to finance the subsidies, and such revenue raising will tend to have an impact on industrial prices and output.[16]

The revenue to finance environmental controls may be raised in several different ways, either through taxation or borrowing schemes. The borrowing alternative has been assumed in other analyses (e.g., d'Arge, 1971), but that approach allows us to slip too easily into the belief that no resource cost at all is involved. Rather resources must in part be attracted away from alternative uses, either through increased interest rates or differential rates of price increases.[17] These considerations are more macroeconomic in nature and a breakdown of their effects on disaggreagate industries has not been attempted here or in next section, but we do consider these issues qualitatively again in the section "Broader Methodological Considerations."

We shall focus on taxation-with-subsidization as a means of financing environmental control alternative to the polluter-pays principle. One type of tax to consider is a value-added tax of the same percentage on all sectors of the economy. Alternatively this might be viewed as a proportional income tax on all employee compensation and property income if we treat depreciation as part of income, and ignore the share of value added accounted for by indirect business taxes.[18]

Operationally, since the environmental cost loadings under the polluter-pays principle are reported by industry as expenditures per dollar of sales, the total revenue required to subsidize environmental control can be approximated by multiplying the vector of cost loadings by the vector of total sales from the input–output table. The value-added (income) tax rate can then be approximated by dividing this total revenue by aggregate value added.[19]

Given a value-added (income) tax rate calculated by this procedure, a set of price–output shocks due to environmental controls financed in this way can be computed. We levy the appropriate tax on each industry instead of the environmental cost loading, taking care to levy it *not* on the dollar value of sales, but rather on value added by industry. In the case of infinitely price-elastic domestic supply curves:

$$\frac{dP}{P} = [I - A^{D'}]^{-1}[T \cdot V] \tag{16}$$

$$\frac{dQ}{Q} = [I - A^{D'}]^{-1}[T \cdot V] \cdot \eta \tag{17}$$

where T is a vector of identical value-added tax rates, and V is the vector of value-added shares in total output by industry. In the case of domestic supply curves with finite price elasticity:

$$\frac{dP}{P} = \left[I - \left(A^{D'} \cdot \frac{\epsilon}{\epsilon - \eta}\right)\right]^{-1}\left[T \cdot V \cdot \frac{\epsilon}{\epsilon - \eta}\right] \tag{18}$$

$$\frac{dQ}{Q} = \left\{\left[I - \left(A^{D'} \cdot \frac{\epsilon}{\epsilon - \eta}\right)\right]^{-1}\left[T \cdot V \cdot \frac{\epsilon}{\epsilon - \eta}\right]\right\} \cdot \eta \tag{19}$$

A set of quantitative price–output shocks from the imposition of environmental controls financed by subsidies and a general value-added (income) tax are reported in the next section.

Proceeding in this simple fashion implies that the origin principle is applied in assessing the value-added tax, rather than the destination principle. That is, the tax is not applied to imports and is applied to exports. Thus we need not allow for any rise in import prices due to the tax, nor need we treat export prices differently from domestic prices. For true value-added taxes, the situation is of course quite the opposite: virtually all "indirect" taxes, including value-added taxes, are levied according to the destination principle. Thus the tax *is* assessed to imports, and rebated on exports. At first glance, one might imagine that there would then be no change in international competitiveness for any United States producer as a result of environmental controls financed by such a tax. The impression is misleading, however. Under the maintained assumption that the supply of *imports* is infinitely elastic, the price of imports must rise by exactly the tax rate: $dP_m^i/P_m^i = T$ for all i. But if domestic supply curves are *not* infinitely elastic, domestic prices will rise by less than the tax rate: $dP^i/P^i \leqq T$, and United States producers will in fact become *more* competitive in export and import substitute markets, not less. Industrial prices would rise, but output would expand. More generally still, if both import supply and domestic supply were less-than-infinitely elastic, industrial prices would rise, but the direction of change in output could not be determined without quantitative information.

On the other hand entirely, value-added taxes are very closely related to income taxes, as we imply above. Income taxes are, however, considered to be "direct" taxes, and cannot be charged against imports or rebated on exports according to the rules of the General Agreement on Tariffs and Trade (GATT). Thus the origin principle holds necessarily. Equations 16–19 and our calculations in the section, "Empirical Results" may be most applicable to this kind of tax.

To highlight the importance of how environmental controls are financed, we consider one other tax that might be used to finance the appropriate subsidies: a turnover, sales, or production tax.[20] The appropriate tax rate in this case, say T^*, can be approximated by dividing total revenue necessary to finance environmental control by aggregate output (production).[21] The price–output incidence of environmental controls financed by subsidies and production taxes can be computed by levying the appropriate tax on each industry. In the case of infinitely price-elastic domestic supply curves:

$$\frac{dP}{P} = [I - A^{D'}]^{-1}T^* \tag{20}$$

$$\frac{dQ}{Q} = [I - A^{D'}]^{-1}T^* \cdot \eta \tag{21}$$

where T^* = a vector of identical production tax rates. In the case of domestic supply curves with finite elasticity:

$$\frac{dP}{P} = \left[I - \left(A^{D\prime} \cdot \frac{\epsilon}{\epsilon - \eta}\right)\right]^{-1}\left[T^* \cdot \frac{\epsilon}{\epsilon - \eta}\right] \tag{22}$$

$$\frac{dQ}{Q} = \left\{\left[I - \left(A^{D\prime} \cdot \frac{\epsilon}{\epsilon - \eta}\right)\right]^{-1}\left[T^* \cdot \frac{\epsilon}{\epsilon - \eta}\right]\right\} \cdot \eta \tag{23}$$

Quantitative price–output shocks from the imposition of environmental controls financed by subsidies and a general production tax are reported in the next section.

One final comment to make with respect to the procedure and data proposed in this section and applied below is that the interindustry flows reported in the most familiar United States input–output tables include both imports and domestically produced goods. This is true regardless of whether we consider the published total-base or domestic-base tables.[22] Unfortunately, we showed above that the appropriate set of coefficients to use in weighting increased-input prices should be those coefficients reflecting only the value of domestically produced good j required to produce one dollar of good i ($a_{ji}{}^{D}$, an element in the matrix $A_{ji}{}^{D}$). Although European countries collect the data necessary to construct such a matrix, the requisite United States data are not readily available. To compensate for this deficiency, we have assumed that all users of a given intermediate input require domestic and imported goods in the same proportion. That assumption implies import shares of the total market are fairly constant, and that the average and marginal propensities to import a good are equal. If these assumptions are approximately true, then each row of the input–output table can be multiplied by the percentage of the total market accounted for by domestic goods, say b.[23] We are then left with an approximation to the pure domestic base table, appropriate for the expressions to be solved above. Using Eq. (11) as an example, the algebraic representation of the procedure is:

$$\frac{dP}{P} = [I - (A \cdot b)']^{-1}E \tag{24}$$

where A is what is called the domestic-base table in United States data. The unattractive aspect of this procedure is that it requires the inversion of a modified input–output matrix. If import shares are not very stable, then the expense of such a step seems unjustified. But if there is some degree of instability in market shares, we believe this adjustment is preferable to using the reported coefficients as they stand, and have employed it in our calculations of price–output effects from Eqs. 11–12 and 14–23.

EMPIRICAL RESULTS

As outlined above, six different illustrative approaches were taken to calculating the short-run displacement of United States industry due to unilaterally imposed environmental controls. In each approach, controls force an industry to raise price, either directly or indirectly, thereby causing it to lose export markets to foreign competitors, and subjecting it to more severe import competition. Our interest is in the differential impact of these environmental controls on prices and output from industry to industry.

Table 4-1 records the estimated price impacts of environmental controls on the 81 industries distinguished in the most familiar (1967) United States input–output table. Table 4-2 records the estimated impacts of the controls on physical output for the same set of industries. For each industry, the price–output incidence of controls is calculated variously under the assumptions: (1) that industries bear the cost of their own environmental clean-up directly (polluter pays); (2) that industries are fully subsidized for the cost of environmental controls, and the subsidies are financed by a general tax on value added or national income; and (3) that industries are fully subsidized as above, but the subsidies are financed by a general turnover, sales, or production tax. Under each of the three financing options, industries are characterized in two ways: either (A) they make no price response to a change in demand (infinite domestic supply elasticities); or (B) they do make price responses, determined by available empirical evidence on supply elasticities and/or domestic price determination.

The percentage increases in prices in Table 4-1 correspond exactly to Eqs. 11, 14, 16, 18, 20, and 22. The percentage declines in physical output in Table 4-2 correspond exactly to Eqs. 12, 15, 17, 19, 21, and 23.

There are several striking generalizations from the illustrative calculations. First, if industrial displacement can be taken to refer both to increased costs and reduced business from environmental controls, then "displacement" is spread more evenly across industries under either of the tax-subsidy schemes than under the "polluter pays" principle. Under the tax-subsidy arrangements, the great majority of industries find that their prices rise and their output declines from 1 to 1.5%.[24] Only a few do better with respect to output—those in agriculture and mining under the (realistic) assumption that their price elasticities of supply are comparatively low. *No* industry suffers more than 2.5% displacement.[25] By contrast, under the "polluter pays" principle, a number of industries suffer from 3 to 5% displacement—among others, livestock, chemicals, plastics, paints, petroleum refining, nonferrous metal manufacturing, and utilities. These displacements are only somewhat dampened by the assumption of finite supply elasticities. They seem in some cases (e.g., nonferrous metals) to be due more to

Table 4-1   Percentage Increases in Domestic Prices from Environmental Controls

| Industry Number and Title | Method of Financing | | |
	Polluter Pays	Value-Added Tax	Production Tax
AGRICULTURE, FORESTRY, AND FISHERIES			
1. Livestock and livestock products	3.03	1.46	1.95
	0.50	0.23	0.35
2. Other agricultural products	2.94	1.48	1.49
	0.63	0.32	0.31
3. Forestry and fishery products	1.53	1.46	1.41
	0.19	0.22	0.21
4. Agricultural, forestry, and fishery services	1.37	1.47	1.42
	0.67	1.12	1.03
MINING			
5. Iron and ferroalloy ores mining	1.72	1.41	1.46
	0.25	0.21	0.21
6. Nonferrous metal ores mining	1.76	1.40	1.43
	0.23	0.19	0.19
7. Coal mining	2.62	1.49	1.34
	0.41	0.23	0.21
8. Crude petroleum and natural gas	0.88	1.50	1.24
	0.13	0.23	0.19
9. Stone and clay mining and quarrying	1.33	1.48	1.35
	0.18	0.22	0.20
10. Chemical and fertilizer mineral mining	1.55	1.48	1.25
	0.22	0.22	0.18
CONSTRUCTION			
11. New construction	1.63	1.45	1.65
	1.39	1.31	1.49
12. Maintenance and repair construction	1.26	1.48	1.38
	1.07	1.37	1.26

Table 4-1 Continued

	Method of Financing		
Industry Number and Title	Polluter Pays	Value-Added Tax	Production Tax

MANUFACTURING

13.	Ordinance and accessories	1.50	1.43	1.56
		1.32	1.33	1.45
14.	Food and kindred products	1.95	1.42	1.97
		0.80	0.77	1.13
15.	Tobacco manufactures	1.13	1.49	1.53
		0.49	1.05	1.08
16.	Broad and narrow fabrics, yarn and thread mills	2.01	1.43	1.94
		1.15	0.89	1.25
17.	Miscellaneous textile goods and floor coverings	2.09	1.40	1.94
		1.28	0.91	1.28
18.	Apparel	1.21	1.45	1.86
		0.75	1.07	1.38
19.	Miscellaneous fabricated textile products	1.50	1.41	2.00
		0.90	0.99	1.44
20.	Lumber and wood products, except containers	0.84	1.39	1.59
		0.51	1.04	1.21
21.	Wooden containers	1.14	1.42	1.63
		0.87	1.13	1.31
22.	Household furniture	1.37	1.44	1.61
		1.14	1.29	1.43
23.	Other furniture and fixtures	1.47	1.44	1.57
		1.26	1.31	1.43
24.	Paper and allied products, except containers	2.85	1.40	1.62
		1.70	0.82	0.95
25.	Paperboard containers and boxes	3.08	1.39	1.68
		1.75	0.77	0.94
26.	Printing and publishing	0.92	1.46	1.48
		0.68	1.33	1.34
27.	Chemicals and selected chemical products	4.00	1.42	1.69
		3.39	1.14	1.38
28.	Plastics and synthetic materials	4.18	1.44	1.77
		3.62	1.20	1.50
29.	Drugs, cleaning, and toilet preparations	2.29	1.46	1.70
		1.95	1.28	1.48

Table 4-1   Continued

	Method of Financing		
Industry Number and Title	Polluter Pays	Value-Added Tax	Production Tax

MANUFACTURING, CONT.

Industry Number and Title	Polluter Pays	Value-Added Tax	Production Tax
30. Paints and allied products	5.12	1.41	1.80
	4.51	1.17	1.52
31. Petroleum refining and related industries	4.78	1.42	1.68
	2.41	0.46	0.65
32. Rubber and miscellaneous plastics products	2.02	1.43	1.60
	1.41	1.04	1.16
33. Leather tanning and industrial leather products	2.23	1.41	1.86
	1.78	1.16	1.55
34. Footwear and other leather products	1.31	1.43	1.67
	1.06	1.27	1.48
35. Glass and glass products	1.79	1.48	1.38
	1.55	1.33	1.22
36. Stone and clay products	2.84	1.47	1.52
	2.50	1.24	1.29
37. Primary iron and steel manufacturing	2.66	1.37	1.54
	2.23	1.43	1.28
38. Primary nonferrous metal manufacturing	3.36	1.25	1.69
	1.75	0.62	0.86
39. Metal containers	2.05	1.40	1.74
	1.63	1.16	1.46
40. Heating, plumbing, and structural metal products	1.89	1.40	1.69
	1.49	1.16	1.41
41. Stampings, screw machine products, and bolts	1.74	1.42	1.55
	1.38	1.20	1.30
42. Other fabricated metal products	1.75	1.42	1.57
	1.36	1.18	1.30
43. Engines and turbines	2.29	1.40	1.70
	1.92	1.19	1.46
44. Farm machinery and equipment	2.23	1.39	1.66
	1.88	1.19	1.43
45. Construction, mining, and oil field machinery	2.17	1.42	1.59
	1.89	1.25	1.40
46. Materials handling machinery and equipment	2.19	1.42	1.65
	1.86	1.23	1.43

Table 4-1 Continued

| | Method of Financing | | |
Industry Number and Title	Polluter Pays	Value-Added Tax	Production Tax
MANUFACTURING, CONT.			
47. Metalworking machinery and	1.94	1.44	1.45
equipment	1.65	1.26	1.26
48. Special industry machinery	2.00	1.40	1.53
and equipment	1.70	1.21	1.33
49. General industrial machinery	2.09	1.43	1.56
and equipment	1.77	1.24	1.34
50. Machine shop products	1.92	1.46	1.41
	1.63	1.28	1.22
51. Office, computing, and	1.27	1.42	1.58
accounting machines	1.01	1.21	1.34
52. Service industry machines	2.35	1.41	1.82
	1.95	1.20	1.55
53. Electric industrial equipment	1.50	1.42	1.53
and apparatus	1.20	1.23	1.32
54. Household appliances	1.79	1.43	1.73
	1.43	1.21	1.48
55. Electric lighting and wiring	1.54	1.44	1.53
equipment	1.20	1.23	1.30
56. Radio, television, and	1.23	1.43	1.51
communication equipment	1.02	1.27	1.33
57. Electronic components and	1.39	1.42	1.54
accessories	1.12	1.23	1.32
58. Miscellaneous electrical	1.69	1.41	1.62
machinery, equipment, and	1.30	1.20	1.36
supplies			
59. Motor vehicles and equipment	2.66	1.40	1.87
	2.42	1.27	1.71
60. Aircraft and parts	1.51	1.43	1.59
	1.34	1.34	1.49
61. Other transportation equipment	1.89	1.40	1.68
	1.66	1.27	1.52
62. Scientific and controlling	4.54	1.42	1.59
instruments	4.01	1.21	1.35
63. Optical, ophthalmic, and	4.31	1.45	1.34
photographic equipment	3.84	1.27	1.15

Table 4-1 Continued

	Method of Financing		
Industry Number and Title	Polluter Pays	Value-Added Tax	Production Tax
64. Miscellaneous manufacturing	2.22	1.38	1.56
	1.95	1.24	1.39

SERVICES, GOVERNMENT, DUMMY, AND SPECIAL INDUSTRIES

65. Transportation and warehousing	1.12	1.47	1.29
	0.97	1.40	1.21
66. Communications; except radio	0.29	1.51	0.99
and TV broadcasting	0.25	1.49	0.97
67. Radio and TV broadcasting	0.58	1.51	1.48
	0.51	1.47	1.44
68. Electric, gas, water, and	5.37	1.50	1.50
sanitary services	5.18	1.33	1.35
69. Wholesale and retail trade	0.71	1.51	1.15
	0.63	1.47	1.11
70. Finance and insurance	0.55	1.51	1.38
	0.50	1.48	1.34
71. Real estate and rental	0.61	1.51	1.12
	0.56	1.46	1.07
72. Hotels; personal and repair	0.93	1.49	1.33
services except auto	0.82	1.43	1.26
73. Business services	0.84	1.49	1.46
	0.74	1.44	1.40
75. Automobile repair and services	1.06	1.48	1.42
	0.93	1.41	1.34
76. Amusements	0.88	1.49	1.43
	0.74	1.42	1.35
77. Medical, educational services,	0.52	1.51	1.19
and nonprofit organizations	0.44	1.46	1.14
78. Federal government enterprises	0.91	1.44	1.26
	0.70	1.33	1.15
79. State and local government	1.18	1.51	1.42
enterprises	1.05	1.43	1.35
80. Business travel, entertainment,	1.83	1.42	2.21
and gifts	1.39	1.18	1.91
81. Office supplies	3.17	1.32	2.16
	2.76	1.12	1.93

Table 4-2 Percentage Decrease in Domestic Output from Environmental Controls

Industry Number and Title	Method of Financing		
	Polluter Pays	Value-Added Tax	Production Tax

AGRICULTURE, FORESTRY, AND FISHERIES

Industry Number and Title	Polluter Pays	Value-Added Tax	Production Tax
1. Livestock and livestock products	3.06	1.47	1.97
	0.51	0.23	0.35
2. Other agricultural products	2.71	1.36	1.37
	0.58	0.29	0.29
3. Forestry and fishery products	2.13	2.03	1.96
	0.26	0.31	0.29
4. Agricultural, forestry, and	1.37	1.47	1.42
fishery services	0.67	1.12	1.03

MINING

Industry Number and Title	Polluter Pays	Value-Added Tax	Production Tax
5. Iron and ferroalloy ores mining	1.76	1.44	1.49
	0.25	0.21	0.21
6. Nonferrous metal ores mining	1.85	1.47	1.50
	0.25	0.20	0.20
7. Coal mining	2.36	1.34	1.21
	0.37	0.21	0.19
8. Crude petroleum and natural gas	0.90	1.53	1.26
	0.13	0.23	0.19
9. Stone and clay mining and	1.38	1.54	1.40
quarrying	0.19	0.23	0.21
10. Chemical and fertilizer mineral	1.61	1.54	1.30
mining	0.23	0.23	0.19

CONSTRUCTION

Industry Number and Title	Polluter Pays	Value-Added Tax	Production Tax
11. New construction	1.63	1.45	1.65
	1.39	1.31	1.49
12. Maintenance and repair	1.26	1.48	1.38
construction	1.07	1.37	1.26

MANUFACTURING

Industry Number and Title	Polluter Pays	Value-Added Tax	Production Tax
13. Ordinance and accessories	1.50	1.43	1.56
	1.32	1.33	1.45

Table 4-2 Continued

Industry Number and Title	Method of Financing		
	Polluter Pays	Value-Added Tax	Production Tax

MANUFACTURING, CONT.

Industry Number and Title	Polluter Pays	Value-Added Tax	Production Tax
14. Food and kindred products	1.99	1.45	2.01
	0.81	0.79	1.15
15. Tobacco manufactures	1.04	1.37	1.41
	0.45	0.97	0.99
16. Broad and narrow fabrics, yarn and thread mills	2.07	1.47	2.00
	1.18	0.92	1.29
17. Miscellaneous textile goods and floor coverings	2.28	1.53	2.11
	1.40	0.99	1.40
18. Apparel	1.29	1.55	1.99
	0.81	1.14	1.48
19. Miscellaneous fabricated textile products	1.50	1.41	2.00
	0.90	0.99	1.44
20. Lumber and wood products, except containers	0.90	1.49	1.70
	0.55	1.11	1.29
21. Wooden containers	1.14	1.42	1.63
	0.87	1.13	1.31
22. Household furniture	1.37	1.44	1.61
	1.14	1.29	1.43
23. Other furniture and fixtures	1.47	1.44	1.57
	1.26	1.31	1.43
24. Paper and allied products, except containers	2.82	1.39	1.60
	1.68	0.81	0.94
25. Paperboard containers and boxes	3.08	1.39	1.68
	1.75	0.77	0.94
26. Printing and publishing	0.93	1.47	1.49
	0.68	1.34	1.35
27. Chemicals and selected chemical products	3.84	1.36	1.62
	3.25	1.09	1.32
28. Plastics and synthetic materials	4.35	1.50	1.84
	3.77	1.25	1.56
29. Drugs, cleaning, and toilet preparations	2.22	1.42	1.65
	1.89	1.24	1.44
30. Paints and allied products	5.12	1.41	1.80
	4.51	1.17	1.52
31. Petroleum refining and related industries	4.74	1.41	1.66
	2.38	0.46	0.64

Table 4-2 Continued

Industry Number and Title	Method of Financing		
	Polluter Pays	Value-Added Tax	Production Tax

MANUFACTURING, CONT.

Industry Number and Title	Polluter Pays	Value-Added Tax	Production Tax
32. Rubber and miscellaneous plastics products	2.10 / 1.47	1.49 / 1.08	1.66 / 1.21
33. Leather tanning and industrial leather products	2.23 / 1.78	1.41 / 1.16	1.86 / 1.55
34. Footwear and other leather products	1.68 / 1.35	1.83 / 1.63	2.14 / 1.89
35. Glass and glass products	1.87 / 1.61	1.54 / 1.38	1.44 / 1.27
36. Stone and clay products	2.95 / 2.60	1.53 / 1.29	1.58 / 1.34
37. Primary iron and steel manufacturing	2.85 / 2.39	1.47 / 1.21	1.65 / 1.37
38. Primary nonferrous metal manufacturing	3.69 / 1.93	1.38 / 0.68	1.86 / 0.95
39. Metal containers	2.05 / 1.63	1.40 / 1.16	1.74 / 1.46
40. Heating, plumbing, and structural metal products	1.88 / 1.47	1.39 / 1.15	1.67 / 1.40
41. Stampings, screw machine products, and bolts	1.74 / 1.38	1.42 / 1.20	1.55 / 1.30
42. Other fabricated metal products	1.78 / 1.39	1.45 / 1.20	1.60 / 1.33
43. Engines and turbines	2.41 / 2.01	1.47 / 1.25	1.79 / 1.53
44. Farm machinery and equipment	2.40 / 2.03	1.50 / 1.29	1.79 / 1.54
45. Construction, mining, and oil field machinery	1.67 / 1.45	1.09 / 0.96	1.22 / 1.08
46. Materials handling machinery and equipment	2.08 / 1.77	1.35 / 1.17	1.57 / 1.36
47. Metalworking machinery and equipment	2.09 / 1.78	1.56 / 1.36	1.57 / 1.36
48. Special industry machinery and equipment	2.08 / 1.77	1.46 / 1.26	1.59 / 1.38

Table 4-2 Continued

	Method of Financing		
Industry Number and Title	Polluter Pays	Value-Added Tax	Production Tax

MANUFACTURING, CONT.

Industry Number and Title	Polluter Pays	Value-Added Tax	Production Tax
49. General industrial machinery and equipment	2.09 1.77	1.43 1.24	1.56 1.34
50. Machine shop products	1.92 1.63	1.46 1.28	1.41 1.22
51. Office, computing, and accounting machines	1.87 1.50	2.10 1.79	2.34 1.98
52. Service industry machines	2.35 1.95	1.41 1.20	1.82 1.55
53. Electric industrial equipment and apparatus	1.49 1.19	1.41 1.22	1.51 1.31
54. Household appliances	1.77 1.41	1.42 1.20	1.71 1.47
55. Electric lighting and wiring equipment	1.86 1.46	1.74 1.49	1.85 1.57
56. Radio, television, and communication equipment	1.22 1.01	1.42 1.26	1.49 1.32
57. Electronic components and accessories	1.67 1.34	1.70 1.48	1.85 1.58
58. Miscellaneous electrical machinery, equipment, and supplies	1.69 1.30	1.41 1.20	1.62 1.36
59. Motor vehicles and equipment	2.88 2.62	1.51 1.37	2.02 1.85
60. Aircraft and parts	1.47 1.30	1.39 1.30	1.54 1.45
61. Other transportation equipment	2.01 1.76	1.48 1.35	1.78 1.61
62. Scientific and controlling instruments	4.72 4.17	1.48 1.26	1.65 1.40
63. Optical, ophthalmic, and photographic equipment	4.44 3.95	1.49 1.31	1.38 1.18
64. Miscellaneous manufacturing	2.71 2.38	1.63 1.51	1.90 1.70

Table 4-2 Continued

	Method of Financing		
Industry Number and Title	Polluter Pays	Value-Added Tax	Production Tax

SERVICES, GOVERNMENT, DUMMY, AND SPECIAL INDUSTRIES

Industry Number and Title	Polluter Pays	Value-Added Tax	Production Tax
65. Transportation and warehousing	1.36	1.79	1.57
	1.18	1.71	1.48
66. Communications; except radio and TV broadcasting	0.29	1.51	0.99
	0.25	1.49	0.97
67. Radio and TV broadcasting	0.58	1.51	1.48
	0.51	1.47	1.44
68. Electric, gas, water, and sanitary services	5.37	1.50	1.50
	5.18	1.33	1.35
69. Wholesale and retail trade	0.71	1.53	1.16
	0.64	1.48	1.12
70. Finance and insurance	0.55	1.51	1.38
	0.50	1.48	1.34
71. Real estate and rental	0.66	1.51	1.12
	0.56	1.46	1.07
72. Hotels; personal and repair services except auto	0.93	1.49	1.33
	0.82	1.43	1.26
73. Business services	0.84	1.49	1.46
	0.74	1.44	1.40
75. Automobile repair and services	1.06	1.48	1.42
	0.93	1.41	1.34
76. Amusements	0.88	1.49	1.43
	0.74	1.42	1.35
77. Medical, educational services, and nonprofit organizations	0.52	1.51	1.19
	0.44	1.46	1.14
78. Federal government enterprises	0.91	1.44	1.26
	0.70	1.33	1.15
79. State and local government enterprises	1.18	1.51	1.42
	1.05	1.43	1.35
80. Business travel, entertainment, and gifts	1.83	1.42	2.21
	1.39	1.18	1.91
81. Office supplies	3.17	1.32	2.16
	2.76	1.12	1.93

unusually pronounced sensitivity to international competition than to unusually severe environmental controls. One implication of this generalization is that from the standpoint of "interindustry equity" alone, environmental controls financed by tax-subsidy schemes might be preferred to those financed according to the polluter-pays principle.[26]

Another generalization that bears on similar issues is that producers of services will prefer environmental controls financed by the polluter-pays principle, while producers of tangible goods will prefer either of our tax-subsidy schemes. This generalization is not surprising, of course, since the particular tax-subsidy schemes we consider tax services industries to help clean up environmental damage in other industries, even though services generally pollute less. The notable exceptions to this generalization—that is, goods producers who will prefer "polluter pays" and services producers who will prefer our tax-subsidy schemes—are crude petroleum and natural gas, wood products, office machinery and computers, communications equipment, electronic components, and utilities.

Not unexpectedly, both the price and output impacts of environmental controls are dampened by the assumption that producer prices vary positively with demand (i.e., the assumption of finite price elasticities of supply). At least a portion of the cost of environmental controls, however financed, is then absorbed into factor rents in the various industries. In general, the difference between displacement under finite supply elasticities and that under infinite supply elasticities is quite dramatic, suggesting the importance of the supply side and pricing behavior for any quantitative study like our own. Even for those industries (such as services) where the assumption of flat domestic supply curves was maintained throughout the tables, there are differences in displacement under the two regimes. These differences arise from the fact that input prices to such industries vary differently under environmental controls according to price elasticities of supply in those input markets.

Finally, although the six approaches in the tables imply fairly striking differences in the extent to which environmental controls displace any given industry through international competition, they do not imply very striking differences at the aggregate level. As a matter of fact, the differences are virtually nonexistent when supply elasticities are finite. The weighted-average percentage increases in prices under the six approaches are:[27]

	Polluter Pays	Value-Added Tax	Production Tax
All $\epsilon^{i\prime}s = \infty$	1.71	1.48	1.52
$\epsilon^{i\prime}s \leqq \infty$	1.23	1.23	1.22

The weighted-average percentage *decreases* in physical output under the six approaches are:

	Polluter Pays	Value-Added Tax	Production Tax
All $\epsilon^{i\prime}s = \infty$	1.75	1.51	1.55
$\epsilon^{i\prime}s \leqq \infty$	1.26	1.26	1.25

BROADER METHODOLOGICAL CONSIDERATIONS

In previous sections of this paper, we have attempted to answer a quite narrowly defined, short-run question: what are the industry-by-industry price–output consequences of environmental controls due to their unfavorable effects on international competitive advantage? That is, we have restricted ourselves to examining the industrial displacement that comes about because of the international scope of most United States markets, and because of the price disadvantage that environmental controls may impose on United States producers. In narrowly interpreting our charge, we have skirted a great many interesting issues that arise from asking the broader, more encompassing question: what are the long-run, industry-by-industry price–output consequences of environmental controls? Given that our narrow question is nested in the broader question, it is no surprise that the answer to the latter depends on international competitiveness. But it also depends on a number of other considerations.

This section of the paper outlines six additional considerations in assessing the general incidence of environmental controls on prices and output by industry.[28] The first two have been touched on implicitly in the preceding two sections; the other four have not. Although we treat these items sequentially, they are hardly independent of each other. And our discussion highlights one particular interdependence at length: the interdependence between each of these other considerations and the international competitive impact of environmental controls. The six are:

1. The severity of controls on one industry relative to others;
2. The method by which the cost of controls is financed;
3. The extent to which the differing severity and industrial incidence of the controls causes users to substitute away from the products of one industry toward those of another;
4. The particular macroeconomic policies that could possibly result from

the effects of the collected industrial displacements on aggregate employment, growth, and inflation;
5. The particular international economic policies that could possibly result from the effects of the collected industrial displacements on the trade balance, balance of payments, and value of the dollar;
6. The technological changes induced or mandated by the controls—which cause alterations in the economy's interindustry linkages and in its investment plans.

The industrial displacement due to differential severity of controls (consideration 1) would seem to be obvious: Those industries subject to more severe controls will be hurt more than others. But the descriptiveness of this regularity becomes increasingly doubtful the more open an economy is, that is, the larger the proportion of its production that competes with foreign production.[29] In open economies, industries that are subject to the most severe environmental controls may be hurt less than others if they are not internationally competitive (i.e., if they produce predominately nontradeables or highly differentiated tradeables). Industries subject to minor environmental controls may nevertheless be hurt severely by these controls if they are internationally competitive—because the slightest tendency for such industries' prices to diverge from world prices causes dramatic changes in their business.[30]

Thus in an open economy, there is no easy one-to-one correspondence between the extent of an industry's environmental despoilation and the cost that the industry bears to "clean itself up"—even under the polluter-pays principle[31] (that has been implicitly assumed in the discussion of consideration 1). The expectations of some who favor polluter pays as the most desirable method of financing environmental control (consideration 2 in our list) may thus be frustrated by international competitiveness. Their (somewhat vengeful) expectations have been that the most severe despoilers would be those most discouraged by the polluter-pays principle: They would be forced into a quandry—to absorb the costs of environmental controls into profits or factor incomes would discourage supply; to pass them on to users in higher prices would discourage demand. Either way, output in such industries would fall, and probably by more than output would fall in less despoiling industries. Even if one grants the acceptability of this argument for closed economies, in open economies there is no guarantee that the polluter-pays principle will be desirable in this sense. Those industries hit hardest by the need to finance their own environmental controls may not be the most severe despoilers, but rather simply those industries whose products are most competitive in world markets. They may be the ones forced into the quandry of choosing between alternatives that reduce supply or reduce demand.

To place this point in perspective, it should be distinguished from the familiar complaint that polluter-pays is inequitable to a country's producers unless all world producers adopt similar environmental controls, all financed by the polluters themselves. Not only is the polluter-pays principle possibly inequitable in this way, but it may also be inequitable in the sense that among a country's industries (rather than *between* them and world producers), the cost of environmental controls from industry to industry, including losses to international competitors, bears little relation to the environmental despoliation for which the industry is responsible. Nor do other methods of financing necessarily improve on polluter-pays from the perspective of interindustry "equity." Contrary to the impression that is sometimes given,[32] there will still be international competitive consequences of financing environmental costs by subsidies to despoiling industries. This is demonstrated for subsidies financed by production or value-added taxes in the two preceding sections.

If, by contrast, the environmental-control subsidies are "financed" by reduced government spending on other goods and services, the price of all such goods and services will tend to fall (more realistically, such prices will tend not to rise as rapidly as others). In this case, industries that are highly competitive on world markets may fare better than others. They can take advantage of any tendency for their prices to fall, and retard the tendency as well, by exporting more to foreign markets or by selling more to would-be importers. Thus they may bear less of the costs of environmental control than industries producing nontradeables or highly differentiated tradeables, which cannot turn toward world markets when the government reduces its spending to finance the control program. The familiar point still holds that the incidence of industrial displacement bears no necessary relation to the extent of environmental despoliation.

All these methods for financing environmental controls entail no striking fiscal policy, however, at most representing balanced-budget increases in taxes and subsidies. One other possibility of financing environmental-control subsidies implies fiscal expansion through purposefully larger budget deficits.[33] Whether fiscal expansion has price effects or not is in part a matter of how much excess capacity exists in the economy at the particular time, and in part a matter of whether the increased budget deficient is financed by government borrowing or by new money creation. To the extent that most prices do rise, once again the more sensitive an industry to the world price of its products, the more likely it is to be subject to above-average environmental costs and above-average displacement. To the extent that most prices do not rise, but interest rates do (as they should if the government increases its borrowing), the industries that bear the greatest cost of environmental control will be those most dependent on borrowing to produce or to carry inventories, and those that are faced with demand that is very interest-responsive. The industrial incidence of environmental-control costs again bears no necessary relation to the industrial incidence of environmental despoliation, although in this case, international competitiveness has little to do with it.

The industrial displacement due to the stimulus that environmental controls create for users to substitute away from the products of one industry, and toward those of another (consideration 3), would again seem to be obvious. Intuition suggests that if the severity of environmental controls is equivalent among heavy polluters, the ones producing goods for which an array of nonpolluting substitutes exist will suffer greater displacement than others. Intuition, however, is again an unreliable guide in an open economy. Heavy polluters producing products for which few available substitutes exist may still be hurt severely by environmental controls if they face stiff world competition in foreign and domestic markets; heavy polluters producing products for which there are many substitutes may be comparatively unscathed by environmental controls if their products are nontraded or highly differentiated from foreign variants. Thus a comprehensive approach to industrial displacement must focus on at least two kinds of price responsiveness (among other things, of course): the responsiveness of demand facing the domestic industry to a change in its price relative to that of foreign suppliers, and the responsiveness of demand facing *all* suppliers in the industry, whether foreign or domestic, to a change in their price relative to those of other industries.[34]

Consideration 4 is more speculative than the others, since it suggests an endogenous determination of aggregate macroeconomic policy for which the behavioral determinants are unlikely to be very stable or predictable. In a closed economy with downward wage-price inflexibility, balanced-budget environmental control (see consideration 2) is almost certain to be simultaneously recessionary and inflationary in its aggregate short-run effects: industries that are impacted severely by the controls will contract, creating unemployment and underutilization of non-labor productive resources; industries that gain from environmental controls (e.g., industries supplying pollution-control equipment or "clean" energy) will be unable to expand quickly, causing a tendency at least for their prices to rise. The result is some recession and some inflation at precisely the same time. In a similar open economy, the recessionary tendency will be exacerbated and the inflationary tendency moderated: Industries that are impacted severely by the controls will also be faced with competition from foreign suppliers not subject to the controls; industries that gain from the controls will be forced to hold down prices somewhat by international competition to "land the new environmental-control business."

In sum, there is a presumption for an open economy that the aggregate recessionary effects of balanced-budget environmental controls will dominate in the short run.[35] What the government chooses to do to reexpand the economy (if anything) is problematical, and probably not susceptible to prediction. Yet the government's aggregate policy response is a crucial consideration in any broad attempt to calculate industrial incidence of environmental controls. Expansion via monetary policy would benefit those industries that rely on borrowing to operate, or whose customers do to buy (housing, consumer durables, etc.). Expansion via fiscal policy could have virtually any imaginable distributional effects among industries, depending on how the fiscal policy is designed. The methodological implication of such unpredictability is that any study designed to calculate the overall effects of environmental controls on an industry-by-industry basis should sensitize the results to several pure but conceivable aggregate policy responses of the government, including at the very least: (A) no response; (B,C) holding aggregate employment-utilization constant while allowing the "price level" to vary (by monetary policy, by "neutral" fiscal policy);[36] (D,E) holding the "price level" constant while allowing aggregate employment and utilization to vary (by monetary policy, by "neutral" fiscal policy).[37]

Consideration 5 is speculative in a similar fashion and for similar reasons. If there are adverse trade performance effects from unilateral environmental-control policy, there will be a tendency for the domestic currency to depreciate on the foreign exchange market. If policy-makers ratify the depreciation by doing nothing, then the industrial displacement caused by controls in industries most sensitive to international competition will be moderated. In industries that are internationally competitive, but less so than average, the depreciation caused by the controls may actually improve their position: instead of facing displacement, their business expands, because the depreciation more than compensates for the control-induced rise in their price. In contrast to all this, however, policymakers may refuse to ratify the depreciation, and choose instead to hold the exchange rate constant by foreign-exchange-market intervention. Or they may avoid the need for such intervention if they find it possible to stimulate inflows of financial capital, say by continuous monetary contraction. In the latter case, the impact industrial incidence of environmental controls is maintained, except for the indirect effects of contractionary monetary policy and possibly higher interest rates on interest-sensitive industries (see the discussion of consideration 4).

Outlining the alternative international economic policies that might be brought on indirectly by environmental controls highlights the same point made earlier with respect to macroeconomic policy: All changes to policy are endogenously determined in reality, but neither the set of determinants, nor their relationship to policy, are likely to be very predictable. The methodological recommendation that is in order once again is that a comprehensive study of the industry-by-industry effects of environmental controls should sensitize the results to several pure but conceivable international economic policy responses of the government, including at the very least: (1) depreciation that offsets the balance-of-payments effects of environmental controls (equivalent to no policy response)[38]; and (2) holding the exchange rate constant by foreign-exchange-market intervention.[39, 40]

Finally, in the list of considerations that have methodological implications for a more comprehensive study of environmental controls, comes changes in production processes themselves due to the controls (consideration 6). In the fashion of Walter (1972), we have assumed that the imposition of environmental controls can be adequately represented by a series of shocks to costs in each industry—and nothing more. We have also assumed that production processes can be represented by a matrix of input–output coefficients that is invariant to the cost shocks caused by environmental controls. Thus, once these cost shocks are passed through the inverse of the stable input–output matrix (in order to record the indirect effects of environmental control costs in one industry on prices in others that use its products), all that is left is to calculate the international competitive impact of the ultimate change in the domestic price vector. In this regime, environmental controls generate precisely the same effects on industrial prices and output as an increase in wages—or in the price of any other primary factor whose income represents an (assumed invariant) share of value-added.

In all probability, these rigid assumptions suit the case of increased wages much better than they suit the case of environmental controls. That is, the technological effects of environmental controls are probably much more pervasive in fact than those of an increase in wages. An increase in wages may be supposed to have some minor effects on both intermediate input–output coefficients (increasing intermediate demands for products produced with comparatively little labor, and decreasing intermediate demands for products produced with comparatively much), and on the final demand vector (increasing investment in plant and equipment that substitutes for labor). However, these are often assumed, as above, to be so minor that they can be ignored. Environmental controls cannot be assumed away so easily: in some cases, they change intermediate input–output coefficients radically, as when electric utilities are forced to switch from coal to petroleum, or when automakers shift from steel to aluminum engine blocks and from steel to Fiberglas bodies. In other cases, they lead to entirely new intermediate demands that vary with current output levels, such as for seedlings on the part of strip miners or for pollution-treatment chemicals on the part of waterfront industries. In still other cases, they make existing plant and equipment entirely obsolete, especially when environmental "standards" are legislated, stimulating first a sizeable short-run boom in replacement investment, and, therefore, in final demand, and then a not-inconsiderable ongoing investment demand. While this ongoing investment demand may be no larger in the long run than it was prior to environmental controls, because both "environmentally dirty" and "environmentally clean" plant and equipment deteriorates and must be replaced, the industry classification of the suppliers of "environmentally clean" machines may differ from that of the suppliers of "environmentally dirty" machines (e.g., more electrical machinery and scientific and controlling instruments; less nonelectrical machinery and motor vehicles). The possibility that the industrial mix of gross investment is different after environmental control than it was before suggests the obvious probability that capital-goods industries producing "environmentally clean" equipment will be cushioned from the burden of environmental controls on them, while capital-goods industries producing "environmentally dirty" equipment will be hit in a double-barrelled fashion by the controls. Mitigating such differential effects among capital-goods industries will be international competition, offsetting somewhat both the tendency for domestic prices and output of "environmentally clean" equipment to rise, and the tendency for domestic prices and output of "environmentally dirty" equipment to fall.

Methodologically, consideration 6 suggests that a broad long-run approach to the effects of environmental control on industrial prices and output should simultaneously (not sequentially): (1) shock total costs in each industry—but only by the increase in the industry's current expenditure on primary inputs for environmental control (e.g., by the increase in expenditure on environmental research-and-development personnel); (2) alter the input–output requirements, and consequently the matrix of input–output coefficients, to the extent that it is known how environmental controls affect current intermediate demands and supplies; and (3) alter the industrial mix of the investment component of the final demand vector. [Data for such an undertaking would *not* appear to be hopelessly unavailable either: the Bureau of Economic Analysis' capital-account-requirement input–output table (Young et al., 1971),[41] and McGraw-Hill's survey of environmental-control expenditures (McGraw-Hill Economics, annual) would seem to be obvious places to start.] Under this more complex but more realistic regime, the imposition of environmental controls is represented by more than just a cost shock; it is simultaneously a shock to costs, to technology, and to final demand.

Taken together, these six considerations suggest a considerably more complex approach to estimating the industrial incidence of environmental controls than are undertaken in the two preceding sections. They also suggest that any attempt to assess the impact of *multilateral* environmental controls, that is, controls undertaken by more than one country at once, must take numerous comparisons into account. Not only must intercountry differences in the severity of environmental controls and the means by which they are financed by recognized (as is well understood in discussions of multilateral environmental control), but attention must also be given to intercountry differences in attitudes toward macroeconomic policy and exchange-rate flexibility. Comparable controls financed by identical methods could still have dramatic effects on international competitiveness, and radically different consequences from country to country, if in the aggregate they provoke quite different policy responses from country to country. In the same vein, comparable controls financed by identical methods also stimulate universal technological changes that translate into alterations in the pattern of comparative advantage. This can in turn have dramatic effects on trade performance, and radically different domestic impacts from country to country. Thus the question, "What pattern of *world* environmental controls places roughly equitable burdens both on industries within a country and between countries?", is an exceedingly difficult one to answer.

CLOSING AND EXTENSIONS

We have outlined an approach in this chapter to estimating the impact of unilateral environmental controls on industry prices and output at a fairly detailed level of aggregation. We have focused particularly on those impacts that can be traced from environmental controls to international competitive disadvantage for domestic producers to domestic industrial displacement and upward pressure on the price level. We have highlighted these linkages in a formal model that was capable of being applied to extant data and parameter estimates. We have also illustrated the model's application to 81 United States industries, and summarized the varying price–output consequences of different methods of financing environmental controls, and of different assumptions regarding domestic supply–price determination. Finally, we broadened our perspective to discuss other considerations in assessing the impact of environmental controls—considerations that we had earlier either ignored or assumed away. We paid special attention to the way in which these other considerations interact with the international competitive effects of environmental controls that played so great a role in our previous illustrative analysis.

Suggestive but tentative answers to a number of interesting questions came from our empirical results. Most importantly, it was possible to answer the question, "Which industries suffer the most severe displacement from environmental controls?" And if one accepts the validity of the assumptions on which these results are based, at least for the time horizon we discussed in the section "Methodology and Framework for an Illustrative Empirical Analysis," the results provide the starting point for an approach to several promising questions beyond the purview of this chapter.

For example, from a political point of view, it may not be the *industrial* incidence of environmental controls that is important, but rather their *distributional* incidence. More precisely, it may be less important to know how environmental controls affect various industries than it is to know how they affect various factors of production or labor groups. One way to approach the impact of these controls on factor or labor requirements is to pass our output effects through a matrix of factor requirements by industry. For example, if labor is broken down into m skill groups, if "capital" is defined to be the plant and equipment produced by n "capital-goods industries," and if labor and capital requirements per unit of output are assumed to be stable,[42] then the impact of environmental controls on factor requirements can be approximated by[43]:

$$\frac{dF}{F} = B \frac{dQ}{Q} \tag{25}$$

where F = an $(m + n) \times 1$ vector of factor requirements, B = an $(m + n) \times 81$ matrix of factor requirements per unit of output, and dQ/Q is the familiar 81×1 vector of output shocks by industry from the first two sections. The proportional change in factor requirements, dF/F, can be treated meaningfully as a vector of m changes in unemployment rates by skill class and n changes in utilization rates on different types of plant and equipment.

A somewhat different, yet equally important aspect of the distributional incidence of environmental controls is their impact on the cost of living of socioeconomic groups (e.g., the poor, the middle class, and so on). Again, it is possible to approximate the answer to this question if budget shares of these socioeconomic groups are known and stable. If, for example, the budget shares of s socioeconomic groups for each of our 81 industries' products were known (an unlikely event, but the principle stands), then the impact of environmental controls on the cost of living of these socioeconomic groups could be approximated by:

$$\frac{dC}{C} = S \frac{dP}{P} \cdot b \tag{26}$$

where C = an $s \times 1$ vector of living costs, S = an $s \times 81$ matrix of budget shares, dP/P is the familiar 81×1 vector of domestic price shocks from the first two sections, and b is one minus the average (marginal) propensity to import [employed in equation (24)]. The proportional change in living costs by socioeconomic groups, dC/C, can be treated meaningfully as a measure of the progressivity or regressivity of environmental controls, as long as relative income levels are closely linked to socioeconomic status.

Without exhausting the questions for which our analysis may provide the starting point, we can demonstrate one more extension. Again from a political point of view, the industrial incidence of environmental controls may be less important than their regional incidence. Certain regions may be much more severely impacted by environmental controls than others. If the location of industry by r regions were known (say for our 81-industry breakdown, although it is generally available only at a higher level of aggregation[44]), then the impact of environmental controls on regional output could be approximated by a rough index of percentage changes in industrial output:

$$\frac{dG}{G} = R\frac{dQ}{Q} \tag{27}$$

where G = an $r \times 1$ vector of regional output indexes; R = an $r \times 81$ matrix of industry shares (assumed stable) in the total output of a given region, and dQ/Q is the familiar 81×1 vector of output shocks by industry from the first two sections. The proportional change in regional output, dG/G, might be treated meaningfully as the short-run change in regional growth rates that environmental controls would bring about.

In sum, both our illustrative analysis and our suggestions for methodological and substantive extensions imply that a great deal of quantitative work remains to be done in assessing the impact of environmental controls.

ACKNOWLEDGMENTS

The authors are indebted to Professor Robert E. Baldwin, who provided illuminating commentary on portions of the paper. John D. Culbertson, Wayne E. Lewis, and Steven Parker were extraordinarily helpful and efficient research assistants. Part of the support for this research was provided by a Ford Foundation grant to the Universities of Wisconsin and Wyoming to study the efficiency, employment, and distribution effects of international economic policy, as one aspect of the Foundation's general support for research assessing the future of international economic order.

Appendix   Behavioral Parameter Values Underlying Calculations in Text[a]

Industry Number and Title	Demand Price Elasticity (η)	Supply Price Elasticity (ϵ)	Environmental Cost Loading as % of Price (E)
AGRICULTURE, FORESTRY, AND FISHERIES			
1. Livestock and livestock products	−1.01	0.40	1.28
2. Other agricultural products	−0.92	0.30	1.92
3. Forestry and fishery products	−1.39	0.32	0.64
4. Agricultural, forestry, and fishery services	−1.00	∞	0.32
MINING			
5. Iron and ferroalloy ores mining	−1.02	0.20	0.82
6. Nonferrous metal ores mining	−1.05	0.20	0.82
7. Coal mining	−0.90	0.20	1.76
8. Crude petroleum and natural gas	−1.02	0.20	0.41
9. Stone and clay mining and quarrying	−1.04	0.20	0.41
10. Chemical and fertilizer mineral mining	−1.04	0.20	0.82
CONSTRUCTION			
11. New construction	−1.00	∞	0.60
12. Maintenance and repair construction	−1.00	∞	0.43
MANUFACTURING			
13. Ordinance and accessories	−1.00	∞	0.53
14. Food and kindred products	−1.02	5.55	0.36
15. Tobacco manufactures	−0.92	8.06	0.18
16. Broad and narrow fabrics, yarn and thread mills	−1.03	4.31	0.38

Appendix Continued

Industry Number and Title	Demand Price Elasticity (η)	Supply Price Elasticity (ϵ)	Environmental Cost Loading as % of Price (E)
MANUFACTURING, CONT.			
17. Miscellaneous textile goods and floor coverings	−1.09	4.31	0.38
18. Apparel	−1.07	8.47	0.19
19. Miscellaneous fabricated textile products	−1.00	8.47	0.19
20. Lumber and wood products, except containers	−1.07	8.50	0.10
21. Wooden containers	−1.00	8.50	0.50
22. Household furniture	−1.00	∞	0.50
23. Other furniture and fixtures	−1.00	∞	0.50
24. Paper and allied products, except containers	−0.99	2.12	1.63
25. Paperboard containers and boxes	−1.00	2.12	1.63
26. Printing and publishing	−1.01	∞	0.08
27. Chemicals and selected chemical products	−0.97	20.00	2.19
28. Plastics and synthetic materials	−1.04	20.00	2.19
29. Drugs, cleaning, and toilet preparations	−0.97	20.00	1.10
30. Paints and allied products	−1.00	20.00	3.29
31. Petroleum refining and related industries	−0.99	1.28	3.73
32. Rubber and miscellaneous plastics products	−1.04	4.17	0.63
33. Leather tanning and industrial leather products	−1.00	174.00	0.95
34. Footwear and other leather products	−1.28	174.00	0.32
35. Glass and glass products	−1.04	33.33	0.86
36. Stone and clay products	−1.04	33.33	1.72
37. Primary iron and steel manufacturing	−1.07	16.24	1.47

Appendix Continued

Industry Number and Title	Demand Price Elasticity (η)	Supply Price Elasticity (ϵ)	Environmental Cost Loading as % of Price (E)
MANUFACTURING, CONT.			
38. Primary nonferrous metal manufacturing	−1.10	2.00	1.76
39. Metal containers	−1.00	12.82	0.53
40. Heating, plumbing, and structural metal products	−0.99	12.82	0.53
41. Stampings, screw machine products, and bolts	−1.00	12.82	0.53
42. Other fabricated metal products	−1.02	12.82	0.53
43. Engines and turbines	−1.05	16.31	1.03
44. Farm machinery and equipment	−1.08	16.31	1.03
45. Construction, mining, and oil field machinery	−0.77	16.31	1.03
46. Materials handling machinery and equipment	−0.95	16.31	1.03
47. Metalworking machinery and equipment	−1.08	16.31	1.03
48. Special industry machinery and equipment	−1.04	16.31	1.03
49. General industrial machinery and equipment	−1.00	16.31	1.03
50. Machine shop products	−1.00	16.31	1.03
51. Office, computing, and accounting machines	−1.48	16.31	0.49
52. Service industry machines	−1.00	16.31	1.03
53. Electric industrial equipment and apparatus	−0.99	17.95	0.49
54. Household appliances	−0.99	17.95	0.49
55. Electric lighting and wiring equipment	−1.21	17.95	0.49
56. Radio, television, and communication equipment	−0.99	17.95	0.49
57. Electronic components and accessories	−1.20	17.95	0.49

Appendix   Continued

Industry Number and Title	Demand Price Elasticity (η)	Supply Price Elasticity (ϵ)	Environmental Cost Loading as % of Price (E)
MANUFACTURING, CONT.			
58. Miscellaneous electrical machinery, equipment, and supplies	−1.00	17.95	0.49
59. Motor vehicles and equipment	−1.08	138.00	1.19
60. Aircraft and parts	−0.97	∞	0.57
61. Other transportation equipment	−1.06	∞	0.72
62. Scientific and controlling instruments	−1.04	14.29	3.37
63. Optical, ophthalmic, and photographic equipment	−1.03	14.29	3.37
64. Miscellaneous manufacturing	−1.22	∞	1.17

SERVICES, GOVERNMENT, DUMMY, AND SPECIAL INDUSTRIES

Industry Number and Title	Demand Price Elasticity (η)	Supply Price Elasticity (ϵ)	Environmental Cost Loading as % of Price (E)
65. Transportation and warehousing	−1.22	∞	0.53
66. Communications; except radio and TV broadcasting	−1.00	∞	0.08
67. Radio and TV broadcasting	−1.00	∞	0.08
68. Electric, gas, water, and sanitary services	−1.00	∞	3.95
69. Wholesale and retail trade	−1.01	∞	0.32
70. Finance and insurance	−1.00	∞	0.16
71. Real estate and rental	−1.00	∞	0.32
72. Hotels; personal and repair services except auto	−1.00	∞	0.32
73. Business services	−1.00	∞	0.32
75. Automobile repair and services	−1.00	∞	0.32
76. Amusements	−1.00	∞	0.32
77. Medical, educational services, and nonprofit organizations	−1.00	∞	0.01
78. Federal government enterprises	−1.00	∞	0.32

Appendix   Continued

Industry Number and Title	Demand Price Elasticity (η)	Supply Price Elasticity (ϵ)	Environmental Cost Loading as % of Price (E)
SERVICES, GOVERNMENT, DUMMY, AND SPECIAL INDUSTRIES CONT.			
79. State and local government enterprises	−1.00	∞	0.08
80. Business travel, entertainment, and gifts	−1.00	∞	0.53
81. Office supplies	−1.00	∞	1.63

^{a} Calculations are made under the assumption of infinite domestic price elasticities of supply disregarded the middle column of Table A1 and assumed all elements to be ∞. (For purposes of computation, ∞ was taken to be 1000.00.) The method for calculating the demand price elasticities is explained in the text, as are the sources for most of the supply price elasticities. In a few cases, for example, agriculture, forestry, fisheries, and mining, supply price elasticities were "guesstimated." The source for most of the environmental cost loadings is Walter (1972, Tables 1 and 2). In a few cases, for instance, government enterprises, environmental cost loadings were "guesstimated." In several other cases, for example, construction and utilities, Walter's (1972) data were supplemented from Leontief and Ford (1972). In the case of Walter's cost loading for "miscellaneous services," a mixed bag of input–output industries, his average figure was disentangled using the supplementary sources listed above.

NOTES

1. Our measure of sensitivity to international competition thus differs from a related measure employed by Walter (1972) to examine the differential effects of environmental controls on "international competitiveness" by industry. He defines "international competitiveness" as trade performance, and measures it by the ratio of an industry's exports to its imports. We, by contrast, are not interested in an industry's trade performance, but in its prices and total output, regardless of where that output is marketed. Thus we focus on an industry's "sensitivity to international competition," measured by the elasticity of demand facing it to a change in domestic relative to foreign prices. "Sensitivity to international competition" is distinguished from "international competitiveness," both conceptually and empirically.

2. In the illustrative work, we maintain the assumptions that neither exchange rates nor international economic policy change, and that the only changes in final demand facing each industry come about because of the loss of international competitiveness, not, for example, because the loss of international competitiveness brings on recession in the aggregate. Both assumptions are made on the grounds of empirical tractability, but the former is consistent with fixed exchange rates, and the latter with government commitment to full employment of labor and other resources. We are probably least happy with the latter assumption, and discuss the analytical and methodological implications of removing it.

3. This property is more technically referred to as want independence or separability. One of its implication is that the income-compensated price change of any good outside the pair of goods considered will have no effect on the demand for either one of the pair of goods. In other words, changes in other prices affect only real income. We have left these other prices out entirely, but have picked up their effect by choosing real income or output as the appropriate scale variable. Such a step is warranted when a very small proportion of total income is spent on any pair of goods.

4. This definition, coupled with the specification of the domestic supply equation, implies a particular method of financing environmental controls that we shall refer to as "polluter pays." That is, every industry is assumed to be directly responsible for the costs of its own environmental "clean-up." Alternative methods of financing are discussed at greater length below.

5. That is, we do not know very precisely how β_m and β (from Eqs. 1 and 3) differ from industry to industry. This problem is hardly insurmountable, and we would not hold rigidly to either this or to the previous justification for ignoring scale effects. As we make clear in the section "Broader Methodological Considerations," we feel these effects should be taken into account in a broader, more comprehensive analysis than we have undertaken here.

6. Exogeneity of import prices implies that $dP_m{}^i/P_m{}^i = 0$. Ignoring income-scale effects implies that $dY^i/Y^i = 0$. Another assumption employed in moving from Eqs. 1 through 5 to 6 through 8 is that $dE^i = E^i$, consistent with our attempt to assess the impact of imposing any and all environment controls. Consequently

$$\frac{d[P^i(1 - E^i)]}{P^i(1 - E^i)} = \frac{dP^i}{P^i} - E^i$$

Still other assumptions are that the input–output coefficients are constant, and that prices of nonentreprenurial primary inputs (W_k) are invariant to the imposition of environmental controls. The latter may be a poor assumption if there is resort to some means of financing environmental controls other than polluter pays, although we maintain it later in this section in our discussion of alternative methods of financing.

7. We thus assume away various types of discrimination between foreign and domestic markets.

8. $Q_d{}^i$ is implicitly set equal to $Q_s{}^i$.

9. Buckler's and Almon's (1972) estimates were made for selected tradeables industries in a 180—sector input–output table. In cases where several of their sectors were contained in a single one of our sectors, an elasticity appropriate to our more aggregated breakdown was obtained by taking a weighted average of Buckler's and Almon's elasticities, the weights being international trade shares of their component industries in the international trade of the particular industry on which we were focusing. In cases where Buckler and Almon reported no elasticity, we assumed it to be zero.

10.   Appendix A also contains the values of E and outlines where they differ from those of Walter (1972).

11.   Of course long-run, *general*-equilibrium supply curves are upward-sloping despite constant returns to scale, so long as relative factor intensities differ from industry to industry at the same relative factor prices.

12.   Also, such delay in imposing controls involves an opportunity cost to society in the form of lower benefits from having a cleaner environment. The tradeoffs involved are an issue well beyond the scope of this paper, as is the welfare loss from particular industries finding it in their interest to lobby for a slowdown in applying pollution control standards (Tullock, 1967).

13.   Equation 15 is the straightforward matrix equivalent of Eq. 9, providing dP/P = the term in the { } brackets, as Eq. 14 claims. That it does can be seen by considering Eqs. 9 and 10 for a single good. Setting the change in demand equal to the change in supply

$$\eta \frac{dP^i}{P^i} = \epsilon \left(\frac{dR^i}{P^i} - E^i \right) - \epsilon \sum_j a_{ji}^D \frac{dP^i}{P^i}$$

Rearranging terms gives

$$\left(\frac{\epsilon}{\epsilon - \eta} \right) E^i = \frac{dP^i}{P^i} - \left(\frac{\epsilon}{\epsilon - \eta} \right) \sum_j a_{ji}^D \frac{dP^i}{P^i}$$

Given that a similar equation can be written for each good i, the equivalent matrix equation is

$$E \cdot \frac{\epsilon}{\epsilon - \eta} = \left[I - \left(A^{D\prime} \cdot \frac{\epsilon}{\epsilon - \eta} \right) \right] \frac{dP}{P}$$

which can be premultiplied by the inverse of the matrix in the [ ] brackets to yield Eq. 14.

14.   Relying on single-equation estimation of the determinants of an industry's price, where no attention is paid to the simultaneous determination of price and capacity utilization, results in derived supply elasticities that are biased upward. We ignore whatever bias has been introduced from this fault in the studies listed as our sources.

15.   The assumption of infinitely elastic supply curves underlying Eqs. 11 and 12 implies in fact that *all* environmental costs are passed on into prices. None *will* be absorbed into factor incomes or profits in the short run; none *can* be so absorbed in the long run because every primary factor, including entreprenurial activity, earns "just-normal" returns; there are no rents to cushion the impact of environmental controls on price.

16.   These statements are expanded in the section "Broader Methodological Considerations."

17.   The only world in which there is no apparent resource cost to environmental controls is an extreme Keynesian one, with unemployed resources of all types. The unemployed resources can be put to work producing environmental control, in essence: no industry need suffer, and no prices need rise. In an equally extreme world of full employment, by contrast, the only source of resources is other industries. Most realistically, of course, resources for the production of environmental control are attracted in part from other industries and in part from the pool of the unemployed.

18.   The income-tax-interpretation of a value-added tax obviously differs greatly from the structure of current income taxes. Our treatment of the VAT (income tax) method of financing also departs from reality by ignoring the existence of other taxes and the possibility that revenue collected from them will decline.

19.   The value-added tax rate is referred to as an approximation, not only because other taxes

are ignored (note 20), but also because no attention is paid to how subsidy requirements will change when taxes are imposed or to how the initial level of transactions will change. Allowing for those factors would require us to solve for the tax rate from the following expression, in the case of infinitely elastic domestic supply curves (T = a vector of identical ad valorem value-added tax rates; V = a vector of value-added shares in total output by industry; Q^0, Q^1 = initial and ultimate output vectors, respectively, $\bar{1}$ = a vector of 1's):

$$(T \cdot V - E)'Q^1 \text{ must } = 0$$

$$\therefore (T \cdot V - E)'\left[Q^0 \cdot \left(\bar{1} - \frac{dP}{P} \cdot \eta\right)\right] \text{ must } = 0$$

$$\therefore (T \cdot V - E)'\{Q^0 \cdot [\bar{1} - ((I - A^{D'})^{-1}T \cdot V) \cdot \eta] \text{ must } = 0$$

The last equation, implied by the requirement that revenues cover subsidies, is a quadratic equation in T that can be solved to give a more precise value-added tax rate than the approximation used in the text.

20. We are not distinguishing the three from each other, and are implicitly assuming that the origin principle is applied again. If the destination principle were applied, there would still be international competitive effects from the imposition of environmental controls. In the case of infinitely elastic domestic supply curves, domestic prices would rise by more than the sales tax rate (say T^*), because of the cascading effects of applying the tax to all purchases, including purchases of intermediate inputs: $dP^i/P^i \geq T^*$. Import prices would rise only by T^*; however, $dP_m{}^i/P_m{}^s = T^*$. Thus domestic producers of import substitutes would be placed at a competitive disadvantage. So would domestic producers of exports, since their rebate, T^*, would fall short of the increase in their price. In the case of finite domestic supply elasticities, matters are more complex, and some domestic producers may *gain* international competitive advantage, as outlined in the text discussion of the value-added tax under the destination principle.

21. T^* will also be an approximation for the reasons outlined in notes 20 and 21.

22. The domestic-base table differs from the total-base table primarily in the way competing imports are treated. The total-base table treats competing imports as if they were produced by the domestic industry and enters them as a transferred input in row 80B. Correspondingly, the industry output is interpreted as including both domestic and imported goods. The domestic-base table does not consider competing imports as part of domestic output, and they are subtracted from the row sum showing how industry output is allocated. Row 80B does not exist since the transferred input interpretation is not accepted. All other transactions between industries, however, include both domestic and imported goods, and appear the same in the individual entries of both tables. The coefficients are different because the transactions entries are divided by different column sums, one inclusive of, and one exclusive of 80B imports.

23. The domestic share of input requirements, b, is calculated as one minus the ratio of transferred intermediate imports (Row 80B of the input–output table) to total intermediate output. "Total intermediate output" is defined as the difference between the column element "intermediate outputs, total" for a given industry and the column element "transfers."

24. That is, their prices rise and their output declines 1–1.5% from what it would have been in the absence of environmental controls. In a generally growing world, any measured decline in output need not necessarily occur, only slower growth; while in a generally inflating world, any permanent change in the rate of inflation need not necessarily occur, only a temporary adjustment to a higher price level.

25. The case can be made that comparing percentage changes in prices and output from industry to industry is misleading. With respect to a number of questions about social benefits

and costs from environmental controls, one should care a great deal more about a 2% decline in business done by the motor-vehicles and equipment industry than about a comparable decline in the household-furniture industry.

26.   There are, however, other arguments than "equity" that would imply the superiority of the polluter-pays principle. See note 33.

27.   The weights are the output shares of each industry in precontrols total output.

28.   We make no claim that our list is exhaustive.

29.   This seems to be an appropriate, although quantitatively difficult, way to measure the openness of an economy. A more measurable and familiar, but conceptually less desirable, way to measure openness is by average propensities to export and import. What makes this measure less desirable is that it neglects the profound impact that any change in a small segment of a homogeneous market has on the entire market—and the more homogeneous the products being marketed, the more profound the influence. In a nutshell, openness, at least with respect to commodity trade, should be measured by some ratio of trade*ables* production to total production, not by the ratio of trade to it. By the former, conceptually preferable, measure, even the United States is a highly open economy.

30.   See Walter (1974, pp. 52, 67) for emphasis.

31.   As discussed in the section "Methodology and Framework for an Illustrative Empirical Analysis," polluter pays is a system of financing environmental costs whereby producers are forced to internalize the external costs of the environmental damage they cause, either by being taxed directly according to the scale of the damage, or by being forced by standards to "clean up" their production so that damage is reduced to some "acceptable" level. The most familiar alternative method of financing to polluter pays is a set of subsidies to polluting industries to finance the costs of environmental control. Baumol and Oates (1975, especially Chap. 12) summarize the historical controversy between the alternatives, and outline analytically the case for the polluter-pays method.

32.   For just one example, see d'Arge and Kneese (1972, pp. 257–258, 273–276).

33.   Thus there is clear interdependence between considerations 2 and 4 (macroeconomic policy), as well as between each one and international competitiveness. If environmental controls are financed by subsidies without any countervailing change in other government budget items, then compared with polluter-pays financing: (1) aggregate unemployment or growth problems caused by environmental controls are mitigated; and (2) aggregate inflation problems are made more troublesome. Therefore the stimulus for further countervailing changes in macroeconomic policy would differ according to the particular financing scheme chosen.

34.   In technical jargon, attention should be paid to every industry's "cross-price elasticities of demand," the percentage change in "its" demand induced by a 1% change in some other industry's "price." Although most familiar from consumer-demand theory, the concept is relevant regardless of the nature of ultimate use, whether by consumers or by producers. We have skirted consideration 3 earlier in this chapter by assuming that all such cross-price elasticities are zero. That is, in a more complete study, it would be useful to remove the assumptions made in Eqs. 1 and 3 that $\gamma_m = \gamma = 0$.

35.   This conclusion differs from the flavor of that of d'Arge and Kneese (1974, pp. 283–289), who found that United States environmental control might be expansionary in the aggregate if the rest of the world adopted a similar program. The difference is largely due to our assumption, underlying the text, that the rest of the world is passive.

36.   Fiscal policy might be defined as "neutral" from a comparative-industry standpoint if it represents changes in government spending on goods and services that maintain every industry's share of total output constant.

37.   As is clear in the first two sections, we have ignored our own injunction. The calculations there are consistent with a "neutral" fiscal policy aimed at maintaining aggregate employment and utilization (but not necessarily the price level) constant.

38.   Basevi (1968) estimates the efficiency loss from United States protection under just such a regime.

39.   We have adopted only this regime in our calculations in the section "Empirical Results."

40.   There is clearly interdependence between considerations 4 and 5, too. Aggregate macroeconomic policies have well-known effects on the balance of payments and/or on exchange rates; changes in exchange rates have well-known effects on aggregate employment-utilization and/or on the "price level."

41.   The capital-account-requirement, input–output table breaks down each industry's gross private fixed capital formation (gross investment), recorded in the "final demand" portion of the conventional input–output table, into the amounts spent on products produced by each of 32 "capital-goods" industries.

42.   The assumption of stable primary factor requirements per unit of output is the physical analog to the assumption of stable intermediate input requirements (in dollar terms) per dollar of output, employed in the first two sections of this chapter. "Capital" requirements per unit of output can be derived from Young et al. (1971), as observed in the next section, "Broader Methodological Considerations." *Census of Population,* among other sources, although perhaps for a different industry breakdown than the one employed here. Work along precisely these lines is being carried out currently by the present authors and Robert E. Baldwin at the Universities of Wisconsin and Wyoming. It is being supported by a grant from the Ford Foundation to foster research in international economic order.

43.   This is essentially the approach adopted by Robert E. Baldwin to estimate the impact of Kennedy-Round tariff reductions on labor requirements by skill class. See Baldwin and Kay (1973).

44.   See, for example, the two-way breakdown of earnings by industry and by state/region from the annual state- and regional-income article in the *Survey of Current Business.*

R E F E R E N C E S

Baldwin, R. E., and D. A. Kay, *International Trade and International Relations,* mimeographed, presented at a Brookings Institution Conference on International Economics and International Politics, January 10–12, 1974.

Basevi, G., "The Restrictive Effect of the U.S. Tariff and Its Welfare Value," *American Economic Review, 58,* 840–852, 1968.

Baumol, W. J., and W. E. Oates, *The Theory of Environmental Policy,* Englewood Cliffs, New Jersey: Prentice-Hall, 1975.

Buckler, M., and C. Almon, "Imports and Exports in an Input–Output Model," *1972 Proceedings of the Business and Economics Statistics Section of the American Statistical Association,* Washington: American Statistical Association, pp. 175–184, 1972; appearing also as Chapter 6 of C. Almon, Jr., M. B. Buckler, L. M. Horwitz, and T. C. Reimbold, *1985: Interindustry Forecasts of the American Economy,* Lexington, Massachusetts: D. C. Heath, 1974.

Carter, A. P., "Linear Programming Systems Analyzing Embodied Technological Change," in *Contributions to Input–Output Analysis,* A. Brodey and A. P. Carter, Eds., Amsterdam: North Holland, 1970.

Council on Environmental Quality, U.S. Department of Commerce, and Environmental Protection Agency, *The Economic Impact of Pollution Control: A Summary of Recent Studies,* Washington: U.S. Government Printing Office, 1972.

d'Arge, R. C., "International Trade, Domestic Income, and Environmental Controls: Some Empirical Estimates," in *Managing the Environment: International Economic Cooperation for Pollution Control,* A. V. Kneese, S. E. Rolfe, and J. W. Harned, Eds., New York: Praeger, 1971.

d'Arge, R. C., and A. V. Kneese, "Environmental Quality and International Trade," *International Organization,* Spring 1972. Reprinted in D. A. Kay and E. B. Skolnikoff, *World Eco-Crisis: International Organizations in Response,* Madison: University of Wisconsin Press, 255–301, 1972.

Eckstein, O., and D. Wyss, "Industry Price Equations," in *The Econometrics of Price Determination Conference,* O. Eckstein, Ed., Washington: Board of Governors of the Federal Reserve System, 1972.

Goldstein, M., "Anti-Inflationary Demand Management in the United States: A Selective Industry Approach," *International Monetary Fund Staff Papers. 19,* 344–94, 1972.

Johnston, J., *Statistical Cost Analysis,* New York: McGraw-Hill, 1960.

Leontief, W., and W. F. Ford, "Air Pollution and the Economic Structure: Empirical Results of Input–Output Computations," in *Input–Output Techniques,* A. Brodey and A. P. Carter, Eds., Amsterdam: Elsevier, 1972.

Magee, S. P., "The Welfare Effects of Restrictions on U.S. Trade," *Brookings Papers on Economic Activity, 3,* 645–701, 1972.

Magee, S. P., and W. F. Ford, "Environmental Pollution, the Terms of Trade and Balance of Payments of the United States," *Kylos, 25,* 101–118, 1972.

McGraw-Hill Economics, *Annual McGraw-Hill Survey of Business Plans for New Plant and Equipment,* New York: McGraw-Hill, 1970–73.

Perry, G. L., "Capacity in Manufacturing," *Brookings Papers on Economic Activity, 3,* 701–42, 1973.

Richardson, J. D., "Estimating Demand and Supply Parameters for Imports Without Import Prices: Methodology and Empirical Results," *1973 Proceeding of the Business and Economics Statistics Section of the American Statistical Association,* Washington: American Statistical Association, 132–141, 1973.

Salant, W., and B. Vaccara, *Import Liberalization and Employment.* Washington: The Brookings Institution, 1960.

Tullock, G. "The Welfare Costs of Tariffs, Monopolies and Thefts." *Western Economic Journal, 5,* 224–32, 1967.

Tweeten, L., *Foundations of Farm Policy,* Lincoln: University of Nebraska Press, 1970.

United Nations Department of Economic and Social Affairs, Statistical Office, *Input–Output Tables and Analysis.* Series F, No. 14, Rev. 1. New York, 1973.

Walter, I., "The Pollution Content of American Trade," *Western Economic Journal, 10* (December), 61–70, 1972.

Walter, I., *International Economics of Pollution,* London: Macmillan and New York: Halstead-Wiley, 1975.

Walters, A., "Production and Cost Functions: An Econometric Survey," *Econometrica, 31:* 1–66, 1963.

Young, A. H., L. C. Malley, Jr., S. R. Reed, and R. A. Seaton, II, "Interindustry Transactions in New Structures and Equipment," *Survey of Current Business, 51,* 16–22, 1971.

Trade, Competitiveness, and Environment: Discussion

The three preceding chapters have pointed out the interconnections between environmental management and international trade. Essentially, the issue involves the allocation of productive resources away from the output of tradeable goods and services and into the improvement of environmental quality. The extent of such reallocation depends on the demand for improved environmental quality relative to the demand for other goods and services that have to be given up to achieve it. It also depends on the ability of environmental resources to assimilate pollutants. As such, environment enters into both the demand and supply side of conventional international trade theory, and will influence short-term competitive relationships and associated adaptation costs, as well as long-term comparative advantage in international trade.

ANALYSIS OF TRADE AND ENVIRONMENT IN THEORY AND PRACTICE

Michel Potier

I shall endeavor to limit my comments to the international aspects of environmental policies, but will not attempt to argue the theoretical merits or drawbacks of the three preceding chapters. Instead, I intend to concentrate on a more pragmatic viewpoint drawing on the experience I have gained by working in an international organization such as the OECD.

From this viewpoint let me state, in a provocative kind of way, that both Horst Siebert's and Herbert Grubel's chapters appear to be interesting contributions to theory. However, at this stage, they do not contribute directly to the daily problems with which decision-makers are confronted, mainly because they basically assume that the information required for carrying out the proposed analysis is available and reliable. As theoreticians they are doing their job, and I cannot blame them for that. However, I would like to stress that from my own viewpoint and from the viewpoint of national administrations, the critical problem is to obtain reliable pollution control cost data for the major polluting industries for both old (existing) and new plants as a prerequisite to any kind of assessment of the international trade implications of environmental policies.

This being said, I would like to divide my comments into two parts: (1) offering some remarks in relation to the assumptions or points made by Professor Siebert in developing his model; and (2) expanding on the practical experience we have acquired in the OECD in our pollution-control cost work.

Limitations of the Theory

There are a number of assumptions specified in the model presented by Horst Siebert that I would like to challenge and subject to some comments.

First, I do not accept the assumption according to which *consumption activities do not generate pollutants*. Certain consumption activities are heavy polluters, mainly the private and public transportation services and household waste in its various forms, including sewage. These activities do represent a significant share of the estimated pollution-control expenditures. As an illustration of this point I recall that, according to the U.S. Council on Environmental Quality, in 1973 one-sixth of the American pollution-control costs will fall on the public sector, predominantly for the construction and operation of municipal sewage treatment plants, whereas one-third of the costs are for private automobile pollution abatement and are essentially paid for directly by the consumer when purchasing and operating his car.

Second, the Environment Committee of OECD has just approved the publication of a handbook on environmental damage functions. In this handbook, the authors, Professors Karl-Göran Mäler and Ronald E. Wyzga, indicate the areas where monetary damage estimates are the most promising, in particular in the field of financial losses such as material damage and lost agricultural productivity. It is clear, however, that one of the major problems encountered in the further development of monetary damage functions is the lack of knowledge about the relationship between emissions and ambient concentrations, and the relationship between ambient concentrations and physical damage. At the same time, I would like to point out that, at least in light of the experience of the OECD countries, the use of effluent charges as an instrument for achieving environmental policy objectives is not as widespread as economists in academic circles might think. It is mainly in the field of water that an effluent charge scheme has been implemented in France and the Ruhr area, as Professor Siebert correctly noted. Effluent charges have recently been implemented in the Netherlands as well.

Third, I would certainly agree with Professor Siebert's statement that factors determining the demand for, and the supply of, assimilative services differ between countries, but I would not agree with the idea that differences in these factors automatically require different effluent charges or emission norms. I would not like to expand on this issue since the matter is dealt with in depth by Jean-Philippe Barde in the following chapter. I would rather turn the proposition around and suggest that, when areas are characterized by different stages of industrialization, different assimilative capacities of the environment, different populations, and the like, it is undesirable and economically absurd to impose, as a general rule, the same emission and process standards. There are cases, however, in which there are valid reasons for harmonizing standards: (1) when there is transfrontier pollution, and (2) in the case of persistent toxic substances. Furthermore, when there is a large volume of trade in the products affected by standards governing their composition, design, or use—and where the standards imposed by a country are liable to raise significant nontariff barriers to trade—there are again good reasons for the harmonization of these standards. In the above-mentioned areas I would certainly have more faith in any kind of international agreement between countries than in mechanisms that will make for an equalization of effluent charges between countries in the very long run as suggested in the paper.

I shall now turn to more practical problems based on the experience we have acquired in the OECD through our pollution-control cost work program. This includes some remarks on the problem of pollution-control costs—some orders of magnitude for a few sectors and a few OECD countries. I shall then turn to the problem of the likely impact of these differences in costs on international trade patterns.

What We Know About Pollution-Control Costs

As pointed out in the Siebert and Grubel papers, given the varying availability of environmental resources between countries and, hence, differences in required controls, differences in costs will be likely to have an impact on trade patterns. The significance of any such change in trade patterns will depend on the extent to which the costs differ, and on the proportion of the overall production costs accounted for by the cost of pollution control. The difficulty we are confronted with here is how to get reliable and comparable data. There are at least three problems facing us: (1) identification or definition of the pollution control measures; (2) joint cost allocation; and (3) participation of the industry in releasing these data.

Pollution-control measures are sometimes difficult to identify. When control measures take the form of the installation of treatment equipment of the add-on type, we can identify fairly well the investment costs, but when the measures take the form of process changes it will be particularly difficult to identify that part of the total investment cost of the process change that would be classified as environmental-control costs. In our work we have tried to handle this problem—particularly in our pulp and paper pollution-control cost study—by reaching an agreement between experts at an international level for the categorizing and listing of all treatment procedures (in plant and add-on measures).

Yet even if we confined ourselves to an analysis of add-on measures, we would run into a joint cost allocation problem. In order for emission-control cost data to be of use to the decision-maker, costs should be expressed by kilogram of discharge reduction. An optimal allocation of discharge reduction between all sources would require that marginal treatment costs per kilogram of discharge were equal for all sources. If we had more than one residual and the treatment cost function for each residual were separable, the economist could leave the decision-maker to determine the discharge reductions necessary for each residual; this could only be done by setting weights (i.e., prices) on the different residuals. For an optimal environmental policy, these weights would of course have to reflect the marginal social damage associated with each residual. However, many treatment processes reduce the discharges of more than one residual at a time, and there is no way to be able to determine treatment cost per kilogram of discharge reduction without a set of weights. As pointed out earlier, these weights (prices) should, ideally, reflect marginal social damage. Thus, in order to be able to allocate emission control costs properly, the economist will need some knowledge of damage functions.

Furthermore, with few exceptions, industries have been reluctant to provide us with certain data for reasons of confidentiality, and because they were afraid that these figures might be used against them, resulting in more stringent controls being imposed upon them.

In spite of these difficulties, we have indeed been able to collect some data that will give you an indication of the differential pollution abatement costs for a few industries, namely the iron and steel, aluminum, and pulp and paper industries.

With respect to the iron and steel industry, we have up to now examined two countries—Sweden and the United States. The study of the Swedish iron and steel industry showed that over the period 1970–1973, the annual costs incurred by existing plants in order to comply with the given emission standards were of an order of magnitude of about 1.3% of 1973 total production costs (including taxes) or roughly S.Kr.52.3 million. These annualized costs are based on an assumption of a 10-year depreciation period and an interest rate of 10%. The government subsidization of emission control investments lowered these costs to about S.Kr.37 million, or to approximately 1.0% of 1973 total production costs. During the same period, roughly 8.5% of the steel industry's total capital expenditures were related to emission control.

For the United States iron and steel industry, the impact of the proposed limitation of emissions is likely to be much greater. In the recent EPA studies it was estimated that compliance with the proposed 1983 standards would cost the industry around $1.474 billion (with $551 million for waterborne and $923 million for airborne residuals) between fiscal year 1977 and 1979 expressed in 1971 prices. This is a level of cost almost five times higher than that presently incurred. Capital expenditures will amount to roughly $3.5 billion. Assuming that total capital expenditures in the iron and steel industry are going to be between $20 and $25 billion over the 10-year period 1974–1983, the proposed emission-control program would account for 14–17% of these capital expenditures. In a country such as Japan, from what we have heard, the pollution-control capital expenditures would appear to be even higher—of the order of magnitude of 20–25% of total new investment. In absolute values, the differential costs have been estimated at $6 per ton in Sweden, $10.5 in the United States, and $12 in Belgium.

With respect to the aluminum industry, I would simply say that from the preliminary information I have received from the International Primary Aluminum Institute, which is carrying out a study in pollution control costs for OECD, the average pollution-control capital expenditures are between 10 and 15% of the total capital expenditures, whereas the annual costs would seem to vary between 2 and 3% of total production costs.

For the pulp and paper industry, the study published by the OECD in 1973 covering Belgium, Canada, Finland, France, Italy, Japan, the Netherlands, Sweden, and the United States showed that the pollution-control costs will increase substantially between 1970 and 1980 at least for some product categories. It also indicated that the cost of controlling pollution will differ widely from one product category to another, and that there may be large differences between estimated pollution-control costs in different countries within the same product category. Furthermore, these costs will not be borne by countries at the same time, because the timetable for implementing the antipollution program will be different in each country. To illustrate this point, let me quote just a few figures. By 1975, averaged over all participating countries, pollution-control costs rose from the 1970 level of about 0.5% of product price to a level of about 1.7% in the paper industry and 2.0% in newsprint. The corresponding figures for sulfate pulp range from approximately 1% in 1970 to a level of 2.6–5.8% in 1975. In sulfite pulp, pollution control costs were expected to rise from a level of about 2% of product price in 1970 to a level of nearly 8% in 1975.

To sum up this point, I would say that we now have incomplete information on pollution-control costs for *some* countries and for *some* sectors. All these figures show that there is a good deal of disparity between countries, and to some extent between sectors as well.

From the figures I have been quoting it seems to me—and these are purely my personal views—that pollution-control programs will undoubtedly affect the capital market, because, if the demand for capital exceeds the supply of investable funds allocated to pollution-control facilities, then these are funds that cannot be spent on productive plant and equipment, even though pollution-control facilities will pay off in other ways. In other words, it is fair to say that pollution-control programs could cause some temporary cash-flow problems for firms. However, expressed in terms of percentage of the total production costs, the additional burden on industry seems to me quite moderate. This conclusion would certainly also hold true in comparison with the burden put on industry by the annual changes in wage rates, raw material prices, and the like.

International Competitive Aspects

What about the international trade implications? Here we have a very difficult question, since after assessing the cost of controlling pollution in one given area and the percentage contribution of such costs to total production costs, it is necessary to assess: (1) the sensitivity of country trade flows to price changes; (2) the manner in which cost changes are normally transmitted into prices that will vary depending upon the competitive nature of the industry investigated; (3) the extent to which the costs borne by industry are offset by some assistance granted for pollution control; and (4) the extent to which other production cost changes are likely to outweigh pollution control costs, so that the relative significance of any impact on international trade is substantially diminished.

In the OECD we have investigated the possibility of building up an analytical framework to measure the impact on prices of a variation in costs due to pollution control. The results so far have been rather disappointing for two main reasons: (1) the inputs or the information requirements were such that it has proved impossible to feed completely any model; and (2) theoretical limitations of the models themselves, which are of a static nature and where cost price elasticities estimated by regression methods through historical series are considered constant, exist.

For example, we applied the methodology suggested by Lo Cascio and Fazio in a seminar held at the OECD in 1971, as a test run, to the case of newsprint in the pulp and paper industry using the data gathered in our study on pollution by the pulp and paper industry. The results of this analysis, which give a quantitative estimation of the maximum-impact effect on exports of newsprint for the main exporting countries caused by the unilateral implementation, showed a very slight reduction in the exports of the main pulp and paper suppliers. Due to the uncertainties of such calculations and the limitations of the method, it is clear that such results will by themselves provide the basis for policy measures.

However, I would say that the findings of this case, valued as an experimental test, are to some extent confirmed by what has been learned by experience at a general level for some specific industries—that environmental policies, at least between the industrialized countries, do not seem to have seriously affected international trade patterns. Let me illustrate my argument by noting two important points.

First, it seems to me that if environmental policy in one country has led to a deterioration in the international competitiveness of that country's industries, there would have been a more concentrated and intensive action on the part of the industries affected to obtain assistance through some kind of bilateral or international negotiation. To my knowledge, nothing of this kind has occurred up to now. In the OECD we have a consultation procedure that could be used by our member countries in the case of any difficulty arising from the implementation of our guiding principles, which include the so-called polluter-pays principle. This procedure has *never* been used, and my guess is that this is because the environmental policies followed by most industrialized countries have not substantially affected the pattern of international trade.

Second, I have had the same impression from discussions with people in the business area. For example, in the aluminum industry I was told that differences in pollution control costs between countries had not affected the relative competitive situation between multinational companies, and that other production cost changes have outweighed the differences in pollution-control costs. What appears to be the major source of difficulties likely to affect the competitive position of companies is that some governments, after issuing a construction permit, withdraw it for reasons of pollution, due to the pressure of public opinion, or that others take an extremely long time before making any decision relating to the granting of such a permit.

To conclude, I would like to stress three points: (1) Reliable and comparable data on pollution control costs on an industry basis are a prerequisite for any kind of policy analysis. We are far from having a good data bank in this field, and without this all of the theoretical analytical framework to which we are referring cannot be used effectively. (2) In the light of my own experience, the impact of international trade of the environmental policies followed by the industrialized countries has been far less important than expected. (3) Thus the difficulties and uncertainties encountered in developing models of a theoretical nature for assessing the impact on international trade of environmental policies are such that, in my own opinion, the expected benefits are perhaps not worth the effort involved at this point in time.

POLLUTION CONTROL AND THE THEORY OF TRADE

Jan Tumlir[1]

The studies contained in this volume are a part of the great flowering of economics in recent years into a large number of specialized subdisciplines, the economics of this and that, from medical care, law, support of the arts, and many other things and activities, to the international economics of pollution control. In most of these new subdisciplines, it was a felt social need for a policy, or for better policies, that attracted economists to the problem. Most of these subdisciplines of applied economics thus started, I should think, from largely empirical research collecting, organizing and classifying the basic data, beginning to analyze them by the most readily available methods, either partial equilibrium or aggregate, and working slowly backwards towards a more general and abstract view of the crucial issues.

This is the context in which I view Herbert Grubel's chapter. It is, I think, an admirable—more, a necessary effort. It is necessary for at least two reasons to test the problems and analyses of the specialized subdisciplines on the rack of pure-theory analysis. It gives confidence to the specialist by forcing him to review the process of abstraction by which he derives, from the complex reality he faces, the simplified analytical assumptions with which he works. Second, the testing of particular problems by pure theory is also a defense against the dangers that specialization necessarily entails. I shall only flag this issue here and return to it later.

An exercise in pure theory always has considerable elegance, and this is particularly true with Grubel's presentation. In fact, it dazzles a bit and blurs an issue that I consider most important. On its own chosen ground, the exposition unfolds in a logical way: a small country, a large country, and then, relaxing an assumption, we come to the third case. I shall emphasize the distinction between the first two cases and the third. They represent two very different classes of problems.

Production generates pollution, and in many, perhaps most, cases this pollution remains local. It does not physically cross national boundaries. Yet efforts to control it at the origin are likely to have economic effects abroad, by affecting trade and investment flows between countries. In this indirect way, some forms of pollution control may be made more or less costly than they appeared at first, and foreign countries may be affected favorably or unfavorably. Problems of this class can be solved by application of economic theory. We want to know, globally, what the least-cost method of achieving a given reduction in pollution generated by certain production processes is; an essentially similar analysis would be used in determining the socially or globally optimal reduction in pollution so generated in a given country or group of countries.

However, production in one country may also generate pollution that physically flows across national boundaries affecting another country or countries or a common property resource directly. Here we are facing a problem of a different nature. The most efficient solution, treating the whole world as one country, is not available. Grubel is only too aware of that. What distinguishes the two classes of problems is that for the first, a general second-best solution within the context of accepted trade theory could be specified or is at least conceivable. For the second class, it is not, and to say "not yet" might be excessively optimistic; it may not ever be possible. In any case, the forms in which the problems of the second class manifest themselves are still too different for us to devise general solutions. What they have in common—the one thing we have so far seen them having in common—is that an agreement between two or more countries on what constitutes the optimal flow of pollution is difficult to achieve, and that power will be exercised in some form in coming to any agreement. And economics is such a friendly, humane science that it is only beginning to learn how to cope with power and threats.

Grubel is clearly aware, too, of the unsatisfactory nature of the only solution left to country A when country B refuses to cooperate. My opinion is that a lot more empirical work is needed in this area before a more general theoretical analysis becomes possible and fruitful. We have to have a much clearer view than we have now of all the forms in which these conflicts may appear and of the main variables involved in each particular instance. Even then it is more than likely that a general approach, to be developed from initially heavily empirical analysis, will not be in the nature of economic theory. It is much more likely to be a legal approach; however, in its formulation the economist will have as much to contribute as the physical scientist. In other words, the second class contains problems for which it may be impossible to find economic-theoretical solutions that are relevant to policy making in a world of sovereign nation states.

This is not to say that economic theory cannot help to clarify thinking about these problems. One can ask, for example, whether two-country general equilibrium models are at all applicable to them. Superficially, it would seem yes. The physical passage of specific pollutants presupposes contiguity; the majority of these problems is, therefore, likely to arise between two countries. But it is the essence of the problem that these two economies, far from representing the world, operate in a global context of which they are, in most cases, only a small part. Country B is likely to be exporting only a fraction of its pollution-generating production of X to its more environment-minded neighbor.

Also, contiguous countries are likely to show smaller differences in average income than far distant ones, and, certainly, what is much more relevant, the contiguous regions of the two countries are likely to be much alike. The problem is, therefore, less likely to emerge from different intensities of demand for a clean environment than from the differences in the relative importance of the polluting industry in the regional economy, and other more specific conditions. (It occurs to me that this class of problems, created by physical flows of pollutants across frontiers, as distinct from problems involving a common property resource, really belongs more to interregional than international economic analysis.) The two-country assumption would be appropriate if this kind of problem polarized industrial and developing countries as groups, but in view of the distances separating them, it will not do that, or only rarely. Most of the problems that pollution-control efforts may create between the two groups of countries fall into the first class of indirect effects via trade and capital flows. Let me at this point return to the previously announced theme: the dangers of specialization.

One of them is the natural, and not so important, tendency for each specialized area to begin to develop its own professional jargon that is a cost to the nonspecialist; more dangerous is the tendency to accept only those propositions that can be derived rigorously from the premises to be found in the field itself. Pure-theory analysis helps to widen the angle of vision; by reminding us of the general interdependence of the system, it keeps the specialization alive to conditions and developments in other areas that may have a bearing on the particular problem the specialist is investigating.[2]

An example of this—result of the tendency of specialized subdisciplines to become autarkic—is the difficulty we have in deciding what effects, in the balance, pollution control in industrial countries may have on the economies of the less-developed ones. Another chapter in this volume demonstrates the difficulty very clearly. Now this is obviously a question that specialists in the economics of pollution control could not answer if they were not aware that their field is only a segment of a much more extensive and complex social and economic change. The problems of environment are intimately and intricately related with the problems of energy, raw materials, and population growth (all of which tend to become specializations in themselves). If they are treated separately, we lose sight of their cumulative aspect.

For example, from the viewpoint of pollution control, by the polluter-pays principle, the metallurgical industries of industrial countries will, on the whole, see their costs rise more than those of other industries. However, they would have been vulnerable even if the environment issue had not arisen. Most of them have been relocated to coasts as it has become more profitable to abandon the mining of relatively depleted domestic deposits and import higher grade ores and fuels from abroad. Thus the increase in the cost of energy, and consequently of transport, also forces a revision of these locational economies, give that highly weight-losing materials have to be transported over long distances, and a part of the processed product transported back. At the same time these industries face the emergence of the so-called "raw material power" in supplying less-developed countries, the possible uses of which I shall discuss in a few moments. I may also mention that, at least in the West European countries, the metallurgical industries show a high proportion of immigrant labor, and in these countries, the long period of free low-wage labor immigration is coming to an end. For all these reasons, each stemming from a different area or aspect of economic development, it is unlikely that protectionist pressures mounted by the polluting industries will achieve much. One point we must grant to the policymakers: dependent as they are on different configurations of specific, sectional interests, they have their own notion of a general equilibrium, and it is not too different from ours.

In international trade policy discussions, changes in comparative advantage caused by the need to reduce pollution generated by the production process have, so far, not been an important issue. They will eventually come to the fore, but, I think, in a different form than we imagine.

In the wake of the Stockholm Conference and the publication of the GATT study, the issue was debated in the GATT Council. So that suitable institutional machinery would be ready to deal with such disputes as might, for example, arise from governments' efforts to stem too large shifts in imports or exports following the specification of obligatory domestic pollution control standards, it was decided to establish a committee to which complaints could be brought. So much was unanimous. A split developed, however, over the way the committee should proceed. One group of countries wished the committee to start meeting immediately to discuss and establish a set of criteria according to which the eventual cases could be disposed as and when they arose. Another group—more, I must admit, in the mainstream of GATT tradition of pragmatism and preference for ad hoc solutions—felt that establishing the committee was a sufficient action for the time being, and that the committee should meet only when a case arose. This second group carried the day, and that is where the matter still stands. No complaint has been made to the committee so far. There has not been, to my knowledge, a case of protection, or export-subsidy, instituted or justified on pollution-control grounds.

I am not saying that the increased cost of production that the pollution-control requirements cause to some industries in some countries is not generating protectionist pressures. There has been, since the late 1960s an almost dramatic rise in protectionist pressures. What I am saying is that pollution control did not furnish a new argument to justify protection. It may be an economist's vanity, but I think that this fact reflects the widespread acceptance of our analysis. Even when they fully conform to the prescribed air and water purity standards, most metallurgical industries, for example, will still be relatively more polluting than, say, machine-engineering, instruments, electronics, and similar industries. The polluting industries are actively campaigning for protection, but on the traditional grounds. They are conspicuously *not* using the pollution-control cost argument. They must have realized that it would be counterproductive in increasingly environment-minded societies.

I expect this argument to emerge in another area of the multilateral trade negotiations now beginning in Geneva—on the other side of the table, so to speak—in the context of negotiations about access to supplies, export controls imposed on raw materials, and related issues. The OPEC action not only greatly dramatized the situation in this area, it also distorted the general view of the most important issues in it. Despite the newly fashionable rhetoric, the major less-developed or industrializing exporters of industrial raw materials are not primarily interested in forming cartels or obtaining other price-raising arrangements. They are well aware of the stringency of the conditions to be fulfilled for a cartel to function, and of the difficulties and costs of administering a single commodity agreement, not to say a range of them. They are mainly concerned with conditions under which they could develop industries for additional processing of the materials that they now export in raw or early processed forms. An important condition for this would be the reduction or elimination of the often very high rates of effective protection that the raw-material importing countries grant to their domestic industries processing these materials. In bargaining for such trade concession, the ability of the raw-material exporters to limit the rate of export, even though only temporarily, is an important leverage. How does pollution control enter into this?

A number of countries in which forestry is an important economic sector maintain taxes or other restrictions on the export of pulp. Transforming pulpwood into wood pulp adds value to the primary product and makes for easier transport. Why should these countries want to discourage the export of pulp? The answer is, simply, because still more value is added to the original ton of pulpwood at the next stage where wood pulp is transformed into paper; they would like to capture that stage and export paper instead of wood pulp.

One of the more important insights opened by the development of the concept of "effective tariffs" is the tendency, alluded to above, for tariff structure in the industrial countries to give margins of protection that increase with the degree of processing, following the tendency for the value added at each successive step in increase. In particular, this tariff structure works against the desire of the raw-material producing countries to stimulate industrialization by further processing prior to export. Taxing the export of the unprocessed product is one way to offset this distortion.

It now also appears that pulping is the most polluting part of the chain of operations in the production of paper, and it is probably true, in general, that the lower the stage of processing, the greater the pollution associated with the particular process. Thus the raw material producers may feel doubly abused; not only are their desires (which would often be in accordance with free-trade comparative advantage) to "move up the processing ladder" partially or completely frustrated by escalated protection abroad, but they are also finding that they have specialized in the dirtiest part of the production sequence.

The study of international trade implications of national pollution control is now well established. It assumes that some national purity standards are laid down as domestic demand for cleaner environment begins to manifest itself, and national industries conform to them. More and more nations will enact such standards and their severity must be expected to rise over time. If we add up the resources that each nation will in this way devote to the maintenance of its environment standards, globally they will come to represent very large sums indeed, but, globally speaking, we still live in a very poor world. And so it is necessary to begin thinking about how the world as a whole can economize on these resources. That, too, is a function of the international trade theorist. Producing paper from pulp generates less pollution than pulping, but it must generate some, probably not inconsiderable, pollution, too. Now there must be scale economics and integration economies in pollution control as well, in the sense that in order to adhere to a given water and air standard, you have to spend more on pollution control as well, in the sense that, in order to adhere to a given water and air standard, you have to spend more on pollution control if pulping and paper-making are locationally separate operations than if they were one integrated process. This must certainly be true in many metallurgical industries when unwrought metal moves from country to country to be reheated again to be processed into wire, sheets, tubes, and other shapes. In this sense, pollution control costs are a force for international restructuring of many industries, a force acting in parallel with the increased energy and transportation costs, as well as with the more conventional sources of change in comparative advantage.

I think we urgently need studies in this area, forward-looking studies, forecasting the global structuring of individual industries in 10 and 20 years' time. Having a notion of the structure to which current development tends, both governments and firms would find the planning of adjustment easier, and the whole process of development would be smoother.

NOTES

1. The author wishes to emphasize that the views presented here are his own and are not to be interpreted as reflecting the views of the GATT secretariat of which he is a member.
2. General equilibrium analysis, as philosophy in other contexts, can be described as reason backing off from a problem taking a few steps back until its angle of vision encompasses all that is relevant. It knows, as does philosophy, that it is not wise to attack a problem head-on.

ENVIRONMENTAL ASPECTS OF TRADE MODELS

Rüdiger Pethig

In the basic model presented in Chapter 2, Herbert Grubel describes the production possibilities of an economy with two private goods in the absence of environmental controls by a concave transformation frontier (Y_0X_0 in Fig. 2-1), as in the standard, neoclassical, two-sector model. He then assumes that the production of one of these commodities generates pollutants, and that in order to reduce or to avoid pollution, environmental controls are implemented that use up some amount of scarce resources. He argues that, in the case of environmental controls, the production possibility frontier shrinks in the particular way indicated by the curve $Y_1P_2X_0$ in Fig. 2-1. This "assumption" is intuitively clear, but, as Grubel states himself, it would be of some analytical interest to derive this phenomenon explicitly within the model instead of presupposing it.

Consider, on the other hand, Professor Siebert's model in Chapter 3. Although it has a similar structure to that of Grubel's model, Siebert chooses a method of analysis that does not refer to the concept of production possibilities. It is the purpose of this comment to make explicit, within the framework proposed by Siebert, how environmental controls affect the production possibilities of the two private consumption goods. More specifically, it will be shown that Grubel's "shrinkage assumption" can be obtained as an implication of Siebert's model, which does not seem to be obvious in view of the two authors' different approaches. Consider first in Siebert's notation, which will be used here throughout, the function

$$R_i = F_i^{-1}[H_i^{-1}(S_i{}^p)] \tag{1}$$

being composed of the inverses of the production F_i and the pollutant-generation function H_i. In a (R_i, $S_i{}^P$) diagram this function can be represented by the continuously increasing curve $0A$ in Fig. 5-1. By construction of Eq. 1 there is an output level Q_i uniquely associated with every point on $0A$ such that we have $Q_i = 0$ at the origin and such that the quantity of good i increases with increasing distance from the origin O.

Now we define by $R_i{}^t \equiv R_i + R_i{}^a$ the total amount of resources used up in the sector i, choose some $\hat{Q}_i \geq 0$, and define $\hat{S}_i{}^P \equiv H_i(\hat{Q}_i)$ and $\hat{R}_i \equiv F_i{}^{-1}(\hat{Q}_i)$. Then by $S_i{}^a \equiv S_i{}^P - S_i$ (from Eq. 5 in Chapter 2) and by the pollution abatement function $F_i{}^a$ we obtain the function

$$R_i{}^t \equiv R_i{}^a + R_i = F_i^{-1}[H_i^{-1}(\hat{S}_i{}^p)] + F_i^{a-1}(\hat{S}_i{}^p - S_i) \tag{2}$$

that defines the "production isoquant" Q_iC for commodity i in Fig. 5-1,

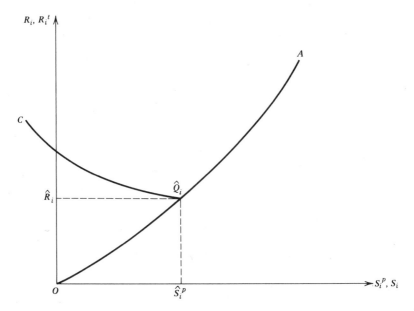

Figure 5-1   The pollution-generation function.

where now the variables R_i^t and S_i, respectively, are plotted on the axes. Since function 2 is defined for every nonnegative Q_i, the plane to the left of $0A$ in Fig. 5-1 is completely covered with such isoquants, whereas the production technology is not defined on the right-hand side of $0A$.

In order to determine the transformation frontier for the case that no pollution controls are enforced, note that the total amounts of pollutants that can be generated in the economy cannot exceed[1]

$$\bar{S} \equiv \text{Max} H_1[F_1(R_1)] + H_2[F_2(\bar{R} - R_1)]$$

$$(0 \le R_1 \le \bar{R})$$

absence of pollution controls, that is, when the production sectors are allowed to produce any feasible level of pollutants they want, the economy's transformation function G is given by[2]

$$Q_1 = G(Q_2; S \le S^*) \equiv F^{-1}[\bar{R} - F_2^{-1}(Q_2)] \text{ for every } S^* \ge \bar{S} \quad (3)$$

If, however, by some collective decision process it is decided that the total amount of pollutants emitted must not exceed $S^* < \max(\bar{S}_1, \bar{S}_2)$, where for $i = 1,2 \ \bar{S}_i \equiv H_i[F_i(\bar{R})]$, then the economy's production possibilities shrink as indicated in Grubel's chapter. This can be illustrated with the help of Fig. 5-2.[3]

Figure 5-2(a) shows a box diagram of size $\bar{R} \times S^*$, where the isoquant system of the production technology of sector 1 (sector 2) is based at origin O_1 (origin O_2), and where the curves O_1BA_1 and O_2BA_2 represent function 1 for sectors 1 and 2, respectively. In Fig. 5-2(b) the transformation curve $\bar{Q}_1B'\bar{Q}_2$ is the graph of function 3 while the transformation curve $\tilde{Q}_1B'\tilde{Q}_2$ is the graph of the transformation function

$$Q_1 = G(Q_2; S \leq S^*), \ \min(\tilde{S}_1, \tilde{S}_2) < S^* < \max(\tilde{S}_1, \tilde{S}_2) \leq \bar{S} \quad (4)$$

Whenever the quantity produced of good 2 is higher than $\bar{Q}_2$, the restriction $S \leq S^*$ is not binding, and, hence, the transformation functions 3 and 4 are identical for every Q_2 within the domain $\tilde{Q}_2 \leq Q_2 \leq \bar{Q}_2$.[4] However, if $Q_1 > \tilde{Q}_1$ (and $Q_2 < \tilde{Q}_2$) both sectors will generally have to devote resources to the pollution-abatement activity in order to attain an efficient production point without violating the upper pollution bound S^*. Therefore, in Fig. 5-2(a), we obtain an efficiency locus connecting B and O_2 (indicated by the dotted line) that is formally equivalent to the well-know efficiency curve in the two-factor, box diagram of the standard, neoclassical, pure-trade model.

It is easily seen from Fig. 5-2 that imposing more restrictive emission standards than S^* (i.e., the right-hand bound of the box in Fig. 5-2a is pushed to the left) increases the shrinkage of the transformation curve, that is, in Fig. 5-2B the point B' moves towards $\tilde{Q}_2$ until, for sufficiently restrictive emission standards, the entire transformation curve lies below the curve $\tilde{Q}_1\tilde{Q}_2$. Thus the real costs of different emission standards can be readily evaluated analytically by the method suggested in Fig. 5-2.

One more remark seems to be in order. In the model discussed here, one

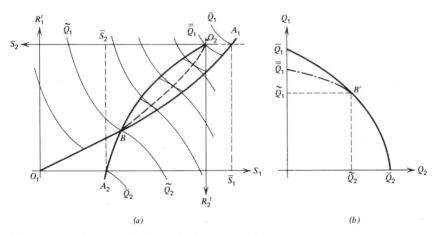

(a)   (b)

Figure 5-2 Production inplications of pollution control.

obtains a different transformation function $Q_1 = G(Q_2; S \leq S^*)$ for every S^* in the domain $0 \leq S^* \leq S$. Since $\bar{\bar{S}}$ is the total net amount of the by-product generated, in order to describe the economy's production possibilities completely one has to consider the three-dimensional space containing the variables Q_1, Q_2, and S. Now suppose, that for some given $S^* \geq 0$, all attainable production points (Q_1, Q_2, S') with $S' > S^* \leq \bar{\bar{S}}$ are "cut off," and that the remaining "truncated" three-dimensional production possibility set is projected into the (Q_1, Q_2) plane. Then the upper bound of this projection is identically equal to the graph of the transformation function $Q_1 = G(Q_2; S \leq S^*)$. Finally, if one is more interested in environmental quality levels (U^s) than in quantities of pollutants (S), by Eqs. 8 and 9 in Siebert's chapter, the production possibility set of the (Q_1, Q_2, S) space can be mapped into the (Q_1, Q_2, U^s) space,[5] which is the domain of the social welfare function introduced by Grubel as well as by Walter.[6]

NOTES

1. By Siebert's assumptions on F^i and H^i, it is not ruled out that function 1 is convex (as drawn in Fig. 5-1). In this case it is possible that

$$\bar{\bar{S}} > \text{Max} \{H_1[F_1(\bar{R})], H_2[F_2(\bar{R})]\}$$

which may lead to some exceptional shrinkage features of the transformation curve, such that neither of its points on the axes move towards the origin. These details will not be pursued here.

2. By its definition, $\bar{\bar{S}}$ is the maximum amount of pollutants being associated with any commodity bundle satisfying Eqs. 3. If $\bar{\bar{S}}$ is not attained at one of the complete specialization points of Eqs. 3, then neither good 1 nor good 2 is uniformly more intensive in its pollution generation than the other good. For the definition of relative pollution intensity see R. Pethig, "Pollution, Welfare, and Environmental Policy in the Theory of Comparative Advantage," *Beiträge zur angewandten Wirtschaftsforschung,* Universität Mannheim, Discussion Paper 45/74, 1974, p. 6.

3. In the following argument the activity of the "environmental protection agency of type A," that is, Equation 7 in Siebert's paper, will not be considered. Its addition would complicate the analysis, but does not seem to cause qualitative changes of the results obtained.

4. Note that $S < S^*$, if in Eq. 4 we have $Q_2 > \tilde{Q}_2$. This is the reason why, in the definition of function 4, the inequality sign is introduced. See also R. Pethig, loc. cit. p. 9 ff.

5. This mapping is applied by I. Walter, "International Trade and Resource Diversion: The Case of Environmental Management," *Weltwirtschaftliches Archiv, 110,* 1974, Fig. 2. For its derivation under some specified assumptions see also R. Pethig, "Umweltverschmutzung, Wohlfahrt und Umweltpolitik in einem Zwei-Sektoren-Gleichgewichtsmodell," *Zeitschrift für Nationalökonomie 35,* 1975.

6. See I. Walter, op. cit. Since Grubel—as opposed to Walter—does not argue within the complete three-dimensional commodity space explicitly, he is forced to use projections of the three-dimensional social indifference surfaces on the (Q_1, Q_2) plane, which are valid only for specific (fixed) environmental qualities, and, thus, may lead to some confusion with respect to their proper interpretation.

SHIFTING THE BURDEN OF RESIDUAL POLLUTION: THE CASE OF A
LARGE COUNTRY WITH ZERO TRANSFRONTIER SPILLOVERS

Jacob S. Dreyer

Although Grubel and Siebert use quite different analytical techniques in
their chapters the problems they address themselves to are very similar. I
shall take advantage of this similarity to pick up some loose ends I perceive
in their treatment. I shall retain the framework set up by Grubel in the section of his chapter entitled, "Large Country, No Spillover of Externalities,"
but I shall use, with some modifications, the relations developed by Siebert.
I shall also use Siebert's notation, unless specified otherwise.

As a point of departure I shall take Siebert's Eqs. 3, 4, 7–9, and explain
why I think this part of his formulation is erroneous.

Because the output, Q_i, is a flow, its joint product, S_i^P, is also a flow, but
then S_i^a in Eq. 4 and S_3^a in Eq. 7, having necessarily the same dimension as
S_i^P, are also flows. Therefore T from Eq. 8, called by Siebert "pollutants
ambient in the environment," must also be a flow. More precisely, it is the
net addition (per time unit) of pollutants to their content in the environment. Yet, if T is a flow, Eq. 9, $U^s = U(T)$, is difficult to interpret. If U^s is,
according to Siebert, the measure of environmental quality, it has to be related not to the net flow of pollutants into the environment in a given time
period, but to their content or concentration in the environment in this period. In other words, by Siebert's definition of environmental quality, it
should be

$$U^s(t_n) = \int_{t_0}^{t_n} U[T(t)]\,dt.$$

As we will see later, this change in the specification of the relation
between the quality of the environment and (ultimately) the levels of output
and abatement in all periods between t_0 and t_n has important consequences
for the formulation of trade policies as they relate to the management of the
environment.

The immediate problem to consider is the following. Suppose that $T(t) >
0$ when $Q_i(t) > \bar{Q}$. This means that, even though the necessary amount of
resources in diverted to abate the pollutants, and despite the positive
assimilative capacity of the environment, $\bar{T}^u$, as long as the production of
the polluting goods exceeds certain levels, the stock of pollutants in the environment increases. In other words, it increases even though we are operating on Grubel's contracted production possibility frontier. In is helpful to
view this irreducible accretion of pollutants in the environment as a consequence of the technological impossibility to reduce their net flow to zero,

above a certain level of output, irrespective of the amount of resources one devotes for this purpose. I shall call $T(t)$ the residual pollution. Suppose now that we have two countries producing two goods: Q_1, tires; and Q_2, transistors. Production of tires entails substantial emission of pollutants; production of transistors is pollution-free. Pollution due to the consumption of the two goods is disregarded. Neither country specializes completely, but the home country exports tires in exchange for transistors, and, thus, enables the foreign country to sustain a lower level of pollution than it would have to accept if it were self-sufficient in tires. If $Q_1 > \bar{Q}_1$ and $Q_1^+ \leq \bar{Q}_1$, as time goes on, the environment of the foreign country remains free of pollution, whereas the quality of the environment in the home country progressively deteriorates. We have to deal, then, with pollution via trade: one of the countries enjoys an opportunity gain by importing the polluting good and thus imposing the burden of residual pollution upon the residents of the other country.

Given the state of technology, the only way for the home country to reduce $T(t)$ is to reduce $Q_1(t)$. If an outright ban on exports of Q_1 is decreed, resources in the home country will be switched toward more production of Q_2, while the foreign country will have to switch resources from the production of Q_2 toward that of Q_1. The same result can be obtained, of course, by imposing a consumption tax on Q_1 in the home country, and using the proceeds to subsidize the production of Q_2. In both cases the two countries in question will move toward autarky; the welfare attributable to consumption will decline in both countries, while the welfare attributable to the degree of cleanliness of the environment will increase in the home country and decrease in the foreign country. The total welfare in the home country may not decrease by assumption.

A justifiable question to ask is whether, instead of an autarkic solution, the residents of the foreign country wouldn't be ready to remunerate the residents of the home country for their being subject to the deleterious effects of the residual pollution, and whether the residents of the home country wouldn't be willing to accept such a remuneration? This can be accomplished by decreeing an export tax collected (indirectly) from foreign importers of home-produced tires.

Such an export tax will leave the domestic price ratio unchanged (if the tax levy is not recycled back into the economy), and will result in a higher price for tires in terms of transistors in the foreign country. If the tax levy is used to subsidize production and/or consumption of transistors in the home country, the world and the domestic price ratios can be made the same. In both cases, the imposition of the tax levy will affect the production points on each country's production possibility frontier as well as the respective consumption mixes. Together, these changes in production and consumption will determine the magnitude, and perhaps even the direction, of the trade flows.

The Model

Let

$$Q_1(t) = C_1(t) + X_1(t) \tag{1}$$

$$Q_2(t) = C_2(t) - X_2^+(t) \tag{1a}$$

$$Q_1^+(t) = C_1^+(t) - X_1(t) \tag{2}$$

$$Q_2^+(t) = C_2^+(t) + X_2^+(t) \tag{2a}$$

where Q_1 and Q_2 stand for outputs of tires and transistors, respectively, C_1 and C_2 for their consumption, and X_1 and X_2 for their exports. The superscript "+" indicates the foreign country.

$$S_1(t) = [HQ_1(t)] \tag{3}$$

$$S_{1+}(t) = H[Q_1^+(t)] \tag{3a}$$

$$S_2 \equiv 0 \tag{4}$$

$$S_2^+ \equiv 0 \tag{4a}$$

$$T(t) = S_1(t) - S_1^a(t) - \bar{T}^a(t) \tag{5}$$

$$\bar{T}^a(t) = \bar{T}^a(t)^+ \tag{6}$$

The above set of conditions say that the production and abatement technologies are the same in both countries, as is the absorptive capacity of the environment. Only production of tires entails emission of effluents. Let $\hat{r}_1$ and $\hat{r}^a$ be, respectively, the marginal cost of resources per unit of output of Q_1 and the marginal cost of resources used to abate the technologically feasible maximum of pollution due to the production of one unit of Q_1.

Also let $v_1(t)$ be a variable border price adjustment (export tax). Then

$$p_1 = \hat{r}_1 + \hat{r}^a + v_1 \tag{7}$$

is the price charged by the home country for exported tires.

If $v_1 = 0$, the price ratios at home and abroad are the same. As an be seen from the Edgeworth box in Fig. 5-3, the home country produces at P and consumes at C. The common price line being DD, the home country exports X_1 in exchange for X_2^+.

When $v_1 > 0$, tires become more expensive in terms of transistors in the foreign country. It moves its production point to $\tilde{P}^+$, where the new price

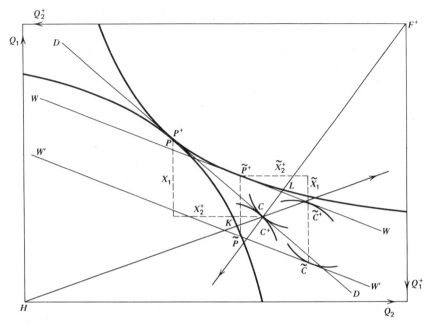

Figure 5-3   Production effects of pollution control.

line WW is tangent to its production possibility frontier while its consumption point is established at $\tilde{C}^+$. The production of tires in the home country decreases accordingly to $\tilde{P}$. The price line $W'W'$, parallel to WW, together with the requirement that the total output of transistors by both countries be consumed, established home country's point of consumption, $\tilde{C}$. At this new set of production and consumption points the home country still exports tires and imports transistors, but the volume of trade is diminished. The new consumption points lie off the implicit contract curve $HKCLF^+$. Both countries are reluctant to produce the maximum possible amount of tires, and, therefore, are forced to consume jointly less of them than would be possible if these countries did not care about pollution. The foreign country is definitely worse off than before the imposition of v_1: its terms of trade deteriorated, its consumption of both tires and transistors decreased, and the pollution of its environment increased because of an increase in output of tires. But the foreign country is still better off than it would have been if it decided to be self-sufficient at point L.

The home country is definitely better off both because of an improvement in its terms of trade and a decrease of a net flow of pollutants into the environment due to the curtailment of the production of tires. The improvement of the home country's position at the expense of the foreign country can be viewed as a partial shifting of the burden of residual pollution by the residents of the home country onto the residents of the foreign country. The foreign country is forced both to increase the output of the polluting good and pay the home country (in the form of the terms-of-trade deterioration) for its suffering the effect of remaining pollution.

The Choice of the Magnitude of the Export Tax

Just how does the home country choose the level of the tax on exports of tires that would maximize its total welfare, that is, the consumption-related and the environment-related utility? In order to analyze this problem we have to specify explicitly the type of social welfare function we want to deal with.

Let us assume that environment-related utility depends on some measure of "cleanliness" of the environment, $Z(t)$, that is inversely related to the accumulated stock of pollutants. In light of our previous definitions

$$Z(t_n) = \int_{t_0}^{t_n} [T(t) \ dt]^{-1}, \qquad 0 \leq Z \tag{8}$$

and the environment-related utility function is

$$V_E(t_n) = V_E[Z(t_n)], \qquad V_E' > 0 \tag{9}$$

As to the consumption-related utility function, we shall assume it to be logarithmic, that is,

$$V_C(C_1, C_2) = \alpha \log C_1 + \beta \log C_2, \tag{10}$$

time invariant and independent of V_E. In other words, the social welfare function, $U(t)$, appropriate for our analysis is additive and weakly separable, or

$$U(t_n) = V_E(t_n) + V_C[C_1(t_n), C_2(t_n)] \tag{11}$$

For the sake of simplicity we can assume that $\alpha = \beta = 1$, so that

$$U(t_n) = V_E\left[\int_{t_0}^{t_n} T(t) \ dt\right]^{-1} + \log C_1(t_n) + \log C_2(t_n) \tag{12}$$

Figure 5-4 is a graphical representation of the relationships spelled out above for a given period of time. The graph in the northwest quadrant is an implicit damage function $Z = Z(Q_1)$, $Z' > 0$, that is, the "cleanliness" of the environment is inversely related to the level of production of the polluting good. In the southwest quadrant the offer curves are depicted, and their intersection point, E, is given by Eqs. 1 and 2. Point $\hat{C}_1$ is the domestic

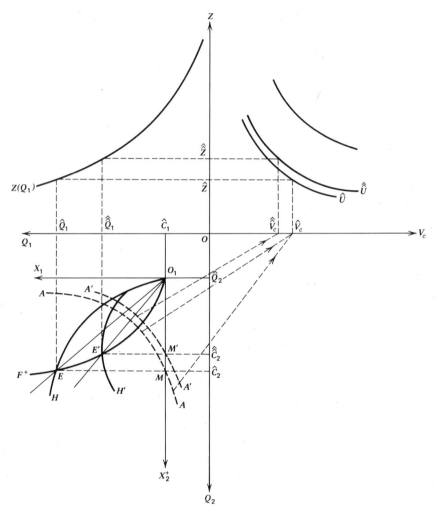

Figure 5-4   Shifting residual pollution via trade.

consumption of tires by the home country, point $\hat{Q}_1$, their total output; $\hat{Q}_2$, domestic production of transistors, $\hat{C}_2$, their domestic consumption. The area of the rectangle $O\hat{C}_1 M\hat{C}_2$ = antilog $V_C(\hat{C}_1, \hat{C}_2)$. The hyperbola AA, being a locus of points such as M for all rectangles with the same area, corresponds to a given level of utility related to consumption. By mapping the (set of) points indicated by AA locus into V_C, we obtain a point $\hat{V}_C$. This is the consumption-related utility associated with the terms of trade given by the slope of the ray $O_1 E$. The volume of exports at these terms of trade corresponding to $\hat{V}_C$ determines the total production of tires, $\hat{Q}_1$, and, via the damage function, the degree of cleanliness of the environment, $\hat{Z}$. In the northeast quadrant we have an indifference map, indicating the trade-off between consumption-related utility and the degree of cleanliness of the environment. The coordinates of points $\hat{V}_C$ and $\hat{Z}$ determine the level of total utility, $\hat{U}$.

Now, if the home country imposes on foreign importers such a payment for its exports that its offer curve shifts from O_1H to O_1H' improving its terms of trade, as indicated by the slope of the ray O_1E', its output of tires will shrink to $\overset{\star}{Q}_1$ and its consumption of transistors to $\overset{\star}{C}_2$. As one can see, although $\overset{\star}{V}_C < \hat{V}_C$, the total welfare $\overset{\star}{U}$ may exceed $\hat{U}$, a condition I indicated by an appropriate mapping of the set given by the locus $A'A'$ into V_C axis. It can be easily ascertained, however, that an increase or decrease in the total welfare of the home country, U, resulting from an imposition of an export tax is continent upon:

1. The elasticity of the foreign offer curve (determining the improvement or deterioration in the terms of trade),
2. The form of the utility function V_C (determining the severity of the drop in consumption-related utility due to the fall in the consumption of the imported goods),
3. The form of the damage function (determining the degree of improvement in the quality of the environment resulting from the curtailment of production of the polluting export good),
4. The parameters of the substitution between improved environment and increased consumption in the total welfare function (the slopes of the U curves),
5. The willingness or reluctance of the foreign country to retaliate when faced with a deterioration in its terms of trade.

These conditions imply that it is by no means certain that a commercial policy aimed at shifting the duress of environmental deterioration upon other countries has to be effective in raising the total welfare of the pollution-afflicted country.

What is to be Maximized?

As was indicated earlier, the answer to this question is of crucial importance in formulating a nation's policy, both domestic and international, toward the environment. More specifically, when formulating these policies at time t_0, what do we want to maximize:

$$U(t_n), \int_{t_0}^{t_n} U(t)\, dt$$

or

$$\int_{t_0}^{t_n} U(t)\, dt + U(t_n)$$

(The symbol t_n stands for the last period in the planning interval, which can also be infinity). Maximizing $U(t_n)$ corresponding perhaps to the desires of some extreme environmentalists, regarding themselves as the guardians of the interests of future, even yet unborn, generations. Maximizing the second expression implies a constant trade-off between consumption- and environment-related utilities over the planning interval, as well as a certain symmetry in treating all generations affected. Maximizing the third expression corresponds to a compromise view, according to which the welfare of earlier generations is subject to a constraint on the quality of the environment inherited by the last generation in the planning interval.

Mathematically, maximizations of the expressions mentioned above are all variants of the general control problem,[1] and with the same initial conditions and constraints will lead to different solutions for the optimal paths of outputs, trade flows, and consumption.

NOTE

1. These variants are usually referred to in the literature on optimal control as the Problem of Mayer, and Problem of Lagrange, and the Problem of Bolza, respectively.

NOTES ON ENVIRONMENT AND TRADE COMPETITIVENESS

Edwin B. Shykind

I would like to open my discussion with several caveats that bear on the nature of my comments. First, since I am in the enviable, or depending on one's viewpoint, the untenable position of ostensibly determining the economic impact of pollution controls on United States industry, as well as the potential international competitive disadvantages occurring from differences in foreign pollution-control standards, and reporting these conclusions to Congress, none of the statements or conclusions that I shall make should be construed as representing United States governmental policy.

Second, I am not an economist and, therefore, am considerably more at ease with a diffusion model for air pollution than I am with an input/output (I/O) model. This is probably because we have not found all the variables in our problems and are not faced with as many caveats as seem to be needed with an I/O model. Consequently I will attempt, in part, to relate my comments to the conclusions and near conclusions we arrived at in our recent Departmental study, *The Effects of Pollution Abatement on International Trade II* (Washington, D.C.: U.S. Government Printing Office, 1975).

The use of I/O studies, such as the one employed in Chapter 4 certainly useful in determining the general trend of prices (excluding the cross-elasticities that were specifically omitted as part of the model's assumptions). The model that we have just completed in the Department of Commerce is in close agreement, across a more limited number of industrial sectors, with similar constraining assumptions. This probably demonstrates that models of this nature are in accord with established theory, and one should not be surprised at the similarity. However, there are several areas where models of this type, even as highly structured as these, may be misleading.

Calculations of price increases due to pollution control, on a strictly national level, are indicators of some potential economic report. Unless additional data on other domestic market relationships that influence decisions on variables—such as capital investment, and existing domestic and international market structures—and some quantitative estimate of the range of pollution-control requirements and the rates of their implementation are available, then the usefulness of models is very limited.

The paired assumptions that costs to industry for pollution control creates an "economic impact" in terms of price increases (with its attendant economic consequences), and that an increase in domestic price may cause a decrease in an existing international competitive advantage are not demonstrated by this particular model. These appear to be general economic truisms that are operative at times and can fluctuate rapidly depending upon other market variables besides price.

Professors Richardson and Mutti do recognize these issues in their general discussion, and it is important to recognize their significance in predicting the outcome of economic situations, whether one uses a model or directly calculates the actual pollution-control costs per unit of pollution on a domestic or multinational basis.

I must confess that I am somewhat puzzled in not finding considerably more discussion of how the domestic price changes will affect our international competitive position. I believe that the authors have reached the limits of interpretation prevalent in most of the current studies, primarily a lack of data on foreign economic structures and environmental controls and policies, each of which affects comparisons across comparable industry sectors.

I see very limited merit in the "industry equity" concept presented to justify a uniform value-added tax on all industries, which would finance pollution-abatement costs largely incurred by a few industries' production activities. Resource misallocation effects would seem to follow such an equity concept in terms of overexpansion of the externality generating productive activities. Since externalities do not distribute themselves in a horizontally equitable fashion across industries, then neither should their tax correction. Equity between generations seems a more appropriate criterion by which to judge the speed with which pollution abatement facilities are installed and the methods by which they are financed. If pollution abatement facilities benefit future generations likely to be richer than ourselves, our financing methods should shift some of the pollution abatement "debt burden" on to them.

However, the economic scenarios in their analysis point out the current national dilemma in investment by most domestic industries: They are affected by requirements for capital expenditures for pollution-abatement devices. There is the parallel problem of many other nations less well equipped financially to meet pollution-control standards as extensive as those of the United States. Certainly the industrial costs are not optimal in all cases, and inferences can be drawn that exceptions to the full internalization of costs by industry may be the best strategy for other nations. Suggested variations and exceptions in implementing the current polluter-pays principle by OECD nations, although perhaps not based on formal models, certainly indicate a much better understanding of the economic consequences of heavy investment (induced by very strict air and water abatement practices). In the case of our own national program, the analysis that Professors Richardson and Mutti have presented points out that there will be larger price increases, in a relative sense, through our adherence to present United States policies toward investment in pollution abatement.

We are currently using a model at the Department of Commerce that compares the "splash" effect of pollution investment on over 40 comparable industrial segments in the United States and West Germany, using the necessary investment in the two national steel industries as the controlling element of the model. Although subject to the same limitations as the model under discussion today, it is interesting to note that the theoretical splash effect through the West German economy is about double that of the United States. Observing this phenomenon, in isolation from all other market factors, the conclusion might be drawn from the Richardson–Mutti analysis that these results could predict a different West German national policy designed to meet both economic and environmental considerations.

Returning briefly to my previous comment concerning price as only one of a number of factors in producing international trade effects, I would like to point out that, at this time, other factors have a much greater impact on export markets and import penetration. Considerations such as transportation and energy costs may mask modest percentage increases due to environmental control. One might ask about the longer-term impact on industrial expansion in light of extensive capital investments for antipollution systems. Certainly the requirement that the United States industries make large investments, in addition to meeting long-range expansion plans, will ultimately create some competitive disadvantage if other nations maintain growth, at 4–5% on a yearly basis, in lieu of heavy expenditures in response to very stringent environmental standards. The United States capital-flows table and capital I/O matrix definitely needs to be reversed in light of more stringent pollution-abatement standards.

Cremeans attempted this in the July 1974 *Survey of Current Business*. The dynamics of the interindustry output and price adjustment process to greater pollution-control capital expenditures require adaptation of one of the various Leontief-type dynamic input–output models currently available.

The comments made earlier by Michel Potier of the OECD, concerning the more pressing problem of national cash flows as perhaps the predominant issue in industrial and national economic impacts, appears to point out long-term capital investment as an area for increased analysis. Consequences of the method by which the cost of the controls are financed, touched on in the analysis in the Richardson and Mutti chapter, are not adequately quantified on a national or international basis to give more than a flavor of potential international impacts. If the calculated increases in prices due to pollution-abatement costs are really significant under any of the scenarios explored in that study, it would be useful to ascertain the nature of these impacts. Perhaps there is some "threshold" value or level of significance associated with the projected price increases in the model that would allow for the "triggering" of more detailed industry analysis leading toward possible policy changes in specific industry sectors.

The Richardson–Mutti discussion of the broader methodological considerations has served to heighten my own frustrations in identifying the most significant factors for the determination of international competitive advantages due to pollution-control differences. In order to derive any meaningful conclusions about either domestic or international impacts one must really place these considerations (or variables) into matrices of priority, or some analytic framework, that will indicate which of the variables may contribute to the distortion within individual industrial sectors. In the absence of much of the required data there are only a few methodologies currently available to allow any conclusions to be drawn, and they are composites of various considerations presented in Chapter 4. We have applied some of these in our own *International Trade Study*.

In order to accomplish the objectives of our Congressional mandate in the absence of cost data, many international control standards, national environmental policies, and fixed implementation schedules, a group of industries, products, and industrialized countries were compared and selected for study. The selection was based on the importance of imports and/or exports and the pollution-abatement investment burden to be borne by the individual industrial sectors. From this group we examined four basic materials industries: basic copper, aluminum reduction, Kraft paper, and phosphate fertilizers. For the most part these industries were analyzed on a plant-by-plant basis. Costs of air-pollution controls were calculated on a unit-product basis under existing or very firm near-term control standards. Extending this process across individual industries and major foreign competitors our "conclusions" bear out a number of conclusions in the methodological section of Chapter 4. However, each industry examined falls into a slightly different domestic and international impact category.

Thus we might add to the list of six considerations for assessing the impact of environmental controls on industry, such as: (1) status of industrial growth and capacity at the time of the imposition of controls; (2) world market prices and demand vs percentage of product cost due to environmental controls; (3) time-phasing of domestic vs foreign antipollution standards; and (4) transportation, energy, and other product- or pollution-related costs.

Examples of how these and other factors have influenced our own analysis can be cited. Hence, if the basic United States copper industry must incur an average 7 cents per pound increase, the domestic and foreign competitive impact on the industry will be large, provided that the international market remains at its presently depressed levels. If existing environmental objectives among the major aluminum manufacturing countries are carried out, there may not be any competitive disadvantage between the major producing countries. The United States fertilizer industry, although requiring a large capital investment for equipment, may not suffer either domestic or international impacts due to pollution controls, provided that world prices for phosphate fertilizers remain at their present elevated levels. Kraft paper products will probably not be seriously affected by current control costs, but diversion of capital from expansion of capacity to abatement equipment may, in the future, produce trade distortions.

Obviously there are many conditional assumptions that must precede the above statements. However, as national policies progress toward stated environmental goals and standards, the complexities and uncertainties in the determination of antipollution costs and possible distortions should be adequately resolved allowing for more definitive conclusions in this area.

In conclusion, the discussion contained in Chapter 4 draws attention to two very important issues: (1) the use of models as a potential factor in the determination of environmental/economic policy; and (2) the complex policy considerations that must be addressed along with the outputs from more comprehensive models, or other analytic work, in order to arrive at balanced and rational decisions in the formulation of economically sound environmental strategies. Further development of this work, in conjunction with new empirical data, will certainly clarify the international trade aspects of environmental control and investment.

PART Two

THE POLICY DIMENSION

National and International Policy Alternatives for Environmental Control and Their Economic Implications

Jean-Philippe Barde

When, in the late 1960s, environmental protection became a serious economic and political concern in the industrialized countries, a number of international issues were raised almost simultaneously. The quality of the environment proved to be a major international issue inasmuch as it highlighted the interdependence between countries. On the one hand, pollution and destruction of common environmental resources call for international cooperation. On the other hand, the new economic constraints may have adverse effects on international trade.

In this chapter a brief account will be made of the major international economic issues relating to environmental protection. Although transfrontier pollution problems are raising important international economic issues, we shall not deal specifically with them. This would go beyond the scope of this chapter, and the issue is tackled in subsequent chapters

137

by Ralph d'Arge and A. Scott. Referring to "environmental protection" we shall in fact concentrate on *pollution control* although an environment policy applies to a number of other activities such as nature conservation and, to some extent, urban planning. We shall also deal with the issues from an empirical and pragmatic viewpoint as they are actually tackled on the international scene.[1]

In this paper we shall deal with two important policy alternatives for pollution control: (1) the cost allocation principles, that is, who should pay environmental costs (control costs and/or damage costs); and (2) the instruments for implementing the policies, that is, how to achieve environmental goals, and how to pay for environmental costs.

THE POLLUTER PAYS PRINCIPLE AND ECONOMIC THEORY

In welfare economics, pollution is generally viewed as an external cost, that is, a cost that is imposed by one economic sector on another without compensation. The logical way to correct this "market failure" is thus to ensure that these external costs, that is, damage caused by pollution, are adequately paid for. This is the so-called theory of "internalization of external costs."

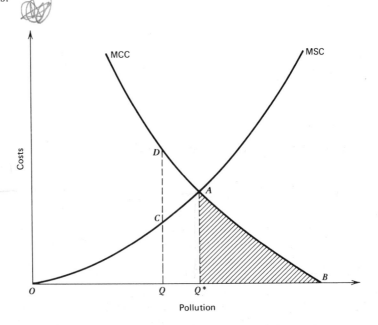

Figure 6-1   Optimum level of pollution.

If we represent on a diagram the marginal social cost of pollution (MSC) and the marginal cost of pollution control (MCC), the optimum level of pollution would be fixed at point Q^*, below which, say at point Q, the costs of pollution abatement (QD) exceed the corresponding social benefits (QC), that is, environment damage avoided ($QD > QC$).

At the optimum level of pollution OQ^*, internalization of pollution-related external costs would imply a payment equal to area OAB. Note that area OAB can be divided into two parts: area Q^*AB, *the pollution-control costs incurred to abate pollution down to level OQ^**, and area OAQ^*, that is, the cost of damage corresponding to the "residual pollution" OQ^*.

Now if the polluter were asked to pay compensation for the total damage inflicted upon the community, he would first abate his pollution down to level OQ^*, and then compensate for the residual damage. In this interpretation, the polluter-pays principle (PPP) implies a *total internalization* of the costs represented by area OAB, but we shall see that at the level of the concrete implementation of environmental policies, the polluter-pays principle, as internationally defined and agreed upon, has a quite different meaning.

DEFINITION AND INTERPRETATION OF THE PPP

It was within the framework of the OECD that the PPP was first internationally adopted. In its recommendation, the OECD Council defines the PPP as follows:[2]

> The principle to be used for allocating costs of pollution prevention and control measures to encourage rational use of scarce environmental resources and to avoid distortions in international trade and investment is the so-called "Polluter Pays Principle." This principle means that the polluter should bear the expenses of carrying out the above-mentioned measures decided by public authorities to ensure that the environment is in an acceptable state. In other words, the cost of these measures should be reflected in the cost of goods and services which cause pollution in production and/or consumption. Such measures should not be accompanied by subsidies that would create significant distortions in international trade and investment.

The principal implications of the OECD's PPP are as follows.

1. If we compare this definition with the total internalization theory, we can see that the OECD does not make reference to the compensation of residual damage, since it states that the polluter should pay for the "pollution prevention and control measures . . . decided by public authorities to ensure that the environment is in an acceptable state." This can be at-

tributed to the fact that, as a general rule, environmental policies are not based on damage compensation. Instead, public authorities decide upon a certain "acceptable" level of pollution and impose corresponding emission standards on polluters. In any case, very little is known about damage costs, and it would not be possible to make polluters pay for the exact social cost they impose on the community, for instance, by using a charge equal to the marginal cost of the damage inflicted.

Hence the PPP as defined by the OECD *is not a total internalization principle.* It merely requires that the polluter bear the costs of pollution prevention and control measures, whatever these are, that is surface Q^*AB in Fig. 6-1. It is implicitly assumed that the pollution level decided upon by the public authorities (e.g., the optimal level OQ^*) leaves the environment in an acceptable state. But the PPP does not preclude the possibility of total internalization. If a country requires from polluters that they pay compensation for residual damage (surface OAQ^*) this would, of course, still be in accordance with the PPP. Note, also, that the use of pollution charges automatically implies total internalization (at the optimum level), since the polluter has to pay the pollution control costs plus the charges corresponding to the residual pollution. Compensation for damage may also be required in specific circumstances, such as the cleansing of an environmental resource after accidental pollution (e.g., the cleansing of a lake).

Among pollution control costs, we must not forget the *administrative costs* of environmental policies, for example, controls, sanctions, and monitoring. These costs may be sizeable, and can be charged to the polluters. For example, the sulfur tax on fuels in the Netherlands is aimed, among other things, at covering 90% of the expenses related to the implementation of air-pollution regulations.[3] Lastly, costs of research and development on pollution-control processes may be paid for either by polluters or by the state. According to OECD definitions, these costs may actually be incurred by the state or subsidized without infringing upon the PPP.[4]

2.   The PPP also requires that internalization of environmental costs take place at the specific level of the polluter. The polluter must be the *first payer.* It does not mean that pollution-control costs are necessarily finally borne by him.

Depending upon market structure—for example, monopolistic, oligopolistic, or competitive—pollution control costs may be totally, partially, or not at all passed on to the consumer. The fact that pollution-control costs may indeed by finally borne by the consumer in no way contradicts the PPP.

3.   It is desirable that prices reflect environmental costs, so that market forces react accordingly. If polluting goods, or goods produced by a polluting process, happen to be relatively more expensive, this price difference

reflects the social costs associated with their production or use. Lower prices—prices not fully reflecting environmental costs—would induce production above the socially desirable level.

4.   As a cost-allocation rule, the PPP is primarily an efficiency principle, but not per se an equity principle.[5]

5.   Who is the polluter, who is the payer? There is no unambiguous answer. It is not always easy to determine where pollution emanates from and responsibilities are often shared. If we take the case of fertilizers and pesticides, the responsibility is shared between the producer and the farmer who may misuse these products. For water pollution, what is the responsibility of households? The detergent producers? Local municipalities?

In the case of automotive emissions, is it the car manufacturer or the user who is responsible? No doubt the user is the physical polluter, but what can he do about it? It is the manufacturer who has the actual power to reduce emissions per mile. In many instances it will be more effective to concentrate environmental action on the economic sector that has the real technical and economic power to abate pollution, rather than to attack directly the physical polluters. In any case, the PPP does not prejudge anything about the identification of the polluter who is, in fact, not defined. It is the role of public authorities to assess where environmental action should most effectively concentrate. The purpose of the PPP is not to define responsibilities, although it may contribute to this end.

From an international viewpoint, it is clear that application of diverging cost-allocation principles by national environmental authorities will tend to result in trade distortions. If one country makes its polluters pay while another systematically subsidizes them, the second country will tend to gain an artificial competitive advantage in trade.[6] International application of a common cost-allocation principle will help ensure that comparative production advantages of different countries are indeed reflected in costs. However, the PPP, as other environmental cost-allocation principles, is subject to a number of exceptions.

THE PROBLEM OF EXCEPTIONS TO THE PPP

Environmental protection may entail high costs to society, at least in certain economic sectors, as well as important structural shifts in the economy. Thus it is quite possible that abrupt and rapid implementation of pollution control measures may cause serious economic and social hardships, as, for example, when a polluting firm cannot afford to comply with the new regulations and must go out of business. Regional development and employment may be directly affected.

Thus it may be regarded as legitimate to introduce a *transition period,* during which assistance may be granted to industries or regions facing special difficulties to ensure more efficient and rational adaptation to the new environmental regulations. This means that the PPP may not always be immediately and fully applied, and may sometimes be subject to exceptions. One has to place environmental policies within the broader context of the overall socioeconomic constraints that exist at a given point in time. The problem of exceptions to the PPP nevertheless raises three important questions: (1) Should these exceptions be limited to specified transition periods, or extended to cover other relevant circumstances however long it takes? (2) Should assistance be granted to any and all plants, or only to *existing* plants—those already in operation when new regulations were passed? (3) How can the exceptions to the PPP be identified, and how can their possible impacts on international trade be evaluated?

In its recent *Recommendation on the Implementation of the Polluter Pays Principle* the OECD Council reaffirms the need for a uniform observance of the PPP, and thus states that, as a general rule, no economic or financial assistance should be granted to polluters.[7] However, for the reasons mentioned above, this recommendation also states that if assistance happens to be necessary, it should comply ". . . with every one of the following conditions:

- It should be selective and restricted to those parts of the economy, such as industries, areas, or plants, where severe difficulties would otherwise occur;
- It should be limited to well-defined transitional periods, laid down in advance and adapted to the specific socioeconomic problems associated with the implementation of a country's environmental program;
- It should not create significant distortions in international trade and investment."[8]

The first two conditions mean that there should not be a permanent, non-defined practice of across-the-board assistance to polluters. Government aids should aim at solving specific and limited environmental problems. Limitation of assistance periods does not mean that such assistance would only be justified during initial periods of the implementation of environmental policies, but confined instead within any specific pollution-control program. In fact, the concept of transitional periods is somewhat broader as it relates to the general idea of *adjustment* periods. There are three distinct kinds of adjustment that may be necessary.

The first and most common case relates to the *initial period* when pollution control measures are implemented for the first time, so that the economy needs to follow some transitional path to adapt to this important change in the rules of the game. In such a case, public authorities will usually set a program, limited in time, and designed to facilitate such adaptation. This has been the case, for example, in Sweden where a specific transition period has been provided, together with the adoption of the basic Environment Protection Act. Under this transitional program, an assistance scheme was designed for a 5-year period (July 1, 1969–June 30, 1974), during which 666.4 million S.Kr. in subsidies were granted to industry and 1014 million S.Kr. to municipalities. For the period 1967–1973 these subsidies have covered an average of 47% of the pollution control investments of the major polluting industries.

The second case occurs when, beyond the normal course of environmental policies, new measures are taken and new program fixed in order to accelerate or strengthen those policies. This would happen, for instance, when environmental standards are significantly strengthened. It may well be, under such circumstances, that adjustment assistance would be required in some sectors of the economy.

The third case relates to the more general occurrence of economic and social hardships when environmental requirements happen to conflict with socioeconomic constraints. Under such circumstances, the only w sector, assistance may be required. We can again take Sweden as a case in point: The original subsidy scheme was limited to 250 million S.Kr. for industry and 450 million S.Kr. for municipalities, but in order to reduce the unemployment that developed during the period 1971–1973, the amount of subsidies were substantially increased (666.4 million S.Kr. and 1014 million S.Kr., respectively), thereby using pollution-control investment as a tool to reduce unemployment. After completion of the initial period, the assistance scheme was extended to 1975.

The last two aforementioned cases place the implementation of the PPP in a dynamic context related to the evolution of environmental programs and the changing economic and political circumstances. It is also worth noting that adjustment programs need not relate to the whole economy, but may instead apply to limited sectors. For instance, in France, the Central Government has introduced so-called "industry contracts" (*contrats de branches*) with specific sectors of industry, whereby the industry involved is bound to achieve specific objectives within a limited period, and, in return, receives exceptional subsidies from the government. Various contracts have been introduced over the last 2 years in the field of water pollution, and others are in preparation. The first was concluded in July 1972 with the pulp and paper industry, which accounts for 20% of water pollution in France. Within a period of 5 years the pulp and paper industry is obliged to abate its pollution by 80%. Out of the 300 million francs (66 million United States dollars) to be invested, about 80% will be subsidized.[9] Since 1972 similar contracts have been signed with potato-starch, yeast, alcohol-distilling, and wool-washing industries.

To which category of plants should assistance be granted? The implementation of new environmental regulations brings with it a rather radical change in economic constraints, so that the related hardships will fall mainly on existing plants that originally invested according to quite different constraints. In the presence of pollution-control regulations, firms adapt their production processes and choose relevant sites. It is thus equitable that *existing plants,* that is, plants that were in existence before the new regulations came into effect, be granted assistance in order to adapt themselves to the new rules of the game.

On the other hand it would appear that *new plants,* plants coming into existence after the implementation of new regulations, should not receive assistance for pollution control since they know beforehand the environmental constraints with which they must comply. Besides, it is less costly to adapt to regulations ex ante rather than ex post since, in the latter case, it may imply substantive changes in the operation of the plant. Also, public assistance given to new plants may induce the proliferation of certain types of plants beyond a socially desirable level, as well as a suboptimal distribution of the investments over time.

But this does not exhaust all policy alternatives for pollution control. To attain a given environmental quality goal an alternative is to accelerate the "catching up" process—the installation of pollution control equipment on existing sources. In this case assistance to existing plants may be required. Another alternative is to impose particularly stringent standards on new installations. In this case the resulting discrimination between old and new plants may justify the granting of assistance to new plants as well. This is what has happened in Japan, where, in the field of air- and water-pollution control, much more stringent emission standards are systematically imposed on new plants.[10]

Generally, in order to avoid economic inefficiencies and international trade distortions the door for subsidies must remain closed as much as possible and assistance should be granted to new plants only under very exceptional circumstances. Otherwise application of exceptions to the PPP will tend to expand dangerously. On the other hand, special circumstances and individual national policies, such as the Japanese one cited above, cannot be ignored. This is the reason why the OECD Council, following the meeting of the OECD Environment Committee at the ministerial level (November 1974), recommended that: ". . . if a Member country, in cases of exceptional difficulty, gives assistance to new plants, the conditions be even stricter than those applicable to existing plants and that criteria on which to base this differentiation be developed."[11] The criteria referred to above are presently in the process of being elaborated.[12]

In the assessment of exceptions and their possible impact on international trade, we have already noted that the PPP has been internationally adopted mainly to prevent environmentally induced distortions of international competition. In order to assess how far the PPP is actually implemented, one not only needs to delineate the scope of exceptions, but it is important also to identify those exceptions that actually occur and to calculate their possible economic effects. This appears simple in theory. In practice it turns out to be extremely difficult and probably impossible in some cases. Difficulties occur at two levels.

First, assistance can take many forms, namely, cash subsidies (to cover capital and/or operating costs), subsidized interest loans, tax benefits, accelerated amortization, and so forth. Whereas it is rather easy to identify cash subsidies, other forms of assistance are much more difficult to identify and evaluate. One could also imagine a hidden form of subsidy as a result of unreasonably low emission standards designed specifically to ease the burden of pollution-control costs on certain sectors.

Second, assistance may be granted under specific pollution-control legislation, or in conjunction with assistance for other social goals, for example, for employment and regional development purposes. In this case when plants benefit from general government assistance, it may prove impossible to identify which part, if any, of this assistance is allocated by the firm to pollution control. One is then faced with a number of practical difficulties for identification and evaluation of the exceptions to the PPP that often make the collection of relevant data rather problematic. The assessment of resultant trade distortions is thus even more subject to uncertainty.

THE PROBLEM OF TRADE DISTORTIONS

The first problem is how to define a trade distortion? From a purely theoretical point of view, international trade is not distorted when trade flows are "naturally" oriented according to the comparative advantages of the different trading partners. Prices should reflect the true productive capabilities of the country—the full social costs involved in production activities. This is indeed the aim of the PPP. If a country has poor hydrological resources and must consequently impose very strict water-quality standards this comparative disadvantage should not be hidden by public assistance to polluters. If, on the other hand, this country benefits from important free space resources it should take full advantage of it by, for instance, imposing relatively less stringent standards for air pollution if it can be adequately dispersed over the available free space.

Since the definition of trade distortion refers to a hypothetical situation of unrestricted competition, it is impossible to define with certainty such a condition in order to compare an actual distorted situation with a previous nondistorted one. Indeed, trade has always been distorted in a number of ways by tariffs, import controls, export subsidies, cartels, and so forth. With regard to the environment, countries are starting with a distorted situation, since prices do not reflect full social costs. Furthermore, because implementation of environmental policies imply internalization of external costs, changes in trade patterns will inevitably result, and, in a sense, it represents a *removal* of distortions. At the same time, if countries are granting assistance to polluters within the framework of a transitional period, it can mean that the original distorted international competitive situation is provisionally maintained.

It may also be mentioned that trade distortions, if any, may actually appear after a certain time lag depending upon the pricing policies of firms. Since most pollution-control assistance by governments appears to take the form of investment subsidies, its impact will be on fixed costs rather than on operating costs. If pricing practice is based on marginal costs, rather than on average costs, the government assistance may have no effect on prices in the short run. However, a distortive effect may indeed develop over the long term.[13]

Finally, it is not possible to elaborate objective criteria to assess trade distortions. One can only make an evaluation when the magnitude of trade changes are likely to introduce "significant" distortions, that is, when assistance entails perceptible impacts on competition and trade. This can be determined on a case-by-case basis when major changes occur or when the price differential involved is sufficiently large to induce an industry or a country to notify the existence of a significant distortion.

In order to monitor the situation on a continuous basis, the OECD is now in the process of implementing a "notification" scheme, whereby member countries will provide regular information on their ongoing or forthcoming environmental-assistance programs. The data collected will be presented in homogeneous form and distributed among member countries through the OECD Secretariat. If a country feels that any program is likely to introduce trade distortions, it can, at any time, ask for a specific "consultation," whereby countries will be able to evaluate further the economic impact of the assistance program and possibly open negotiations.

But environmental policies are still in a preliminary stage (the costs may increase along with more stringent standards), and our knowledge is still very limited so that no definitive conclusion as to the nature and extent of trade distortions can be drawn as yet.

ENVIRONMENTAL STANDARDS

Policy alternatives for pollution control do not only include cost-allocation principles, but the so-called *instruments* for policy implementation. There exist a rather wide range of such instruments, and their national and international economic implications can be quite different.

The issue of instruments is crucial to environmental policies and requires exhaustive analysis that would be beyond the scope of this paper. We shall, therefore, concentrate on a limited number of issues, particularly relevant to international trade.

It is now quite common to differentiate between *regulatory instruments* and *economic instruments* for pollution control. While the first mainly introduces the problem of nontariff barriers to trade, the second, in some cases, may again raise the question of cost-allocation principles. Regulatory instruments mainly set environmental standards.

The important international economic issue related to environmental standards is to know whether these standards should be internationally uniform, or at least harmonized. Supporters of harmonization state that it would yield important benefits such as: (1) avoidance of nontariff barriers to trade; (2) reduced costs through common research and development of pollution-control technologies; (3) reduction of production costs for firms due to mass production of uniform products; and (4) prevention of transfrontier pollution problems.

Although, at first glance, these statements would seem quite reasonable, they are, in fact, less straightforward in reality, and need to be examined further in the light of the different kinds of standards that exist, and the environmental and regulatory conditions prevailing in various countries.

FACTORS GOVERNING DIFFERENTIATION OF STANDARDS

Environmental standards to some degree reflect the comparative advantages of countries and regions as they fit the environmental resources and the social preferences.

With regard to environmental resources, standards must be adapted to the prevailing natural conditions, like the assimilative capacity of the different media—water, air, and soil. Availability of water resources and space forms a determining factor of environmental policy. For instance, abundant water will enable a country or region to issue relatively nonstringent standards for organic matter if they can be easily assimilated through natural processes.

Population structure is, of course, of major importance. Densely populated areas induce both high-pollution concentrations and increases in damage probability. For example, with regard to natural resources and population, environmental constraints will be completely different in countries like the Netherlands, with highly concentrated population densities together with limited environmental resources, and Scandinavian countries that benefit from the reverse situation.

The nature of economic development also plays an important role. Growth patterns in various countries can be relatively more or less pollution intensive, and concentration of industry can also be quite different.

Last, but not least, social preferences ultimately determine the level of environmental standards. A country might wish to accept more pollution for the sake of a certain type of economic growth, or in order to achieve short-term development objectives. In some countries the public demands a much higher level of environmental quality than in others. Due to all of these factors there are no reasons why environmental standards should a priori be similar internationally or made so. Indeed, common sense would require a wide differentiation between standards, not only between countries, but also among regions within a single country.

As a matter of fact "national standards" hardly exist, that is, standards that would be applicable throughout a given country. At most, one can find national standards in the form of general guidelines or minimum requirements for policy makers. At the implementation level, decision-makers will have to fit those standards to local conditions. When environmental policies are implemented through direct regulations, standards are often imposed on polluters on a case-by-case basis with due consideration to the natural and socioeconomic conditions prevailing in a given area at a given time.

SHOULD ENVIRONMENTAL STANDARDS BE HARMONIZED?

The fact that environmental standards should match local conditions implies that internationally uniform standards would mask comparative advantages, and thus work against an efficient patterns of international trade. But this has to be analysed separately for each kind of standard.

Environmental Quality Standards

Environmental quality standards specify the main characteristics to be maintained in the environment, that is, "the maximum permissible levels of pollution in the receptor media namely air, water and soil."[14]

For reasons mentioned above, quality standards will vary between countries as well as within countries. Moreover, quality standards represent an *objective* for environmental policies rather than an instrument, and will have to be achieved by means of other types of standards. It is, therefore, when these quality objectives are set that social preferences enter into consideration.

Uniform quality standards between countries would, therefore, mean uniform policies, and uniform policies would be economically justifiable only when all things are equal. One can, however, identify a limited number of cases where some kind of harmonization could be necessary: when different countries decide to join in an integrated economic and political union with a common set of preferences and objectives—and in the area of transfrontier pollution. Beyond purely economic considerations, there may also be grounds for common quality standards to ensure an international control of persistent toxic substances, and in order to seek basic levels of protection that apply to all countries.[15]

Emission and Process Standards

Both emission and process standards aim at abatement of pollution from *stationary sources*. Emission standards impose an obligation to achieve a certain *result* by specifying the maximum quantity of pollution that may be discharged into the environment, whereas process standards impose an obligation to use certain *methods* for pollution abatement, for example, certain production processes, modes of operation, or pollution treatment technology to achieve a given objective.

Emission and process standards are the most common instruments of environmental policies, and as such have to be adopted to every quality objective and every local condition. Not only do these standards differ between regions, but they may also vary within a single locality. Under a licensing procedure, permits to pollute are granted on a case-by-case basis, and very often after a rather complicated impact assessment weighing the pros and cons of each project—not only with regard to the environment per se, but also with due consideration of local socioeconomic conditions.

Emission and process standards can be efficient only if they are sufficiently flexible to match local conditions. Uniformity in such standards, even within a single country, would be economic nonsense. The only conceivable international harmonization would be an agreement on minimum standards as general guidelines, but this would mean no more than falling into line with a least common denominator. Extensive studies undertaken by the OECD on major pollution sources show that diversification of standards is the most appropriate method.

For the pulp and paper industry, for example, one is faced with a diversity of manufacturing processes and a diversity of emission standards according to local conditions.[16] With regard to sulfur oxides, an OECD report states that it is "unlikely that common action throughout the OECD countries will be a satisfying solution"[17] due to the necessity of flexible standards. This, also, is very much true for eutrophication control, which needs an extreme adaptation to particular conditions.[18]

We must also note that making standards uniform would not mean uniform production costs, since pollution control is only a small component of overall production costs.

Emission and process standards cannot induce trade distortions. The only exception would be if standards would be set at a deliberately low level in order to yield a competitive advantage in trade. This would, in fact, amount to a disguised subsidy. This can take the form either of low pollution standards or of deliberate nonenforcement of existing standards, but the necessary strengthening of standards to remove the distortion is less a harmonization than an adaptation to the real local conditions.

Table 6-1 maps out a number of possible situations between two countries, A and B. It shows that differentiation in emission and process standards cannot lead to trade distortions with the exception of situation 5. These cases refer to a perfectly competitive market, where the demand for environmental quality (social preferences) is fully revealed and taken into account. One could imagine different situations where pressure groups could induce the setting of "abnormal" wear standards in certain sectors compared to others (given the state of technology). In such cases, standards may be fixed with regard to trade considerations rather than to respond to social preferences for environmental quality. In other words, a number of malfunctions in the market, other than subsidies, may be distortive of international trade.

Product Standards

According to OECD definition, product standards prescribe: "(a) the physical or chemical properties of a product (with particular reference to its content of polluting or harmful matter); (b) the rules for making up, packaging or presenting a product so as to ensure consumer protection and make the product identifiable; (c) the maximum permissible polluting emissions from the product during its use."[19] The problem associated with product standards is that they give rise to nontariff barriers to trade. This would be the case, for instance, if standards related to automobile nuisances (pollution and noise) of country A would prevent country B exporting its cars to country A if they did not comply with the standards of the importing country.

Table 6-1 Harmonization of Environmental Standards

Case	Country	Quality Objective	Emission and/or Process Standard	Subsidy	Price Effect	Distortion	Harmonization of Standards
1	A	high	high	No	Strong	No	Not required
	B	high	low[a]	No	Weak		
2	A	high	high	Yes	Weak	Yes	Not required
	B	high	low[a]	No	Weak		
3	A	high	high	No	Strong	No	Not required
	B	low[b]	low	No	Weak		
4	A	high	high	Yes	Weak	Yes	Not required
	B	low[b]	low	No	Weak		
5	A	high	high	No	Strong	Yes	Required
	B	low[c]	low[c]	No	Weak		

[a] Due to greater assimilative capacity of the environment.
[b] Due to social preferences.
[c] Deliberately low due to trade considerations only.

Another type of nontariff barrier may arise from testing and control measures for the traded products, for example, if one country does not recognize the validity of the testing measures performed in the exporting country. In the case of automobiles, there are two "driving cycles" for measuring motor vehicles' emissions, the so-called "European cycle" versus the "American cycle," (i.e., specific driving conditions simulated in laboratories for testing vehicular emissions).

Another argument in favor of harmonization of product standards is production-cost minimization. It could be too costly for firms to diversify too much their products according to the different standards enforced on foreign markets. However, producers have given ample proof of their capability to diversify their products for purely commercial purposes, and this may not prove to be a major competitive drawback.

Although product standards are less subject to regional variations than emission standards, and are usually uniform throughout a single country, they may be subject to regional variations in some cases—such as the sulfur content of fuels or detergents designed to match local environmental conditions. Harmonization of product standards may also be necessary when transfrontier pollution problems are involved, for instance, in the case of aircraft noise.

The problem of nontariff barriers is important, but one must not forget that product standards also reflect comparative advantages and social preferences in various countries. Harmonization of product standards should be considered in the light of the costs and benefits related to both the environment and to trade. Trade benefits must not be offset by the environmental costs incurred.

POLLUTION CHARGES

There are many economic issues surrounding the subject of pollution charges, and we shall very briefly mention the international issues.

Pollution levies should be designed to induce the polluter to abate his discharges into the environment up to a certain level. Although many arguments plead for the use of pollution charges (cost minimization, permanent incentives, etc.) they are actually being applied only in a limited number of cases. There is, however, growing interest in this policy instruments, and a number of countries envisage implementation of charges in different areas such as air, water, and noise.

When pollution levies are actually in operation they usually take the form of so-called redistributive charges. Economic theory shows that an optimal charge should have a rate per unit of pollution equal to the marginal social cost of pollution. Since evaluation of a monetary environmental damage function is subject to uncertainty, an "efficient" solution could be devised by equalizing the rate of the pollution charge with the maginal cost of pollution abatement at a level corresponding to an objective fixed by public authorities.[20] However, a number of practical difficulties remain to be surmounted. On the one hand, we have very little knowledge of marginal pollution control costs. On the other hand, an efficient rate of effluent charge often turns out to be too high to be suddenly imposed on polluters. Politically and economically, to start with low nonefficient rates and increase progressively over time appears to be a reasonable solution. In such cases, charges play a redistributive role, that is, they may be used to finance a fund managed by a specialized agency that invests the funds within the framework of a specific pollution-control program run by the agency.

This approach is mainly used in the field of water management. River basin agencies levy charges and redistribute the proceeds in the form of subsidies to help polluters to invest in treatment plants (or in changing their production process) or to finance collective treatment plants. This form of policy is mainly used in France and in the Netherlands.

Since redistributive charges in many instances aim at financing subsidies, there has been some controversy about the compliance of such systems with the PPP.[21] Also, a nonincentive rate can simply mean nonenforcement of pollution control, since it is thus more profitable to polluters to pay the charge than to abate pollution. In fact, such redistributive schemes can be acceptable with regard to the PPP in the following circumstances.

First, setting low rates for charges must be a transitional measure, that is, the rates must increase up to an efficient level over the transitory period of implementation of the policy.

Second, the redistributive scheme must be implemented in an efficient manner; that is, it must minimize the real cost of pollution control within a basin. For example, if 500 polluters discharge 500 units of pollution, and if the target of the basin agency is to abate 400 units, the most efficient solution would be to have the abatement carried out by say the 100 most efficient polluters, that is, those who are able to perform the most efficient abatement. Thus subsidies granted to these 100 polluters would, in fact, amount to the *purchase of a service* financed by the nonefficient polluters who pay more pollution charges to the extent that they do not treat their effluents. In other words, the efficient polluters perform treatment for the others and are compensated by subsidies.

To conclude, we should mention a particular international aspect of pollution charges that may become an important issue in the future.

In the specific area of aircraft noise, recent studies tend to prove that aircraft noise charges would be an effective complementary measure to the present ICAO (International Civil Aviation Organization) regulations. These charges would be especially useful during the catching-up period, since noisy, noncertified aircraft are likely to be in operation up to the year 1985.[22] In France, aircraft noise charges are levied (at Paris Airport, Roissy-Charles de Gaulle), and several countries are making studies of this matter. Aircraft noise charges must have two purposes: (1) at the local (airport) level they can provide funds to finance local noise-protection measures; (2) at the global level they may induce aircraft companies to scrap or to retrofit their noisy aircraft and/or to change the distribution of their fleet according to the noise charges levied on different airports. It is obvious that the greater the number of airports levying charges, the more efficient will be the charge. Aircraft noise being largely an international problem, uniform international application of such a scheme would be most desirable.[23]

CONCLUSIONS

In summary, provided environmental policies in different countries are based on a common cost-allocation principle, no significant trade distortion should arise. Taking due account of diversities between different countries and regions is, in fact, an important condition for efficient environmental management, both at a national and an international level, since each policy must fit as much as possible into the environmental conditions, social preferences, and economic structures prevailing in each country. This diversity of situations calls for a diversity of policy instruments, whether in the form of pollution standards or charges.

Nevertheless, there may be circumstances where some kind of uniformity may be necessary. This would be the case where transfrontier pollution occurs, and for the management of common resources such as lakes and seas. Harmonization of objectives and policies may also be required when a number of countries are part of an integrated economic union (as are the European communities).

The uniform application of the polluter-pays principle as a common cost-allocation system may be faced with important difficulties when environmental objectives conflict with other socioeconomic goals. Although this may occur mainly during the initial periods of implementation of environmental policies, such hardships may occur at any other times as well. Exceptions to the PPP in the form of aids to polluters may thus be required, but in order to limit the distortive effects on trade, such exceptions should be limited in time and in scope. One problem is to know how long such transitional periods will last. During the initial phase of environmental policies, the most difficult tasks relate to the so-called catch up of pollution control and to ensuring that each pollution source, which was in existence before new regulations were passed, is adequately equipped for pollution abatement. That is, the most difficult task relates to the equipping of an existing "stock" of pollution sources. Once this "stock" is equipped one enters upon a situation of "pure flux," a situation where only new potential sources have to be equipped. This latter situation would be much easier to handle than the previous one. However, it may happen that environmental objectives are considerably strengthened at a later stage, so that the catch-up phase and, consequently, adjustment measures would be required again. It is, therefore, likely that a number of changes in environmental objectives, and consequently in trade patterns, will occur during the coming decade, inasmuch as the recent energy "crisis" will probably entail both short-term and long-term changes in environmental policies.

Finally, there is one important point we have not mentioned, because it would have gone beyond our scope—one which will be of critical importance in the future. It relates to the impact of environmental policies of industrialized countries on the developing countries. For instance, it may happen that certain product standards (the ban of DDT in food products for example) will negatively affect the trade of developing countries; government expenditures for environmental protection may be detrimental to the development assistance; industrialized countries are tempted to export their polluting industries to the developing world. Since many key sectors of the economy, such as the iron and steel industry, the chemical industry, and the cement industry are among the most polluting, the development process may in itself be particularly detrimental to the environment of the poorer countries. On the other hand, the oil price increase may result in a new valuation of natural products such as rubber, cotton, and copra (as less polluting substitutes for synthetic products) to the benefit of developing countries.[24]

The Stockholm Conference (1972), stressed that the environment is a new factor of interdependence between countries. Growing environmental concern, together with growing energy scarcities, are making these links between countries all the more confined.

NOTES

1. Although we shall refer mostly to the work undertaken at the OECD, this should in no way imply the statement of any official OECD viewpoint; needless to say, any error or misjudgment in this paper would be the author's entire responsibility.

2. *Recommendations of the Council on Guiding Principles Concerning International Economic Aspects of Environmental Policies*, C(72) 128, OECD, Paris, June 6, 1972. The Eu-

ropean Communities have adopted a text on the PPP in January 1975 which shows a few differences with the OECD definition (see doc. R/12/75, ENV.2) January 1, 1975.

3. These costs include:

- The costs of granting licences and inspection costs
- Government staff and institutions' costs
- Compensation for irrecoverable losses due to air pollution
- Compensation to firms confronted with disproportionately high pollution control costs
- Costs of R&D
- Cost of monitoring and emission recording

4. See *Note on the Implementation of the PPP*. op. cit. and *Recommendations of the Council on the Implementation of the PPP*, OECD, Paris November 21, 1974, C(74)223.

5. The European Communities state that the PPP satisfies both "efficiency and equity criteria."

6. Provided the exchange rate fixed.

7. C(74)223, Paris, November 21, 1974.

8. C(74)223, Paris, November 21, 1974, para. III-2.

9. This percentage represents the maximum subsidy which a polluter can receive, taking into account subsidies granted by River Basin Authorities (*Agences Financières de Bassin*).

10. For instance in Tokyo Bay area the maximum average discharge of COD is 110 ppm for plants constructed before April 1972, whereas it amounts to only 25 ppm for plants constructed after this date.

11. Op. cit. para. III-3.

12. The European Communities have taken a quite different view in this respect since they explicitly state that no aids whatsoever should be granted to existing plants or for existing products. It is also stipulated that aids could be granted as compensation when particularly stringent standards are imposed on certain polluters in order to obtain an "exceptional degree of purity in the environment." This could be the case, for example, if a polluting firm would be located in the vicinity of a national park [Document R/12/75 (ENV.2) Annex-I para. 6(a) and 7(b)].

13. But subsidizing fixed costs may lead to a lower marginal cost insofar as capital must be borrowed to finance the initial purchase of fixed assets. In this way, pollution abatement subsidies will find their way into pricing decisions. (I am indebted for this point to Tracy Murray).

14. OECD, *Environmental Standards: Definitions and the Need for International Harmonization*, (Paris: OECD, 1974).

15. See OECD, *Environmental Standards, op. cit.* para. 30.

16. See, *Pollution by the Pulp and Paper Industry*, OECD, Paris, 1973.

17. Report and Conclusions of the Joint Ad Hoc Group on Air Pollution from Fuel Combustion in Stationary Sources, OECD, Paris, 1973.

18. *Report by the Water Management Sector Group on Eutrophication Control*, OECD, Paris, 1974.

19. See OECD, *Environmental Standards, op. cit.*

20. See Baumol and Oates, "The Use of Standards and Prices for Protection of the Environment," *The Swedish Journal of Economics, 73*, March 1971.

21. See, An Examination of the Polluter Pays Principle Based on Case Studies" in *The Polluter Pays Principle—Definition–Analysis–Implementation* (Paris: OECD, 1975).

22. See A. Alexandre and J-Ph. Barde, "Aircraft Noise Charges" in *Noise Control Engineering, 3,* September–October 1974.

23. In one of the ten recommendations following the Environment Committee meeting at ministerial level, the OECD Council recommends that "the possible value of various other means of aircraft noise control such as charges on noisy aircraft, the institution of zoning policies around airports and of associated land use planning and control" be considered. (Recommendation of the Council on Noise Prevention and Abatement—C(74)2177-Paris 21st November 1974).

24. See G. Destanne de Bernis, "L'impact sur les pays sous developpés des politiques d'environnement des pays developpés," *Analyse et Prévision,* April 1974.

Commercial Policy Implications of Environmental Controls

H. Peter Gray

The institution of measures designed to reduce the degree of environmental despoilation by one or many nation states must induce a change in the global mix of international trade in both commodities and services. Both the volume of trade and the distribution of gains from trade are likely to be different under the new, environmentally protective regime than under the old regime in which environmental despoilation was freely tolerated. The purpose of environmental protection is to improve the social welfare by introducing into the cost calculus an important element that has been ignored. The gains in welfare achieved by making the costing framework more inclusive must not be lost or lessened by a failure to carry the reallocation of resources over to the international level.

The restructuring of the mix of international trade that follows the introduction of environmental protection must be allowed to take place or, at least, not to be unnecessarily countered by measures arising out of narrow national or sectoral interests. The key word here is unnecessarily. It seems unreasonable to expect that the whole set of antipollution expenditures will be completely trade-neutral, even though the OECD has adopted the polluter-pays principle (PPP) very largely on the basis of its trade neutrality. The problems of environmental protection are too complex and too variable among regions and among industries for the PPP to be adhered to without exception.[1] Complete trade neutrality is, therefore, beyond our reach. But it is important to eliminate unnecessary or avoidable trade biases.

INTRODUCTION

In order to consider in a useful way the potential role of impediments to international trade, overt or covert, that could follow from the imposition of environmental controls is national states, it is useful to distinguish among the three different ways by which such measures will improve social welfare. These are best illustrated with a simple diagram showing pollution on the horizontal axis and real output of material goods and services on the vertical axis (Fig. 7-1). The four rays from the origin denote average amounts of pollution per unit of material output. The ray *LF* shows the

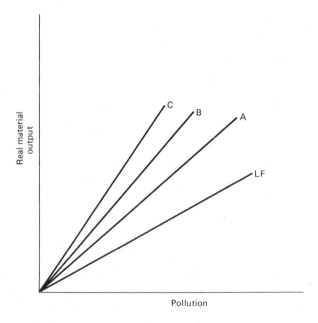

Figure 7-1 The pollution-real output ratio.

relationship that exists under laisser-faire conditions (that is, before the institution of environmental controls). Ray A denotes the corresponding relationship that results from the institution of pollution-abating equipment in different sectors: the higher the effluent fee the larger the shift from ray LF to ray A. Ray B denotes the increased improvement that is obtained when the costs of environmental protection are passed on to the set of prices of final goods (as is achieved by PPP), and the consumption or absorption mix changes in response to the different set of prices. Finally, the ray C shows the additional improvement that can be attained if international resources are reallocated in accordance with different national targets and assimilative capacities. It is the shift from B to C that can be countered by commercial policy measures in their broadest sense, and it is with the why and how of such potential impediments that this chapter is concerned.

There are several ways of incorporating the existence of pollution controls into an analysis of international trade. One approach is to regard clean resources (air, water, and soil) as inputs into the production process that are used up when they are polluted. The price of clean resources is determined by the national sensitivity to polluted resources and to differences in environmental assimilative capacity. The traditional influences of tastes and resource endowments determine the autarkic price of the input as shown in Fig. 7-2. The particular type of pollutant generated by a production process determines the marginal product of a unit of clean resources in that process and, therefore, the additional variable cost. As with any other input, steps will be taken to increase the productivity of that input until the cost-saving derived from increased productivity is equal to the added cost involved. Since the gain from increasing the productivity of an input is positively related to the unit price of that input, the higher the effluent fee, the greater will be the attempts to reduce pollution. The price of a unit of clean resources—the effluent fee—is determined by the intersection of the marginal social benefit curve, and by the marginal cost of pollution removal. The greater is the nation's assimilative capacity, the further to the right the cost curve will lie. The greater the tolerance of the population for polluted resources, the further to the left the marginal social benefit schedule will lie, and, consequently, the lower the price of a unit of clean resources. There is a reasonable presumption that rich countries will tend to impose higher prices on clean resources than will poor or developing nations. The values underlying the MSB schedule are those that contribute to the marginal rate of substitution of material income for the quality of the environment. Material income will encounter only very slowly diminishing marginal utility until some threshold level of income has been reached. Additionally, the longer history of manufacturing in most developed nations will have contributed to the stock of pollution so that, other things being

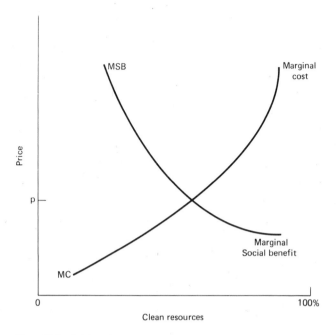

Figure 7-2   Pricing clean-resource inputs.

equal, the assimilative capacity of a rich nation will be less than that of a poor nation. While this relationship is likely to be observable in a general sense, it can in no way be relied upon for any particular nation. It may also be complicated by the fact that, in many nations, local (state, provincial, or even smaller subdivisions) authorities may have a significant role to play in environmental regulation and legislation. There is room, then, for sizeable international variation in environmental standards.

Just as with any other factor of production, relative prices in different countries will indicate relative scarcity, and the country that is more plentifully endowed with clean resources will tend to export those goods that use clean resources more intensively (goods with a higher pollution content) in a free-trade world. There is likely to be a desire to interfere with the natural gains that accrue from the redistribution of international production (and trade) following the introduction of environmental costs. This desire will derive from *the co-operating factors* of production in those industries that use clean resources most intensively, since it is these industries that will suffer cutbacks in domestic production and replacement of that production by imports.

The more industry-specific the human and physical capital involved in these industries, the more intensive will the attempt to use commercial policy measures to protect their positions be. These types of defensive or compensatory measures are designed to perpetuate a production mix at odds with comparative advantage, and they must be prevented if the full benefits of environmental protection are to be achieved. (It is worth noting here that comparative advantage is a static concept, and that the problem of adjustment from one well-established production mix to a new one may well justify some temporary impediments to uninhibited resource reallocation.) In his codification of nontariff barriers (NTBs), Ingo Walter distinguishes three types of commercial policy:[2]

I.   Measures designed primarily to protect domestic industry from import competition, to restrict exports, or to strengthen domestic industry in competing with imports or competing for export markets.
II. Trade-distorting policies and practices that are imposed primarily with the intent of dealing with non-trade-related problems, but which are periodically and intentionally employed for trade-restrictive purposes.
III. Policies and practices applied exclusively for non-trade-related reasons, but which unavoidably serve to distort international competitive conditions and hence affect trade.

The third type of policy is likely to result from the justifiable departures from PPP examined by Barde.[3] They are of no concern in this paper. Type-II measures do present problems of legitimate concern to any analysis of the commercial policy implication of environmental controls, if the trade considerations are an influential determinant in the selection of the measure. Such decisions will almost always concern the choice of instrument, and will, therefore, embody all trade-dominated decisions to substitute a subsidy for an effluent fee. This type of measure is clearly counterproductive. Finally, type-I measures include the imposition of tariffs and (explicit or identifiable) NTBs designed to protect the industry made vulnerable to foreign competition by the introduction of pollution costs into the social pricing calculus. Type-I measures particularly tariffs, will be more easily recognized for what they are than type-II measures. The existing international agreements governing the imposition of tariffs, and authorizing countermeasures together with the avowed emphasis in the imminent Tokyo Round on reducing NTBs, may cause any pollution-induced type-I measures to be converted to NTBs that are more difficult both to identify and to remove.

The improvement in world living standards that can be achieved by the combination of environmental controls and a global reallocation of resources may not be achieved. If poor or developing nations were to impose as high a price for clear resources upon their economies as do the rich manufacturing nations, there would be no global reallocation of resources. In terms of Fig. 7-1, ray B will be the minimum ratio of pollution to real material output obtainable. There are three possible reasons for such a policy on the part of poor nations. First, it is possible that the poor/ developing nations may be concerned with some sort of reservation demand, and wish to preserve the clean resources for their future generations. This decision could be rational and, under such conditions, there would be no loss in world welfare. It does, however, seem an unlikely decision since it implies a perfectly inelastic demand for clean resources with respect to income over what may be a substantial range of income as well as having interesting time-preference connotations. A second reason might be that the poor, developing nations were persuaded by rich, manufacturing nations to place a high price on clean resources because of the danger to the rich nations or to the global ecosphere of additional transfrontier pollution. There is no a priori reason why the poor countries should reduce their pollution in order to reduce the severity of environmental controls borne by rich nations. Finally, rich nations may attempt to persuade poor nations to impose severe pollution controls simply because the rich nations recognize the implication of unequal effluent fees upon the terms and pattern of trade. To the degree that rich nations are successful in persuading poor countries to impose effluent fees that are higher than those dictated by the rational demands of the poor country, the persuasion amounts to a propagandistic commercial-policy device and will reduce global welfare.

The costs of adjustment from an established output-mix to a new one are an important problem area in the analysis of the imposition of environmental protection in a closed economy—both from the adjustment generated by an actual initiation of environmental controls as well as by an increase in the standards required of industry (a rightward shift in the MSB curve in Fig. 7-2). Problems of adjustment will be amplified by the global reallocation of resources that the law of comparative advantage will require. There is, in both the domestic and the international dimensions, an argument for moderation in attaining the new ultimate pattern of resource allocation and output-mix. This problem can be called the dynamic aspect of environmental control and may be contrasted with the static aspect, which analyzes the role of commercial policy in the determination of the ultimate pattern of resource allocation.

The approach of this chapter is to examine, first of all, the static implications of environmental controls for commercial policy. An analysis of the dynamic considerations will follow. Finally, the analysis considers the potential for commercial policy in the imposition of product standards that are directed largely toward what is generally known as consumption-pollution.[4]

THE STATIC ANALYSIS

The introduction of another input into the costing process that underlies international trade in commodities and services must enlarge the potential for impediments to the free flow of trade. Not only is the whole existing range of familiar policy tools available to protect the nation's industries and interest, but there are likely to be others that have reference only to the new input. This section identifies potential new tools, considers ways in which the old measures can be used in a new form or to a new purpose, and examines whether the introduction of environmental controls generates any systematic effect on established instruments of commercial policy.

The reasons for expecting that national governments will quickly come to perceive the uses for commercial policy following the application of environmental controls are that nations will anticipate adverse movements in their balance of trade (and accompanying current-account deficits), and that some industries may be completely eliminated if exposed to unlimited foreign competition. Since the purpose of environmental controls is, *inter alia,* to bring about the movement of polluting processes from nations with high-cost environmental resources to nations with low-cost environmental resources, commercial policy measures that frustrate the change in the global pattern of production will impair global welfare.

However, commercial policy and environmental control charges have another similarity. They operate, as it were, in the same dimension. As a result of the failure of a nation to protect its environment by effluent fees, private and social costs of commodities diverge. The existence of tariffs or of NTBs causes a similar divergence, so that consumers are not given a socially valid basis for making expenditure decisions. The distinction between the two sets of externalities is that commercial policy measures are sins of commission, while the failure to protect the environment is a sin of omission. The imposition of environmental costs in a nation with a high price for clean resources is equivalent to a negative tariff, and works counter to existing tariffs. The total protective effect (p) is simply the sum of the commercial policy measures less the effluent fees:

$$p = t + n - g$$

where t is the *ad valorem* tariff rate, n is the rate of nominal protection afforded by NTBs, and g is the level of pollution costs (all measured in percent of the private cost).

There is one new means by which nations can protect vulnerable industries from international competition resulting from environmental protection. The pricing of clean resources is, in practice, an administrative decision. The computation of the marginal products of clean resources in terms of the different types of pollutants generated by different industries is not only an administrative decision, but one that is likely to be made quite difficult and even arbitrary as a result of the sheer difficulties in measurement that are required.

In a world in which no difficulties of measurement exist, each pollutant would be given a multiple that would apply to the basic price fixed for clean resources. In this way, sulfur emissions might be costed at three times the rate applied to, say, soot. A government concerned with preserving one of its industries from foreign competition might deliberately depart from its best estimate of the proper weighting system and invoke a low multiple for a particular kind of emission produced by the vulnerable industry. The preventive for such an NTB is for the weighting system to be internationally agreed upon and established by environmental scientists ignorant of the economic repercussions associated with the weights actually chosen.

There is a more general aspect of this problem. Governments employ a great number and wide variety of measures to modify the structure of domestic industry in the absence of environmental controls. These "interferences" may range from tax concessions to regional development programs, export promotional facilities, access to subsidized capital, and preferential treatment in government contracts because of the defense-status of the industry. The introduction of a covert measure to assist an industry in maintaining its international competitiveness will not be easily identified, and governments will be able to subvert the purpose of environmental controls—at least as far as it involves the international reallocation of resources.

It is probable that the introduction of environmental protection by means of a schedule of effluent fees (and in conformity with the PPP) may systematically reduce the degree of effective protection that was built into the commercial policy structure in earlier years. The degree of protection (or omission of taxation) provided to a good or process in the early stages of production can have a magnified effect on the degree of protection afforded to the next stage of processing for any given nominal rate of protection to that product. This is the now-familiar question of the difference between the nominal and effective rates of protection.[5] Drawing from an indicative study by Ingo Walter,[6] the environmental costs imposed upon United States goods will represent a decrease of 27% to the existing level of protection afforded those goods. Using the basic formula to measure the net rate of protection (p^n) of a nation's industry provided by the tariff structure is:[7]

$$p_j^n = t_j - \sum_i a_{ij} t_i / 1 - \sum_i a_{ij}$$

where t_j is the tariff on industry j, t_i is the tariff on an input, i, and a_{ij} is the proportion of final sales values of output j contributed by input i. Using n and g as above, the composite net rate of protection (CNRP) embodying all three types of differences between private and social costs of production (tariffs, NTBs, and environmental costs), Walter estimated the weighted average effects of t and n to be 0.15 and of g to be 0.04.

$$\text{CNRP} = \frac{t_j + n_j - g_j - \sum_i a_{ij}(t_i + n_i - g_i)}{1 - \sum_i a_{ij}}$$

Despite assiduous and imaginative gathering of raw data by Walter, the shortcomings of his data do reduce the reliability of his estimate.[8] In particular, several NTBs were inevitably omitted from the computation, and the methodology assumes that foreign suppliers impose no pollution control measures of their own. The United States is, perhaps, a leader in the development of a coherent, long-range plan for environmental control, but the omission of foreign environmental controls from the estimating procedure will have exaggerated the effect of United States pollution costs. If these are introduced into the definition of CNRP as f_j and f_i, the change in CNRP resulting from environmental protection will be less stark.

$$\text{CNRP}_j = \frac{t_j + n_j - g_j + f_j - \sum_i a_{ij}(t_i + n_i - g_i + f_i)}{1 - \sum_i a_{ij}}$$

Note here that the value of f_j and f_i must mean the increase in the cost of the relevant commodity from the cheapest supplier before and after the imposition of environmental charges. The value of f may be less, therefore, than the effect of the effluent fee in the established supplier and could, if one potential supplier imposed no effluent fee at all, amount merely to the difference in private costs between the original supplier and the new supplier.

To the extent that processes in the early stages of production have higher pollution contents than the finishing processes (irrespective of industry), there is a possibility that the introduction of environmental charges will tend to offset the commonly accepted practice of "cascading" tariff structures. A tariff structure is cascaded when the nominal tariff rates increase as the imported good approaches the finished stage. Cascading is the most important single source of sizeable differences between effective and nominal rates of protection and systematic differences between the values of g and f will tend to have a reverse, magnifying effect.

To this point the assumption has been tacitly made that all nations adhere to PPP and, therefore, that the costs of environmental protection are passed on to the ultimate user. It is possible that some nations will adopt alternative means of financing the costs of environmental control. The most important alternative means is the payment of a subsidy to the industry concerned. Such a decision may be based on reasons other than international competition, but a discrepancy between the way in which environmental costs are financed may have serious repercussions for the international competitiveness of the two industries. If one nation levies an effluent fee, and the other pays a subsidy, the difference in the direct cost of the goods in the two countries (and, therefore, in the market prices) could change by the amount of the environmental charge. Such a change in relative prices will not reflect a difference in comparative advantage, and will, therefore, be a potntial cause of a global misallocation of economic resources.

Nations that levy taxes as a means of ensuring that the environmental charges are passed on to the ultimate user (in accordance with PPP) will have a valid reason for imposing countervailing duties whether or not international competitiveness reasons were the basis for the recourse to subsidy by the trading partner. A difference in the means of financing the costs of environmental protection amounts to "dumping." As Haberler pointed out, "the outcry against dumped imports is far greater than the facts warrant."[9] Provided that the exporting country is prepared to continue to deliver the goods at less than social cost, the importing country has no particular reason to complain. The costs incurred by the importing nation derive from the possibility that the dumping seeks to weaken a domestic industry or is being used merely to disencumber a nation of excess inventory. If a nation chooses to subsidize one of its industries in the amount of the costs of environmental protection, export sales are sold abroad at below national social cost. This will harm the size and/or the growth of the industry in the importing nation. But once the nation has adjusted to that, it has the benefit of a favorable shift in the terms of trade.

The costs of adjustment and the health of the competing domestic industry are the crux of departures from the PPP by foreign trading partners. There is an obvious temptation to counter such an export subsidy with a countervailing duty of some kind. Such duties are already part and parcel of international agreements on commercial policy and can be adopted when the need is severe.

The main danger is not that nations might, possibly misguidedly, seek to counter apparent departures from PPP, or even to offset differentials in environmental charges on a case-by-case basis. It is, rather, that nations will refuse to permit the kind of reallocation of resources on a global basis that stems from differences in the marginal rate of substitution of clean resources for material income or from differences in assimilative capacity. There will be a temptation to see in such differences a Machiavellian opportunism. As a result, nations may be tempted to apply a so-called scientific tariff that will obliterate all of the possible gains. For example, the United States has gone part of the way in that direction. Section 6 of the Federal Water Pollution Control Act Amendment of 1972 explicitly instructs the Secretary of Commerce to determine:[10]

> ... The probable competitive advantage which any article manufactured in a foreign nation will likely have in relation to a comparable article made in the United States if that foreign nation—
> (a)   does not require its manufacturers to implement pollution abatement and control programs,
> (b)   requires a lesser degree of pollution abatement and control in its programs, or
> (c)   in any way reimburses or otherwise subsidizes its manufacturers for the costs of such programs; alternative means by which any competitive advantage accruing to the products of any foreign nation . . . may be (a) accurately and quickly determined, and (b) equalized, for example, by the imposition of a surcharge or duty, on a foreign product in an amount necessary to compensate for such advantage; and the impact, if any, which the imposition of a compensating tariff or other equalizing measure may have in encouraging foreign nations to implement pollution abatement and control programs.

THE DYNAMIC ANALYSIS

A modern economy has certain built-in rigidities, so that the costs of adaption to a shock or disturbance can be quite significant. Any disturbance, originating at home or abroad, brings with it the need to change the output mix. The costs of such a change will vary positively with the size of the disturbance and with the speed with which the reallocation of resources and the redistribution of income are to be achieved. Some small rate of change can probably be accomplished without cost, but once the required rate exceeds that minimum it is reasonable to postulate that the social costs of adjustment are positively related to the magnitude and rate of change, and that the second derivatives with respect to both variables are both positive and large.[11] Adjustment requires that some industries be sent into decline, and that others grow at above average rates. Adjustments induced by the adoption of environmental charges will tend to be industry-specific rather than general, and the costs will be concentrated in the declining industries. As a result, the burden may bear quite heavily upon a relatively small segment of society.

The institution of environmental charges (or a sudden increase in the rate) can jeopardize the continued existence of some industries if they are left unprotected against foreign competition. This risk is particularly great if the foreign competitors either do not impose environmental charges because of a relatively greater preference for material income, or if they welcome foreign capital that brings with it an export market and the necessary technology. To preserve these industries from a precipitous decline constitutes a potentially valid reason for granting them some sort of temporary assistance. Even so enthusiastic a champion of PPP as Barde (see Chapter 6) has acknowledged that (domestic as well as international) transitional problems can warrant a short-run departure from trade neutrality,[12] but any such assistance must be temporary and the ultimate attainment of the gains from the international reallocation of resources must not be denied. The (inverse) similarity between environmental charges and commercial policies is apparent in the analysis of this policy problem, as well as in the static analysis.

If one of a nation's industries (or a marginal firm) is to be eliminated by the requirements of pollution control, and the product imported from suppliers in another nation, the costs of contraction in that industry could be socially damaging. The capital, both physical and human, that is specific to the industry will become worthless very quickly. To the extent that the capital is industry-specific and completely nontransferable, individuals will bear unseemingly large shares of the adjustment burden and the society's total stock of capital will be reduced at a time when the society is already undergoing a reduction in its material income. By preventing the sudden demise of the industry, the social costs of adjustment will be reduced in total and more widely distributed. Such an industry can be described as senile in that its useful life is seen as finite. The useful life is now limited to the time needed to reallocate to other industries or to depreciate fully the physical and human capital employed.[13] The important characteristic of the assistance to be provided to the industry is that it shall allow the capacity of the industry to decline, and that it shall have some prespecified maximum duration. The purpose is to phase the industry out and not to preserve it.

The assistance can take three forms. The nation can impose an avowedly international impediment to competition such as a quota or a tariff. The quota could be increased year-by-year according to some predetermined formula, so that a reduction in the capacity of the domestic industry would be gradually enforced. The tariff would originally be levied at an *ad valorem* rate equal to the environmental charge, and the rate would gradually be reduced to zero over the life-span of the senile industry. A domestic alternative would be to subsidize the industry, so that the pollution would be reduced without the industry losing its competitiveness. The subsidy would, therefore, have the rate equivalent to that of the tariff. Finally, there exists the possibility of delaying the imposition of environmental charges on emissions for a specified period, so that the industry's mortality would become apparent to entrepreneurs and workers alike.[14]

The delay in imposing the environmental charges reduces the gain from the introduction of environmental protection legislation. As such, it prevents the attainment of ray A in Fig. 7-1 for a period of time. The subsidy has the disadvantage that there will be no increase in the price of the pollution-causing product, and, therefore, no discouragement of its use. This represents a clear departure from PPP, and in this way delays the attainment of ray B in Fig. 7-1. The international measures prevent only the attainment of ray C. There is an apparent argument in favor of international controls over their domestic equivalents, since they interfere least with the efficient allocation of resources.[15] This conclusion is, at best, tentative and does not make any allowance for repercussions abroad.

Explicit recognition of the costs of adjustment adds another dimension to the already-strong case for international cooperation in the introduction of environmental protection. The benefits to be derived from agreements on the legitimacy of certain counteractions to departures from PPP are self-evident. An agreement to set the "equilibrium" levels of charges for a long period of time—say seven years—at the first instigation will reduce the domestic problems of fear of increases in the rates of effluent fees and will allow both nations and entrepreneurs sensibly to plan their adaptive strategies. The agreed-on level of charges would also allow the problems of adjustment to be recognized and, it is hoped, to be approached with a spirit of tolerance. Finally, the institution of environmental charges would take place in many nations simultaneously. This simultaneity will reduce the adjustment required by some industries as their ultimate reduction in competitiveness will amount only to the net difference between the charges levied at home and abroad. There will be less danger of overreaction in the phasing-out or phasing-down of polluting industries.

Adjustment to a new global set of environmental charges is reminiscent of the sets of negotiations of tariff reductions conducted under the auspices of the GATT. There is a good argument for approaching the problem of the harmonization of environmental procedures in a similar way. Certainly the dynamics of adjustment to the institution of environmental charges is the same as the adjustment to widespread tariff reductions. The emphasis on adjustment assistance in the United States Trade Act of 1974 that provides the authority for the ongoing Multilateral Trade Negotiations (MTN) in Geneva will have to be included in any international agreement on adjustment to environmental protection. The "burden of proof" approach that was a key concept in the philosophy of "linear reductions" in the Kennedy

Round, could play a valuable role in any justification of departures from PPP. Lastly, the concept of senile industry protection with its emphasis on gradual adjustment, may enable nations to achieve higher levels of agreement if long-term adjustment protection of this type were to be built into the negotiating framework.

PRODUCT-POLLUTION

Up until this point, the discussion has concerned itself completely with process-pollution or production-pollution, in which the environmental damage results from the transformation of raw materials or inputs to the next stage in the production process. The implications of environmental protection for commercial policy are perhaps greater for this type of pollution than for product-pollution (or consumption-pollution), which is concerned with the creation of pollutants in the use and/or during the disposal of the final good. Consumption-pollution is important in its own right, and has its own set of implications for commercial policy. As a general statement, product-pollution offers far fewer qualifications to the adoption of the polluter-pays Principle.

To reduce the quantity of product-pollution, definitive standards are developed to set limits of acceptability for the physical or chemical composition of a product, they set maxima for pollution emissions and prescribe conditions for the elimination of packaging material. Setting standards of this type can preclude certain imports simply because they fail to meet absolute standards. The standards constitute, in such instances, straightforward embargoes on the importation of certain goods. Thus the means by which the standards are decided upon and instituted can have important implications for the freedom of international trade. Foreign suppliers can be put at a disadvantage compared with domestic producers, and the institution and administration of the standards can open up possibilities for the imposition of covert NTBs exclusively for mercantilistic purposes.

The imposition of absolute standards on final goods can put foreign suppliers at a disadvantage in two ways: (1) If the export market is only a small proportion of the output of a firm (or of an optimally sized plant), the adaptation of a domestic good to higher foreign standards can impose important diseconomies of small-scale production. (2) It is possible that the basis for setting and measuring standards will differ among nations. The design needed to serve a foreign market may be substantially different from that required in the home market. Under these conditions, few firms will invest in the product design necessary for exporting, and the volume of international trade will be unnecessarily curtailed.

The first impediment to trade is an inevitable consequence of differences in national tastes and resource endowments. Nothing can be done about this potential reduction in the volume of global trade. The second impediment is the result of the failure of nations to harmonize the bases by which product standards are set. This impediment could be avoided by an intelligent degree of international cooperation, unless it reflects a real intercountry difference in tastes or environmental endowment.

It is possible for the means of enforcing these standards to vary among nations. According to PPP, the charge should be levied on the pollutant-creating act. But it is possible that the charge will be levied on the product that contributes to the emission rather than on the act itself. If the charge is levied on the act, there are no international implications. If the charge is levied on the product in one country and the act in another, the contradictory situation can be remedied by appropriate border taxes and rebates.

The danger that product-standards could serve as a basis for NTBs is very real. Such NTBs would be purely mercantilistic in intent and would impair the global allocation of resources in the same way as any other commercial policy measures. In essence, the basic strategem by which NTBs are instituted in a complication of the standards and the consequent creation of uncertainty in the minds of potential exporters. If standards are clearly defined beyond any cavil of doubt, foreign suppliers will not be discouraged from tooling up for the export market. Important in the definition are the acceptability of certain designs and materials, a reasonable constancy of regulations, explicit descriptions of the means of testing materials as to their compliance with regulations. Inconsistency in customs and consular procedures and classifications are another source of uncertainties. Unfortunately, it is almost impossible to distinguish those NTBs instituted by sheer bureaucratization and those by mercantilistic intent.

Where the tax is levied on the pollution-creating act, there will be no international implications only if the tax does not discriminate in some way by the source of the good. Thus, the effluent fee must be a species of excise tax rather than a tariff.[16] There is no reason for offering domestic producers or polluting substances or commodities protection from their foreign competitors, particularly if the net result of such protection would be to keep the price lower than it otherwise would be.

CONCLUSION

The most apparent feature of any joint consideration of commercial policy and the imposition of environmental charges is their virtual equivalence as far as international trade is concerned. The consequence of this similarity is that commercial policy measures are capable of providing an almost perfect means of lessening the impact of environmental-protection legislation upon certain industries. The general adoption of the Polluter Pays Principle reflects the virtues of trade neutrality as a norm, but economists must be fully aware of the temptations to depart from principle in search of expediency.

There is a distinction to be drawn between the ultimate impact in process-pollution or in product-pollution and the adjustment to the new basis for computing costs. The use of commercial policy to reduce the degree of ultimate impact introduces a trade distortion in the same way that any tariff distorts trade under any circumstances. As such, measures of this kind will prevent the socially optimal global allocation of resources from being attained, and will reduce the gains inherent in the recognition of the social costs of pollution. However, in lessening the social costs of adaptation to a new set of cost data, the equivalence between environmental charges and commercial policy measures can serve a useful purpose. Commercial policy can be used to reduce the costs of adjustment by excluding any additional effects that derive from foreign competition. These measures, however, must be temporary, and the danger is that they will, like infant industry tariffs have been known to do, achieve a counterproductive permanency.

NOTES

1. See the detailed description of the need for departures from PPP given by Jean-Philippe Barde in "National and International Policy Alternatives for Environmental Control and their Economic Implications," Chapter 6.

2. See Ingo Walter, "Nontariff Barriers and the Free-Trade Option," *Banca Nazionale del Lavoro Quarterly Review,* March 1969, p. 20.

3. See Chapter 6.

4. These are the type *A* and type *B* functional sources of environmental despoilation in Ingo Walter's, "Environmental Control and Patterns of International Trade and Investment: An Emerging Policy Issue," *Banca Nazionale del Lavoro Quarterly Review,* March 1972, pp. 84–85.

5. For a thorough discussion, see Herbert G. Grubel, "Effective Tariff Protection: A Non-specialist Introduction to the Theory, Policy Implications and Controversies," in *Effective Tariff Protection,* H. G. Grubel and H. G. Johnson, Eds., Geneva: General Agreement on Tariffs and Trade and Graduate Institute of International Studies, 1971, pp. 1–15.

6. Ingo Walter, "Pollution and Protection: U.S. Environmental Controls as Competitive Distortions," *Weltwirtschaftliches Archiv,* March 1974, pp. 104–113.

7. Data limitations forced Walter to analyze the effect in terms of industries rather than the more appropriate measure of processes. In a strict sense, it is the process or stage of production that receives effective protection, and not necessarily the final product.

8. Walter is, of course, completely aware of these limitations and qualifies his estimate appropriately.

9.   Gottfried Haberler, *The Theory of International Trade*, New York: Macmillan, 1950, p. 314.

10.   Committee on Public Works, 93rd Congress, 1st Session, *The Effects of Pollution Abatement on International Trade*, Washington, D.C.: U.S. Government Printing Office, 1973, p. 1.

11.   See H. Peter Gray, *An Aggregate Theory of International Payments Adjustment*, London: Macmillan, 1974, pp. 98-104.

12.   Loc. cit., Section 1.3.1.

13.   H. Peter Gray, "Senile Industry Protection: A Proposal," *Southern Economic Journal*, April 1973, pp. 569-574; Geoffrey E. Wood, "Senile Industry Protection: Comment," and Gray, "Senile Industry Protection: Reply," *Southern Economic Journal*, January 1975, pp. 535-541.

14.   Note that the delay in imposing environmental charges is equivalent to a tariff.

15.   See the reference to the work of H. G. Johnson and J. Bhagwati in H. G. Grubel, "Some Effects of Environmental Controls on International Trade: The Heckscher-Ohlin Model," in Chapter 2 of this volume.

16.   This is shown, within the limitations of his model, by Herbert G. Grubel, in Chapter 2.

Environmental Policy and Multinational Corporate Strategy

Thomas N. Gladwin and John G. Welles

Excluding centrally planned economies, multinational corporations (MNCs) are estimated to contribute roughly one-fifth of world GNP.[1] Output of MNCs has been expanding at a rate of about 10% per year in real terms, while gross world product has been expanding by only about 5% a year.[2] Some observers speculate that, before the close of the century, some 300 of the largest MNCs will produce more than one-half of the world's goods and services.[3]

Even though simplistic extrapolations of this type lack credibility,[4] one current conclusion is inescapable—the industrial operations of the world's MNCs necessarily have a substantial influence on the quality of the global environment. They are found in some of the most pollution-intensive industries, and are responsible for much of the world's generation of residuals. The influence that MNCs have on world environmental quality underscores the need to understand the nature of the multinational enterprise, the logic that underlies their behavior in the environmental area, how public policy may and may not influence them, and the directions in which their environmental behavior may evolve.

The objective of this chapter is to examine the adaptations of MNC behavior in response to widely divergent environmental conditions and policies at the local, national, and international levels. The emphasis rests more with patterns of *organizational* behavior than with *economic* behavior more narrowly defined. An understanding of the behavioral characteristics and response-patterns of MNCs is a prerequisite to appreciating the international economic dimensions of environmental management, and to the design of effective public policies for anticipating, avoiding, and resolving conflicts. Primary attention is given to the traditionally pollution-intensive industries such as petroleum, chemicals, and metals. Our consideration is limited largely to pollution control or "residuals management" problems, although the general approach and conclusions apply to other types of environmental disruption as well. The focus is on general patterns—the peculiarities, idiosyncracies, and irrationalities that are so important in explaining specific behavior of individual MNCs are largely set aside in the search for the basic forces and tendencies. Finally, the bulk of the chapter presents original, largely unpublished, empirical findings from recent research conducted separately by both authors.[5]

THE STATE OF EMPIRICAL RESEARCH

Corporate adaptation to public environmental policy has only recently emerged as a focus of conceptual and empirical analysis. The relevant theory remains in an embryonic state, and much of the empirical research to date has tended to be largely exploratory, descriptive, and superficial. The literature on the international corporate strategy–environmental policy nexus may be divided into several distinct but related categories, and includes work specifically focused on the behavior of MNCs per se, as well as work more narrowly focused on the response patterns of these same firms in a single nation, typically the United States.

One category consists of questionnaire-type research on corporate pollution-control expenditures, capital budgeting techniques, financing methods, and organizational patterns. It is generally rather long on description and short on analysis and interpretation. In addition, its validity is sometimes suspect, given "data sensitivity" problems and the potential for "response error." Nonetheless, such work is useful from an international perspective because it broadly describes the response patterns of firms to environmental policy "shocks" in the United States, and the behavior of these same firms abroad can usefully be compared with this "benchmark" United States behavior. Examples of such questionnaire research include the annual McGraw-Hill surveys of United States corporate pollution-control expenditures[6] and three Conference Board studies concerned with organizational aspects of corporate pollution control.[7] These studies reveal a great deal about the response patterns of firms operating in the United States. Additional United States-oriented questionnaire-type research has been concerned with the general impact that the environmental movement has had on corporations,[8] the capital budgeting techniques employed in making pollution-control expenditures,[9] and the way in which some of these expenditures have been financed.[10]

A second category of research includes surveys of corporate environmental practice provided in the "business press." Treatment of the topic in such surveys is typically shallow, but as a total package they represent a valuable source of examples, case-studies, and insights. They cover a wide range of environmental management organizational activities and trends in United States and European enterprises.[11]

A third category of research related to the MNC-environmental policy interface consists of the theoretical work related to: (1) corporate adaptation in response to social demands, (2) MNC behavior under internationally heterogeneous conditions, and (3) environment-induced international shifts in industrial location. Corporate adaptation (i.e., changes in organizational structures, processes, and behavior) in response to social pressures such as ecology, minority employment, and consumer protection has only recently received research attention from organizational theorists. The social response process in large divisionalized United States firms seems to follow a general pattern, and typically begins with attempts from the top to accomplish change—ending, if the organization is adaptive, with the institutionalization of the new corporate social policy at the operating level.[12] The conversion of social responsiveness from policy to action typically involves various phases including top management concern, creation of staff specialists to handle the problem, and finally full integration into operating divisional management. MNC behavior in a world of diversity has also received a fair amount of conceptual and empirical attention, particularly concerning global business strategy formulation under unifying and fragmenting influences, and has provided valuable insights into the influence of multinational operations on business strategy, finance, organization, and marketing.[13] In contrast, the body of theory directly focusing on the topic of environment-induced international shifts in industrial location is rather sparse, although some good conceptual work has been done.[14]

The final category of research, and the one on which most of this chapter is based, is that of descriptive interview research conducted with MNC managers on the subject of adaptation in response to environmental policy.

One researcher examined how seven large United States-based MNCs chose to carry out decision-making in the area of pollution control.[15] The study was largely concerned with curative approaches to current problems rather than with preventive approaches for avoiding future problems, and was not internationally oriented. Two other studies, by the present authors, extensively surveyed North American and European MNCs with regard to their response to emerging issues and constraints of environmental protection. One study involved interviews in eight nations with representatives of MNCs, industry associations, consulting firms, banks, and governmental organizations at the national and international level, and explored possibilities for international cooperation among industry associations and intergovernmental organizations.[16] The other study involved interviews in nine nations with executives of 17 major petroleum, chemical, and metals MNCs, and focused primarily on organizational arrangements for dealing with environmental management problems and on the current role of ecological considerations in project planning.[17]

THE CONCEPTUAL FRAMEWORK

The guiding framework of this essay consists of four components: (1) the nature of the multinational enterprise, (2) strategic behavior, (3) the environmental policy system, and (4) the structure of international diversity. We shall briefly examine and define each of these components, and at the same time construct the framework of description and analysis that will be employed in this paper.

First, we define the MNC in managerial terms as a firm whose international operations are substantial, which operates facilities in a number of countries, which exercises managerial control over assets abroad, and which attempts, at least in part, to follow a central optimizing strategy across national boundaries.[18] This conception clearly applies to such firms as EXXON, Royal Dutch Shell, British Petroleum, Dow Chemical, BASF, Imperial Chemical Industries, Alcan Aluminium, Rio Tinto-Zinc, and Pechiney. We view these firms as having two essential roles in the world economy: (1) the development, transmission, and application of resources internationally (e.g., technology, management, capital, and so on), and (2) the development of unified systems of industrial activities among several nations.[19] As such, our attention will primarily rest with environmental policy-induced adaptation in international resource transfers and in organizations of transnational operating systems.

Second, strategic behavior is rather loosely conceived as defining how a

MNC combines and employs resources in the conduct of its operations.[20] We view a firm's overall "strategy" as the composite of its strategic behavior in such areas as marketing, production, logistics, finance, ownership, government relations, research, technology, and so forth. Two major areas of strategic behavior are broadly examined in this paper: (1) organization and, (2) investment. These two areas were chosen for examination basically for two reasons. First, most of the public policy issues that have been raised on the connection between MNC strategy and environmental policy relate to one or both of these two areas of strategic behavior. Second, most of the existing empirical research has been addressed to these two issues. Our focus is on adaptation in patterns of strategic behavior over time, across geographic boundaries, among corporate functions and divisions, and vertically throughout the organization.

Third, a national environmental policy system is defined as the interrelated package of formal and informal actions of organized publics taken in a nation to mitigate, correct, or prevent environmental problems. These "organized publics" may be legislative bodies, executive agencies, judicial bodies, industry associations, or citizen interest groups. The actions relate to indirect and direct social controls such as standards, subsidies, prohibitions, tax incentives, environmental impact statement requirements, citizen law suits, land use plans, enforcement procedures, and so forth. We shall focus on institutional arrangements and policy instruments capable of influencing MNC behavior.

The fourth and final component of our conceptual framework is international environmental policy diversity: the lack of homogeneity in the substance, intensity, and timing of environmental policies among nations. For reasons more fully discussed elsewhere,[21] the relevant norms, priorities, techniques, and timing associated with environmental policy systems differ substantially among nations, not withstanding harmonization efforts at the international level. An in-depth examination of the character and probable determinants of environmental policies in twelve nations resulted in the generalized model of environmental policy determination shown in Fig. 8-1.[22] The policy system of a nation, in this representation, can be viewed as a complex product of the impact of causative actions arising from its "technological–economic system" on its receiving "natural system" as interpreted and mediated by characteristics in its "political system" and "social system." Given the wide present and projected intercountry variations in the "determinants," the resulting environmental policy systems are, thus, likely to exhibit concomitant variation. The international diversity can be "structured," however, by sorting nations into groups based on similarities and differences in policy system components.[23]

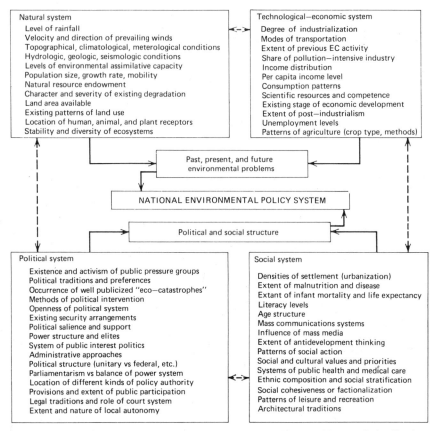

Source: Thomas N. Gladwin, "The Role of Ecological Considerations in the Multinational Corporate Project Planning
       Process: A Comparative Study of North American—and Western European—Based Petroleum, Chemicals
       and Metals Firms" (unpublished Ph.D. dissertation, Graduate School of Business Administration, The
       University of Michigan, 1975), App. D.

Figure 8-1 Determinants of national environmental policy.

ORGANIZATIONAL STRATEGY

The first area of environmental policy-induced strategic behavior to be
examined is organization. We are interested in six structural elements: corporate objectives, role assignment, performance measurement, surveillance-
information systems, research and technology programs, and interorganizational relations. Each of these represents a point of leverage in the system of
MNC decision-making behavior. If such behavior is to become "environmentally oriented," then each must first undergo adaptation in order to
exert the appropriate influence.[24]

Our survey reveals that adaptation of organizational structure along environmental lines is an evolutionary process. Except for a few leading corporations, most MNCs interviewed have not yet fully modified their structures in order to bring about environmentally sound planning and decision-making on a global basis. The environmental management function in most MNCs is currently handled in a decentralized, fragmented manner, but the direction of movement is towards greater global standardization in policy and practice.

Environmental Objectives

The majority of MNCs contacted have formulated written statements of corporate environmental objectives or policies. Such statements are more commonly found in large rather than in small MNCs, in North American rather than in Western European MNCs, and in chemical and petroleum rather than in metals MNCs. Their contents vary widely, and frequently consist of generalities, such as, "We will comply with all governmental laws and regulations," or "We will be a good neighbor or citizen."[25] Some include direct references to planning or decision-making: "We are dedicated to sound environmental planning"; "We will make environmental considerations an integral part of our decision-making process"; and "We will do an environmental impact assessment for all new projects." Only a few proclaim an expressed objective of "leadership and excellence in the field of environmental protection." Few say anything about going above and beyond the law or express a desire to go beyond current social-political expectations.

Environmental protection is generally not viewed as a positive opportunity, but rather as a reluctantly-approached hurdle or operating constraint. MNC environmental policies are frequently modified or revised from time to time, and in some firms they appear to be in a continual state of evolution. In sum, short-term financial pressures appear to demand short-term MNC planning horizons and concomitant environmental management behavior.

Geographically, most MNCs have made no attempt to develop a consistent set of environmental policies applicable to their global operations. Such environmental objectives and policies as have been developed and applied pertain almost exclusively to their home countries. Even where the policies have been made global in coverage, as in the case of Dow Chemical's "Global Pollution Control Guidelines,"[26] the interpretation and implementation of these policies is tailored to the local situation. "Our environmental policy and practice is adjusted to the different laws, attitudes, interpretations, esthetic values, and environmental conditions found in each nation," stated the conservation adviser of one European petroleum firm. "We respond when and where there is social concern for ecological balance," states an aluminum company vice-president. "We try to make sure that our operations and products are compatible with community needs and environmental, social, and economic aspirations," states the policy document of one large petroleum MNC. In general, the environmental objectives of MNCs in their overseas operations appear to be a matter of local adaptation or accommodation.

In a few situations, economic forces produce uniform results on a global basis. Examples include uniform installation of a chemical process that is designed to meet the most stringent environmental requirements among multiple, new plant locations, and products produced uniformily for global marketing but which meet the standards of the most stringent nation. In these situations, it is cost saving and not MNC environmental policy that results in uniformity.

Environmental Role Assignment

Corporate level environmental directors, advisors, or coordinators are found in most pollution-intensive MNCs. These functions sometimes consist only of one individual, but more frequently involve small staff groups with such names as: Environmental Control Center, Industrial Ecology Department, or Office of Environmental Affairs. The senior environmental officer and staff unit typically reports to either the president, one or more senior vice-presidents, or to the research or technical director.

These staffs serve coordination, watchdog, advisory, clearing house, external relations, and communications functions. The units typically act as "energizers" or "catalysts," but not as "problem-solvers." Most MNCs have decided that the development of a centralized cadre of generalist "environmental managers" is not the way in which environmental problems will be solved. Rather, they have chosen to force the issue into the operating line manager's decision system, while providing him with access to highly specialized resources, both internal and external to the firm. In the view of many MNC executives interviewed, a large centralized environmental problem-solving group would tend to: (1) generate staff-line organizational conflict by threatening the autonomy of operating management, (2) give line managers the impression that environmental management is not their problem, and (3) be inefficient because its members would lack familiarity with the intricacies of the countless processes, products, effluents, and practices encountered at the operating level.

The creation of a corporate-level, environmental coordinating staff unit appears to represent an instrumental, but perhaps transitional, phase in the process by which issues of environmental protection are internalized within the MNC.[27] Strong evidence of this is encountered in some environmentally progressive MNCs. One petroleum MNC has recently eliminated the position of Environmental Conservation Coordinator. In one chemical MNC, the position of Manager of Environmental Affairs has been converted to Manager of Public Issues, and the areas of consumerism, minority hiring, and other social concerns were added to compensate for the greatly diminished need for a catalytic role in the field of ecology.

In addition to staff units, many MNCs have corporate level top management committees concerned with environmental problems. These are employed for policy formation, catalytic, and progress-review purposes. One chemical MNC, for example, has an overall, top-level, environmental quality committee, a manufacturing environmental committee, a product environmental committee, and an occupational safety and health committee. Committee representatives are viewed as "focal points" and "linking pins" through which the firm's environmental communications network functions. Top management committees, just like environmental staff units, also appear to be transitory organizational mechanisms for bringing about institutionalization of environmental concerns. In many MNCs contacted, these committees meet less frequently now than they did previously, and in a few MNCs they have withered away entirely.

Environmental functions that appear more permanent than the generalized coordinating and committee roles described above have been integrated by most MNCs into their corporate-level engineering, research, legal, and public-relations staff groups. Almost every MNC has added highly trained environmental science professionals to its engineering, technical services, and research units. Environmental lawyers have been added by some of the MNCs, particularly those corporations having a large share of the operations in nations such as the United States, where citizen-group law suits and the courts have played a large role in the environmental movement. Environmental public-relations specialists have also been added, most typically by the large petroleum and/or United States-based MNCs employing "high-profile" environmental image strategies.

Most MNCs have created environmental advisor or technical specialist positions in units of the firm below the headquarters level. One petroleum MNC, for instance, has at least one qualified technical person whose time is fully committed to environmental affairs in all major facilities, operating regions, divisions, and affiliates. MNCs with global environmental policies and regional organizational frameworks typically have an environmental advisor at the regional headquarters level.[28]

MNC environmental role assignments in any particular country seem to depend on a number of factors, including: size of the operation, nature and range of activities, degree of ownership, local organizational structure, and, most critically, the stringency of the applicable environmental regulations, intensity of citizen action, and extent of governmental reporting requirements. One petroleum MNC, for example, has four environmental coordinators for its United States operations, four in West Germany, two in Canada, and only one-half of one man for all of Latin America. Just as we saw environmental objectives to be a matter of "local adaptation," so too is a MNC's environmental role assignment.

Environmental Performance Measurement

Most of the MNCs contacted have not yet been successful in adapting their performance measurement, evaluation, and reward systems to handle the issue of environmental protection. A few, however, especially some of the American firms that have been under heavy public pressure for increased "social auditing,"[29] are actively wrestling with the problem, but the practical and conceptual difficulties are formidable.

Limited attempts at measuring environmental performance in plant and operations are being made by some MNCs. In a few, the results of plant-level residuals output monitoring are periodically sent into the corporate level environmental staff unit. A few have added an environmental section to their "monthly operating review forms" or added environmental criterion to their annual "stewardship reviews." "Citation and complaint lists" are maintained by some environmental coordinators on a plant-level basis. Some of the larger chemical and petroleum MNCs have relatively well-developed systems for reporting spills of oil and hazardous substances, especially in their United States operations.[30] Most of these performance measurement mechanisms are only utilized by the MNCs in their home country operations. Most have not yet attempted to extend environmental performance measurement to overseas operations. It should also be noted that the mechanisms both formal and informal, employed in any firm typically vary considerably from division to division and from function to function.

Environmental performance has generally not been formally added as a criterion in the MNC executive evaluation, promotion, and compensation systems. In most MNCs, environmental considerations enter into executive performance evaluation, if at all, only in a very informal and subjective way. Whereas cost control, profitability, employee morale, and safety are typically checkpoints in plant supervisor performance appraisal, environmental protection has not yet been added explicitly to the list. In addition, according to many of the MNC executives interviewed, the distribution of rewards and punishments has not been related systematically to environmental performance.

Environmental performance measurement of plants and managers, both nationally and internationally, is fraught with difficulty. Performance measurement systems in MNCs are predominantly financial in their orientation, and measures of environmental performance simply do not mesh very well with "bottom line" logic and cost-accounting-oriented systems. The primary problem involves establishment of valid indicators. Wide variation in applicable laws and regulations, and intracompany variation in the age, size, and residuals output characteristics of plants, creates such situational diversity that comparisons between the environmental performance of one plant versus another becomes almost impossible. Environmental performance is not an easy thing to communicate or to understand, and is generally not amenable to corporate-wide aggregation. Finally, company-wide environmental performance measurement can be logically inconsistent with the existing policies of "local adaptation" embraced by most MNCs (i.e., managers have in essence been instructed to perform against different national or even local yardsticks).

Environmental Surveillance and Information Systems

Staff has been assigned, in most of the MNCs interviewed, for the purpose of monitoring trends and events in the "turbulent" areas of environmental legislation and technology. The effort is more extensive and formalized in some MNCs than others, however. The external monitoring job is done by different kinds of personnel in different MNCs. Most typically it is done by the environmental coordinator or members of his staff. In other firms, this activity is carried out by environmental lawyers on the corporate legal staff, by the top management environmental committee, or by members of the public affairs office. The pattern of external monitoring is similar in most firms: international trends and events are monitored at headquarters, national trends at the national subsidiary level, and local trends at the local plant level. In many MNCs, the results of local and national monitoring are periodically sent into the headquarters environmental staff unit and are analyzed and collated into a broad-based global trend report that is then redistributed back to the field. In a few of the MNCs contacted, the volume of external monitoring activity has recently diminished, and they have shifted from a "full" to an "exception" system of monitoring and reporting.

The monitoring of external developments is done in many different ways.

Media reports of legal and administrative trends are read weekly by most environmental coordinators. Many of the MNCs included in our research have representatives (e.g., public affairs specialists, lawyers, and lobbyists) in capital cities of major countries in which they operate, and these individuals are utilized as antennas for detecting change. Trends in environmental technology are followed by means of journals, professional meetings, and information supplied by manufacturers of pollution-control equipment and services. Industry trade associations are used by many MNCs, especially in Europe, for the purpose of tracking the winds of change in the environmental area.

Although few MNCs engage in frequent "direct," face-to-face contact with citizen environmental organizations, most maintain some form of indirect liaison. The environmental director of one United States firm, for example, is a member of seven environmental groups. "Being a member of these groups and receiving all of their literature allows me to keep my finger on the pulse of the environmental movement," he stated in an interview. Another United States-based metals firm has an "environmental information specialist" on its staff unit whose full-time job is to keep track of the activities, viewpoints, and legal maneuvers of all environmental groups active in the United States. Finally, informal communications channels between company environmental personnel and their counterparts in other firms, and with governmental civil servants represents the means by which most of the developments are first detected.

The information acquired from external surveillance activity is formally and informally disseminated within most MNCs. Environmental trend reports, bibliographic bulletins, and house organs devoted entirely to environmental issues are produced in many of the larger MNCs. Environmental "key words" have been added to the sophisticated "selective dissemination of information systems" of some of the MNCs, which distribute abstracts or complete articles to personnel based on a computerized key-word identification system. Most of the information acquired via external monitoring, however, is probably disseminated through informal channels of communication between the receiver and user.

Environmental Research and Technology Programs

Environmental issues appear to be receiving increasing attention in the research and development (R&D) programs of most MNCs, although the amount of funds and manpower allocated to these issues varies widely by industry and by company. Most MNCs have formally created environmental studies sections in their R&D units. The research effort is primarily of an "applied," rather then "basic" character. The R&D activity tends to be concentrated for the entire MNC in a single facility or at a very few locations. The principal research facility is invariably in the home nation for the following reasons: reduction of overhead costs, proximity to "familiar" governmental and university centers of environmental research, access to government-financed environmental research, scale requirements of relevant R&D activity, enhancement of managerial control, proximity to the bulk of company operations having pollution problems, ease of recruitment of specialized environmental professionals, and likelihood of capturing spillovers from the firm's other R&D activities, which also tend to be concentrated in the home nation. One is probably safe in estimating that 90% of the Western World's environment-related R&D is conducted in six nations: United States, Sweden, Netherlands, West Germany, United Kingdom, and Japan.

In addition to engaging in their own in-house, environment-related R&D, many MNCs also participate in joint industry environmental research programs. These kinds of programs are most evident in Western Europe, according to many observers interviewed. In industry terms, cooperative efforts are most noticeable in the petroleum industry, due to commonality of product, activity, and process-related environmental problems faced in this industry as compared to the more diverse problems found in industries such as chemicals and nonferrous metals. One example of a joint industry research program is CONCAWE (The oil companies' International Study Group for Conservation of Clean Air and Water in Western Europe), which today has twenty participants, representing about 80% of the refining capacity in Western Europe. CONCAWE's basic function is to examine and to promote the use of means for preventing air, water, ground, and noise pollution attributable to the oil-refining industry and to the use of oil products reflecting conducive policies by industry and regulatory authorities to competition.[31] products.[31]

The emphasis in many in-house and joint industry environmental research programs has recently shifted from production processes to products. This new emphasis on issues of product environmental impact is probably explained by the increasing list of "environmentally-banned" products,[32] the growing awareness of the need for less energy-intensive products,[33] and the movements in the United States and Europe towards the control of toxic chemicals and towards better operational health and safety.[34] A few chemical MNCs have recently formed product environmental committees and expanded their product research programs. Dow Chemical, for example, has created a formalized program of product environmental safety which it calls "product stewardship." This program involves inputs from the R&D, manufacturing, and marketing departments of the company, and consists of an integrated program of product impact research, creation of product impact data profiles, education of salesmen, and communications to distributors and customers.[35] New joint industry programs with a specific product impact focus have also been created. ETAD (The Ecological and Toxicological Association of the Dyestuff's Manufacturing Industry) in Europe and ICT (The Institute for Chemical Toxicology) in the United States represent two prime examples.[36]

The main source of advanced environmental technology can today be found within the confines of the large MNCs. The MNC is also probably the dominant institution transferring environmental technology across national borders. MNC affiliates can potentially draw upon the environmental knowledge of the entire organization of which they are part. In practice, full and instantaneous intrafirm transfer does not usually take place. Environmental technology may not be suitable for use by the affiliates. In addition, given the "local adaptation" environmental strategy of most MNCs, newly developed environmental technology is frequently not desired by the affiliate, and is rarely forced on them by the parent company.

The transfer of environmental technology via the MNC takes place in many direct and indirect ways.[37] New, foreign direct-investment normally results in the transfer of considerable technology to the host nation and MNCs generally move abroad with their most efficient, and usually their cleanest, process technology, for reasons discussed below. Relevant skills acquired in a stringent nation—such as environmental-impact assessment, or oil-spill recovery and prevention programs—are occasionally transferred when the MNC believes that their utilization will provide an advantage in the eyes of host governments over the behavior of indigenous or third-country firms. Cross-border flows of information and environmental personnel (e.g., trend letters, consulting teams, inspection tours, annual meetings, international conferences, transfer of operating managers, etc.) can also result in considerable technology transfer.

The international transfer of environmental technology by MNCs is not entirely an intrafirm process. Through the effects of observation, imitation, emulation, demonstration, and external sales, the MNCs stimulate, internationally, the transfer and adoption of environmental technology by governments, as well as by other industrial organizations. Many MNCs currently market their environmental systems and know-how externally. In most firms contacted such external selling is a relatively minor activity, but in a few of the chemicals MNCs, this kind of activity has become a significant line of business.[38] Some of these firms proceeded by means of external acquisition of pollution-control firms, but the predominant pattern has been one of internal development. According to some executives, outside commercialization tends to act as a stimulant to further in-house R&D.

Pressure to maintain a sound corporate environmental image and the ability to spread environment-related R&D costs over a wider market are major contributing factors.

Interorganizational Environmental Relations

In contrast with the five variables examined above that are primarily intraorganizational, the final structural element to be examined is interorganizational in character. Interorganizational relations strategies—defined here as exchanges of information and influence between a MNC and organizations external to it—vary widely among countries, industries, and firms.

Many MNCs actively participate in national and international intraindustry, interindustry, and government-industry groups on environmental matters. Some of these are listed in Table 8-1, together with selected intergovernmental organizations concerned with environmental matters. The extent of such participation is generally higher for European than for United States-based MNCs, reflecting differing antitrust regulations and differing views on the role of industry-wide collaboration. The extent of cooperation is also generally higher among firms in the petroleum industry than in other industries, probably reflecting the homogeneity of environmental problems. One European petroleum executive added the following rationale: "Pollution control in our industry, at least within Europe, is not perceived as a competitive area; by sharing experience and exchanging information the duplication of effort can be minimized; a common industry stance on environmental issues gives us strength when urging consideration or adoption of certain ideas or proposals; finally, when the industry stands united on an issue the government can't use the strategy of divide and conquer."

Most MNCs have direct and frequent contact with governmental bodies, especially regulatory agencies, on environmental matters. The extent of this contact is similar in Western Europe and North America, but its "character" and timing varies widely. As a general rule, the contact processes in Western Europe are often cooperative in character, involving a relatively high degree of mutual trust and respect, while in the United States they are typically competitive or adversary and suspicious in nature. This is most evident in the setting of environmental standards; MNCs appear to have a stronger influence in Europe than in the United States. Much of the industry–government contact in Europe takes place *prior* to the passage of enforcing legislation, and takes the form of cooperative negotiations, joint research and consultation into possible technical solutions, and relatively free flowing communication. With some exceptions, much of the contact in

Table 8-1 Selected Intergovernmental and Industry Groups Dealing with Environmental Issues[a]

Intergovernmental Organizations

Commission of The European Communities
Council of Europe
Food and Agricultural Organization (via Industry Cooperative Program)
General Agreement on Tariffs and Trade
Inter-American Development Bank
Inter-American Economic and Social Council
Inter-Governmental Maritime Consultative Organization
International Bank for Reconstruction and Development
International Civil Aviation Organization
International Joint Commission
International Labor Organization
International Organization for Standardization
North Atlantic Treaty Organization (Committee on the Challenges of Modern Society)
Organization of American States
Organization of Economic Cooperation and Development (via Business and Industry Advisory Committee)
United Nations Development Program
United Nations Education, Scientific, and Cultural Organization
United Nations Environment Program
United Nations Economic Commission for Europe
United Nations Economic Commission for Latin America
United States Agency for International Development
World Health Organization
World Meteorological Organization

Chemicals Industry

American Chemical Society
The Ecological and Toxicological Association of the Dyestuffs Manufacturing Industry
European Council of Chemical Manufacturers' Federations
Institute for Chemical Toxicology
Manufacturing Chemists Association
Synthetic Organic Chemical Manufacturers' Association
The Swiss Society of Chemical Industries

Metals Industry

American Institute of Mining Engineers
American Iron and Steel Institute
American Mining Congress
European Primary Aluminum Association

Table 8-1 Continued

German Steel Industries Association
International Iron and Steel Institute
International Primary Aluminum Institute

Petroleum Industry

American Petroleum Institute
Interindustry Emission Control Program
International Petroleum Industry Environmental Conservation Association
International Tanker Owners Pollution Federation
North Sea Operators Committee
Oil Companies International Marine Forum
Petroleum Association for Conservation of the Canadian Environment
The Petroleum Association of Japan
Petroleum Industry Environment Executive (Australia)
Stichting CONCAWE
U.K. Institute of Petroleum

General Industry

American Institute of Merchant Shipping
Chamber of Commerce of the U.S.A.
Committee for Economic Development
Conference Board
Confederation of British Industry
Council of European Industrial Federations
Council of Netherlands Economic Organizations
Federation of Belgian Industries
Federation of German Industries
Federation of Swedish Industries
International Center for Industry and the Environment
International Chamber of Commerce
International Organization of Employers
Japanese National Committee of the I.C.C.
National Academy of Engineering
National Academy of Sciences
National Association of Manufacturers
Union of Industries of the European Community
U.S. Council of the I.C.C.

[a] Source: Thomas N. Gladwin, *The Role of Ecological Consideration* loc. cit., Chapter VI.

the United States takes place *after* the controlling legislation and standards have been drafted, and frequently is antagonistic in character and sometimes results in dilatory efforts to delay implementation.

Most MNCs interviewed have not attempted to centralize the governmental contact process at the headquarters level, but rather have generally created a "structure of decentralized contact." Contact with local and regional bodies is usually carried out by local plant management; contacts with national governmental bodies by managers from the national subsidiary or affiliate; and contacts with international governmental bodies by personnel from the firm's world headquarters. This symmetrical, or parallel, structure, which matches level of government to level of corporation, is occasionally altered, especially during crisis situations in which the intervention and influence of top level corporate personnel are needed. In addition, a few of the larger MNCs attempt coordination by requiring headquarters notification of all meetings between company managers and governmental officials at all levels.

MNCs and their industry associations are only beginning to deal with intergovernmental organizations concerned with environmental issues. Industry associations made almost no effective contributions, for example, to the preparatory process for the United Nations Conference on the Human Environment in Stockholm in 1972.[39] One week before the United Nations Conference began, the International Chamber of Commerce staged a World Industry Conference on the Human Environment in Gothenburg, Sweden—4 months after the substantive preparations were completed and 6 months after practical opportunities to be of real assistance had passed. Most MNCs we contacted during this period either underestimated the potentials of the Stockholm Conference, or were unprepared and unorganized to interact effectively.

Since the Stockholm Conference, and with the urging of officials of the United Nations Environment Programme (formed as a result of the Conference), MNCs have begun to organize for more effective cooperation with international governmental organizations. On a horizontal basis, the International Center for Industry and the Environment was formed in 1973, under sponsorship of the International Chamber of Commerce, with offices in Paris and Nairobi.[40] Members include the horizontal national industry associations in several of the Western industrialized nations, and a number of vertical international industry associations. Several of the latter have also been formed recently to deal with environmental matters, including the International Petroleum Industry Environmental Conservation Association (IPIECA).[41] These industry associations serve not only the interests of MNCs, but also the requirements of intergovernmental organizations. When quick responses are needed to technical environmental questions, intergovernmental organizations simply do not have time to go through the cumbersome protocol of contacting governmental members to identify and reach industry expertise at the national level.

Some Observations on Organizational Strategy

MNC organizational strategy, in response to the internationally heterogeneous structure of environmental policy, is *dynamic, decentralized, and fragmented.* In the MNCs we contacted, adaptation was found to be a dynamic process in which:

1. Internal objectives and policies are progressively formulated, refined and extended.
2. Environmental staff positions are created as a catalytic device, allowed to serve their purpose, and then phased out if they are successful.
3. Resistance to complicating the existing performance measurement and reward systems by adding environmental criteria is at first steadfast, but gradually erodes if top management strongly demonstrates its commitment and provides clear signals to middle managers.
4. Efforts to "map" the uncertain and turbulent trends in the field are at first exploratory, then typically voluminous, and finally "routinized" in an exception system format.
5. Emphasis in environmental R&D shifts in response to awareness to new environmental problems, and R&D efforts undertaken to solve internal problems are often later converted into products, processes, and services for external commercialization.
6. Institutional arrangements, such as industry environmental associations, are created and joined by MNCs in response to new governmental initiatives so that their interests can be effectively articulated.

The adaptation or institutionalization process clearly extends over time, varies in different divisional, functional, and geographic parts of the organization, involves many vertical organizational levels, may be painful and frustrating, and is progressively managerial in character.[42] Our findings also show that the speed at which the process proceeds in the MNC as a whole, or in any one divisional or geographic unit, appears to depend on the overall adaptiveness of the organization in question, as well as on the intensity of environment-related external conflict, pressure, and trauma experienced by that organization.[43]

In most MNCs, environmental management is a divisionally, functionally, and geographically decentralized decision area. Environment is viewed as a line management responsibility, and MNCs have generally been reluctant to disturb the existing decentralized structure of decision-making that has been successful in managing global product-market diversity. The tendency to decentralization is strongly reinforced by the desire for autonomy on the part of local management. "What do those environmental fellows in our New York office know about conditions in Belgium?," was the way a European vice-president of a United States chemical firm expressed it. In short, the lack of strong headquarters intervention in this area implies that for any MNC there are typically as many environmental strategies as there are foreign subsidiaries.

Most MNCs have not yet found real benefits in a unified multinational approach to environmental management. The differences among nations in competitive situations and in the substance, intensity, and timing of national environmental policies are commonly viewed as being so great that little can be gained from standardizing MNC environmental objectives, policies, and programs. Environmental affairs in the MNC today are handled in a manner similar to the way marketing and advertising were handled during the 1960s—strategy in each country is most typically viewed as a strictly local problem.[44]

A gradual movement towards greater standardization is apparent, however, and the way is being led by a few of the larger North American chemical and petroleum MNCs who hold "integrated operations" philosophies of international business. Social and economic trends, particularly gradual convergence and harmonization of national environmental policies, are working in favor of more, rather than less, standardization in MNC environmental strategies. This is especially evident in the product area in which cost savings are often possible.

INVESTMENT STRATEGY

Some of the most important environmental aspects of MNC business policy relate to corporate investment patterns, especially locational decisions and project design. From a review of recent MNC locational behavior, foreign direct investment motivations, "pollution haven" characteristics, energy and engineering factors, and MNC executive perceptions, we conclude that MNC locational decisions are *not* likely to be particularly sensitive to near-term intercountry variations in environmental standards and their application. From a review of the broader question of what role environmental factors are currently playing in the MNC project planning process, we conclude that the practice of "environmentally oriented" project planning is still in its infancy. In reaching this conclusion we examine, in turn, the manner in which environmental factors have been considered, the extent to which they have been incorporated, and the reasons that appear to lie behind the current environmental planning behavior of MNCs.

Environment-Induced Locational Shifts

An issue that has received a great deal of interest and has bristled with controversy concerns environment-induced locational shifts on the part of MNC production facilities. The argument in its simplest form is well known: "Investment will be driven out of nations having high environmental standards that result in high costs, and will be attracted by nations having low standards with low costs."

For a number of reasons, we feel that the importance of such "pollution haven" considerations has been grossly exaggerated by government officials, citizen groups, and the media. Predictions of massive "locational flight" on the part of pollution-intensive MNCs appear to be based on incomplete and/or simplistic reasoning. They generally reflect a misunderstanding of: (1) recent MNC locational behavior, (2) the motivations for foreign direct investment, (3) the character of "pollution havens," (4) the importance of energy and engineering factors, and (5) the behavioral and perceptual characteristics of MNC executives. Although environmental differentials may seem persuasive when viewed in isolation, under *ceteris paribus* assumptions, their significance for inducing "real-world" locational spillovers can be properly appraised only within the complete structure of costs, risks, and returns that are considered when investment location decisions are made.

RECENT MNC LOCATIONAL BEHAVIOR. There is little solid evidence of international locational spillover activity, with exceptions in the cases of certain copper smelters and petroleum refineries in the United States, chemical plants in certain European countries, and heavy industry in Japan as part of its program of industrial decentralization.[45] Most locational spillovers to date have stemmed from explicit or implicit blockage of preferred sites, which has occurred largely in high density and/or high per capita income regions such as the Mid-Atlantic and Northeastern states of the United States, the Rijnmond and Amsterdam areas of the Netherlands, the Rhein, Ruhr, and Elbe River valleys of West Germany, and the States of Victoria and New South Wales in Australia. Participatory activism, marked by a profusion of citizen groups willing to oppose projects subject to administrative approval, can be viewed as the major reason for locational impasse in most of these regions. Representative blocked projects involving

MNCs include Progil's proposed carbon disulfide plant near Amsterdam, Hoesch–Hoogovens' proposed steel mill near Rotterdam, Shell's proposed refinery in Delaware, and BASF's proposed petrochemical complex in South Carolina.[46]

Strident environmentalist opposition in congested, developed areas has not generally led to automatic international spillovers of discouraged investment. A review of over 50 cases of preproject MNC-environmental group conflict reveals that most projects have only been delayed, not totally blocked.[47] Moreover, intranational, rather than international, shifting is still feasible (e.g., to the Southeast in the United States, the North in the Netherlands, the West in Australia, etc.), and is an option that appears to be heavily utilized.[48] Rather than face the socioenvironmental problems associated with breaking virgin land for plant sites, many MNCs have chosen to expand, if at all possible, at existing sites.[49] In sum, expansions at present sites, internal shifts at the national level, and acceptance of time-consuming delays appear to be site-location options that are attempted before resorting to alternate foreign locations.

FOREIGN DIRECT-INVESTMENT MOTIVATIONS.   Predictions of environment-induced international shifts in industrial location are usually based on either simple multiplant locational theory, classical profit differential capital movement theory, or competitive international trade theory with its emphasis on factor prices and factor endowments. Each of these models is of only limited utility in explaining the level and pattern of postwar foreign direct investment (FDI).[50] Investment decisions are usually the result of a complex amalgam of factors, with costs in rival locations frequently playing only a minor role.[51] As shown in Fig. 8-2, the determinants of FDI are many and varied.[52] Factors relevant to explanation of FDI fall into six categories: industrial organization, international economics, locational economics, organizational behavior, political science, and business investment. The significance of differentials in the environmental factor, included in Fig. 8-2 in the locational economics group, for flows of FDI can only be properly appraised when simultaneous consideration is afforded to the many other independent variables that bear on plant siting decisions.

The most powerful determinants of FDI lie in the realm of industrial organization.[53] The bulk of FDI occurs in oligopolistically structured industries, with horizontal investments typically being made in the pursuit and protection of markets, and vertical investments typically being made in the pursuit and protection of controlled sources of raw materials supply. FDI is often based on "monopolistic advantage" in the form of managerial, technological, or marketing know-how and experience, and as such is only loosely related to national factor endowments or comparative advantage.

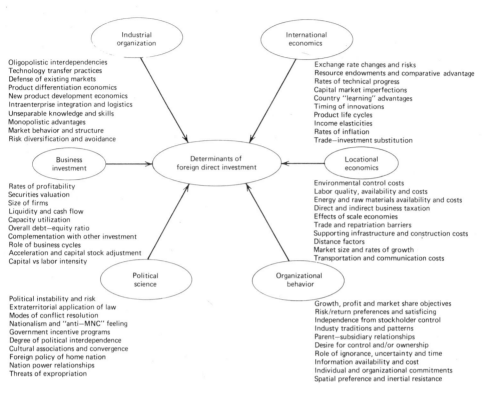

Figure 8-2   An eclectic view of the determinants of foreign direct investment.

Also, oligopolistic responses may play a dominant role in the behavior of FDI, with the phenomenon of "cross-hauling" (i.e., simultaneous FDI by firms in the same industry, from different home countries, in each other's markets) representing a classic example. The recent investments in the United States by Pechiney, Alusuisse, British Petroleum, BASF, Akzo, ICI, Hoeschst, Ciba-Geigy, Bowater, Dunlop, and Georgetown Steel, for example, certainly are evidence that nonenvironmental FDI criteria were sufficiently well satisfied to decide in favor of a nation with stringent pollution-control standards. In short, FDI is motivated by profit expectations, but these are broadly conceived as involving more than rate of return on investment narrowly defined, and are viewed in a long-term (5–10 years), rather than a short-term (1 or 2 years) fashion. The emphasis on long-term, strategic, and oligopolistic factors strongly implies that the flow of FDI is unlikely to be sensitive to environmental policy differentials that are either of a short-term nature or give the appearance of being tentative or impermanent.

CHARACTER OF "POLLUTION HAVENS."   Another problem is the higher cost and/or higher degree of risk entailed in "pollution haven" investments. If we equate "pollution havens" with developing countries in Latin America, Africa, Asia, and the Middle East, then certain cost/risk factors are present. Strong nationalistic sentiment and "anti-MNC feeling" has been evident in many of these nations. Recent events involving oil in the Middle East, copper in Latin America, and aluminum in the Caribbean dramatize the deterioration of "investment climates" in this part of the world, and some of the relevant governments may be politically unstable as well. Most of these countries are poor, lacking the necessary market size and purchasing power to provide indigenous demand for large scale manufacturing plants with low unit costs. If the investment is to be export-oriented, then frequently large transport costs will be incurred in getting the product to market. Supporting infrastructure, both for industry and foreign management, is often lacking with the result, for example, that plant construction costs and necessary management compensation can be 15–50% higher than in home countries. Rampant inflation, rapidly depreciating currencies, constraints on profit repatriation, demands for local content, threats of expropriation, and so on, may also be factors to consider. In short, the political and economic disadvantage to such nations may easily counterbalance gains in reduced environmental costs.

ENERGY AND ENGINEERING FACTORS.   Analysis of pollution-intensive industries must take into account that these industries are typically energy-intensive, capital-intensive, technology-intensive, industrial-market-intensive, and transport-intensive. The relative importance of pollution control as a cost element is often exaggerated by expressing it as a percentage of capital investment; in all but a few of the most pollutive industries, pollution-control costs amount to less than 5% of the value of plant shipments.[54] Energy or transport costs often outweigh this element by a factor of three to four. It may thus be realistic to focus instead on energy-induced locational shifts of certain industries; for many MNCs, declining availability and steeply rising costs have made energy a principal factor in site selection. A movement of petrochemical and chemical firms that depend on low-cost energy and low-cost hydrocarbon feedstocks to the Middle East seems already to have begun.[55]

Just as industrial location may be constrained by energy or feedstock considerations, it may also be constrained (or determined) by such factors as access to deepwater port facilities, access to existing industrial facilities, or location of ore bodies and other raw materials. All of these factors further reduce the "freedom" of MNCs to seek out low-environmental-cost locations. Engineering factors may also be biased against locational flight. Multicountry sourcing patterns, with goals of interchangeability in source of supply in case of strikes, rebellions, and the like, frequently demand similarity in quality control and production processes in plants in different countries. Moreover, new industrial plants are designed by professional engineers, who, preferring to work at the forefront of technology, are biased towards high quality, more efficient, and more automated process technologies. Process technology selection for overseas plants has been found to be rather insensitive to leniency of environmental regulations; MNCs generally move abroad with "off-the-shelf" plant designs and with their newest, most efficient process technologies.[56] Finally, correcting environmental problems in existing plants at future dates with "band-aid" remedies to meet increasingly stringent pollution regulations can frequently be more costly and inefficient than building preventive antipollution measures into the plant design right from the start.

MANAGERIAL BEHAVIOR AND PERCEPTIONS.   Except for export-oriented investment projects, alternative locations do not generally play an important role in the FDI process. MNC managers typically investigate a *specific* investment opportunity only in response to a *specific* threat to their existing operations in the local market.[57] Managers frequently exhibit a home-country preference, and often overestimate the risks and underestimate the returns of FDI.[58] Since plant lives usually extend anywhere from 15 to 40 years, the time horizons in new FDI are typically long-term (5-10 years ahead), and FDI is thus influenced more by prospects for long-range profit than by immediate short-term gain.

The attitudes and perceptions held by MNC managers, indeed, often run counter to the locational spillover argument. Current intercountry differences in environmental norms are viewed by many executives as only transient in nature. Most expect substantial convergence to occur over the next 10 years, especially within the developed world, but also with regard to nations such as Mexico and Brazil.[59] Further, some executives are fearful that locational shifting might backfire, in terms of giving rise to home country commercial policy measures that block the products of "locational flight" and "environmental sweatshops." Other executives note that poor environmental performance in a developing country may provide just another target for cries of "exploitation" and "imperialism" by ambitious politicians or national elites. Perhaps more significant, many executives believe that current discouragement of new industry in the developed countries is only a transitory phenomenon. Many point to the setbacks to environmentalists caused by the recent energy crisis hysteria as an indication that strident opposition to new plants may soon decline.[60] Finally, probably nothing is more effective against opposition to plant expansion than unemployment; if joblessness continues to rise, undoubtedly those MNCs still desirous of expansion in home countries will encounter less opposition.

SUMMARY: ENVIRONMENT-INDUCED SHIFTS IN LOCATIONAL POLICY. Predictions of MNC behavior are notoriously unreliable. Not withstanding this caveat, we offer this assessment of the international locational spillover issue: Flows of foreign direct investment do not appear, as yet, to differ substantially from what would be expected in the absence of environment-induced locational shifts except in a few instances. More importantly, we do not expect a flow of environment-induced FDI of any real significance to materialize in the future. For the reasons obviously demonstrated by Fig. 8-2 and discussed above, we believe the elasticity of FDI with respect to environmental differentials to be rather low. A slight shift at the margin has, indeed, been introduced into the locational calculus of FDI, but for most MNCs the shift will not be significant enough to counterbalance the higher costs and risks involved in seeking out a developing nation "pollution haven" for major new facilities. MNCs will of course try to locate in areas in which all costs (energy, environmental, political, labor, transport, etc.) are minimized. FDI will of course, continue to flow to developing nations, especially those with stable governments and indigenous natural resources, but for intrinsic reasons largely unrelated to lower environmental costs.

Environmentally Oriented MNC Project Planning

While MNC locational decisions will not generally be very sensitive to the stringency of environmental laws and regulations, this represents only one component of the broader role that environmental factors play in MNC project planning. In what manner and to what extent have environmental considerations been incorporated into MNC project planning, and why? Some answers to these questions are provided by one of the research efforts supporting this chapter that investigated whether an environmentally oriented mode of planning was being utilized by MNCs in the overall process of project design.[61] Twenty-one recently planned projects were studied in the field research. These ranged in cost from $35 million to $5.5 billion, were executed by 15 different MNCs in the chemical, metals, and petroleum industries, originated in six different home nations, and were directed to 13 different host nations.

IN WHAT MANNER HAVE ENVIRONMENTAL FACTORS BEEN INCOR-
PORATED? Table 8-2 provides the percentage results of measuring and
classifying the surveyed projects on the basis of 26 indicators of environmentally oriented planning behavior, grouped into six dimensions. These dimensions and indicators were derived from a fusion of principles of effective
preproject environmental-impact assessment into the behavioral characteristics of the MNC project planning process.[62] Keeping in mind that
specific behavior varies widely, as reflected in the distribution of
percentages across the three categories on all of the indicators, the following brief observations can be offered with regard to the typical manner in
which environmental considerations have been injected into the process of
MNC project planning.

Environmental Science Professionals are Frequently Involved. Most of
the involvement consists of part-time advice and assistance, but occasionally of full-time membership on the planning team on the part of
internal environmental engineering staff personnel. For reasons of needed
expertise and "credibility," external environmental professionals are also
frequently brought into the planning process, but usually at a late stage for
investigations at the site location.

Some Use is Made of Systematic Methods. Systematic residuals discharge monitoring and prestart-up baseline surveys, both apparently done
for essentially defensive reasons, are quite commonly employed. Systematic
preproject environmental-impact assessment and poststart-up ecological impact monitoring are employed much less frequently, and rather reluctantly,
in order to satisfy the planning approval process.

Attention is Given Only to Process Pollution. Planning attention is
usually focused on issues of process-related residuals discharge, with only
shallow attention generally being directed to potential environmental consequences associated with other project actions such as construction and
transportation. Attention to pollution control in the selection of process
technology is most significant when the project involves a new engineering
challenge or unsolved environmental problems. In addition to being primarily focused on residuals-discharge, environmental factors are typically
brought into the planning process in a rather fragmentary, compart-
mentalized fashion. Integrative and holistic environmental impact thinking
is rarely found.

Project Planning is a Closed, Nonparticipatory Process. MNC project
planning is typically secretive, exclusionist, low profile, and "official-chan-
nels-only" in character. Participation of potentially affected publics is
rarely solicited. Such efforts are made (if at all) just prior to any formal
public hearing, with few exceptions.

Consideration of Environment is Usually Only at a Late Stage. The in-

Table 8-2 Environmentally Oriented MNC Project Planning Behavior (Dimensions, Indicators, and Findings)[a]

| | % of MNC Projects Scoring | | |
| | Low or No | Medium or Partly | High or Yes |
Dimensions and Indicators			
Professional Involvement			
1. Current involvement of internal corporate environmental staff	7	40	53
2. Current involvement of external environmental professionals	33	13	53
3. Current involvement of multi-disciplinary environmental expertise	40	7	53
4. Previous relevant involvement of environmental professionals	27	20	53
Systematization			
1. Prestart-up ecological baseline survey	33	7	60
2. Formal preproject environmental-impact assessment	53	20	27
3. Program of residuals discharge monitoring	7	7	87
4. Program of site location environmental media monitoring	53	20	27
5. Previous relevant environmental investigations	20	27	53
Inclusiveness			
1. Comprehensive prestart-up ecological baseline survey	40	7	53
2. Environmental-impact criteria employed in site selection	40	40	20
3. Environmental-impact criteria employed in process technology selection	20	27	53
4. Comprehensive scope of environmental impact causing actions considered	47	20	33
5. Environmental-impact criteria previously employed in design of process technology	13	53	33

Table 8-2 Continued

	% of MNC Projects Scoring		
Dimensions and Indicators	Low or No	Medium or Partly	High or Yes
Public Participation			
1. Utilization of locally based environmental consultants	33	20	47
2. Surveys of local environmental values and perceptions	67	20	13
3. Active seeking of community and citizen group input	40	33	27
4. Initiation of community information program	47	27	27
5. Initiation of special educational efforts	53	7	40
6. Previous relevant interaction with publics on environmental aspects of project	7	47	47
Continuousness			
1. Early citizen participation in planning process	47	33	20
2. Early ecological baseline survey in planning process	33	40	27
3. Early inputs on environmental impact from previous experience	33	27	40
Formalization			
1. Environmental section in formal project proposal	20	13	67
2. Top management environmental review and approval	53	33	13
3. Corporate environmental staff environmental review and approval	0	47	53

[a] Source: Thomas N. Gladwin, *The Role of Ecological Considerations* loc. cit., Chapter IV.

corporation of environmental considerations is discontinuous in nature, coming largely at very late stages in the planning process. Most site-location, ecological baseline research, for example, is done only after approval has been received, preliminary construction activity has already begun, and the range of choice has been narrowed to a single favored project design. Project design choices are principally guided by the "pool of accumulated environmental knowledge" possessed by the MNCs by virtue of similar prior project planning experience and previous environmental research and remedial efforts carried out at similar existing facilities. MNCs appear averse to building into their planning processes the time necessary for thorough preproject, on-site environmental research.

The Process is Formalized on the Matter of Environmental Spending. Many MNCs have established formal rules and procedures for considering environmental factors during planning, but these largely relate to pollution-control expenditure considerations and late stage environmental staff office project reviews. MNC top managements rarely review separately the environmental aspects of a proposed project, but generally consider these matters, if at all, in the context of the regular capital appropriation and review procedure.

TO WHAT EXTENT AND WHY HAVE ENVIRONMENTAL FACTORS BEEN INCORPORATED?   On the basis of calculated composite "scores" for each project across all six dimensions and associated indicators, a wide range of behavior was discovered.[63] Environmental factors have been incorporated quite exiguously in some MNC project planning processes, moderately in others, and quite extensively in still others. In terms of modal behavior, however, it can be concluded that the practice of environmentally oriented MNC project planning is still in its infancy. In only a little over one-third of the cases was careful thought and attention being accorded to environmental effects and costs during the course of planning. The intellectual exercise of asking, analyzing, and answering the question, "what impact will this project have on the environment?" has generally not yet been made an integral part of MNC project planning.

What explains the extent to which a MNC's project planning process is environmentally oriented (i.e., a high composite score achieved across all of the indicators in Table 8-2 versus a low score)? Table 8-3 contains a listing of possible explanatory variables and their correlation coefficients with the composite index of environmentally oriented project planning. In short, the field work on which this table is based showed that the extent to which environmental considerations are embodied in a given MNC project planning process is a function of an interaction among: (1) the nature of the project; (2) the internal organizational context of the project planning process; and

Table 8-3 Environmentally Oriented MNC Project Planning Behavior (Explanatory Variables and Correlations)[a]

Explanatory Variable	Rank Order Correlation with Composite Index of Environmentally Oriented Planning[b]
Nature of Project	
1. Project Cost (total cost of the project)	0.6952*
2. Project Type (relative severity and range of potential, associated adverse environmental impacts)	0.5820*
3. Site Location Type (extent to which the site location of the project is currently nonindustrial in character)	0.3892***
4. Project Ownership (extent of project ownership by firm)	−0.0587
5. Project Year (year in which project was undertaken)	−0.1040
Organizational Characteristics	
1. Environmental Objectives (extent to which firm is committed to objectives of environmentally responsible behavior)	0.5087**
2. Environmental Surveillance and Interaction (extent of surveillance of, interaction with, and internal dissemination of information about plans of external environmental reference groups)	0.4938**
3. Company Investment Intensiveness (relative size of firm's capital spending program; capital expenditure to total asset ratio 1971–1973)	0.4252**
4. Environmental Role Assignment (extent to which firm has assigned personnel to formal environmental roles)	0.3086
5. Company Size (relative size of firm; average sales 1971–1973)	0.2706
6. Company Profitability (relative profitability of the firm; profit to sales ratio 1971–1973)	0.1933
7. Environmental Performance Measurement (extent to which plant and managerial environmental performance is measured and evaluated)	0.1627
8. Environmental Research and Technology (extent to which firm has researched and developed environmental technology relevant to the project)	0.1014

Table 8-3   Continued

Explanatory Variable	Rank Order Correlation with Composite Index of Environmentally Oriented Planning[b]
Public Policy Characteristics	
1. Project Associated Public Pressures (intensity of project-associated public pressures for environmental protection)	0.5648*
2. Environmental Conflict Experience (extent of conflict over environmental issues experienced by the firm during the 5 years prior to the project)	0.4080***
3. Public Project Examination (extent of environmental impact related public project examination via hearings, impact statements, permissions, etc.)	0.4046***
4. Home Country Environmental Policy (extent of governmental intervention, amount of public attention, and duration of intervention and attention in firm's home country)	0.2530
5. Host Country Environmental Policy (extent of governmental intervention, amount of public attention, and duration of intervention and attention in host country receiving the project)	0.1561

[a] Source: Gladwin, *The Role of Ecological Considerations*, loc. cit., Chapter VIII.
[b] Kendall Rank Correlation Coefficients (Tau); Significance Levels: * = 0.01 level, ** = 0.05 level, *** = 0.10 level.

(3) the public policy context of the firm and the given project being planned.[64]

The Influence of Project Nature.   As shown in Table 8-3, two aspects related to the nature of the project being planned are highly correlated with environmentally oriented project planning behavior.[65] Greater *project cost* seems to be associated with greater top management attention to the environmental path of the planning process, and also appears to motivate the early incorporation of environmental factors for risk-reduction purposes (i.e., avoidance of delays and terminations). The relative severity/range of potentially adverse environmental impacts associated with the *type of project* involved also appears to be important. More time and energy is generally devoted to the consideration of environmental factors when the project has the potential of creating more serious environmental problems.

The Influence of Organization. Environmentally oriented project planning is more likely when: (1) the MNC's *objectives for environmental protection* have been made formally explicit, expressed in leadership terms, applied globally, and backed by considerable evidence of top management support; and (2) the MNC engages in considerable external *surveillance of, interaction with, and internal dissemination* of information about the actions and plans of government environmental agencies, industry environmental organizations, and citizen environmental groups.[66] Firmly held corporate objectives for environmentally responsible behavior appear to provide project planners with considerable guidance in incorporating environmental factors. External surveillance and interaction facilitate such incorporation. Such interorganizational interaction implies greater exposure to new ideas of advance environmental planning, more feedback on the satisfactions and intentions of normative environmental reference groups, and greater access to the exponentially increasing body of research and knowledge concerning environmental impact. Objectives and surveillance thus appear to represent necessary conditions for environmentally oriented planning, as well as for other aspects of MNC's environmental management structure—such as role assignment, performance measurement, and research and technology programs.

The Influence of Public Policy. As partly indicated by the correlations shown in Table 8-3, but more fully via an extended partial correlation analysis, much of the motivation for environmentally oriented project planning behavior appears to be either directly or indirectly derived from public policy variables.[67] *Public pressures* for environmental protection in the locality, and especially resistance to the specific project—from government environmental agencies, citizen groups, and the media—appear to strongly induce environmentally oriented planning behavior on the part of MNCs. Such behavior is induced both in anticipation of expected pressures, and in reaction to actual felt pressures. The extent to which institutional arrangements are available for *public examination* of the project also appears to be a powerful motivator. Dramatically more time and energy is generally devoted to the consideration of environmental factors when the MNC knows that it will be required to disclose and articulate the basis of its environmental-impact judgments and control plans in a public forum. Public pressures and public examination largely explain the close relationships observed above between environmentally oriented planning and project cost and project type. Pressures are typically more intense, and the public scrutiny more comprehensive, the larger the scale (cost) of the project, and the more severe the potential environmental consequences associated with the type of project.

Perhaps the most interesting public policy finding is that the amount of *prior external conflict* (in the form of project delays and terminations, forced plant closing, adverse publicity, and litigation) experienced by the MNC on environmental issues with publics and governmental bodies, represents an important determinant of current environmentally oriented planning behavior. Such prior conflict appears to create well-perceived "performance gaps," to catalyze top management attention, and to emphasize the relative advantage of innovative planning behavior. In addition to stimulating the adoption of innovative environmental planning practices directly, the extent of prior conflict also has an indirect influence. The MNCs that currently possess the most deep-seated environmental objectives, have the fullest environmental role assignment, and engage in the most environmental surveillance are generally the same ones which have experienced the most prior environment-related external conflict. Some of the strong relationships discussed above under organization can thus be partly explained by the antecedent influence of prior conflict. In sum, concern for environmental protection is generally further institutionalized, and applied in the course of planning, in those MNCs that have experienced the greatest amount of conflict in the past.

CONCLUSIONS AND PUBLIC POLICY IMPLICATIONS

Conclusions

Seven interrelated conclusions can be drawn from our review of MNC strategic behavior patterns in response to diversity among national environmental policy systems.

EMBRYONIC STATE OF RESEARCH. The body of theory and empirical research regarding MNC strategic adaptation in response to environmental policy is in a formative state. We are only beginning to understand the system of economic, organizational, and political forces that determine the behavior of MNCs in this area. If we want to be able to better explain, predict, and control the key variables associated with their behavior, then more knowledge is required. At the descriptive level, more needs to be known about how MNC managers relate their firms to environmental problems and the difficulties of doing so. At the normative level, alternative conceptions of the role of the MNC in relation to global environmental problems need to be formulated and systematically explored.

"UNECOLOGICAL" BEHAVIOR AND RESISTANCE TO CHANGE. MNCs have been spending large sums of money on pollution control in recent years, with some abatement efforts extending back several decades. A few of the MNCs included in our field research are compiling commendable records in environmental activities. However, the findings show that the decision-making and planning behavior of the bulk of MNCs contacted can still be characterized as being "unecological." Continuous, careful thought and attention is not being given to environmental impacts in project planning or product development. It is of course unreasonable to expect immediate behavioral adaptation, but the fact remains that in most MNCs the practice of environmentally oriented planning is still in its infancy. The major forces impeding environmental reorientation are organizational inertia, insensitivity, and resistance. MNCs appear resistant to complicating or "contaminating" traditional management patterns—particularly in areas of operating autonomy, decentralized planning, and financially oriented performance measurement and evaluation—that have been quite successful in the past.

FRAGMENTED AND DECENTRALIZED APPROACHES TO ENVIRONMENTAL MANAGEMENT.   MNCs included in our research have responded to a structure of environmental policy diversity among nations, with a pattern of strategic behavior that closely mirrors this diversity. The environmental management function is handled by MNCs in their various countries of operation in a typically fragmented, "local adaptation" manner. This is true for most areas of organizational environmental behavior, including objectives, role assignment, pollution abatement, performance measurement, public and governmental relations, and research and development. In addition to being fragmented, the environmental managment function is also handled as a decentralized decision-responsibility area. The "locus" of decision-making is decentralized not only geographically, but divisionally and functionally as well. So far, very few MNCs have found real benefits in, or real pressures for, a multinational approach to environmental management controlled and directed from headquarters, although a movement in this direction can be discerned.

ADAPTATION AS A DYNAMIC, EVOLUTIONARY PROCESS.   MNC behavioral adaptation in response to pressures for environmental protection was found to be a dynamic, evolutionary process in the firms contacted. Corporate environmental objectives and policies change over time. Environmental staff roles are created and eliminated. Efforts to "map" external environmental pressures are at first exploratory, then extensive, and then routinized. Attention is sequentially focused on curing problems in existing operations, and only later on preventing problems in prospective operations. Emphasis in environmental R&D shifts in response to awareness of new problems. Industry organizations are created in response to governmental initiatives so that MNC interests can be articulated. The institutionalization process advances at different rates in different geographic, functional, and divisional parts of the MNC. Within any one part, the speed of adaptation appears to hinge on the overall adaptiveness of the unit as well as on the intensity of external pressures. Concern for environmental protection is generally institutionalized further in MNCs that have been exposed to the influence of progressive national environmental policy and that have experienced a great deal of prior external conflict over environmental issues (adverse publicity, blocked or delayed projects, and so forth).

DOMINANT HOLDER AND TRANSFER AGENT OF ENVIRONMENTAL TECHNOLOGY. MNCs are the dominant source and developer of technology and expertise needed for solving the world's industrial environmental problems. They are also the dominant institutions transferring, directly and indirectly, such resources across national borders. Although the international transfer of environmental technology within a MNC is not instantaneous or complete due to the fragmented and decentralized approach of these firms to environmental matters, it is clear that MNCs are serving to accelerate the international diffusion of such technology. MNCs are geared to the pragmatic issues of engineering and managing change. These capabilities are directed towards solving environmental problems when clear and effective public policies have been designed within a nation to guide or constrain corporate behavior.

INSENSITIVITY OF MNC LOCATIONAL DECISIONS TO ENVIRONMENTAL FACTORS. Our findings indicate that most MNC locational decisions are not sensitive to near-term intercountry variation in environmental standards and programs. The importance of environment-induced "locational flight" to "pollution havens" has been overestimated. A review of the complete and complex structure of costs, risks, and returns that guide foreign investment decisions indicates that the elasticity of flows of foreign direct investment with regard to environmental differentials in likely to be fairly low in all but a few special cases. Recent MNC locational behavior, the motivations of foreign investment, the characteristics of "pollution havens," various energy and engineering factors, the dependence of MNCs on well-developed, infrastructures, and the perception of MNC executives all appear to be biased against environment-induced locational shifting.

NARROWNESS OF PRESENT MNC ENVIRONMENTAL BEHAVIOR. In the MNCs examined, environmental thinking and action is focused primarily on residuals-discharge or pollution control. The broader concepts included in the term environmental management are seldom applied.[68] Mindful of the cost-benefit tradeoffs involved, most MNCs have a great deal of room for innovating in such areas as: incorporating ecological factors in plant siting and project design analyses; adopting a mode of planning that is environmentally more open and participatory; substituting nonpolluting materials for polluting ones; designing processes, products, and facilities to conserve energy and materials; and designing products for ease of maintenance, long life, reuse, reclamation, and recyling. In the longer run, complex questions dealing with the total system of the energy–resources–food–population–pollution–technology problems confronting mankind will inevitably be added to the agendas of MNCs. At stake, given recent trends, will be how to achieve a long-term sustainable relationship, in the broadest sense, between MNCs and the Earth. Consideration of this issue will require reexamination of traditional economic concepts about growth, capital incentives, interest rates, corporate standards of performance, and tax and regulatory policy. Consideration of this issue, in short, will require rather fundamental changes in present management and political thinking, and may necessitate acceptance of rather revolutionary notions about stewardship of the planet's resources by MNCs.[69]

Public Policy Implications

A number of implications for public policy emerge from the research findings and conclusions presented in this chapter. The implications relate to environmental problems caused by MNC behavior, as well as to economic problems induced by this behavior. Attention is first addressed to environmental and economic policy implications at the international level, and then briefly directed to environmental-policy implications at the national level. Discussions of national economic implications (e.g., adjustment assistance programs, commercial policy measures, etc.) can be found in other chapters in this volume,[70] and discussions of corporate policy implications can be found in other works by the authors.[71]

AT THE INTERNATIONAL LEVEL. Do we need international regulation of the environmental behavior of MNCs? The answer appears to depend on the character of MNC-created problems in question. Where the environmental consequences are locally confined, the answer is probably no. Where the problems are transnational, such as sulfur dioxide in Northern Europe,[72] the answer is probably that regional attention or regulation is required. In the case of truly global problems, such as threats to the oceans, persistant pesticides, and carbon dioxide in the atmosphere, the answer is probably yes.[73] Truly international action with regard to MNC behavior would seem to be most appropriate only for MNC-induced problems relating to international common property and public-good resources. In such cases, equitable and effective solutions cannot be achieved without mutual consultation, coordination, and concerted action on the part of all nations concerned.

Are MNCs desirous of international environmental regulation? The answer is clearly no. MNCs as a group have exhibited no great enthusiasm for a coordinated approach by sovereign states to environmental policy, with some exceptions in the product areas that are discussed below. MNCs appear to prefer to deal with issues of environmental policy on a national or even a "local accommodation" basis, without trying to elevate these matters to the intergovernmental level. They tend to fear their flexibility of action (i.e., factor cost exploitation and resource allocation) would be constrained by international regulation. This implies that pressure for international agreements or regulations is likely to come from governments and not from MNCs.

Do we need harmonized or even uniform national environmental policies to mitigate the economic problems induced by MNC behavior? For reasons discussed above,[74] the substance, intensity, timing, and enforcement of environmental policies differs substantially between nations. Many have argued that this diversity will lead to trade distortions, locational spillovers, and "foot dragging" on the part of both governments and MNCs.[75] Concern with competitive dislocations has lead to proposals for establishing uniform environmental standards in different countries.

MNCs are well equipped to exploit differences in factor costs in various national jurisdictions, including opportunities afforded by differences in environmental standards. We have seen that such differentials are indeed exploited in current operations (i.e., local adaptation), but are not likely to induce a massive relocation of existing or prospective operations. To the extent that such environmental relocations do occur, however—given no transnational externalities and heterogeneous but "optimal" national environmental standards[76]—they are probably desirable from a global efficiency viewpoint. The efficiency gains would result from an improved resource allocation that reflects differences in comparative advantage based on different social preferences and environmental assimiliative capacities. Uniform standards of a process emission variety would serve to reduce the amount of locational spillovers, and hence the size of associated efficiency gains. Uniform standards on process emissions, assuming no transfrontier effects, would thus fail to achieve Pareto optimality in the international allocation of environmental resources. Such standards, besides being institutionally impossible to achieve, would clearly be inconsistent with the objective of maximum welfare for the international community.[77]

The case for uniform standards in controlling MNC behavior is not, however, completely negative. Certain kinds of uniform standards, in certain situations, can be useful and effective.[78] This is so because the assumptions used above of "no transnational externalities" and "optimal national standards" are often unrealistic. Where the environmental effects induced by MNC activity in one location cross national boundaries into a shared airshed or watershed, the imposition of uniform standards could be useful in establishing the ambient concentration of emissions in these common property resources. Where the national standards are less than optimal, the induced locational spillovers are likely to result in an inefficient international allocation of environmental resources. This implies that uniform standards could be useful in establishing certain minimal baseline standards that would prevent this from occurring. Uniform international standards for maximum permissable human biological exposure and concentration (e.g., in the cases of heavy metals, radiation, insectides, toxic chemicals, etc.) would be appropriate for this role.

Although MNCs are opposed to uniformity in production process emission and effluent standards, they will often support harmonization efforts in the area of product performance, operating and disposal standards when wider markets and reduced costs can be attained. Seven European automotive manufacturers, for example, fearful that export manufacturing costs would get out of hand if separate production lines or runs were required to meet differing national environmental and safety standards, banded together in 1972 to push for harmonization.[79] Here the common standards are being motivated not by an international agreement, but by market forces.

In light of the regulation and harmonization arguments discussed above, what are the bases for effective international action? The logic of symmetry between government and the governed has led some to propose a supranational environmental protection agency to regulate the environmental behavior of MNCs.[80] This notion is probably neither feasible nor desirable at present. Given the currently deep-seated differences among countries on environmental policy and strong resistance to erosion of sovereignty in this area, it is unrealistic at this stage to expect that nations would voluntarily cede sovereignty in this area to an international body.[81] There is presently little conviction on the need for such an agency on the part of those who would have to create it. If created, it would certainly suffer from massive problems of surveillance and enforcement.

Others have proposed the extraterritorial application of national environmental policy to cover the foreign operations of home-based MNCs.[82] This might involve prohibiting the overseas sale of environmentally hazardous substances banned at home, environmental-impact statements for overseas projects requiring prior approval or facilitation by the home government, required disclosure of environmental spending in overseas plants, and so forth. Such unilateral action to regulate the behavior of MNCs abroad would surely run into problems regarding extraterritorial applicability of national law.

Still others have advanced the idea of self-regulation through codes of conduct. Recently the International Chamber of Commerce promulgated a set of 34 rather broad-guage "Environmental Guidelines for World Industry."[83] While such voluntary guidelines undoubtedly will have some educational value, just how influential they will be is difficult to judge. It is easy for a MNC to commit itself to the guidelines because of their general nature and the lack of a monitoring mechanism.

While the changes of effective international regulation appear remote, the forces for harmonization of environmental policies among nations, at least within the industrialized world, are already at work. The Organization for Economic Cooperation and Development (OECD), despite inefficiences due to a diffusion of interests, has drafted and adopted the Polluter Pays Principle, and is encouraging its 21 member nations to formulate national policy accordingly.[84] In practice it is proving extraordinarly difficult to define what this principle means and how it should be applied. In another move for harmonization, the Environment Ministers of the OECD nations recently adopted ten recommendations for guiding the formulation of environmental policy.[85] The European Economic Commission (ECC) is also seeking to achieve harmonization of environmental policies and legislation. Through its Program of Action it is beginning to lay down "quality objectives" at the community level, and to establish "basic protection levels" for a range of pollutants.[86] The United Nations Environment Programme (UNEP), is another force on the side of harmonization, and appears to be well launched in providing a framework and the means for international cooperation of a global scale.[87]

AT THE NATIONAL LEVEL. In our opinion, several themes running through the foregoing discussions should be taken as given in the background of national environmental policy-making.
These are:

- As supranational regulation will be slow in coming, the individual nation state will remain as the primary locus of power over the environmental behavior of MNCs into the indefinite future.
- MNCs have a substantial impact on global environmental quality— directly in terms of resource consumption and residuals generation, and indirectly in terms of consumer use and disposal of their products.

- Little can be expected from altruistic, voluntary behavior—MNC environmental behavior is largely determined by economics except as modified by measures adopted by public authorities.
- Adaptation of MNC behavior along environmental lines is a dynamic, evolutionary process, the pace of which is largely determined by exposure to progressive public policy and conflict on issues of environmental impact.
- MNCs are the dominant sources and developers of technology needed for solving industrial environmental problems. Subsidiaries are able to tap this pool of resources and will do so when pressed by host country demands.
- International locational spillovers attributable to local and regional environmental policies are not likely to be very significant as long as the policies are within reasonable bounds. Threats of locational shifting on the part of MNCs need not be taken very seriously except when clean-up costs are unusually heavy, for example, nonferrous metal smelters.
- Attention to environmental degradation, despite recent erosion as a result of increased economic difficulties and the energy crisis, is now deeply and irrevocably implanted as a major public concern in most developed countries.

The behavior of MNCs depends, in short, on the environmental management capabilities of national and local governments. The concrete institutional arrangements and social controls appropriate for any particular political jurisdiction will of course rest on a number of political, economic, social, and ecological conditions. Some of the more powerful techniques for reorienting MNC behavior that might be considered, however, include: (1) incorporating environmental-impact criteria into MNC entry evaluation and review procedures, by means of an environmental-impact statement requirement;[88] (2) establishing the citizen's right, where it does not exist, to bring suit against, and investing the courts with authority to review, MNC actions;[89] (3) reducing the many barriers to citizen participation in public decision-making on MNC projects subject to administrative approval;[90] (4) broadening control over the use of land, and developing comprehensive regional land-use plans that allow MNC planners to gauge the long-run compatability of their proposed projects;[91] and (5) creating and maintaining effective environmental policy-making and policy-implementing organizations within the nation.[92] All of these techniques represent powerful levers for motivating MNCs to find ways of minimizing or avoiding damage to the environment.[93] As with all endeavors, however, it is to be hoped that reason will prevail in the use of such levers, since environmental quality is but one of society's many aspirations.[94]

ACKNOWLEDGMENTS

The authors express their appreciation to the following institutions which either supported or facilitated the research on which this article is based: Tennéco Inc., Institute for International Commerce in the Graduate School of Business Administration at the University of Michigan, Centre d'Etudes Industrielles, Business International S.A., Colorado School of Mines, University of Denver Research Institute, and the Secretariat of the United Nations Conference on the Human Environment. The authors also thank Dr. Ingo Walter of New York University for his invaluable comments on an earlier draft of this chapter. The views expressed, of course, are those of the authors alone, and do not necessarily represent the views of the reviewers and supporting organizations identified above.

NOTES

1.   United Nations Department of Economic and Social Affairs, *Multinational Corporations in World Development,* ST/ECA/190, New York: United Nations, 1973, p. 13.

2.   The Diebold Institute, *Business and Developing Countries: A Study of the Role of Private Enterprise in Economic Development* (New York: Praeger, 1973, p. 5.

3.   Richard Eells, "Do Multinational Corporations Stand Guilty as Charged?" *Business and Society Review,* 11, 1974, p. 82.

4.   See: Stephen Hymer, "Is the Multinational Corporation Doomed?" *Innovation,* 28 1972, pp. 10–17; and Norman Macrae, "The Future of International Business," *The Economist,* Jan. 22, 1972, pp. xxi–xxii.

5.   The relevant research of both authors is briefly described in the second section. Only part of the research by Welles has been previously published. See: John G. Welles, "Multinationals Need New Environmental Strategies," *Columbia Journal of World Business, 8,* 1973, pp. 11–18. The research by Gladwin has only recently been completed. See: Thomas N. Gladwin, *The Role of Ecological Considerations in the Multinational Corporate Project Planning Process: A Comparative Study of North American- and Western European-Based Petroleum, Chemicals and Metals Firms,"* unpublished Ph.D. dissertation, Graduate School of Business Administration, The University of Michigan, Ann Arbor, Michigan, 1975. (Hereinafter referred to as *The Role of Ecological Considerations*).

6.   Economics Department, McGraw-Hill, "Annual McGraw-Hill Survey of Pollution Control Expenditures," New York: McGraw-Hill. (Released each year in May: 1968–1974). For data on overseas EC spending by U.S. firms see: Economics Department, McGraw-Hill, "Overseas Operations of U.S. Industrial Companies," New York: McGraw-Hill. (Released each year in August: 1971–1974).

7.   John H. Watson III and Barbara Flower, "Pollution Abatement in Industry: Policies and Practices," *The Conference Board Record,* December 1966, pp. 35–42; Richard A. Hopkinson, *Corporate Organization for Pollution Control* (New York: The Conference Board, 1970); and Leonard Lund, *Corporate Organization for Environmental Policy-Making,* New York: The Conference Board, 1974.

8.   Harold W. Henry, *Pollution Control: Corporate Responses,* (An AMA Management Briefing), New York: AMACOM, 1974.

9.   Azmi D. Mikhail, "Capital Budgeting for Pollution Control, *Journal of General Management, 1,* 1973, pp. 32–44; and George William Trivoli, "Evaluation of Pollution Control Expenditures by Leading Corporations," *Financial Management, 2,* 1973, pp. 19–24.

10. Pamela Archbold, "Pollution Control Financing Grows Up," *Corporate Financing,* July/ August, 1972, p. 21–27.

11. See, for example, Irvin Schwartz, "More of Management Moves into the Environment Picture," *Chemical Week,* February 14, 1973, pp. 57–62; Elizabeth Hennessy, "The Other Side of the Pollution Story," *The Director,* March 1972, pp. 334–337; Peter Gaskell, "Pollution: Cleaning Up Costs Money," *Vision,* December 1971, pp. 28–34; and Jacqueline Aloisi de Larderel and Anne-Marie Boutin, "How do European (and American) Companies *Really* Manage Pollution?" *European Business,* Winter 1972, pp. 56–73. Examples of Press Reports include: "Uniform Rules Urged as Pollution Becomes a Worldwide Problem," *Wall Street Journal,* November 26, 1971, pp. 1ff; and "Equalizing Pollution: Environmental Meeting Struggles with Issue of Worldwide Rules," *Wall Street Journal,* June 9, 1972, pp. 1ff. See also Business International S.A., *The Ecological Challenge: A New Element in European Corporate Planning,* Geneva: Business International S.A., 1972; "Organizing Antipollution Action: Corporate Examples in Europe," *Business Europe,* June 18, 1971, pp. 196–197; and "The Stockholm Conference on Pollution: What it Means for Companies in L.A.," *Business Latin America,* June 22, 1972, pp. 193–194.

12. Robert W. Ackerman, "How Companies Respond to Social Demands," *Harvard Business Review, 51,* 1973, pp. 88–98. See also Melvin Anshen, Ed., *Managing the Socially Responsible Corporation,* New York: Macmillan, 1974, for some practical management problems attributable to social demands.

13. See *inter alia:* John Fayerweather, *International Business Management: A Conceptual Framework,* New York: McGraw-Hill, 1969, Chapter 5; Raymond Vernon, *Sovereignty at Bay: The Multinational Spread of U.S., Enterprises,* New York: Basic Books, 1971; Michael Z. Brooke and H. Lee Remmers, *The Strategy of Multinational Enterprise: Organization and Finance,* London: Longman, 1970; Sidney M. Robbins and Robert B. Stobaugh, *Money in the Multinational Enterprise: A Study of Financial Policy,* New York: Basic Books, 1973; John M. Stopford and Louis T. Wells, Jr., *Managing the Multinational Enterprise: Organization of the Firm and Ownership of the Subsidiaries,* New York: Basis Books, 1972; and Vern Terpstra, *International Marketing,* New York: Holt, Rinehart and Winston, 1972.

14. See: Ingo Walter, *Environmental Control and Consumer Protection: Emerging Forces in Multinational Corporate Operations,* Occasional Paper No. 2, Washington, D.C.: Center for Multinational Studies, June 1972; Ingo Walter, "Environmental Control and Patterns of International Trade and Investment: An Emerging Policy Issue," *Banca Nazionale del Lavoro Quarterly Review, 100,* March 1972, pp. 82–106; Ingo Walter, "Environmental Mangement and Optimal Resource-Use: The International Dimension;" *in* Herbert Giersch, Ed., *Das Umweltproblem in Ökonomischer Sicht,* Tübingen, J. C. B. Mohr (Paul Siebeck), 1974; William J. Baumol, *Environmental Protection, International Spillovers, and Trade,* 1971 Wicksell Lectures, Uppsala: Almquist & Wiksell, 1971; Ralph C. d'Arge and Allen V. Kneese, Environmental Quality and International Trade," in David A. Kay and Eugene B. Skolnikoff, Eds., *World Eco-Crisis: International Organizations in Response,* Madison: The University of Wisconsin Press, 1972, pp. 255–301; General Agreement on Tariffs and Trade, *Industrial Pollution Control and International Trade,* Geneva: G.A.T.T., July 1971; Clifford S. Russell and Hans H. Landsberg, "International Environmental Problems: A Taxonomy," *Science, 172,* June 25, 1971, pp. 1307–1314; "Founex Report on Development and Environment," *International Conci-*

liation, 586, January 1972, pp. 7–36; Thomas N. Gladwin, "The Response of Multinational Corporations of Global Environmental Diversity," a paper delivered at the Public Hearing on the Multinational Corporation and the Worker in the Environment, for the United Nations Conference on the Human Environment, University of Detroit, April 8, 1972; and Roger M. Troub, "The Stockholm Conference and Beyond: Implications for Multinational Enterprise," a paper delivered at the Annual Meeting of the Association for Education in International Business, Toronto, December 29, 1972.

15. Steven C. Wheelwright, "Developing a Corporate Response to Pollution Control," *European Business,* Summer 1973, pp. 64–72.

16. John G. Welles, "Multinationals Need New Environmental Strategies," op. cit.

17. Thomas N. Gladwin, "The Role of Ecological Considerations," loc. cit.

18. The ideas of Ruediger Naumann-Etienne on the definition of the MNC are gratefully acknowledged by the authors.

19. See: John Fayerweather, "The Internationalization of Business," *The Annals, 403,* 1972, p. 3, for an extended discussion of these roles.

20. The term "strategy" is usually interpreted more broadly. According to one definition it is "the determination of long-term goals and objectives of an enterprise, and the adoption of courses of action and the allocation of resources necessary for carrying out these goals." See: Alfred D. Chandler, Jr., *Strategy and Structure,* Cambridge: M.I.T. Press, 1962, p. 13.

21. See: Walter, "Environmental Control and Patterns of International Trade and Investment: An Emerging Policy Issue," loc. cit., pp. 82–84.

22. This model is more fully developed in Gladwin, "The Role of Ecological Considerations," loc. cit., Appendix. D.

23. This is done in Gladwin, "The Role of Ecological Considerations," loc. cit., Appendix D.

24. For two discussions of the influence of these "leverage points" on corporate behavior see: Joseph L. Bower, *Managing the Resource Allocation Process: A Study of Corporate Planning and Investment,* Boston: Division of Research Graduate School of Business Administration, Harvard University, 1970; and Yair Aharoni, *The Foreign Investment Decision Process,* Boston: Division of Research, Graduate School of Business Administration, Harvard University, 1966.

25. For examples of such statements see: Henry, *Pollution Control: Corporate Responses, loc. cit., and* Hopkinson, *Corporate Organization for Pollution Control,* loc. cit.

26. The Dow Chemical Company, *1972 Dow Annual Report to Stockholders,* Midland Michigan: The Dow Chemical Co., p. 17.

27. For additional evidence supporting this proposition see: Ackerman, *op. cit.*

28. For a discussion of how one MNC, E. I. DuPont de Nemours & Co., Inc., has organized at the European regional level for environmental management see: "DuPont's Environmental Men in Europe," *Environmental Science and Technology, 8,* 1974, pp. 118–120.

29. See: Raymond A. Bauer and Dan H. Fenn, Jr., "What is a Corporate Social Audit?" *Harvard Busiess Review, 51,* 37–48, 1973; and Milton Moskowitz, "The Social Audit: Redemption Through Mathematics," *Business and Society, 5,* October 31, 1972), pp. 1–4.

30. This is probably explained by the stringent reporting requirements of section 333, paragraph (5) of the U.S. Federal Water Pollution Control Act (33 U.S.C. 1251, et seq. PL 92-500, enacted by Congress Oct. 18, 1972).

31. Stichting CONCAWE, "What is CONCAWE?" (4th Revised Edition) Report No. 1/72, The Hague: CONCAWE, December 1972).

32. See: "Shell Loses a Round," *Chemical Week,* October 9, 1974, p. 14; "VCM Aerosols

Ban On," *Chemical Week*, October 16, 1974, p. 20; Janice Crossland, "Aerosols," *Environment 16*, 16–26, 1974; "European Industry Engages in Preventive Antipollution Campaign," *Business Europe*, November 11, 1971, p. 368; and "Beating the Ban: Many U.S. Companies Sell Products Abroad That are Banned Here," *Wall Street Journal*, February 11, 1971, pp. 1ff.

33. John Rivoire and John M. Winton, "Energy and the Product Mix," *Chemical Week*, November 11, 1974, p. 29; and Juhan McCaull, "Back to Glass," *Environment, 16*, 6–11 1974.

34. See: "Events Force Toxic Substances Issue," *Environmental Science and Technology, 8*, 408–409, 1974, and "Moving Toward Control of Toxic Chemicals," *Business Week*, May 11, 1974, pp. 112–114.

35. See: "Dow's Big Push for Product Safety," *Business Week*, April 21, 1973, pp. 82, 85; and "Product Stewardship: Responsibility Never Ends," *Chemical Week*, October 3, 1973, pp. 45–46.

36. See: "A New Dyestuffs Industrial Group," *Environmental Science & Technology 8*, 783, 1974; and "Chemical Companies Team Up For Early Warning on More VCMS," *Chemical Week*, January 29, 1975, pp. 44–45.

37. See: James Brian Quinn, "Technology Transfer by Multinational Companies," *Harvard Business Review, 47*, 147–161, 1969.

38. See: "Payoff for Pollution Control," *Chemical Week*, February 2, 1972, pp. 37–38, and "Turning Their Problems Into Profits," *Chemical Week*, January 10, 1973, pp. 35–38; For reviews of the EC business of two chemical MNCs, Dow and Union Carbide respectively see: "Interview: McKennon on Dow's ECS (Environmental Control System) Business," *Environmental Science & Technology 8*, 495–497, 1974, and Joseph J. Fenley, "Ecologists' Target Also a Big Pollution Fighter," *Industry Week*, April 24, 1972, pp. 41–48.

39. For a study of the involvement of transnational, nongovernmental associations in the international decisions leading to the Stockholm Conference see: Anne Thompson Feraru, "Transnational Political Interests and the Global Environment," *International Organization, 28*, 31–60, 1974.

40. "World Environment and Industry," *Environmental Science & Technology, 9*, 100–101, 1975.

41. For a fuller discussion of this organization see: J. D. Moore, "IPIECA," *Esso European Review, 4*, 10–11, 1974.

42. A full discussion of the process of institutionalization can be found in Ackerman, op. cit. Also see his "Putting Social Concern into Practice," *European Business, 40*, Winter/Spring, 1974, pp. 31–35.

43. See: Gladwin, "The Role of Ecological Considerations," loc. cit., Chapter VII.

44. See: Robert D. Buzzell, "Can You Standardize Multinational Marketing," *Harvard Business Review, 46*, 102–113, 1968.

45. See: "Some Mining States Outdo U.S. Standards in Air Pollution War," *Wall Street Journal*, February 10, 1972, pp. 1ff; "Oil: Refiners Gamble on Offshore Plants," *Business Week*, April 14, 1973, p. 42; "The New England Oil Rush," *Business Week*, March 9, 1974, p. 130; "Europe Antes Up for Chemicals," *Chemical Week*, May 22, 1974, pp. 45–50; "Low-Country Plant Builders Head for Hinterlands," *Chemical Week*, July 11, 1973, pp. 34–36; "Chemicals in the Third World," *Petroleum Press Service*, August 1972, pp. 295–297; "Ecology and Acrimony in Stockholm," *Wall Street Journal*, June 15, 1972, p. 14, and "Equalizing Pollution: Environmental Meeting Struggles with Issue of Worldwide Rules," *Wall Street Journal*, June 9, 1972, pp. 1ff.

46. See: "Dutch Demonstrators Put Pressure on Polluters," *Chemical Week*, August 23, 1972, p. 35; "The Antipollution War Intensifies; Higher Costs Jeopardize Plans," *Business*

Europe, September 3, 1971, p. 288; "A Debate Over Delaware's Tough Coastal Use Law," *Business Week,* March 2, 1974, pp. 71–73; and Oliver G. Wood, Jr., et al., "The BASF Controversy: Employment vs. Environment," *Essays in Economics, 25,* November 1971 (Bureau of Business and Economic Research, College of Business Administration The University of South Carolina).

47. Gladwin, "The Role of Ecological Considerations," loc. cit., Appendix D.

48. John M. Winton, "Plant Sites 1975: Social Concerns are Complicating the Choosing," *Chemical Week,* October 23, 1974, pp. 33–52.

49. John M. Winton, "Plant Sites '74: They're Building Close to Home—If They Can," *Chemical Week,* October 17, 1973, pp. 29ff.

50. For a brief critique of these traditional theories of FDI see: Thomas N. Gladwin and Ian H. Giddy, "A Survey of Foreign Direct Investment Theory", Working Paper No. 86, Ann Arbor, Michigan: Division of Research, Graduate School of Business Administration, The University of Michigan, November 1973.

51. See: Raymond Vernon, "Future of the Multinational Enterprise," in Vernon, *The Economic and Political Consequences of Multinational Enterprise: An Anthology,* Boston: Division of Research, Graduate School of Business Administration, Harvard University, 1972, p. 209.

52. For an extensive bibliography on this topic see: C. Michael Aho, "Bibliography on Foreign Direct Investment," Paper No. 2, Project on International Business, Cambridge: Center for International Studies, Sloan School of Management, M.I.T., August, 1974.

53. See: Richard E. Caves, "International Corporations: The Industrial Economics of Foreign Investment," *Economica, 38,* 1–27, 1971; Stephen H. Hymer, "The International Operations of National Firms: A Study of Direct Investment," unpublished Ph.D. dissertation, M.I.T., 1960; Charles P. Kindleberger, *American Business Abroad,* New Haven: Yale University Press, 1969; and Frederick T. Knickerbocker, *Oligopolistic Reaction and Multinational Enterprise,* Boston: Division of Research, Graduate School of Business Administration, Harvard University, 1973.

54. This point is stressed in Welles, op. cit., p. 15.

55. More than 150 oil refinery, gas liquefaction, and petrochemical ventures are reportedly now slated for the Mideast. See: John M. Winton, "Mideast Pulls Chemical Crowd," *Chemical Week,* July 24, 1974, pp. 31–44.

56. See: Gladwin, "The Role of Ecological Considerations," loc. cit., Chapter IV.

57. This has been found in many studies of FDI behavior. The most extensive documentation of such behavior appears in: Yair Aharoni, *The Foreign Investment Decision Process,* loc. cit.

58. For a theory of FDI which deals explicitly with "inertial resistance" to investing overseas see: J. David Richardson, "On Going Abroad: The Firm's Initial Foreign Investment Decision," *Quarterly Review of Economics and Statistics, 11,* 7–22, 1971.

59. Brazil, for example, which maintained a steadfast position that it was "its turn to pollute" at the Stockholm Conference, a year later turned around and began enacting environmental legislation. See: "Turn to Pollute," *New York Times,* February 23, 1972, p. 38, and "Brazil Enacting Pollution Curbs," *New York Times,* March 11, 1973, p. 24.

60. See: "Where the Tradeoffs come in the Energy Crisis," *Business Week,* November 17, 1973, pp. 66–68; "Environment in an Energy Crisis," *Business Week,* December 15, 1973, pp. 53–54; "Energy Crisis Brings Setbacks and Windfalls to Environmentalists," *Wall Street Journal,* January 2, 1974, pp. 1ff; "Environmentalists at Bay," *Wall Street Journal,* January 3, 1974, p. 10.

61. Gladwin, "The Role of Ecological Considerations," loc. cit.

62.   For a good discussion of principles of environmental impact assessment see: Richard N. L. Andrews, "A Philosophy of Environmental Impact Assessment," *Journal of Soil and Water Conservation, 28,* 197–203, 1973.

63.   For a presentation of the composite scoring system and the results see: Gladwin, "The Role of Ecological Considerations," loc. cit. Chapter IV.

64.   See: Gladwin, "The Role of Ecological Considerations," loc. cit. Chapter II for the theoretical foundations of this model.

65.   See: Gladwin, "The Role of Ecological Considerations," loc. cit. Chapter V for a full discussion on the influence of project nature.

66.   See: Gladwin, "The Role of Ecological Considerations," loc. cit. Chapter VI for a full discussion on the influence of organization.

67.   See: Gladwin, "The Role of Ecological Considerations," loc. cit. Chapter VII for a full discussion on the influence of public policy.

68.   Environmental management at the intergovernmental level has been defined by the United Nations as ". . . activities considered to include those measures which provide for international cooperation to facilitate and support the management of man's activities that may have impact on the environment as well as the management of certain environmental resources. The objective is to harmonize the complex relationships and interdependencies between man's actions and the quality of the environment. It strives to develop approaches fo meeting human needs without creating environmental degradation for present and future generations. The process includes the interacting functions of goal-setting, planning, development of criteria and standards, and the adoption of economic, legal, and other measures to achieve multiple objectives." United Nations Conference on the Human Environment, *An Action Plan for the Human Environment,* A/CONF. 48/5, February 9, 1972, p. 33.

69.   See: Maurice Strong, "The Case for Optimism," *Saturday Review/World,* December 14, 1974, pp. 7–11, and John G. Welles, "On Sustaining Industrial Societies," *ROMCOE Forum, 1,* 2–3, 1974.

70.   See especially the chapters by Barde, Grubel, and Richardson & Mutti.

71.   See: Welles, "Multinationals Need New Environmental Strategies," op. cit., and Gladwin, "The Role of Ecological Considerations," loc. cit. Chapter IX.

72.   "Who 'Exports' and Who 'Imports' Pollution?", *The O.E.C.D. Observer, 70,* June 1974, pp. 12–13.

73.   Such global problems are discussed in: Carroll L. Wilson and William H. Matthews, Eds., *Man's Impact on the Global Environment: Assessment and Recommendations for Action,* Report of the Study of Critical Environmental Problems, Cambridge: The M.I.T. Press, 1970.

74.   See Fig. 8-1 on the determinants of national environmental policy.

75.   See for example: Seymour Halpern, "A Major Obstacle to Worldwide Environmental Accord," *Atlantic Community Quarterly, 10,* 239–246, 1972.

76.   By "optimal" we mean policies designed to reduce pollution to the level where the marginal costs of doing so equal the marginal benefits.

77.   For a discussion of the negative welfare effects of uniform environmental standards see: A. Majocchi, "The Impact of Environmental Measures on International Trade: Some Policy Issues," pp. 201–218, in O.E.C.D., *Problems of Environmental Economics,* Paris: O.E.C.D., 1972.

79.   James Ensor, "A Car Safety Standard for Europe," *The Financial Times,* November 15, 1972, p. 23.

80.   See: George F. Kennan, "To Prevent A World Wasteland: A Proposal," *Foreign Affairs,*

48, 401–413, 1970; Richard A. Falk, *The Endangered Planet: Prospects and Proposals for Human Survival*, New York: Random House, 1971; Gaylord Nelson, "We Need a New Global Agency to Confront the Environment Crisis," *War/Peace Report, 10*, 3–5, 1970, and Charles Cheney Humpstone, "Pollution: Precedent and Prospect," *Foreign Affairs, 50*, 325–338, 1972.

81. This problem was evident during the creation of the United Nations Environment Program. See: The Editors, "The Stockholm Conference: A Synopsis and Analysis," *Stanford Journal of International Studies, 8*, 31–78, 1973.

82. See: Eugene V. Coan, Juilia N. Hillis, and Michael McCloskey, "Strategies for International Environmental Action: The Case for an Environmentally Oriented Foreign Policy," *Natural Resources Journal, 14*, 87–102, 1974.

83. "New Environmental Guidelines Framed for Broad Application," *Journal of Commerce*, July 25, 1974, pp. 1ff.

84. "Environment: A New Programme of International Cooperation," *The O.E.C.D. Observer, 58*, June 1972, pp. 27–29.

85. "10 Recommendations of O.E.C.D.'s Environment Ministers," *The O.E.C.D. Observer*, No. 72, October/November 1974, pp. 9–11.

86. For a full discussion of these programs see: Commission of the European Communities," Declaration of the Council of the European Committee and of the representatives of the Governments of the Member States meeting in the Council of November 22, 1973, on the programme of action of the European Communities on the Environment," SEC (74) 10014, Brussels, January 30, 1974.

87. For a review of the progress and problems of UNEP see: Maurice F. Strong, "One Year After Stockholm: An Ecological Approach to Management," *Foreign Affairs, 51*, 690–707, 1973.

88. See: Frederick R. Anderson, *NEPA in the Courts: A Legal Analysis of the National Environmental Policy Act*, Baltimore: The John Hopkins University Press, for Resources for the Future, Inc., 1973.

89. See: Joseph L. Sax, *Defending the Environment: A Handbook for Citizen Action*, New York: Vintage Books, 1970.

90. For a discussion of these barriers in the context of power plant siting see: Barry M. Mitnick and Charles Weiss, Jr., "The Siting Impasse and a Rational Choice Model of Regulatory Behavior: An Agency for Power Plant Siting," *Journal of Environmental Economics and Management, 1*, 150–171, 1974.

91. For a collection of articles expressing this theme see: Donald M. McAllister, Ed., *Environment: A New Focus for Land-use Planning*, Washington, D.C.: RANN-Research Applied to National Needs, National Science Foundation, October 1973.

92. See: Lynton K. Caldwell, "Organization and Administrative Aspects of Environmental Problems at the Local, National and International Levels," in U.N. Department of Economic and Social Affairs, *Organization and Administration of Environmental Programmes*, ST/ ESA/16, New York: United Nations 1974, p. 19 for some principles of effective organization.

93. The potential role of each of these techniques is discussed in Gladwin, "The Role of Ecological Considerations," loc. cit., Chapter IX.

94. See: Irving Kristol, "The Environmentalist Crusade," *The Wall Street Journal*, December 16, 1974, p. 14.

Chapter

9

Environmental Aspects of
International Income Distribution

Jaleel Ahmad

Recent concern with environmental controls in major industrial countries, particularly the United States, has brought into prominence the need for a systematic appraisal of the likely consequences of environment-related matters on economic relationships between developed and developing countries. This chapter explores the implications of global environmental protection as viewed from the standpoint of the developing countries, with particular reference to its income distributional aspects. The basic question posed is whether the developing countries will be better or worse off, on balance, by the increasing trend toward pollution control in the industrialized world, and how they themselves will fit into the pattern of environmental protection.

This formulation of the problem involves numerous questions relating to environmental management and their relationship to the international economy. How would a unilateral pollution-control program in the developed countries affect their economic relationships with developing countries in the field of trade, payments, and productive-factor movements?

Will the manner and the speed with which environmental controls are instituted influence to any significant degree the likely changes in structure, volume and terms of trade, balance of payments, and the choice of production locations? In what manner would these changes affect the developing countries' prospects for growth and development? Is it reasonable to expect internationally uniform standards of pollution control, or could one distinguish between groups of countries on the basis of differences in environmental quality in their demand for social goods? And finally, will an uncoordinated pursuit of environmental quality make the rich richer and the poor poorer? These and related questions should be considered in a framework that is not only *efficient* in encouraging a steady expansion of economic relations between the developed and the developing countries, but also *equitable* in its income-distributional impact.

INTRODUCTION

There has emerged in recent years a growing literature encompassing a wide variety of environmental issues. However, the question of probable impact on developing countries has received only modest attention. Consequently, the state of knowledge in this area is not only rudimentary, but it is also devoid of empirical content and provides, at best, only the narrowest basis for generalization. The following analysis will, therefore, eschew attempts at generality and will instead address itself to a narrower, though important, range of policy issues.

In order to provide a proper perspective for the distributional aspects of environmental controls and to keep clear distinctions between problems and solutions, it is necessary to underline the following general considerations at the outset.

First, the pressing priorities of the developing world constitute a very different set of environmental problems from those encountered by the developed countries. Environmental problems familiar in the developed countries take such forms as the pollution of atmosphere by sulfur dioxide, nitrogen oxides, and particulates, water pollution by oil, lead, and mercury, as well as the depletion and destruction of valuable, and often nonrenewable resources. By contrast, the common developing country problems are of meager and contaminated water supplies, eroded soils, poor sanitation and nutrition, debilitating disease, inadequate housing and transport, and the like. In general—and at the cost of some oversimplification—it may be said that developed country environmental problems are caused by an overindulgent and wasteful pattern of consumption (and production) without considering environmental spillover, while developing country environmental problems are the result of poverty and underdevelopment. Consequently, the two would require quite different means of correction.

The foregoing remarks may be distinguished from two opposing points of view frequently encountered in policy discussions. The first is the assertion that developing countries have an *equal* stake in environmental problems as they are being dealt with now in the industrial countries. The second dismisses environmental problems as merely an internal "housecleaning" for the developed countries, and, as such, should be of no concern to the developing world. Neither of the two viewpoints is distinguished for its accuracy and realism. It is evident that both the developed and the developing countries have a *common* interest in international measures of pollution control, even though their degree and manner of participation will inevitably take different forms.

The developing countries are recipients of global environmental disruption caused largely by the (geographically smaller) industrialized part of the world, and must take an active part in measures of its abatement. Moreover, the growth of large productive capacities in industry and transport in the developing countries, and the resulting urban concentration, is likely to induce environmental disruptions not dissimilar to those encountered in the developed countries. Late-comers on the industrial scene can learn from the mistakes of the presently industrialized countries, and can avoid the creation of environmental damage that these countries have inflicted upon themselves. And in an interdependent world economy the effects of environmental measures in industrial countries will be transmitted to the developed countries in as yet unclear ways through trade in final and intermediate products, through capital movements, and through changes in international comparative costs. These latter consequences will be spelled out in some detail below.

The importance of environmental issues to the developing countries in ways sketched above need not detract from the fact that the developing countries have priorities of their own and will not accord a comparable status to environment if it is in conflict with their overriding social concerns. The major, and perhaps the only, area of potential conflict between environment and developing country priorities is likely to arise in the context of their efforts to produce a rapid industrialization. This potential conflict gives rise to profound implications, and will pose serious problems to many developing countries.

The second point concerns the current structure of international trade and of international distribution of income and wealth, within which the impact of environmental policies should be evaluated. Firstly, the major part of international trade takes place within the group of developed countries, and despite assertions to the contrary, it is here that the major impact of environmental measures will find its way into trade.[1] Secondly, developing countries, by and large, are major suppliers of raw materials and agricultural products to the developed countries in exchange for manufactured goods and services.[2] Their own exports of manufactures are largely labor-intensive and do not make a damaging use of the environment in their production. This implies that the developed countries are specialized in the production and export not only of goods whose consumption entails a pollution-causing diseconomy, but also in processes that are pollution-ridden.[3] As a reflection of the above, the major proportion of the costs and benefits of environmental measures will tend to be localized within the developed countries.

It requires very little statistical evidence to show that the distribution of income and wealth between the developed and the developing countries is anything but equitable. The developing countries among themselves contain three-fourths of the world's population, but only a fraction of its total income. By the same token, the per-capita consumption of commodities damaging to the environment, as well as consumption in general, is far lower in the developing than in the developed countries.[4] These disparities in levels of income and wealth are not unconnected with the structure of international trade, and constitute an important source of instability in the international economy. It is important that the emerging environmental policies at least do not exacerbate these differences.

Finally, few economic phenomena in the developing countries can be viewed without reference to their influence on the rate and character of economic growth. Economic development and growth is such an overriding objective in most of the developing countries that virtually all economic events must be evaluated in terms of their impact on the rate of economic growth, and environmental concerns are no exception.

ENVIRONMENT CONTROL AND MARGINAL UTILITIES

Baumol (1972) has drawn attention to the fact that rich and poor countries do not have the same stake in measures to protect the environment. He argues that the ratio of marginal utility of environmental protection to the marginal utility of "other goods" to the rich is greater than that for the poor. If this is true, international measures to improve environmental quality yield disproportionately large benefits to the richer countries, while benefits to poor countries may be minimal or even negative. Pollution-control measures in the rich countries may, therefore, turn out to be regressive, and may have the effect of redistributing real income from the poor to the rich.

This conclusion, while perhaps valid for the domestic economy, requires strong assumptions of trade-off between environmental quality and "other goods" for its application to the problem of income distribution between the developed and the developing countries. In other words, it requires the assumption that enhancement of environmental quality in the developed countries will deprive the developing countries of goods substitutable with environment and, conversely, that the developed countries will somehow make the "other goods" available to the developing countries. Additionally, it requires the assumption that environmental quality, or the lack of it, in the developed countries is subject to "externality" and spill-over into the developing countries—an assumption valid only in the case of frontier pollution. Neither of the assumptions can be defended for the particular case of the developed and the developing countries. The differences in marginal utility of environmental quality between the developed and the developing countries that undoubtedly exist are not sufficient to conclude that developed country efforts to preserve their environment will necessarily be regressive to the developing countries. Even if regressive elements do arise indirectly through trade and productive-factor movements, appropriate redistributive measures can be envisaged for their correction. In the latter case, it would be possible to argue that environmental protection measures can be made "Pareto-optimal" through appropriate compensatory devices.

It is generally recognized that the level and depth of environmental protection measures will differ between the developed and the developing countries, and will generally be lower in the latter (GATT, 1971; Walter, 1972). Further, Cumberland (1972) has argued that indiscriminate imposition of uniform standards could generate unnecessary trade disruptions and result in higher costs than benefits. However, there is the more practical question: Barring uniformity, how much lower are the developing country environmental targets likely to be? In order to answer this question, one must examine the underlying bases for preferring differential rather than uniform standards.

The preference for differential norms rests on differences in (1) pollution assimilative capacities, and (2) "weights" of pollution-free environment in social welfare functions, between the developed and the developing countries. In general, pollution assimilative capacities would seem to be higher, and preference for environmental quality lower, in the developing than in the developed countries. These propositions, while perhaps basically correct, must be qualified on a number of grounds. The proposition relating to higher assimilative capacities rests on the reasoning that excessive industrial activity causes pollution, and since the developing countries have very little industry they must have a higher unused capacity to assimilate pollution. In fact, however, developing countries have serious environmental problems of their own, albeit of a different kind (Osmaston, 1971; Whitcomb, 1972; Blair, 1972). The essential point is that if additional pollution through noxious production activities were added to the existing forms of pollution, the overall environmental disruption may reach unacceptable levels. In certain essential respects, the physical environment in developing countries is perhaps even more fragile than in the developed ones. Moreover, the relative scarcity of knowledge and technical capacity to deal with environmental pollution in the developing countries implies that even minor problems may cause serious dislocations.

Second, the fact that the ratio of private marginal utility of environment to that of "other goods" is low does not mean that governmental agencies in developing countries cannot, and will not, assign a higher value to the environment in their social preference functions than is believed likely now. One need only witness the existence of social welfare and labor legislation in many developing countries, which is frequently ahead of growth of productivity, and is certainly more advanced than that which the advanced countries had at a comparable stage in their own economic development.

Third, the paramount cause of mounting environmental problems in the developed countries is that the cost of external diseconomy occasioned by certain types of production and consumption is not reflect in private costs. The thrust of contemporary environmental policies through agreement on the polluter-pays principle (see Chapter 6) and so forth, has been to reintroduce this cost into private accounting which will provide "correct" price signals to consumers and producers. It would be inconsistent and self-defeating it one were to argue that correct prices for the use of environment should not be included in private costs in the developing countries. If they are not, the "real" costs of production activities will be understated, leading to an overuse of environment and its cumulative deterioration. If the fact of learning from the developed countries has any meaning, it is clear that full cost of environmental use in the developing countries should be reflected in private balance sheets and income statements.

The conclusion that may be drawn from all this is that, differences in assimilative capacities and social preference for environmental quality notwithstanding, the developing country norms of pollution controls will tend to be higher than is generally believed to be the case. This will undoubtedly pose serious problems of conflict with developing countries' efforts towards industrialization, and will also modify some of the current conclusions with regard to distributional aspects of environment controls. These problems are discussed in the following section.

TRADE CONSIDERATIONS

As the externalities caused by consumption and production of pollution-causing goods are internalized through effluent charges or other menas, the relative prices of internationally traded goods will change. The change in relative prices will in turn induce changes in the structure, volume, and terms of trade between the developed and the developing countries. The direction and degree of these changes is not known with any precision at this time, and only general predictions can be laid down.

If the consumption of polluting goods in the developed countries is curtailed by nondiscriminatory taxes or by outright ban, this will reduce consumption and trade in such commodities. UNCTAD (1972) has drawn attention to cases of bans on imports of fruits and vegetables carrying traces of DDT and other pesticides. Such measures may have serious effects on trading prospects of certain developing countries, and may hurt them more than do current health and safety standards. However, there is little that the developing countries can do about it. On the other hand, environmental standards are likely to lead to substitution of natural products for synthetics, and the developing countries that are major exporters of such products may experience both a rise in volumes of exports and, depending on elasticities, in prices. This favorable circumstance may, to a certain extent, be hindered by resource-recovery and recycling efforts in the developed countries. However, the scope for significant amounts of recycling seems to be limited due to lack of efficient and cheap techniques (see Chapter 14) so that developing country prospects on this score appear to be quite good. Since an overwhelming proportion of developing country exports consist of primary commodities, they are likely to experience a favorable change in terms of trade and, hence, an improvement in real incomes.

The most immediate impact of environmental controls on developing countries may be through increased cost of imports of manufactures, chiefly of intermediate and capital goods. Regardless of the manner in which environmental controls are instituted, a general rise in prices of tradeable goods in the developed countries is foreseen (Walter, 1973; Magee and Ford, 1972).[5] Since the developing countries acquire a majority of their manufactures from the developed countries, the former may experience a decline in their terms of trade as import prices rise. This will represent a real-income transfer from the developing to the developed countries—income allocated to pollution control—since the former will have to release a larger volume of real resources in order to obtain a given amount of import goods. However, this unfavorable circumstance may be wholly or partially offset by a corresponding rise in prices of natural commodities following the displacement of synthetics, as noted earlier.

It is difficult at this stage to know the precise magnitude of price rises due to environmental measures. GATT (1971) had estimated that capital expenditures for air and water pollution control in the United States manufacturing sector were expected to be about 4% of total expenditures for new plant and equipment. The highest rises were expected in iron and steel (9.8%), followed by pulp and paper (9.1%) and stone and clay (5.9%). Similarly, the cost increases for compliance with the U.S. Clean Air Act were estimated to be 16.8% for nonferrous metals, 7.3% for utilities, and 3.5% for iron and steel. For most other manufacturing industries the estimate is for a price rise of less than one per cent. The estimates provided by the U.S. Council on Environmental Quality (1972) range from 5–8% for smelting industries to 0.7–1.5% for steel making.

These values suggest that export price rises will be significant in the *short* run. However, it cannot be presumed that they will continue to be high in the long run, since environment-related cost increases may be offset by increases in productivity.

More difficult problems are likely to arise in the realm of commercial policy. Domestic industries facing competition from imports may mount successful pressures for protection by tariffs or quantitative import restraints against products using "cheap" foreign environmental resources. There is, therefore, the possibility that stricter environmental controls in the developed countries may be used as the pretext for discriminatory trade policies. Historically, trade barriers in the developed countries tend to be erected as soon as developing countries start exporting at competitive prices, and the practice may be repeated in the case of products with which the comparative advantage has shifted to developing countries due to imposition of environmental standards. If so, the use of environmental measures as a rationalization for trade protection will not only reduce trade, but will nullify the real objectives of environmental management (Walter, 1972; d'Arge and Kneese, 1972; GATT, 1971).

The increase in cost of developed-country exports, as well as the possible emergence of new trade barriers due to environmental controls, may harm the developing countries' industrialization efforts more than they do through changes in terms of trade. Developed countries are the major source of capital goods for the developing countries, and an increase in import prices will simply raise the real costs of capital formation. However, this may help the contemporary import substitution programs in the developing countries by lowering the level of effective protection for industrial goods and, thereby, fostering domestic production.

There do remain some doubts as to whether environment-induced cost increases are sufficient to erode the competitive position of the developed countries in the export of goods for which they are major suppliers. The present author believes this erosion to be quite small, if present at all. The reason is that international trade in manufacturers is not simply a matter of minute differences in cost, but of "product differentiation," quality, standardization, marketing, and a host of other nonprice factors. If so, environmental control per se will not seriously affect the competitive position of developed countries in established lines of production. This conclusion is bolstered by Walter's (1973) findings that "EC measures bearing on respective suppliers of U.S. exports and imports will be trade-neutral, or at worst only marginally biased against the U.S." (p. 67).[6] It would thus seem that the anticipated shift in comparative advantage to the developing countries would be illusory. For this reason, no dramatic changes in the structure of trade between the developed and the developing countries can be foreseen.

COMPARATIVE ADVANTAGE AND CAPITAL MOVEMENTS

It is generally believed that, due to differences in assimilative capacities and in environmental preferences, developing countries will experience a shift in comparative advantage for production of pollution-intensive goods (GATT, 1961; Beckerman, 1972; Walter, 1974). This follows from a Heckscher–Ohlin type of model (e.g., Siebert, 1973) where differences in factor endowments guide the allocation of resources according to comparative advantage (see Chapter 2). Since the cost of pollution will tend to be lower in developing countries, a shift of polluting activities from the industrial to the developing countries can be envisaged. This is supposed to have beneficial effects on developing country growth through increased employment of resources, economies of scale, and backward and forward linkages.

However, given the questions pertaining to the empirical validity of factor-proportions model, it is difficult to accept any strong presumption originating from such a model. The following points may be offered in defense of the author's scepticism.

Firstly, the generalizations of Heckscher–Ohlin model are strictly valid only in the two-factor case. Firm conclusions are not possible when the number of factors is increased. For example, if one were to include environment as an additional and complementary factor (in addition to the usual capital and labor), it does not necessarily follow that developing countries will have a comparative advantage in pollution-intensive goods, solely on the basis of "cheaper" environment. This is so because the processes that use the environment intensively also tend to be intensive in their use of capital, which is scarce in developing countries and has a high opportunity cost. Since the number of alternative processes requiring different factor proportions is limited, it may not be possible to locate labor-and-pollution intensive processes on the production function.

Second, since environment is a public good, no market prices may exist for determining its optimal use, particularly in an intertemporal sense. The use of "shadow" prices to express relative scarcities may depend on the solution of a full-scale general equilibrium problem that is never a practical matter.

Third, developing country economic plans tend to encompass the short and medium range, and ignore the external diseconomies arising in the long run from the use of environment (Sachs, 1970, 1972; Blair, 1972; Reichardt, 1970). Less environmentally disrupting patterns of growth will inevitably raise the price of environment, and its relative abundance may then not be quite so apparent.

Finally, Heckscher–Ohlin theory points only to a *tendency* for specialization in line with factor endowments. Whether actual specialization will take place cannot be deduced without explicit knowledge of factor efficiencies and demand conditions. If the relative demand for pollution-free goods in higher, production in both groups of countries will shift to pollution-free goods. It may just be possible that demand may gradually shift away from pollution-causing goods or from goods whose production entails pollution. This situation is not as far-fetched as it may appear, and the substitution of natural products for synthetics is a case in point.[7]

What is more likely is simply that, as environmental quality standards rise in the developed countries, there would be a tendency for the flow of capital and technology from environment-tough countries to environment-soft countries. International location of industries and firms guided by differential pollution costs in different countries may transfer certain "dirty" processes in developing countries. This could be done either by locating dirty processes within a firm's vertically integrated system of operations in developing countries or by transferring the whole operation to such a country. In either case, the motivations for doing so would be analogous to those that lead to locating unskilled or semiskilled labor intensive processes in developing countries, namely to reduce costs and increase profits (for the opposite view, see Chapter 8). This process of transfer of productive activities will enable developing countries to acquire private capital investments and technology, but important qualifications have to be made before this process can be visualized to confer real and not illusory benefits to the developing countries.

The escape from high-standard environment to "pollution havens" may simply be an extension of the developed countries' domestic production structures into selected pockets of the international economy, and may exacerbate all the well-known problems of "dual economy" in the developing countries. Since the multinational corporations are likely to be at the center of such a transfer of activities, the whole process involves a host of real and potential conflicts between them and the developing countries. In the absence of appropriate controls, foreign firms may pay cheap prices for the use of environment, repatriate profits to parent countries, and transfer pollution-ridden technology. They may engage in the production and export only of pollution-intensive commodities whose exports do not compete with exports of parent companies. If so, the dependence of the developing countries on exports of certain types of products, viz., those that are pollution-intensive, will be perpetuated and will be a source of additional difficulty in their production and trade structure.

If all this is allowed to happen uncorrected, environment-related transfer of capital and technology may be detrimental to the long-run development prospects of the Third World, and may increase the international income inequalities. The role of transfer of technology is particularly crucial in this regard, since technological progress is cumulative in character and affects the long-run course of development. Moreover, a transfer of polluting industries, if it takes place at all, may tend to favor the most industrialized of the developing regions, and may hasten the process of environmental despoilation. However, it is possible to avoid the worst features of this so-called "new international division of labor" through appropriate international action.

ENVIRONMENT CONTROLS AND FOREIGN AID

Before concluding this paper, it is necessary to dispose of a "nonproblem" that has occupied a great deal of attention in the literature. This concerns the developing country fears that funds for environment development purposes will come at the expense of foreign economic aid (Founex Report, 1972, Stockholm Conference, 1972, UNCTAD, 1972; Schneider-Sawiris, 1972; Nicholls, 1973; MacLeod, 1974), hence, the demand that funds necessary for environmental action should be independent of, and "additional" to, those provided for economic development. The concept of "additionality" is devoid of practical meaning since development and environment concerns are closely intertwined, as was pointed out in the introduction to this paper. If measures for improvement of environment in the developing countries result in the most advantageous use of resources over time, the distinction between development and environment virtually disappears.

CONCLUSIONS

One of the dangers of rapid swings in intellectual fashions is that certain notions become accepted before their implications have begun to be explored. One such notion is the conflict between continuing industrialization and maintenance (or enhancement) of environmental quality in the developing countries. The issue is largely posed as to whether developing countries should throttle growth for the sake of environment and avoid the experience of the developed countries, or whether they should continue to industrialize and hence pollute the environment. Behind this crude sort of choice lies the assumption that industrialization must necessarily lead to pollution.

One must recognize that industrialization is not an alternative to a nonindustrializing path of development, but is instead an essential ingredient in the raising of living standards of the majority of people in those countries. Moreover, a steady pace of industrialization is the only solution for most of the environmental problems in the developing countries. Problems of public health, sanitation, and an adequate management of natural resources cannot be solved without progress in industrial activity. Too stringent enforcement of environmental standards to the point where it chokes off nascent industrialization will, in effect, mean condemning the majority of world's population to continuing poverty. This will naturally be seen as an attempt to make the world a pleasant place to live for prosperous people—both in the developed and the developing countries.

Is industrialization in developing countries compatible with pollution-free environment? Environment, like any factor of production, has a cost, but because of externalities this cost is not properly reflected in the private costs of production. Once the social costs of environment use are accounted for, the nominal costs of industrial activities will rise. However, there should be no question about their feasibility. A significant degree of industrialization, with social costs of environmental properly accounted for, would still remain viable in large parts of the developing world. There is no presumption that the developing countries would be unwilling to pay the cost of keeping their environment clean. Professor d'Arge (1971) believes that economic growth and environmental quality are compatible in the long run, if a significant portion of investment is directed toward recycling wastes and increasing the assimilative capacity of the environment.[8]

Further conclusions of this paper may be summarized as follows: First, the main general impact on developing countries of environmental controls in the developed countries will arise not through trade, but through capital movements. The rise in the cost of industrial imports caused by environmental-control measures will very likely to matched by a rise in prices, and developing countries may not be greatly affected. There is the possibility that due to price rises and the emergence of new trade barriers, the volume of trade between the two groups of countries may fall even further. If this materializes, the developing country prospects for industrialization may suffer.

Second, shifts in the locus of production, if done with full regard to the developing country's interests offers more potential benefits to the developing countries. This has led Walter (1974) to conclude that "growth effects of environmental management tend to serve as an equalizer, helping to redress the imbalance in real income levels between the developed and the developing countries" (p. 17). Walter's conclusion may be a little too optimistic, because if environmental concerns have a growth-retarding effect in the developed countries, growth must also slow down in the developing countries if comparable environmental goals are achieved.

It will also be necessary to approach the problem of "pollution havens" with great caution, since it can lead to inequitable consequences and to permanent instability. Moreover, it is contrary to the spirit of the 1972 Stockholm Conference on the environment, which called for control and elimination of pollution and not merely for its relocation to the developing countries.

Third, the irreversibility and long-term consequences of ecological despoilation are equally relevant for the developing countries. For this reason, there is likely to be a gradual convergence in the demand for environmental quality between the developed and the developing countries, although Walter (1974) considers it unlikely in the near term. This convergence will arise, because the demand for environmental quality is income-elastic within narrow limits that may be further shortened for the developing countries by an international demonstration effect together with social policies of governments, which may diverge from private environmental preferences.

Environment controls in industrial countries may create some difficulties in the short run for the growth efforts of developing country, but in the long run it will benefit them by correcting a number of market distortions that affect international trade and factor movements. There is no evidence that environment controls will lead to a prolonged transfer of resources from the poor countries to the rich or vice versa. It is certainly difficult to confirm the conclusion of Castro (1972) that world-wide environmental policies will tend to perpetuate the gap between the developing and the developed countries.

NOTES

Remark: The views expressed in this paper are those of the author and not necessarily those of the United Nations Conference on Trade and Development.

1. The developed countries (excluding socialist countries) exported a total of $273.1 billion worth of goods or services in 1972, out of which $211.2 billions were intra-developed country exports and only $50.6 billions to the developing countries. (United Nations, 1974).

2. Primary commodities (SITC 0-4) constituted 78.9% of developing country exports in 1971–1972, while the share of manufactured products (SITC 5-8 including nonferrous metals) amounted to 16.5% of the total. (United Nations, 1974).

3. Walter (1972) provides contrary evidence in that "the product-profile of American exports does not seem to be systematically more or less pollution-intensive than the product-profile of American imports" (p. 67). But, since he uses the United States input–output table to derive the environment coefficients ("overall EC loading"), his results may be subject to the biases familiar to the readers of "the Leontief Paradox."

4. As an example, per capita energy consumption ranges from 11,244 kg of coal equivalents in the United States to a low of 186 kg in India. Even in the wealthier developing countries, it is 2518 kg in Venezuela and 1270 kg in Mexico. (United Nations 1974).

5. In general, the relative efficiency of different environmental control measures will depend on the type of pollution and as to whether it is dealt with by specific effluent charges, subsidies, or outright ban. The OECD countries have accepted the polluter-pays principle in order to internalize the diseconomy caused by polluting units, although serious difficulties remain in quantifying these costs. On the whole, one would expect that the trade consequences of pollution taxes would be more widespread than those caused by general subsidization of environmental quality, but subsidies are not costless either and would probably entail a general rise in price level.

6. The average annual "overall EC loading" of United States exports during 1968–1970 was estimated at about $751 millions or 1.75% of total exports. The corresponding figure for imports was $609 millions or 1.52% of total imports. For details, see Walter (1972).

7. Indeed, the demand shift away from pollution-ridden goods and processes may be the logical culmination of heightened pollution-consciousness.

8. On this, also see Corea (1972), Kulig (1972), and Majocchi (1972).

REFERENCES

Baumol, W., "Environmental Protection and the Distribution of Income" in OECD, *Problems of Environmental Economics,* Paris, 1972.

Beckerman, W., "Economic Development and the Environment: A False Dilemma," *International Conciliation*, No. 586, January 1972.

Blair, T., "The Environmental Crisis in the Third World," *Intereconomics*, No. 2, February 1975.

Castro, J. A., "Environment and Development: The Case of the Less Developed Countries," *International Organization*, 26, No. 2, 1972.

Corea, G., "Development Strategy and the Environmental Issue," *International Conciliation*, No. 586, January 1972.

Council on Environmental Quality, *The Economic Impact of Pollution Control*, Washington, D.C., 1972.

Cumberland, J. H., "The Role of Uniform Standards in International Environmental Management" in OECD, *Problems of Environmental Economics*, Paris, 1972.

d'Arge, R. C., "Essays on Economic Growth and Environmental Quality," *Swedish Journal of Economics*, 73, No. 1, 1971.

d'Arge, R. C., and A. V. Kneese, "Environmental Quality and International Trade," *International Organization*, 26, No. 2, 1972.

Founex Report, Development and Environment, Report and Working Papers of a Panel of Experts convened by the Secretary-General of the United Nations Conference on Human Environment, Mouton, Paris, 1972.

GATT, *Industrial Pollution Control and International Trade*, Geneva, 1971.

Kulig, J., "Environment Policies for Developing Countries and their Development Strategy," in *Founex Report*, op. cit., 1972.

MacLeod, S., "Financing Environmental Measures in Developing Countries: The Principle of Additionality," *IUCN Environmental Policy and Law* Paper, No. 6, Morges, Switzerland, 1974.

Magee, S. P., and W. P. Ford, "Environmental Pollution, the Terms of Trade and the Balance of Payments of the United States," *Kyklos*, 25, 1972.

Majocchi, A., "The Impact of Environmental Measures on International Trade: Some Policy Issues," in OECD, *Problems of Environmental Economics*, Paris, 1972.

Nicholls, I. I., "Source Book: Emergence of Proposals, for Recompensing Developing Countries for Maintaining Environmental Quality," *IUCN Environmental Policy and Law Paper*, No. 5, Morges, Switzerland, 1973.

Osmaston, H., "Pollution in the Tropics," *New Scientist*, June 8, 1972.

Reichardt, R., "Dilemmas of Economic Behavior vis-à-vis Environmental Pollution," *Kyklos*, 23, No. 4.

Sachs, I., "Environmental Concerns and Development Planning," *International Conciliation*, No. 586, January 1972.

Sachs, I., "Development Planning and Environment: The Case of the Countries of the Third World," *Social Science Information*, 9, No. 5, 1970.

Schneider-Sawaris, S., "The Concept of Compensation in the Field of Trade and Environment," *IUCN Environment Policy and Law Paper*, No. 4, Morges, Switzerland, 1972.

Siebert, H., "Environmental Protection and International Specialization," *Weltwirtschaftliches Archiv*, 110, No. 3, 1974.

UNCTAD, "Impact of Environment Policies on Trade and Development, in Particular of the Developing Countries," Report by the Secretariat, Santiago, Chile, TD/130, March, 1972.

United Nations, "Report of the United Nations Conference on Human Environment," held at Stockholm June 5–16, 1972, A/CONF. 48/14, New York, July, 1972.

Walter, I., "The Pollution Content of American Trade," *Western Economic Journal, 10,* No. 4, 1972.

Walter, I., "Environmental Control and Patterns of International Trade and Investment: An Emerging Policy Issue," *Banca Nazionale del Lavoro, Quarterly Review, 25,* No. 100, 1972.

Walter, I., "International Environmental Policy and Economic Development: The Issues Reconsidered," in S. Chee and K. Mun, Eds., *Malaysia and the Multinational Corporations,* Kuala Lumpur: Malaysian Economic Association, 1973.

Whitcomb, E., "Development Projects and Environmental Disruptions: The Case of Uttar Pradesh, India," *Social Science Information, 11,* No. 1, 1972.

The Policy Dimension: Discussion

The foregoing chapters have shown that international economic repercussions of environmental management are essentially a product of policy decisions at the international, national, state/local, and enterprise level. Some of these decisions are "active" in the sense that they purport to translate the public will into environmental action through a political mandate. Others are "passive," to the extent that the decision-makers involved are the recipients of environmental dictates, and must decide how best to bring about the desired change. In this chapter three discussants who are respectively corporate, national, and international-organization decision-makers consider these questions in response to the issues raised earlier.

ECONOMIC IMPLICATIONS OF NATIONAL POLLUTION CONTROL POLICIES

Judith Marquand*

First, I should like to commend Jean-Philippe Barde's chapter as an extremely clear account of the polluter-pays principle, particularly as

_____
* The opinions expressed are those of the author and should not be taken as providing any indication of U.K. policy.

adopted by OECD, and as a valuable presentation of many of its implications. He has discussed some aspects of environmental standards too, and there are several problems at which he has hinted, arising out of the incompleteness of the polluter-pays principle alone as a guide to cost-allocation policy, and the corresponding need for some careful negotiating and explicit decision-making on an international level. It is these problems and the interrelationship of the polluter-pays principle with questions of standards to which I should like to draw attention in my comments.

The Cost-Allocation Principle

The source of the problem is that the polluter-pays principle—regarded as in the OECD and EEC purely as a "no-subsidy" principle—is incomplete as a prescription for allocating costs. It only concerns the allocation of the costs of achieving what is termed an "acceptable state" of the environment. The problems begin to arise because of differing views as to what should count as acceptable, hence the interrelationship with questions of standards. The definition of the principle recognizes the "acceptable level" as that which is laid down by "the competent authorities." Let us assume that the authorities are indeed competent in the practical sense as well as in the legal sense. Nonetheless, there are good reasons why these acceptable levels may vary, both from region to region within a country and between countries. Mr. Barde mentions these reasons, but he does not, I think, give sufficient emphasis to them or to their consequences.

Variations from region to region within a country as to what is regarded as acceptable tend to arise for two main reasons. First, even if there are uniform environmental quality objectives, differences in the assimilative capacity of the environment and in the burdens that polluters wish to place upon it lead to different acceptable emission levels or process standards. Second, there may be varying environmental quality objectives from one region to another arising out of broad land-use decisions that lead to industrial zones, recreational zones, and so on. Given the assumption of a "competent" administration (in both the senses mentioned above), the differences from one region to another will arise as the consistent reflection of a specific set of preferences and of a specific set of given environmental assimilative capacities.

However, when considering the variations in what is counted as an acceptable level from one country to another, we have to add to the reasons for variation within a country, the possibility or even the probability that the countries concerned have differing sets of preferences. These differing preferences, as well as any differing land-use policies and any differing assimilative capacities, will all give rise to differences in the "acceptable levels" as laid down by the competent authorities. However, none of these differences give rise to anything that could properly be termed a "distortion" of trade. Indeed, it is the unhampered expression of the consequences of these differences that is precisely what is intended if distortions in trade are to be moved, so that comparative advantage and differences in preferences from one country to another are able to determine what trade shall take place.

However, we run into certain problems if we set about removing distortions in trade simply by attempting to apply the polluter-pays principle to the point where each authority regards the environment as acceptable. The difficulties do not arise from differences in the assimilative capacity of the environment—these represent a fundamental given factor in environmental policy. Indeed, optimizing the use of the assimilative capacity of the environment is the objective of most environmental economic policy. It is the consequences of differences in preferences that give rise to a whole range of problems. An additional complication is that such differences, for reasons familiar to all economists, are often closely associated with differences in income between one country and another.

What are these various problems? Firstly, let me remove from the discussion the whole question of toxic persistent pollutants of global significance. For these, no country is an island. Whatever the set of preferences within a country, emission standards that lead to emissions that exceed the assimilative capacity of the environment are as unacceptable in any one place as in any other. The world as a whole can and should be regarded as a decision-taking standard-setting unit. Anyone who will not bear the costs of abating such pollutants to whatever level has been agreed internationally to be tolerable should refrain altogether from the processes that generate these pollutants. Whether there is any adequate way of formulating or enforcing such decisions is another matter. The United Nations Environment Programme (UNEP) is the appropriate forum for discussion of these questions, but so far it is only discussion, as opposed to decision and enforcement, that has proved possible.

For other products and processes, the argument that tends to be put forward by the rich countries is that, if the poorer countries are to have low environmental standards, then "pollution havens" tend to be set up. Polluting industry deserts the rich countries to go to the poorer ones, who do not require the industry to abate its pollution to the same extent. However, this argument is simply the other side of the comparative advantage coin. It is impossible to have both sides at once. If we are sure that the poor countries genuinely prefer the marginal unit of wealth to the marginal unit of health, and if we believe it important for them to have health too, then the logical policy—which is indeed appropriate according to traditional economic welfare criteria—is for the rich countries to give them extra aid. If we are not prepared to aid them, then we cannot grumble about their own allocation of their own resources. Admittedly, there may be some special problems that arise under some circumstances if multinational enterprises choose to produce in ways that give rise to few spillover benefits in those countries in which costs of production are lowest.

The argument concerning distortions has also to be subject to a proviso concerning product standards for goods that enter into trade. These standards tend to be justified, quite properly, in terms of the protection of consumers in importing countries, and do not necessarily have any particular degree of pollution associated with the processes by which they are produced. If product standards set for the protection of health constitute barriers to trade, I do not think they are barriers about which we need to feel defensive.

International Differences in Environmental Preferences

If the legitimacy of different preferences in different countries is accepted, at least two points follow. First, it follows that only a certain proportion of transfrontier pollution problems are appropriately solved by the adoption of common standards by the countries affected. Countries may have perfectly valid reasons for wishing to have different standards. Even where good-will is present, if resources differ greatly between the countries concerned, there may be no determinate solution to the transfrontier pollution problem without a transfer of resources from one country, the richer country, to the poorer country. Even then, once we abandon simple two-dimensional models, there may be only a range within which a solution might be reached by bargaining rather than a single determinable point. However, in any case, in welfare terms, it may be perfectly appropriate for the rich country to make a larger proportionate contribution to removing the transfrontier pollution than the poor country. This may be the only satisfactory solution to the problem, but such solutions are notoriously difficult to negotiate.

Second—and only the assumption of differing assimilative capacities is necessary for this result, although it is reinforced by different preferences—internationally set emission and process standards as opposed to environmental quality objectives or standards *can* induce trade distortions. Countries with similar preference functions may be rendered unable to take advantage of their natural endowment of assimilative capacity, and forced to settle for nonoptimal positions. Where countries, in addition, have different sets of preferences, the nonoptimality may or may not be compounded, but certainly there is no reason to expect the two sources of nonoptimality to cancel out. Thus I cannot agree with some of Mr. Barde's argument (p. 146), unless he is referring only to domestically determined emission standards. I would note that Table 6-1 (p. 151) omits the cases where both countries have similar emission or process standards—high or low, as the case may be—and that in these cases distortions may arise if the standards have been set internationally without regard for environmental quality.

I have argued that the application of a common cost-allocation principle (a no-subsidy principle) itself is insufficient to ensure the appropriate reflection of pollution-abatement costs in prices. Consideration has to be given also to the nature of the "acceptable level" to which pollution has to be abated, and there is no reason why different countries should arrive at similar or even so-called "harmonized" definitions of this level. Even if we were living in a world where all that is required is to operate a static neoclassical model of the economy, the application of a common cost-allocation principle would be necessary, but not a sufficient condition, for distortions of trade to be removed and optimal environmental decisions to be taken.

Even if the domestic optimum where marginal costs of abating a further unit of pollution equal marginal benefits of so doing is chosen, none the less such an optimum is not necessarily uniform from one region to another, let alone between countries. Indeed, an administratively determined standard is more likely to be uniform than an economic optimum. This in no way prevents the achievement, in principle at least, of an optimal amount of trade, but what variations in "acceptable levels" do make difficult is the empirical determination of whether countries are in some way manipulating the choice of what is to count as acceptable and so creating conditions conducive to distortions of trade.

If we now abandon a static neoclassical model, and think in terms of an economy that moves along a growth path without even achieving a static optimum position, it might well be that the means of moving along the optimum path do not even include the polluter-pays principle as a necessary condition. It might well be that some second-best solution would be found that embodied, perhaps, some rather complex system of subsidies. In discussions at OECD, this possibility has been raised, but no one has yet grappled with it.

Because this is probably a more realistic picture of the world than that presented by the static model, the question is raised directly as to what exceptions to the polluter-pays principle should be permissible. Jean-Philippe Barde has mentioned (p. 196) that it is important to identify cases where exceptional payments are being made. I would add that it is of prior importance to describe and delimit very carefully what kinds of measures are to count as exceptions, and to define such concepts as that of "severe difficulties" if the polluter-pays principle is to have any international economic role. The problem here is closely analogous to that of deciding what is to constitute a distortion of trade. For most purposes, this is interpreted as providing aid for exports that is withheld from other products so that countries who wish to aid exports selectively have to use all their ingenuity to devise general instruments that happen to help exports more than anything else. When is such an instrument a distortion?

The difficulty can perhaps best be described by pointing out that there is a distinction between the domestic application of the polluter-pays principle and its international application. The domestic application can be justified in terms of ensuring that the polluter takes the effect of his activities upon the environment into account when making his decision to pollute. In an international context, justification is wider and rather different. Distortions of trade, given a comparative static model, can indeed arise to the extent that polluters in one country are subsidized, while in another country they are forced to bear the costs of abating pollution themselves. However, I have argued that in general there are no legitimate economic grounds for concern by other countries if one country has a less active environmental policy than others so that, in effect, even though that country applies the polluter-pays principle, its polluters bear only a small burden in relation to that borne by polluters in other countries. Only when countries agree jointly as to what should be allowed to constitute an acceptable environment is it appropriate to insist on common standards, whether these are environmental quality objectives or emission or process standards under similar circumstances to those between one country and another.

Problems of Implementation

As Mr. Barde mentions, the EEC is able to adopt a much more definite position than OECD. The commitment to the concept of basic protection levels and, ultimately, to the adoption of common environmental quality objectives makes it possible for the EEC to use the polluter-pays principle as one part of the means of preventing "pollution havens" within the Community. Without some such common basis for agreement, the application of the polluter-pays principle rests on sands that are prone to shift. The insecurity of the foundations tends to become apparent as soon as exceptions start to be identified and delimited.

In a situation where countries have no firm commitment to common environmental and other economic policies in matters of detail, the problem of agreeing what should count as an exception is one which can only be solved where there is the goodwill to solve it. While many OECD countries have regional policies, industrial policies, or research and development policies, there are certain areas of policy that are not necessarily closely similar and, indeed, where major divergences may appear. The clearest example of this, given in Chapter 6, is the Japanese requirement that new plants be allowed to be subsidized within the framework of exceptions to the polluter-pays principle. As far as I have been able to understand it, the Japanese argument is either concerned with distributing the burden of pollution abatement equitably, in which case it could readily have been accommodated within the polluter-pays principle by a system of redistributive charges, or it is simply that if the new plants are not subsidized there will be unacceptable employment consequences. It would thus have accorded more closely with the way in which many OECD countries operate if the attempt to justify the subsidy had been made in terms of some sort of employment policy. Instead, the Japanese have driven a large coach and horses through the application of the polluter-pays principle. That they should have succeeded in doing this is an illustration of the limitations of OECD in the particular bargaining context that is appropriate to the drawing up of international rules for applying the polluter-pays principle. This is one aspect of the point I have been trying to make, that OECD countries as a group are *not committed to any common approach* to problems of environmental policy, once the level of very broad generality is passed. I find that, in this last point, I am talking as a practitioner rather than an academic.

The Practitioner's Dilemma

I would like to conclude by attempting a succinct exposition of the practitioner's predicament. From a purely national point of view, there are very good reasons why the polluter-pays principle is a desirable policy domestically. Given that we wish to impose it domestically, and that we do care about the condition of our own environment, we have a strong interest in ensuring both that our competitors apply the polluter-pays principle domestically, and that they adopt environmental policies that are at least as tough as our own, whatever this may turn out to mean when attempts are made to spell it out in detail.

Accordingly, the basis for a negotiated agreement with them exists, but only to the extent that our competitor countries are prepared to adopt environmental policies that are at least as tough as our own, and to regard the same range of types of policies as acceptable in achieving their environmental objectives, and the same range of types of policy as acceptable in mitigating any incidental ill effects. This still provides only a fragile basis for an agreement, which can easily be broken, as in the Japanese example. The process of definition of permissible exceptions is a delicate diplomatic one rather than an exercise in applying economic theory.

As far as the countries that are not our competitors are concerned, a narrow view of our own national interest as a country that imports their raw materials would be that we are not particularly worried if they choose to adopt minimal environmental policies. Indeed, to the extent that their exports are, thereby, rendered cheaper, we stand to gain. Problems only arise when countries with low environmental standards turn into competitors. However, if such countries do not consider it in their own interests to achieve a clean environment, there is really very little that the rest of the world can do about it unless it wants to pay them directly to clean up. And the recipient countries may well prefer to use foreign aid for other purposes. The UNEP approach, of building up monitoring networks and dealing with the problems of persistent pollutants of global significance, is the only direct environmental way forward. For the rest, it is necessary to fall back on the importance of helping such countries to develop for a variety of other reasons, and on the observed phenomenon that rising levels of real income tend to carry with them a rising concern for the condition of the environment within which people live and work.

What the developed world must not try to do is to persuade the rest to adopt the developed world's own set of preferences. This is as inappropriate where environmental protection is concerned, as it has been in many other areas of social endeavor—including the whole area of development policy.

ENVIRONMENT AND MULTINATIONAL CORPORATE STRATEGY

Howard S. MacAyeal

From a multinational "practitioner's" viewpoint, the paper by Thomas Gladwin and John Welles is a thorough piece of scholarship. While the authors admit their findings lack intensity, the conclusions drawn from the findings and their commentary on the conclusions are highly objective and should be well received.

The key element in the paper, and in the subject itself, is the observation that: "At stake, given recent trends, will be how to achieve a long-term sustainable relationship, in the broadest sense, between MNC's and the Earth." The relationship at present is in what one might best describe as a state of unstable equilibrium. Gladwin and Welles quite rightly discover that there is no clear and consistent attack on the problem, no management technique yet ground through the american management process and emerging as a standard approach with coherent decisional guides. In short, there is no policy foundation for the trade-offs required between industrial development and human welfare.

People who are outside the MNC do not know what to expect from people who are inside, and the lack of perspective is mutual. When a problem of global proportions appears, as in the case of environmental deterioration, both populations tend to institutionalize their ignorance of each other. Solution methods quickly deescalate from a cooperative plane to an adversary plane. Officialdom on both sides adopts defensive, hard-line positions. The problem becomes a battleground in propoganda.

Gladwin and Welles see the dilemma in this. They note that the allocation of authority to cause remedial behavior at the institutional level is significantly counterproductive and perhaps unworkable. The inference is that they intuit, although they do not explicitly recognize, two forces at work. One force is the evolution of MNC management capability. The other is forebearance of public anxiety about the abuse of special interest capability. Let's examine the two forces.

As said, and as reflected in the Gladwin/Welles findings, MNC management response to environmental disturbance is in a state of flux, but management has been there before, in an array of "surprise" problems that basically date from the creation of fictional corporate society as a surrogate of real society.

In the late 1950s, public concern materialized over product-related deaths and debilitations. Management of the then nacent MNCs (who were really going from regional to continental marketing systems) took two fundamental ad hoc approaches: either lean on the risk averaging system represented by actuarial underwriting; or rely on the lag effect of law reform in the *stare decisis* system of the judicial process. Neither approach worked out ultimately, although the populist pressure to apply the principle of "negligence pays" did not work out either. What happened was the development of a field of compromise, in which intermediate events began to characterize the perception of final solutions. The process goes on, both from the standpoint of product modification, and from the standpoint of public pressure. Today nobody is alarmed at the daily recital of automotive recalls; yet today nobody in management is publicly arguing the penumbra of *caveat emptor*. The duty is being assimilated through collective experience.

The process through which corporate management evolved its attack on the product liability problem was largely a function of group synthesis. The commentator participated in the early stages of developing safe product standards for industrial lift trucks. The early meetings were confrontations over need, anticompetitive "rub offs," assertions that fork lift drivers are always unskilled and nontrainable, and the like. Later meetings began to shift confrontation to the minimal axis between the industry and society, which may parallel the management evolution stage today as it relates to environmental concerns. But finally, over 10 years and under increasing liability pressure, the industrial truck industry evolved product standards that safeguard all but the most unforeseeable events. And the standards are ritual in product design.

Other evolutionary phases of MNC management response can be cited as parallels, such as the problem of occupational safety, retirement, and, in fact, competition itself. The point is that under reasonable pressure the management response mechanism works, and it is a proactive force of change.

On the other side lies the forbearance doctrine that allows world citizenry to be patient with active progress. This is a more difficult force to manage. Consider for example, that perhaps as many as 300 million people now alive on earth will starve to death regardless of the planning or execution of any countersolution now known to science. Consider that a statistical percentage, however small, of all risk-oriented catastrophes will happen regardless of risk-elimination procedures. In an inappropriate forum, the paradox is raised to the level of ritual fate. The French notion of "triage" will not do. Hence the engineering principles inherent in ordering the social function are likely to become evolutionary in reverse.

Gladwin/Welles appear to realize this, and to caution against an overly institutional approach towards meeting the environmental challenge from the public sector. They point out that international environmental regulation may simply counter the converse forces involved in local adaptation. They correctly surmise that the current flux in environmental management methodology evidences a lack of concern for the impact on investment decisions of environmental issues—a part of the present equilibrium that may well keep the worst from happening (i.e., pollution-related industrial migration).

It seems likely that environmental management will begin to fit more exactly into the mechanics and law of land-use planning as time goes on, and that MNCs will have a positive influence on this trend. MNCs, after all, are not entrepreneurial, although they continually search for entrepreneurial stirrings in the management system. Their confrontations with society are not as likely to be visceral as were the battles between entrepreneurial real-estate developers and communities during the late 1940s and 1950s. In fact, cases exist that suggest that communities that do not learn the difference between the single-mindedness of the entrepreneur and the complex reasoning of a MNC management system can suffer from that ignorance. The impact of gasoline shortages in New England during the winter of 1974 traces in part to disbelief that the refinery safeguards offered by MNCs were any more credible than those offered by tick-tack housing developers. The field of rational accommodation is wide open, but its traverse requires sharp identification, at the situs level, of real attitudes on both sides.

Further, it requires a ground rule understanding on the part of society that the cost/benefit equation can never be reduced to zero as long as the industrial process continues, and that the industrial process cannot discontinue without a massive eradication of human life. In the trade-off between industrial wealth and human welfare, the optimal point always excludes the last few percentiles of achievement on either side. Thus while clean air may again be general, the air will never again be as generally clean as it once was. This condition will affect someone, perhaps some few, but the concern of society shifts to naked humanitarianism as the number of adverse effects reduces.

In this sense, finally, the problems of abatement and the problems of design are divergent, and the commentator would like to see Gladwin and Welles address this further. In many instances, pollution effects are the result of second-generation discoveries, and the product of well-intentioned design. The abatement process has an impact on the economics of standing investment while it stimulates design innovation for new investment. The problem, on the one hand, is to avoid or minimize unwanted side effects on employment and revenue, and, on the other, to design an optimum cost/benefit relationship. When the two problems are treated as one problem, a tradeoff develops in forensic terms between employment and new investment. This, it seems to the commentator, is a false issue. The goal of the job-hungry community should be to gain new investment at state of the art designs, even though the designs may become suboptimal as the state of the art advances. The goal of the abatement-hungry community should be to install state of the art technology compatible with the technology in place. Either avenue will produce exceptions, but both will bring environmental concerns on stream rather than over the dam.

PROBLEMS OF ENVIRONMENT AND DEVELOPMENT

Jeremy J. Warford

Despite an introductory statement to the contrary, the chapter by Jaleel Ahmad addresses itself to a wide range of policy issues, and makes a number of generalizations about the impact of environmental-control measures on the distribution of income between developed and less developed countries. A major difficulty with the paper is that it essentially consists of a series of ideas about the possible impact of environmental controls on trade, product prices, and welfare, with little analysis to substantiate them. The paper seems to fall between two stools. On the other hand, it fails to develop in a rigorous way the theoretical conditions under which such measures will effect a redistribution of income between rich and poor countries.

If anything, the paper discusses the second of these approaches, but the effort put into its preparation seems misplaced. I am unhappy with a number of the generalizations that form its base, but even the development of a theoretical model probably includes little that is innovative to students of international trade theory. It seems to me that the consequences of environmental-control measures for international trade can theoretically be dealt with in much the same way as any other change in relative factor scarcities, and in a way rather more useful than the approach taken by the author. It also seems to me that the attention of economists in this area should be directed primarily at the collection and analysis of empirical data by analyzing, for example, the relationships between the physical effects of pollution, pollution-control measures, and economic indicators, and then applying standard theories of international adjustments.

I, therefore, have a basic problem with the concept of Professor Ahmad's chapter. Moreover, on points of detail there are numerous statements with which one could take issue or that appear to be inserted randomly in the text. For example, what is the point of the distinction between pollution caused by "over-indulgent and wasteful" consumption and production patterns in developed countries and that due to poverty in LDCs? Why do they require different corrective devices? And if so, what are they? And consider the following statement: "In certain essential respects, the physical environment in developing countries is perhaps even more fragile than in the developed ones." (p. 000) It is not clear what these respects are, or what consequences follow from them.

I also have a number of difficulties with the discussion of the importance of the polluter-pays principle, which may or may not be implemented by means of effluent charges that vary with the amount or type of waste discharged by those responsible. If the burden of pollution is placed upon those who create it, and if they happen to be the manufacturers of exportables, one would obviously expect export prices to tend to rise. However, if one looks at the overall efficiency of the economy it might be argued that, because devices such as effluent charges tend to improve efficiency in resource allocation, they will tend to keep production costs (possibly including costs of exportables) lower than they would otherwise be. More generally, if the benefits of pollution-control measures exceed their costs, and if the benefits are cost-saving, then, no matter how the improvements are financed, one might expect there to be a tendency for the cost of at least some exportables to fall. In any case, the conclusion of this section of Professor Ahmad's is somewhat weak, and one wonders what purpose it serves, that is, that LDC norms of pollution control will tend to be "higher than what is generally believed to be the case." I am not quite as optimistic as the author, and in this regard it is useful to recall the distinction made earlier in the paper between the type of pollution encountered in LDCs and that in developed countries. In the former it is easy for the rich (the policy-makers) to escape pollution by moving, installing sanitary facilities, and so on. In developed countries one might argue that pollution is more pervasive, and, therefore, becomes increasingly the concern of those in a position to remedy it.

In Professor Ahmad's discussion of the magnitude of price rises due to environmental measures, there is an implication that increased productivity is likely to be associated in particular with those activities subject to environment-related cost increases. I do not understand why this should be so. Perhaps some explanation is in order. However, it turns out that the preceding discussion is unimportant since the author states that the structure of trade is unlikely to be affected anyway. Moreover, if the costs of pollution control are so slight that there is likely to be little change in trade patterns, one might also expect, since the same forces are involved, that capital movements may also be insignificant. This is not the conclusion arrived at in the paper—again for reasons that are not clear.

I have a number of problems with the section on comparative advantage, but I shall leave it to the academic exponents of two product–two factor models to take issue with the author on his criticism of the Heckscher–Ohlin concept. In any case, whatever the shortcomings of such models, the superficial critique of their validity does not do much to destroy the intuitive argument that LDCs will tend to have an increasing advantage in the production of pollution-intensive goods. Similarly on shadow pricing no one expects perfection in the estimation of shadow values, and in any case failure to be accurate in shadow pricing does not in any way deny the opening statement of this section. I also question the implication that less environmentally disrupting patterns of growth will raise the price of environment. And finally, if the polluter pays, the shift away from pollution-intensive goods and events such as the substitution of natural for synthetic products is exactly what one would expect to tend to happen: Why does the author seem so surprised?

Lastly, with respect to foreign aid, I would disagree with the author's contention that in practice, "additionality" is a nonissue. To the extent that international/bilateral aid agencies earmark funds for certain types of projects, the failure of a country to accommodate itself to the aid agency's whims may certainly involve an important opportunity cost to the country.

PART Three

THE TRANSNATIONAL DIMENSION

Transfrontier Pollution:
Some Issues on Regulation

Ralph C. d'Arge

Transfrontier pollution is quite simply the non-market-reflected transfer of one or more sovereign nations' residuals—and/or their effects—to other nations. The residuals may be in the form of water-borne or air-borne residuals, or may be inadvertantly transmitted through commodities (trade) or through a consumer property medium such as the air waves. Examples in Western Europe are plentiful, and in North America there are a few classic examples including pollution of the Great Lakes, Trail Smelter emissions, and salt loads in the Colorado River.

The important economic and political aspects of transfrontier pollution in a taxonomic sense can be identified by examining three central questions: (1) Are the polluting and receptor nations identifiable? To what extent? (2) Are damages and control costs known by all involved and noninvolved nations? With what accuracy? (3) Are there guiding international principles on who pays for damage incurred, and how much? Is there substantial international agreement on their efficiency and equity characteristics?

The variations in answers to these questions on individual cases of transfrontier pollution will undoubtedly determine how they may be resolved, if at all. The Trail Smelter case was resolved through international adjudication of rights and responsibilities. The Great Lakes pollution problem is being arbitrated through the United States–Canadian International Control Commission. The salts in Colorado River water are being reduced through bilateral intergovernmental agreement. The OECD countries have adopted the polluter-pays principle, establishing that the identifiable polluter within a country is responsible for payment of control costs (but not residual or other damages, as has been adopted in Japan) *within* the country. The case of transfrontier pollution was explicitly excluded in applications of the OECD polluter-pays principle.[1] A new principle of nondiscrimination in transfrontier pollution has emerged from OECD, where such "pollution should be subject to legal or statutory provisions no less severe than those which would apply for any equivalent pollution occurring within the polluting country."[2] Also, the principle states unequivocally that, whenever the country imposes the polluter-pays principle, it should be imposed without regard to whether impacts are in fact internal or transnational in location.

It may be appropriate to proceed by first examining the problem of transfrontier pollution and its unique aspects in very general terms, and then proceed to discuss a special case, aircraft emissions into the stratosphere. In so doing, we hope to demonstrate how important the answers to the free foregoing questions are in predicting how transfrontier pollution will be regulated.

TYPES OF TRANSFRONTIER POLLUTION

A taxonomy of cases for transfrontier pollution can perhaps be identified through differentiation by certain characteristics such as: (1) number of polluting countries; (2) number of receptor countries; (3) reciprocal external effects; (4) one-directional external effects; (5) ownership of the transmitting medium; and (6) the magnitude and measurement of potential or actual damages and control costs.

A particular transfrontier pollution problem can be identified on a scale for each of these characteristics. For example, Colorado River salt pollution involves one polluting and one receptor country with one-directional external effects and no legal definition of the Colorado River as a common property, but complete entitlement identified within national boundaries. Alternatively, nuclear-weapons testing may involve several polluting countries, many receptor countries, both regional and one-directional effects, and at least implicit agreement as to the common property character of the stratosphere.

Viable economic negotiation of transfrontier pollution problems along with guiding principles for resolution may be vastly different as is suggested by the examples given. The Trail Smelter case of air pollution had only two countries involved, effects were one-directional, ownership of the transmitting medium was recognized by both nations to be commonly held, and damages or control costs did not constitute a more than insignificant amount of wealth or income for either country and were easily measured. The case was resolved by the International Court of Justice in The Hague, and both nations accepted the outcome. In the case of fallout from nuclear testing, control costs from the standpoint of national defense may have been huge, damages were not easily measured and would not become evident immediately, the number of receptor countries was large and not organized, and the effects were largely (although not completely) one-directional. Another case is the pollution problem in the Baltic Sea, where several nations are both emitters and receptors, where common property ownership of the transmitting medium is implicitly recognized, the magnitude of damages and control costs are of significant magnitudes in relation to national economic activity, and at least a partial resolution of the problem occurred through unilateral action by the reciprocal incentive effect of generating states. Alternatively, pollution of the Rhine River—because of its one-directional nature, with few nations included and difficulty in establishing damage estimates or control costs—predicted a very slow rate of movement toward solution even with full polluter liability already established by international precedent. Ongoing, often bitter disputes over the Icelandic and other fisheries indicate that the sheer magnitude of potential damages and control costs may be an overriding factor in determining how transfrontier pollution problems are resolved.

Given these observations on important differentiating characteristics of transfrontier pollution, can any general observations on their effects be made in isolation? In other words, other things being equal, will a larger number of receptor nations, better-defined ownership patterns of common property resources, or more accurate measures of damages and control costs make substantial differences in the resolution of transfrontier pollution patterns? The answer would appear to be obvious, and in later sections of this chapter I shall endeavor to show how they individually suggest that an overriding general guiding principle for solving such problems is not only unlikely, but also inefficient. Before proceeding to general efficiency aspects, it may be appropriate to reemphasize several problems concerning transnational common property resources.

The classic economic solution to externality problems was to "internalize" them by either developing a well-defined market for the "spill-overs" or controlling them through collective provision of regulations. Neither of these possibilities appears easily amenable to the problem of transfrontier pollution in general, and environmental externalities in particular. First, environmental externalities have arisen because most dimensions of the natural environment on a regional or global scale are resources without rigidly defined or enforceable ownership rights. The oceans, atmosphere, and electromagnetic spectrum are typical examples. These resources are viewed as being commonly owned or not owned at all. A nation that agreed to a particular pattern of ownership of these resources could potentially lose some of its implicitly controlled resources and, thereby, its national wealth.[3] As long as international entitlements are obscure, any nation can lay implicit claim to the common property resource exceeding any equitable share it may presume to receive if entitlement were made explicit. This is not to say that once some other nation impinges on a country's perceived implicit entitlement, that it will not find a negotiated settlement and, thereby, explicit entitlement to be superior to an implicit one. However, the impinging nation, in negotiating, must revise downward its own perceived ownership of the common property resource. In consequence, proceeding from a situation of implicit entitlements of common property resources to explicit regulation and, thereby, ownership means of common property resources to explicit regulation and, thereby ownership means that some (or all) nations must revise downward their expectations of national wealth, stemming from the resources that each implicitly believes it controls.

A second aspect of a major importance arises from the concept of national sovereignty. Not unlike consumer sovereignty as conceptualized by economists, national sovereignty implies the idea that governments, acting in their own interest—omitting deviations in power or information implying political or economic monopoly—will achieve the greatest welfare for all by independently pursuing autonomous goals and interacting through international markets. The belief in national sovereignty as an ideal is so imbedded that it is impractical to presume it will be easily given up or seriously impinged upon.

Coupling the concepts of national sovereignty in decision, and the idea that implicit, as opposed to explicit, entitlement of international common-property resources yields a greater perceived wealth for nations, is suggestive that resolution of transnational externality problems will generally entail the following restrictions:

1. No nation will easily accept international agreement on entitlement of significant common property resources without compensating payments

to retain its perception of national wealth. Hence, the classical answer to externality problems of internalizing the decision-making process for the resource is not easily transferable to transnational problems. A new overriding element of distributional gains and losses must be simultaneously included in efficiency considerations.

2. Unidirectional, transnational externalities, if they are of substantial importance to the polluting country as a method of waste disposal, will in general be resolved by some form of compensation system in which compensation flows from the victim country. The nonliability case (or victim-must-pay principle) will generally be dominant.[4] This is to be contrasted with the reciprocal environmental externality case in which compensation may flow in either or both direction.

3. International court settlements of transnational externalities are not likely to yield satisfactory results. There appear to be three almost insurmountable problems. First, how are damages to be measured and damage payments assessed? The victim country's social values may be strikingly different than those of the polluting country. In consequence, there may not be a social welfare index that is applicable to both. For the victim country, international trading prices, at least at the margin, offer a measure of welfare loss. However, if the impact is on individual citizens with no market prices representing their losses, then a measure of welfare loss is not available except through direct examination and questioning with consequent "free rider" difficulties. In addition, there may be uncertainty as to the magnitude of loss unless the externality is allowed to continue to the point of maximum damages, that is, threshold levels of fish populations.

Given the sovereign rights of nations, no nation can be forced to pay environmental damages. The tradeoff here is in terms of loss of international prestige and goodwill, or increasing the possibility of conflict, versus monetary payments based on possibly misrepresented public preferences in the victim nation.

There also is basically the chicken-and-egg problem of historical precedent most dramatized by airports and noise pollution. An airport is built drawing in people that are then adversely affected by airport noise. Who is responsible? Who is the polluter referred to in the polluter-pays principle? As environmental problems increase in severity and potential damages induced between countries rise, it seems that assigning responsibility will become increasingly difficult. In this context, there is also the problem of assigning damages when more than one nation's waste residuals contribute to total damages. If the different nations' residuals are synergistic or if damages are nonlinear relationships of waste intensity, then there is no easy method of determining how much responsibility each nation should assume even under the polluter-must-pay principle. Thus it can be anticipated that international courts or international commissions will have difficulty in arbitration, even if such institutions are given some degree of regulatory powers.

ECONOMIC EFFICIENCY AND TRANSFRONTIER POLLUTION

Figure 11-1 depicts a hypothetical polluter river. Prior to pollution controls being established, a certain configuration of industrial locations and population clusters can be envisioned in the two countries. With internal pollution controls of the polluter-pays type, water polluting industries in Country A will have incentives to relocate downstream, that is, move closer to an international border where presumably controls further downstream do not

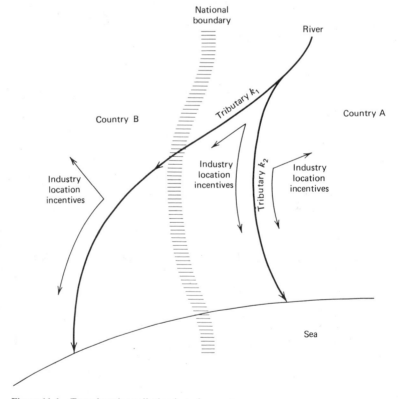

Figure 11-1   Transfrontier pollution in a river system.

matter. However, there may be countervailing movements to take into account population clusters and the river's assimilative capacity. Both Countries A and B have incentives to achieve the lowest internal cost of pollution abatement. If sea pollution is a recognizable *internal* problem to either country, then there may be additional justification for relocation upstream. The incentive in both countries is quite straightforward, letting the sea "assimilate" a relatively greater share of the waste load.

The OECD principle of nondiscrimination strongly suggests that Country A require water quality to be no worse when the waters cross into Country B than elsewhere in the country with "equivalent pollution." This principle of course allows A to divide up its heavily polluting industries, locating part of them on tributary k_1 near the border and part of them on tributary k_2 near the sea and assert "equivalent pollution" on each small reach of the tributaries. Likewise, Country B has the incentive (although perhaps not the inclination) to relocate damaged parties (firms or water users) in such a configuration that they replicate some "equivalent pollution" problem within the polluter country. As has been demonstrated in other cases, it is unlikely that such unilateral actions taken by firms, industries, or countries will be efficient from a global perspective. With only internal actions taken by the countries, outputs of water pollution-intensive commodities will be generally too large in Country A and too low in Country B, since A's firms are not paying full opportunity costs of production, and vice versa for B's.[5]

Cooperative solutions to the river pollution problem in a case such as this depend on the acceptance of a guiding principle by both nations. We shall briefly compare the efficiency of four possibilities:

1. Victim pays principle = no liability to polluter.
2. OECD principle of nondiscrimination = partial liability for control costs and consistency.
3. Full cost polluter-pays principle = complete liability without proper incentives.
4. Third party charge-subsidy principle = complete liability with proper price incentives.

In the context of the discussion thus far we have examined only internal incentives to the countries involved with slight reference to internal relocation when the OECD principle of discrimination is adopted. Which principle is most efficient from a global perspective? It cannot be decided universally without reference to the cost of transactions and agreements among countries, information costs, and costs associated with losses in national sovereignty. From a pure efficiency price perspective with zero information, transactions, and sovereignty costs do not matter. Any such principle is as efficient as any other because, through costless trading by all parties and nations, prices will reflect opportunity costs of production and consumption. The ideal of production being on the world production possibility frontier will be achieved.[6]

The only relevant issue is *who* pays and *who* benefits, a distributional problem not easily resolved. With positive information and transactions costs, only under the victim-pays principle do both countries have incentives to "discover" the extent and impact of pollutant emissions. This is because each will have an expected gain from additional information. Alternatively, any polluter-pays principle offers no (and in fact negative) incentive for identification and problem-solving by the polluting country. This basic *asymmetry* in incentives may make it worthwhile in some circumstances to adopt a victim-pays principle. For example, such a principle may be more appropriate when it is impossible for countries other than the polluting country to know rates of pollutant emissions.

It can be assumed that for most cases of transfrontier pollution, emitter and receptor nations will have different amounts of information on pollution damages and control costs. Polluting firms, and by implication the sovereign state they are located within, will be more knowledgeable about control costs at the source than other nations, while the victim nations should have more information on damages and costs of avoidance. Thus, in terms of a bargaining solution, information is not likely to be identical across "frontiers." As has been pointed out, there are strong incentives for the emitter to advocate no control, and the receptor to advocate complete control.[7] However, this "asymmetry" in information further accentuates complications in bargaining, since it clearly pays in uncertain bargaining situations for the victim to overstate damages and its own avoidance costs, and the polluter to overstate source control costs if any of the polluter-pays principles are adopted.

This leads to the possibility of game-strategic approaches for resolving transnational pollution problems that generally cannot be studied *in vacuo*.[8] However, with less than full liability (as set forth in the OECD polluter-pays principle) less importance might be attached to deception or costs for creating misinformation. Under the victim pays principle deception and misinformation have value only to the victim, who may be able to pay less if it can convince the polluting nation that its control costs are low enough (when in fact they are not), such that the emitter is compensated near or equal to actual control costs—but not more.

It has been demonstrated that none of the above principles, with the exception of the third party charge-subsidy principle, will be globally efficient if resources are transferable between nations and transaction costs are not zero; in other words, only the directly affected parties negotiate.[9] That is because, through simple full liability, partial liability, or nonliability rules, *payments between* parties will continue to distort prices in the sense that too few or too many resources will be committed. To remove the distorting payments there are a number of options:

1. The victim nation may sell all pollution rights to the emitter nation;
2. The emitter nation may sell such rights to the victim nation, where in each case the buyer agrees to sell the resource on a nondiscriminatory basis;
3. The payment between nations being held by the nation and *not* transferred to affected private firms or consumers except through lump sum transfers. Even if such an agreement on lump sum transfers is made, it may still pay for one country to attempt to maximize that transfer without cognizance of differences in pollution-control costs between nations. For example, it may pay the polluting country to overstate source-control costs so long as they were less than downstream avoidance costs;
4. With the third-party principle, each nation transfers operational authority of common property resources with transfrontier pollution aspects to a "disinterested" third party or commission;
5. Another unrealistic alternative would be for each nation to fully regulate entry and exit, and location decisions of firms and individuals in consort with optimum use of the international common property resource. None of these solutions appears highly palatable to cases of transfrontier pollution in which there are many emitter and receptor nations, and potential damages and control costs are more than insignificant proportions of national wealth. In each case, there is a prescription of loss in national sovereignty and decision-making.

The full cost polluter-pays principle as set forth in the Trail Smelter case leads to inefficiencies in revenue allocation directly, because of the difference between marginal and average damage payments. In the special case in which damage functions are linear, no inefficiency is implied. Because marginal damages do not equal average damages, the polluting country need not pay as much as would be necessary to achieve an optimal production level internally. Thus, with full cost liability, the polluting country's output will be too large and in consequence domestic (and perhaps international) prices of the polluting commodity too low. However, this principle does not necessarily imply the removal of sovereign rights, nor does it induce directly the national incentives for locational distortions inherent in the OECD "principle of nondiscrimination." Alternatively, with regard to transaction costs problems, the full cost polluter-pays principle, unlike the victim-pays principle, may induce expenditures by the emitter country to misrepresent its contribution to pollution.

POLLUTION FROM STRATOSPHERIC FLIGHT

For the past few years there has been growing concern over pollution of very substantial common property resources, including the oceans, troposphere, and stratosphere. The nature of transmission embodied by the stratosphere was first recognized when widespread radioactivity was observed following nuclear explosions. The stratosphere, which is generally delineated as that part of the atmosphere from 11 to 60 km above the Earth's surface, is characterized by laminar layers of air moving at reasonably high rates of speed. Unlike the troposphere, which has very substantial vertical and horizontal mixing of air currents, there is little vertical mixing in the stratosphere at an elevation of 15–20 km, and a particle may be retained for as long as 3 years. Alternatively, such a particle emitted in the troposphere at say 2 to 5 km, through vertical mixing and rains may be airborne for only a matter of weeks.

Estimated residence times by latitude and height are depicted in Fig. 11-2. Thus pollution of the stratosphere may normally have a much longer retention time than pollution into the troposphere. If amounts of particle or aerosol pollution are allowed to accumulate in the stratosphere, a shielding effect may occur causing less solar radiation to penetrate to the Earth's surface. Such a reduction in solar radiation may cause a change in the Earth's climate, which can be global in extent.

Another and related aspect of stratospheric pollution is the effect of water vapor injected at stratospheric altitudes. Water vapor apparently has a counteracting impact to aerosols or particulates in that water vapor in the stratosphere causes a "greenhouse" effect that may lead to a warming effect at the Earth's surface. Still another recognized impact is the possible alteration of the ozone profile within the stratosphere. It is hypothesized by a number of scientists that if a substantial amount of NO_x (and fluorocarbons) accumulated in the stratosphere, through a complicated set of chemical reactions, this would cause a reduction in the amount of ozone. In consequence greater amounts of ultraviolet radiation would be anticipated to reach the Earth's surface.

The central question is whether various kinds of human activities would induce a pollution load into the stratosphere large enough so that substantial climatic and biological changes occur. Activities that have been identified thus far as either actual or potential sources of such emissions include space transport systems that pass through the stratosphere, military

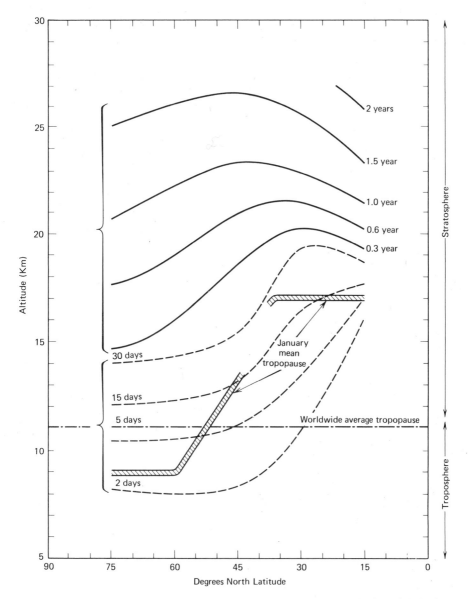

Figure 11-2 Mean stratospheric residence times, as a function of altitude and latitude, January inflection.

aircraft, fluorocarbons, commercial aircraft that now occasionally fly within the stratosphere, nuclear weapons tests, and finally supersonic aircraft that must for technical reasons fly within the stratosphere. In Fig. 11-3, optimal engineering height calculations are given for various aircraft currently or potentially flying in the tropopause or above. Of course, natural injections occur because of vertical mixing between the stratosphere and troposphere, and also through volcanic injections. There is substantial evidence that the eruption of Krakatoa in 1873 had very significant effects on the global climate a year later. This eruption apparently had a large negative impact on temperature, as indicated through the study of tree rings and in observed reduction in agricultural yields on other continents.

It can be tentatively concluded that the stratosphere is truly a global common property resource. That is, decisions by any one country to inject pollutants into it will cause repercussions on *all* other nations. There has yet to be identified substantial, man-induced injections into the stratosphere from nonmilitary sources.

Both common law and international agreement (implied in the Chicago Convention of 1944) state that airspace above each sovereign nation is controlled exclusively by that nation. The stratospheric pollution problem, at least in terms of an institutional setting, can be viewed as somewhat analogous to the pure mining problem in which there are owners of land above the common pool that underlies each unit of owned land, and the common pool can be tapped by any one owner. Pumping by one owner will affect all other owners directly through pumping pressures and future supplies. Conventional wisdom asserts that each individual will have very strong incentives to exploit the resource, and use it more intensively than is socially desirable. In the case of stratospheric pollution, there is the added dimension that each individual nation's decisions will not only affect others, but also itself; if an individual nation should decide to pollute the stratosphere, it would not only influence the climate of other nations, but also its own. Consequently, there would be some incentive for each nation acting individually to restrict it emissions. For truly global common property resources—like the oceans and stratosphere—positive or negative impacts are unlikely to be one-directional in effect and incentive, but more likely to have this feedback effect.

For the stratosphere, two of the three questions posed in the introduction to this chapter can be answered quite simply at this time. Those nations that designed supersonic aircraft must, by definition, be identified as polluters; this list currently includes the Soviet Union, Great Britain, and France. The receptor or affected nations can also be identified: the global grouping of all nations, including the polluting countries. The question of damages and control costs is much less easily examined. Some very rough estimates of

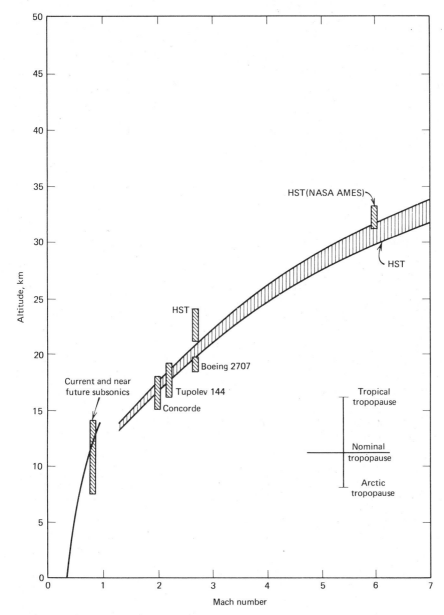

Figure 11-3 Estimated optimal altitude by type of aircraft as a function of velocity).

control costs, both in the form of costs of air pollutants emitted into the stratosphere and foregoing faster flight, are available. Current estimates of control costs could be in error by a factor of at least two, as will be noted below. It should be obvious that with any kind of substantial change in global climate there will be exceedingly large number of both positive and negative economic impacts. At least for now, it can be concluded that damage estimates for *individual* receptor nations are not available.

With regard to guiding international principles, who pays and how much, it appears that there are no existing precedents except the various observations on conflicts over nuclear testing. Individual nations, through their sovereign rights to the airspace above them, and with some degree of individual autonomy, have the right to impose regulations, provided these individual countries are willing to accept some sort of potential retaliation, economic or otherwise, and ban supersonic flights or subsonic flight in the stratosphere over their geographical area. Individual nations also have the right through bilateral agreement outside of the International Civil Aviation Organization (ICAO) to prohibit landing of any form of aircraft that they believe constitutes present danger. The upper limit to airspace is roughly defined by customary international law and observation during the first decade of the space age. It was recognized that the U2 aircraft flying reconnaissance flight at 60,000 feet (18.3 km) was in sovereign airspace. It was accepted as sovereign airspace, because it was navigable by aircraft. On the other hand, states have *passively* permitted spacecraft satellites to orbit over their territory without claims of violation of their sovereign rights. Thus it appears that individual states can regulate emissions from stratospheric flight that occur within their sovereign boundaries, including boundaries at sea. What individual states will not be able to control are emissions over the oceans, which do not constitute sovereign airspace, and over nations agreeing to allow stratospheric flight. This might lead one to speculate on the feasibility of flying from Moscow, using the Arctic Ocean as a pivotal point for entering other oceanic airspaces, and being able to land at almost any coastal city in the world without violating sovereign national airspace. In consequence, it appears unrealistic to assume that stratospheric flight can be regulated through assertions on the rights and laws of sovereign airspace, even though the aircraft typically will be flying at altitudes within currently recognized sovereign boundaries.

There is an emerging legal question as to whether an agreement among the ICAO nations can be made in the future to regulate emissions from supersonic flights and aircraft outside sovereign territories without conflict with other international agreements. The 1958 Geneva Convention on the high seas provides for freedom of flight over the high seas.[10]

The fundamental dependence between economic activity and the atmospheric environment is well understood by everyone either adapting to or living in adverse climates, and it is obvious that climate is one of the underlying determinants in economic systems. Human settlements, location and density, value of agriculture, physical health, and even recreational pursuits are partly the result of climatic changes. It is clear that if substantial climatic changes do occur, the economic impacts will be diverse. For example, increased temperatures could mean decreased heating costs, counteracted by increased air-conditioning costs. Lower temperatures may mean a decrease in productivity of agriculture. In the past two years there has been an attempt by researchers to examine costs and benefits associated with climatic change, under the auspices of the Climatic Impact Assessment Program, U.S. Department of Transportation.

It is impossible to examine all economic effects without a complete global general-equilibrium analysis of benefits and costs. However, the approach was taken of examining a more or less representative sample of major agricultural crops, major fisheries, and major commercial forests in order to assess the (partial equilibrium) adjustment to climatic change and its implied associated benefits and costs. Studies were completed on world corn, cotton, wheat, and rice production, on forest production in the United States, Canada, and the U.S.S.R., and for 13 commercial fisheries species worldwide. For assessing effects in the nonnatural resource area, a set of cost and benefit measures were made for residential, commercial, and industrial fossil-fuel demands, for electricity in commercial and residential buildings, for housing and clothing costs, for road repair and snow removal costs, and finally in aesthetic costs (or benefits) associated with preferred weather patterns. In addition, studies were made of the health-cost impacts.

Cost or benefit measures were developed utilizing the concept of consumer surplus, where applicable, and direct changes in costs or savings where consumer surplus appeared not to be applicable. For comparative purposes, a 1°C change in mean annual global temperature is assumed to occur over a 30-year interval 1990–2020. Of course, the interval 1990–2020 is entirely arbitrary dependent upon the pollutant injection rate assumed.

Table 11-1 is presented only to illustrate magnitudes of benefits and costs of this arbitrary global temperature change. For those categories of economic activity analyzed, net cost is approximately 8.5 billion dollars on an annual basis, or 170 billion dollars on present value basis. It is important to note that there is incomplete coverage of economic sectors as well as omitted sectors, except possibly for rice and cotton production. Each estimate was developed independently, so there are no corrections for sectoral or categorical interdependence, such as the effect of increasing scarcity of rice on the demand for wheat, and there is no consideration of possible future technological changes.

Table 11-1 Estimates of Economic Costs of Climatic and Biologic Changes (1°C Change in Mean Annual Temperature, No Change in Precipitation, 5% Interest Rate Assumed)

Impact Studied	Investigators	Annualized Cost— 1974 (in Millions of U.S. Dollars, Negative Sign Denotes Benefit)
Corn production	Schulze, Ben-David	−21
Cotton production	Schulze, Ben-David	11
Wheat production	Mayo, McMillan	92
Rice production	Bollman	956
Forest production	Schrueder	
United States		661
Canada		268
U.S.S.R. (softwood only)		1383
Douglas Fir production	Schmidt	475
Marine resources	Bell	1431
Health impacts (excluding skin cancer)	Anderson, Lave, Pauly	2386
Water resources	Bollman	−2
Urban resources		
Wages	Hoch	3667
Residential, Commercial and Industrial Fossil Fuel Demand	Nelson	176 lower bound 232 upper bound
Residential and Commercial Electricity Demand	Crocker et al.	−748
Housing, Clothing Expenditures	Crocker et al.	507
Public Expenditures	Sassone	24
Aesthetic Costs	Bradley, Larsen	−219

For illustrative purposes a 1°C mean-annual decrease in temperature corresponds to roughly a 72–200 km movement of existing human settlements northward. The magnitude of measured damages suggests that slight changes in the atmosphere that affect the Earth's temperature will have very large economic repercussions.

Table 11-2 presents additional direct costs for a 1°C change in the mean-annual temperature in the United States with a measure of the wage dif-

Table 11-2 Urban Resource and Health Costs: Comparison of Wage Differentials and Estimated Direct Additional Costs for the United States of a 1°C Decrease in Mean Annual Temperature, No Change in Precipitation, 5% Interest Rate Assumed

Potential Impact	Method of Measurement	Annualized Cost Estimate (Millions of U.S. Dollars)
Wage differences	Cross section (by state) multiple regression analysis by skill category	3667
Additional direct costs		
1. Residential, commercial industrial fossil fuel demand	Cross section (by state multiple regression analysis for each use, differences in expenditure	387
2. Electricity use in commercial buildings	Regression analysis of data on individual commercial buildings	−707[a]
3. Electricity use in residential buildings	Derived from commercial electricity demand regression	−41
4. Personal budget costs (clothing, housing, miscellaneous)[b]	Cross section regression analysis of income-expenditure data	507
5. Public costs on roads, snow removal, etc.	Cross section regression analysis by state	24
6. Materials weathering	Not measured	—
7. Aesthetic costs of preferred weather patterns	Questionnaire on recently moved families	−219
8. Health costs	Cross section regression analysis of health expenditure and crude mortality rates	2386
Sum of additional estimated direct costs, noting that potentially important cost and benefit estimates are omitted		2558

[a] Estimate is probably too high since no adjustment is made for substitution of future buildings to less costly energy sources.
[b] Some double counting.

ference observed between climatic zones of the United States when other nonclimate adjustments are made on wages. These calculations presume a gradual change in temperature over the interval 1990–2020, reaching an equilibrium. In terms of economic theory, wage differentials among regions when adjusted for the large number of other socioeconomic factors, should at least partially reflect differences in the cost of living associated with climatic differences. Thus we should expect that the sum of measured differences in direct costs of living in one climate versus an alternative climate should be approximately equal to the wage differential that is observed between the climates.

In Table 11-2 we observe that for the United States wages would have to increase by about 3.7 billion dollars per year to compensate workers for a minus 1° change in temperature. The measured additional costs for living in the United States with a reduction of 1°C change in temperatures is about $2.6 billion on an annual basis. They are close enough to at least lend some support to the hypothesis that a negative change in temperature will induce a rise in the cost of living or a social loss. It cannot be argued that these estimated costs (and benefits) are necessarily accurate or scientifically defensible. However, they do shed some light as to the order of magnitude of damages that might be associated with unregulated stratospheric flight or other types of emissions into the stratosphere that could markedly alter the Earth's climate—particularly surface temperature.

Examination of Tables 11-1 and 11-2 suggest that the *incidence* of benefits and costs across countries will not be identical. Who will benefit and who will pay for stratospheric pollution cannot be assessed at this time. It appears that the Soviet Union would have one of the greatest probabilities of being harmed through both reduction in acreage of marginal producing wheat areas and increased capital expenditure for farm equipment to compensate for shorter growing seasons. Alternatively, the United States would benefit through greater comparative advantage in wheat production as well as increased yields due to the reduction in "hot-spots" during the summer months. In Fig. 11-4, one illustrative relationship of yield changes for winter wheat in the Soviet Union is given. For very small negative changes in temperature there would be a positive in yield. If temperatures continue to decrease however, yield changes at one point might become negative. A central question for regulation of the stratosphere is how much temperature change on a global basis is tolerable both to the emitter and receptor countries.

In Tables 11-3 and 11-4, a very preliminary benefit–cost analysis based on the *measured* damages and control costs is given. Table 11-3 contains estimates of the damages avoided by desulfurization of jet fuel used in supersonic aircraft (from climatic change imposed by aerosols) along with the

Table 11-3 Climate Change—Preliminary Estimates of Costs and Benefits for Fuel Desulfurization

| Number of Planes[a] | Present Value Cost 1974 5% Rate of Interest (Millions of U.S. Dollars) | |
	Damages Avoided	Desulfurization
200	240	92
400	480	186
600	720	278
1000	1200 (−0.007°C probable change)	464

[a] Second generation supersonic aircraft flying in the year 2020.

costs associated with sulfur removal. It is seen that for various fleet sizes of supersonic aircraft in the year 2000 the benefit–cost ratio for desulfurization exceeds 2.5. However, it is to be noted that damages avoided are computed on the basis of proportionality from 0–1°C to 0–0.007°C. The mean temperature change resulting from the various possible fleets is now very uncertain. Some scientists have indicated the most likely change is negative, but very slight, between 7/1000 and 14/1000°C. It is conceivable, but not probable, that the negative change could be as high as 0.5°C. There is an

Table 11-4 Ozone Depletion—Preliminary Estimates of Costs and Benefits for Engine Redesign

| Number of Planes[a] | Present Value Cost 1974 5% Rate of Interest (Millions of U.S. Dollars) | |
	Damages Avoided	Redesign Costs
200	560	110
400	1040	150
600	1600	190
1000	2760	270

[a] Second generation supersonic aricraft flying in the year 2000.

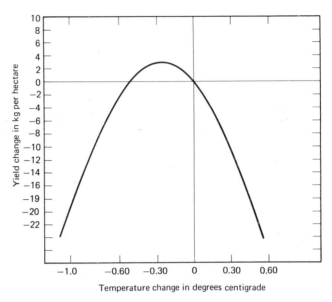

Figure 11-4   Winter wheat changes for (+) and (−) temperature changes (USSR).

additional problem in that fuel desulfurization takes account of the aerosol impact on climatic change, but the counteracting impact from injection of water vapor, which on balance is predicted to raise surface temperature via the "greenhouse" effect, is not considered. Desulfurization alone could conceivably induce an even greater warming effect from water vapor injections. Until more precise meteorological models can be constructed on a global basis so that the joint effect of water vapor and aerosols can be more accurately predicted, the benefit–cost ratio for sulfur removal must be extremely qualified.

Economic costs induced by alteration in the amount ultraviolet radiation contacting the earth were estimated for skin cancer (nonmelanoma) and materials. Materials weathering costs associated with increased uv radiation were estimated for plastics, textiles, paints, and other surface finishes. Many other potential impacts including increased skin aging, sunburn, and biological processes dependent on the ultraviolet spectrum, were not measured. Table 11-4 lists measured damages avoided and estimated costs associated with redesigning jet engine combustors to reduce NO_x emissions by a factor of 6.

For fleet sizes from 200 to 1000 airplanes, all computed benefit–cost ratios exceed 4. Among countries, ozone depletion effects are highly diverse since incidence rates for skin cancer are much greater for light-skinned

Caucasians and for individuals who spend large amounts of time in the sun, such as farmers and construction workers. For countries in which there is relatively little activity out of doors, changes in ultraviolet radiation should have only minor effects on incidence rates. Alternatively, for nations with very substantial levels of outdoor recreational activity, incidence rates may increase. Because of the likely negative impacts of ozone depletion on areas that were not included and the method of estimating damages, a greater degree of confidence might be placed in the estimated benefit–cost ratios than for temperature change. In the benefit–cost estimates presented for ozone depletion and for climatic change, there is a substantial difference in the sheer magnitude of damages that may occur. However, the climatic estimates are subject to a much greater degree of uncertainty.

A central question is concerned with whether the meager evidence presented allows deduction as to how the stratospheric pollution problem might be resolved, and how the stratosphere can be feasibly managed as a global common-property resource. Hopefully, it is clear from this very tentative benefit–cost analysis that: (1) The stratosphere is a resource that is potentially sensitive to man's activities, and not enough is known about it to accurately predict consequences either in an efficiency or distributional sense. (2) Suspected impacts are negative and of a long-term character. Increased exposure to ultraviolet radiation today means an increased probability of contracting skin cancer in 30 years, and gradual buildup in aerosols in the stratosphere may require 60 years to be noticeably reflected in long-term trends of surface temperature. It is suggestive that an international regulatory body for the stratosphere is urgently needed. There are few incentives now for adequate regulation because of the lack of identifiable international precedent on rights, and because of the great uncertainties in actual benefits and costs.

NOTES

1. OECD, *Recommendation of the Council on Guiding Principles Concerning International Economic Aspects of Environmental Policies,* Annex, Paris, May 26, 1972.

2. OECD, *Recommendation of the Council on Principles Concerning Transfrontier Pollution,* Paris, November 21, 1974.

3. Christy draws a very useful distinction between the production of wealth, and distribution or ownership of wealth with regard to ocean fisheries. The first concept involves issues of access and free use while the second involves specification of shares. The discussion in this paper will be centered on the use issues although some comments will be directed on access. See F. T. Christy, Jr., "Fisheries: Common Property, Open Access, and the Common Heritage," *Pacem in Maribus,* The Royal University of Malta Press, 1971, Chapter 6.

4. The appearance of reciprocity may negate this statement, particularly in those cases where an external diseconomy in one direction between countries is offset by an external economy in the opposite direction.

5. See, Ralph C. D'Arge, "Observations on the Economics of Transnational Environmental Externalities," in *Problems in Transfrontier Pollution,* OECD, Paris, 1974, p. 173.

6. P. Samuelson, "The Gains from International Trade Once Again," *Economic Journal,* December, 1962.

7. See, Anthony Scott, "Transfrontier Pollution: Models of Separate and Joint Abatement," University of British Columbia, April 1974, mimeographed.

8. See, d'Arge, op. cit., for some simple examples.

9. See, R. d'Arge and W. Schulze, Appendix 1 of R. d'Arge, op. cit.

10. See, Convention on the High Seas signed at Geneva, Switzerland, April 29, 1958.

Chapter

12

International Externalities:
The Ocean Environment

Charles Pearson

Transnational pollution is defined as the physical movement of pollutants generated in one country that are transported outside its territory, and that degrade the environment of other countries or an international common property resource. Marine pollution is a special and important category of transnational pollution, and can be described as reciprocal external diseconomies of an environmental nature that affect an international common property resource, the oceans.[1] While the laws of gravity have made natural sinks of the oceans, the failures of domestic and international law, and market failure, have assisted in this process.

  The purpose of this chapter is to analyze, from an economic perspective, some aspects of ocean environment deterioration and corrective measures, drawing on the literature of the economics of environmental management.[2] The first section presents background information on types and sources of marine pollution, and identifies some of the major United States international measures for environmental control (EC). The next section focuses

Table 12-1 Major Ocean EC Measures by Type of Pollution and Method of Introduction[a]

	Method of Introduction									
	Marine-Based Sources					Land-Based Sources				
	Ocean Transport								Atmos-	
Type of Pollutant	Routine	Acci-dental	Dredg-ing	Off-Shore Petroleum Exploitation	Other	Dirty River Dis-charge	Marine Outfalls	Ocean Dump-ing	pheric Blowoff	Other
Petroleum	1a	1a		12		7		2, 3, 4		
Industrial waste (general)	1b, 1c	1b, 1c				7		2, 3, 4		
Pesticide, insecticide residuals (halogenated hydrocarbons)	1b, 1c	1b, 1c				7, 9		2, 3, 4	9	
Sewage and garbage	1d	1d				7		2, 3, 4		
Heavy metals						7	7	2, 3, 4		
Dredge spoils			2, 3, 4					2, 3, 4		
Radioactive wastes	10				5, 6			2, 3, 4	5	10
Thermal discharges										11
Others									8	

[a] Identification key to Table 12-1: Major Ocean EC Measures.

1a. International Convention for the Prevention of Pollution from Ships (1973) Annex I. This mandatory annex contains design and operating standards, and effluent discharge limits for tankers. Provisions are designed to reduce both routine and accidental petroleum discharges from tankers and other ocean-going vessels. The Convention has not been ratified and is not in force.

1b. International Convention for the Prevention of Pollution from Ships (1973) Annex II. This mandatory annex established effluent discharge limits in ocean transport of noxious liquid substances.

1c. International Convention for the Prevention of Pollution from Ships (1973) Annex III. This optional annex deals with ocean transport of containerized noxious wastes.

1d. International Convention for the Prevention of Pollution from Ships (1973) Annex IV, V. These two optional annexes deal with vessel's sewage and garbage, respectively.

2. Convention on the Prevention of Marine Pollution by Dumping of Wastes and other Matter (1972). More commonly, the Ocean Dumping Convention. The Convention established a blacklist of substances for which dumping is prohibited, but leaves considerable discretion to national authorities in controlling the dumping of other wastes. The Convention has been ratified by the United States, but is not yet in force.

3. Regional ocean dumping conventions including the 1972 North Sea Ocean Dumping Convention and the 1974 Convention on the Protection of the Marine Environment of the Baltic Sea Area. The North Sea Convention is similar to the Ocean Dumping Convention; the Baltic Sea Convention covers land-based sources and vessel sources of ocean pollution.

4. United States Marine Protection, Research and Sanctuaries Act of 1972, and subsequent implementing regulations established by the EPA. This legislation designates the EPA as the primary permit-granting agency for ocean dumping, but the Army Corps of Engineers retains permit-granting authority over its own activity of dredging operations.

5. Treaty Banning Nuclear Weapons Tests in the Atmosphere, in Outer Space and Under Water (Partial Test Ban Treaty). Signed and entered into force, 1963.

6. Treaty on the Prohibition of the Emplacement of Nuclear Weapons and Other Weapons of Mass Destruction on the Sea-Bed and the Ocean Floor and in the Subsoil Thereof (Sea-Bed Treaty). Signed 1971 and entered into force, 1972.

7. United States Federal Water Pollution Control Act Amendments of 1972.

8. Major air pollutants (sulfur dioxide, particulate to matter, carbon monoxide, hydrocarbons, nitrogen oxides, photochemical oxidents) are controlled in the United States by the Clean Air Act Amendments of 1970 and the 1974 Energy Supply and Environmental Coordination Act.

9. United States Federal Environmental Pesticide Control Act of 1972. While not directly intended for marine EC, it may indirectly reduce land-based sources.

10. The disposal of radioactive wastes from nuclear power plants is regulated by the Nuclear Regulatory Commission. The NRC also has the responsibility for licensing the operation of all marine vessels with nuclear reactors.

11. The EPA sets standards for thermal discharges through the Federal Water Pollution Control Act.

12. For the United States, the Interior Department is responsible for leasing territory on the Outer Continental Shelf, and for monitoring the safety of drilling. The environmental-impact statement provisions of the National Environmental Policy Act (NEPA) are, of course, involved.

on the two broad questions of ocean environmental management determining pollution-abatement (environmental-quality) objectives, and selecting control instruments. The third section sets forth certain additional considerations in formulating ocean EC policy, and presents tentative conclusions. Throughout, special attention is given to the two major international EC measures negotiated recently, the 1972 Ocean Dumping Convention and the 1973 Prevention of Pollution from Ships Convention.[3]

OCEAN POLLUTION: TYPES, SOURCES, ENVIRONMENTAL MEASURES

Ocean pollution can be usefully classified by pollutant and by method of introduction into the marine environment. The usefulness of the classification scheme rests in part on the fact that ocean EC measures are fragmented and piecemeal, and are not comprehensive as to source and type of

Table 12-2   Estimated Sources and Quantities of Oil Pollution of the Oceans[a]

	Metric Tons	%
Tanker Operations		
LOT cleaning/ballasting[b]	84,499	2.4
Non-LOT cleaning/ballasting	455,708	13.2
Product tankers using shore reception facilities	19,492	0.6
Product tankers *not* using shore reception facilities	63,832	1.9
Ore/bulk/oil carriers cleaning and ballasting	119,543	3.4
Additional cleaning and disposal prior to drydocking	91,895	2.7
Tanker bilges	9,573	0.3
Tanker barges	12,787	0.4
Terminal operations	31,933	0.9
	889,262	25.8
Other Ship Operations		
Bunkers	9,055	0.3
Bilges, cleaning, ballasting, etc.	292,481	8.5
	301,536	8.8

Table 12-2 Continued

	Metric Tons	%
Vessel Accidents		
Tankers	104,268	3.0
Tank barges	19,803	0.6
All other vessels	48,972	1.4
	173,043	5.0
Offshore Activities		
Offshore drilling	118,126	3.4
	118,126	3.4
Nonmarine Operations and Accidents		
Refinery-petrochemical plant waste oils	195,402	5.7
Industrial machinery waste oil	718,468	20.8
Automotive waste oil	1,034,588	29.9
Pipelines	25,574	0.7
Overall Total	3,455,999	100.0

[a] Source: D. Charter & J. Porricelli, "Quantitative Estimates of Petroleum to the Oceans," paper presented at the May 1973 Workshop on Inputs, Fates and Effects of Petroleum in the Marine Environment, National Academy of Sciences, National Research Council, and quoted in C. Pearson, op. cit.

[b] LOT—Load on Top, a technique in which oily water ballast is collected in slop tanks with the heavier seawater settling to the bottom and being released. Fresh oil is then loaded directly on the oil residue in the slop tanks.

pollutant.[4] No attempt is made to present here a complete taxonomy of marine pollution and related EC measures. Rather, the purpose is to set forth as background information the major pollutants, methods of introduction to the marine environment, and associated EC measures, and to illustrate the diversity and complexity of the phenomenon.

Table 12-1 attempts this description of pollutants and methods of introduction. The first column lists major ocean pollutants. The categories are not entirely mutually exclusive, for example, dredge spoils may contain heavy metals, as can sewage sludge.[5] The horizontal stub lists channels through which pollutants enter the marine environment. The major division is between land-based and marine-based waste generating activities. It is clear that some channels are more deliberately used than others as, for example, marine outfalls and ocean dumping. Finally, we have attempted to identify some of the major domestic (United States) and international EC measures according to the type and source of pollution that they attempt to abate. This is an imperfect exercise, as we do not comprehend all EC measures, and ambiguities in the classification interfere.[6] Naturally, the existence of an EC measure does not mean that the pollution problem is resolved.

Tables 12-2 and 12-3 extend this description by considering in greater detail a major ocean pollutant, oil, and a particular channel for pollution, ocean dumping. Both are now subject to international conventions.[7] Table 12-2 presents estimates of petroleum reaching the marine environment. The data are classified according to method of introduction. Note that there are no estimates of ocean pollution arising from atmospheric blowoff, although this is considered to be a major source by most observers.[8] Also, observe that, even if atmospheric blowoff is excluded, land-based sources are extremely important, accounting for 57% of oil pollution of the oceans. The significance, explored below, is that international EC measures have been

Table 12-3   United States Ocean Dumping: Types, Locations, Amounts, 1968 and 1973[a]

Waste Type	Atlantic		Gulf of Mexico		Pacific		Total	
	1968	1973	1968	1973	1968	1973	1968	1973
			(thousands of tons)					
Dredge spoils	15808	NA	15300	NA	7320	NA	38428	NA
Sewage sludge	4477	5429	0	0	0	0	4477	5429
Industrial wastes	3013	3997	696	1408	981	0	4690	5405
Construction and demolition debris	574	1161	0	0	0	0	574	1161
Solid wastes	0	0	0	0	26	0.2	26	0.2
Explosives	15	0	0	0	0	0	15	0
Total	23887		15966		8327		48210	

[a] Sources: Council on Environmental Quality, *5th Annual Report*, 1974, Table 11, pg. 150 and Council on Environmental Quality, *Ocean Dumping: A National Policy*, Washington: GPO, 1970.

Note: These data do not include wastes piped to sea (marine outfalls). Note also that 86,758 containers of radioactive wastes were dumped between 1946 and 1970, but at a greatly reduced rate in recent years. The practice has now been apparently discontinued.

blocked by national sovereignty in reaching back to control major land-based ocean pollution.[9]

Table 12-3 presents data on United States ocean dumping by dumped material, and by location, for 1968 and 1973. The data do not include dumping incidental to normal ships operations, nor marine outfalls. By weight, dredge spoils dominate, but these vary considerably as to degree of contamination. Sewage sludge, industrial wastes (waste acids, refinery wastes, pesticide wastes, paper mill wastes, etc.), and construction and demolition wastes are up 21, 15, and 102%, respectively, from 1968 to 1973. Solid-waste dumping was down, and the dumping of explosives (by scuttling old Liberty Ships) was zero in 1973.

Finally, as background information we reproduce in Table 12-4 an alternative classification of sources and types of marine pollution that attempts to describe the importance of particular sources for each pollutant. The information is based on the work of the Joint Group of Experts on the Scientific Aspects of Marine Pollution (GESAMP), and was cited by Shinn.

OBJECTIVES AND INSTRUMENTS

It can be argued that, in principle, the economic explanation for ocean environment deterioration is no different than domestic environmental deterioration; it is the failure of a common property legal regime to account for external diseconomies. Moreover, the formulation of ocean EC measures must confront the same fundamental decisions as domestic EC measures—the choice of pollution-abatement (environmental-quality) objectives, the selection of control instruments having the lowest social cost, and evaluating the effects of EC measures on the distribution of welfare.

In four important respects, however, the formation of ocean EC policy differs from the domestic process. First and most obvious, the oceans beyond territorial jurisdiction are under no effective national or international authority. Restrictive international law is very weak, with a strong tradition of laissez-faire, embodied in the doctrine of freedom of the seas, free access, and rights of capture. Accordingly, ocean EC measures will only come about through negotiations among sovereign states and the development of international law, or as the almost incidental side effect of national measures designed to improve domestic environmental welfare. While all EC measures have welfare distributional consequences, the traditional separation of allocative efficiency and distributional consequences that characterizes much of domestic EC policy, and which derives ultimately from the authority of government to take action to promote the social

Table 12-4 Principal Sources of Marine Pollution[a,b]

Category of Pollutant	Manufacture and Use of Industrial Products—Disposal via Direct Outfalls and Rivers	Domestic Wastes—Disposal via Direct Outfalls and Rivers	Agriculture, Forestry, Public Health—Disposal via Runoff from Land	Deliberate Dumping from Ships	Operational Discharge from Ships in Course of Duties	Accidental Release from Ships and Submarine Pipelines	Exploitation of Seabed Mineral Resources	Military Activities	Transfer from the Atmosphere
Domestic sewage including food-processing wastes	+	++	– –	+	(+)	– –	– –	– –	– –
Pesticides									
Organochlorine compounds	+	+	++	(+)	– –	0	– –	?	++
Organophosphorus compounds	+	(+)	+	– –	– –	0	– –	?	++
Carbamate compounds	+	– –	(+)	– –	– –	0	– –	– –	– –
Herbicides	+	(+)	++	– –	– –	0	– –	+	+
Mercurial compounds	+	– –	++	– –	– –	0	– –	?	?
Miscellaneous metal-containing compounds	++	(+)	(+)	– –	– –	0	– –	– –	?
PCBs	++	(+)	– –	(+)	– –	–	?	– –	+
Inorganic wastes									
Acids and alkalis	+	– –	– –	+	– –	+	– –	– –	– –
Sulfite	+	– –	– –	–	– –	– –	– –	– –	(+)
Titanium dioxide wastes	0	– –	– –	0	– –	– –	– –	– –	– –
Mercury	++	+	– –	+	– –	0	?	?	++

	1	2	3	4	5	6	7	8	9
Copper	++	(+)	(+)	(+)	—	(+)	—	—	—
Zinc	+	—	—	+	—	(+)	—	—	—
Chromium	++	—	—	?	—	0	—	?	—
Cadmium	++	—	(+)	—	—	0	—	?	—
Arsenic	++	—	—	+	—	0	—	?	?
Radioactive materials	++	(+)	—	(+)	—	+	+	(+)	0*
Oil and oil dispersants	++	—	—	+	+	+	+	+	—
Petrochemicals and organic chemicals									
Aromatic solvents	++	—	—	(+)	—	(+)	—	?	?
Aliphatic solvents	+	—	—	(+)	—	(+)	—	?	?
Plastic intermediates and byproducts	++	—	(+)	+	—	(+)	—	?	?
Phenols	++	(+)	—	+	—	0	—	(+)	—
Amines	++	—	—	(+)	—	0	—	—	—
Polycyclic aromatics	++	—	—	+	—	0	?	—	—
Organic wastes including pulp and paper wastes	++	++	+	+	?	—	—	—	—
Military wastes	?	—	—	?	?	?	—	?	?
Heat	++	—	(+)	—	—	—	—	—	—
Detergents	++	++	—	+	++	(+)	—	+	—
Solid objects	+	+	—	+	—	(+)	(+)	+	—
Dredging spoil and inert wastes	+	—	—	+	—	—	++	—	—

[a] Key to symbols: ++ important; + significant; (+) slight; ? uncertain; -- negligible; 0 potentially harmful; * dependent on extent of weapons testing

[b] Source: Joint Group of Experts on the Scientific Aspects of Marine Pollution, *Report of the Third Session*, Rome: FAO, February 1971, UN Doc GESAMP III/19, pp. 19–22. Cited by Robert Shinn, *The International Politics of Marine Pollution Control*, his Table 1.2.

welfare, cannot be assumed on the international level. Neither the element of compulsion nor the redistributional mechanisms that are present domestically, are available in the international context. Consequently, distributional considerations play a much larger role in the negotiation of abatement objectives and the choice of instruments.

Second, ocean environment questions are closely linked to other ocean issues. The resolution of these issues through the current Law of the Sea negotiations will result in fundamental alteration of the legal regime governing ocean space. The environmental issue of increasing economic efficiency in the use of oceans by restricting access for waste disposal, is hopelessly enmeshed in the scramble of countries to appropriate to themselves new wealth from the oceans—offshore oil, manganese nodules, fisheries resources, and so forth.[10] Moreover, the traditional interests of naval and maritime states, such as the United States, in unimpeded marine transport and naval mobility have a profound impact on ocean EC policy. For this reason, we cannot expect ocean environmental policy to be established independently, and on its own merits. Environmental and economic purists should become aware of this.

Third, international ocean EC measures will require implementing regulations by domestic authorities. This introduces an intervening layer of authority between an international agreement and the pollution source. In some respects this may be an advantage. Discretionary authority accorded to national governments can provide desirable flexibility in EC standards, and allow local standards to conform with local-benefit cost calculations. The serious disadvantage is that the mechanisms for compelling compliance with international instruments are far weaker. At the extreme, complete discretion given to national authorities reduces to a parochial cost-benefit calculus, with no reduction in external international diseconomies, unless joint-reduction benefits are seen.

Fourth and last, it should be pointed out that ocean environmental deterioration does not conform to simple models of transnational pollution that assume a simple unidirectional flow of damages. Damages are generally reciprocal. The number of states affected is usually large.[11] Nor is international law as clear with respect to right assignments in ocean space as it is with direct transnational pollution. The principle that a state should not undertake activities that directly damage the territory of another state is stronger when prospective damage is to an international common property resource such as the oceans. The large number of affected parties, the mutuality of the damage flows, the greater uncertainty surrounding the assignment of rights, and the continued importance to states of jealously guarding national sovereignty, all suggest that transaction costs for negotiating and enforcing international EC measures will be substantial.

To a greater or lesser degree, these four special aspects of negotiating ocean EC measures influenced the form and substance of the Ocean Dumping Convention, and the Prevention of Pollution from Ships Convention. They will continue to be felt as new ocean EC measures evolve.

ABATEMENT GOALS

With this introduction, an important question to tackle is whether globally optimal, ocean-pollution-abatement goals will be approximated by actual abatement levels given the absence of any supranational authority having the power to compel compliance. The high transactions costs and the primitive nature of international compensation networks suggests doubt.

Consider first a situation in which two countries, A and B, share an international common property resource for beneficial uses (recreation, transport, etc.), and A pollutes and B does not. Assume "normal" marginal abatement cost and benefit functions in which, as abatement approaches 100%, marginal costs increase and marginal benefits decrease. Finally assume that no compensation flows between A and B. The situation is depicted in Fig. 12-1.

Marginal benefits from abatement to A are indicated as MB_A, marginal benefits to B as MB_B and global benefits as MB_{A+B}. Marginal abatement

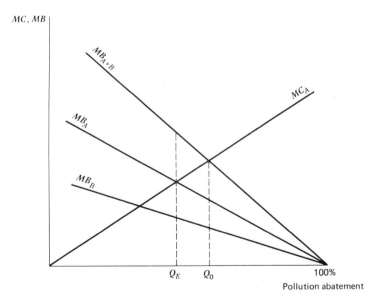

Figure 12-1 Setting abatement levels: one polluter.

costs, borne entirely by A, are MC_A. In maximizing its own welfare, A will undertake abatement up to level Q_E, but this will fall short of global optimum abatement level Q_0 where $MC_A = MB_{A+B}$. Just as the flow of damages from A to B is unrecorded in A's calculations, so too will the benefit from A's abatement conferred on B be given zero weight. The degree to which the unilateral action by A falls short of the optimum ($Q_0 - Q_E$) will be less: (1) The steeper the slope of MC_A; (2) The steeper the slope of MC_B; (3) The steeper the slope of MB_B; and (4) The lower the position of MB_B.

The economic interpretation is clear—if abatement costs rise rapidly, if marginal damages to others fall rapidly, and, especially, if ocean pollution is mostly *local* in the sense that most damages fall on the polluting state, then unilateral action maximizing the welfare of the polluter may be close to the global optimum.

The situation is more complex when both A and B are polluters, and contemplate entering into a mutual agreement to reduce pollution, but no compensation payments can be made. In general, the knowledge that others will undertake to reduce pollution should permit individual states to balance larger benefits against their own abatement costs, and, therefore, pursue higher abatement goals. However, countries may falsely report their benefits and costs in order to enjoy a "free ride." Consider Fig. 12-2.

We assume for simplicity that prior to any *EC* measures, A and B contribute equal quantities of pollutants, that their marginal-abatement costs (MC_A, MC_B) differ (due perhaps to different availability of alternative

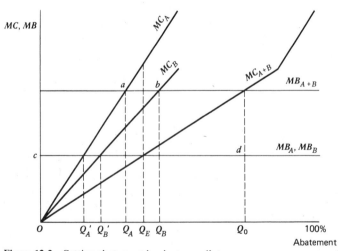

Figure 12-2   Setting abatement levels: two polluters.

disposal sites or mediums), and for simplicity, that the marginal benefits from abatement (MB_A, MB_B) are independent, constant, and equal in the two countries. The global marginal-abatement cost curve, MC_{A+B}), has been constructed so that at all levels the division of pollution abatement between the countries is optimal ($MC_A = MC_B$). It is thus a minimum marginal-abatement cost curve. The global optimum level is Q_0 ($MC_{A+B} = MB_{A+B}$). Note that if each country abated to its parochial optimum ($MC_A = MB_A$ and $MC_B = MB_B$), the total abatement would be OQ_A' plus OQ_B' $= OQ_E$, which would be less than the global optimum, OQ_0. Given the slopes and positions of the curves as drawn, and if the only alternative confronting A and B were no abatement or abatement at Q_0, it is clear that both states would be better off to abate to the optimal level (Q_A for A, Q_B for B). The net welfare gain to A is the area under its marginal benefit curve less the area under its own marginal abatement cost curve ($O \ Q_0dc - O \ Q_Aa$), and for B is ($O \ Q_0dc - O \ Q_Bb$).[12]

However, the solution calls for a greater percentage and absolute reduction by B ($OQ_B > OQ_A$), and might be resisted. In contrast, an agreement for the same optimal abatement level OQ_0, and equal percentage and absolute reductions would be Q_E for each and this would be inefficient with $MC_A > MC_B$. The flexibility exhibited in the ocean dumping convention is a necessary condition to account for differential abatement cost (and damage) functions. At the same time it may weaken the confidence of individual states that they will benefit from others' abatement. Perhaps more importantly, unequal abatement burdens may offend notions of equity, and be precluded for this reason.

To this point we have drawn abatement benefit functions for the two countries which do not explicitly disaggregate the damage by source. In practice, the spatial nature of pollution and of beneficial uses of ocean resources is such that pollution abatement benefit functions should distinguish between pollution sources, and between recipients of benefits. We have attempted to illustrate this in Fig. 12-3. We assume (1) countries A and B contribute equal amounts of pollution, (2) that marginal abatement costs are the same in both countries, (3) that B is a major beneficial user of ocean resources and, hence, suffers greater relative damages than A from pollution, (4) that the folow of damages from A to B exceeds the follow of damages from B to A (A's pollution less local than B's).

Let MC_i be the marginal costs for the ith country. Let MB_{ij} be the marginal benefit to the ith country from abatement by the jth country. By assumption, MC_A depicted in panel 1 equals MC_B depicted in panel 2 for all abatement levels. For ease of exposition we have assumed that all marginal benefits are constant, and that $MB_{AA} = MB_{AB}$ and $MB_{BB} = MB_{BA}$. Additionally, to accord with our assumptions that B is a major beneficial user of

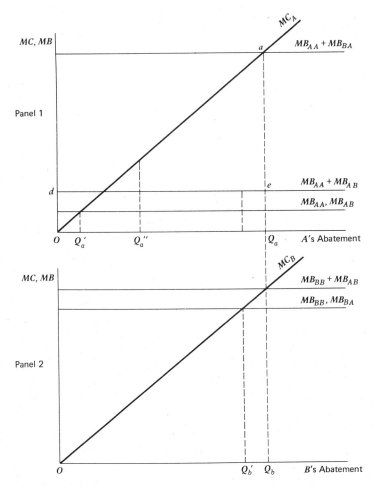

Figure 12-3   Setting abatement levels: two polluters, assigned damages.

the oceans, and that the flow of damages from A to B exceeds the flow of damages from B to A we have shown total marginal damages to B, $MB_{BB} + MB_B$, greater than total marginal damages to A, $MB_{AA} + MB_{AB}$, and the flow of damages from A to B, MB_{BA}, greater than the reverse flow, MB_{AB}.

To maximize global welfare, marginal abatement costs in A are equated to total marginal benefits, or $MC_A = MB_{AA} + MB_{BA}$. In country B this optimum is found at $MC_B = MB_{BB} + MB_{AB}$. The globally optimum abatement levels are then Q_a and Q_b, respectively. (The equality of abatement levels results from our assumption of equal marginal assumed equality of MB_{AA} and MB_{AB}, and MB_{BB} and MB_{BA}.)

Assuming that the only choice were between no abatement and abatement to the optimum levels Q_a and Q_b, and that no compensation could be paid, the global optimum would not be achieved. With the reasonable constraint that no country would enter an agreement that makes it worse off, abatement would be suboptimal, because at the global optimal levels A would be worse off. A would incur a cost of O_aQ_a that exceeds its benefits of $OdeQ_a$.

If we allow for intermediate abatement levels between zero and the global optimal, the negotiations and outcome become more complicated.[13] For example, if A were certain that B would move to its parochial optimum of Q_b', equating MC_B with MB_{BB}, then A would move to its parochial optimum, Q_a' ($MC_A = MB_{AA}$), but would have no incentive to go further. The bargaining might be such, however, that B "demands" that A move to a higher level, say Q_a'', in exchange for going to Q_b'. This outcome is feasible as both countries would be made better off.

Alternatively, A could attempt to "extort" a payment from B in terms of B's abatement that carried it past its optimum level Q_b. Such an arrangement could leave both A and B better off than initially or at their parochial optima, but by assumption would be globally suboptimal. Game theory analysis is suggested.

The conclusion, then, is that, when no compensation payments can be made (or when the only "currency" for making payments is in units of abatement), it is unlikely that the globally optimum level of abatement will be attained. This conclusion becomes important when there are substantial differences among the ocean users with respect to their beneficial use of the oceans, the extent to which their pollution is local, and the availability of low-cost, alternative disposal sites.

In a broader sense, the issue of choosing optimum abatement levels is serious because restrictive international law is weak, the mechanisms for international transfers are primitive, and there is no effective resort to compulsion. The presumably necessary condition that no country be made worse off appears constraining. In this situation the optimism of the Coase Theorem with regard to allocative efficiency regardless of initial rights allocation is not enough.[14] Even with zero transactions costs, mechanisms for compensatory transfers are insufficient for a priori confidence in internationally negotiated abatement levels.[15] One may argue, of course, that the international arena is rich with nonenvironmental "payments" that can be made, ranging from trade concessions to granting fishing rights, and that the inclusion of environmental matters in the inclusive Law of the Sea Conference (LOS) provides a wealth of opportunities for one type of side deal or another. My preliminary opinion, however, is that the inclusion of environmental questions in LOS negotiations will not provide the avenue for compensation, but rather will tend to sacrifice environmental interests for others that have stronger voices within national delegations.

SETTING ABATEMENT GOALS: THE CONVENTIONS

The Ocean Dumping Convention and related United States legislation, and the Prevention of Pollution from Ships Convention can illustrate these propositions. With respect to United States dumping, it can be argued that most of the damages are local, harming United States interests. Accordingly, it is not surprising that the United States instituted dumping controls simultaneously with the negotiations of an international agreement, and would have proceeded on a unilateral basis if necessary. Furthermore, the structure of the global convention, which leaves considerable discretion to national authorities (except for certain blacklisted substances), would probably not be a serious barrier in the case of the United States, to establishing optimal levels if the assumed local character of United States dumping is correct.[16] At the same time the discretionary nature of the agreement reflects the absence of an international compensation mechanism. No country is compelled to go beyond its parochial cost–benefit calculus, but is given encouragement to do so.

The situation is quite different in European waters where pollution damages may not be predominantly local. In such circumstances one could not rely on unilateral action to approach a global optimum. The multilateral commitment represented by the global convention (supplemented by the regional North Sea and Baltic conventions) becomes necessary. One is, however, less confident in the discretionary nature of the global agreement, particularly in the absence of any compensation schemes (which were not included), and the possibility for free riders.

Compensatory transfers were not a part of the Prevention of Pollution from Ships Convention either. However, the structure of that agreement is very different, and the issue of attaining optimum abatement levels takes a quite different form. In contrast to the Ocean Dumping Convention, this latter agreement lays down very specific provisions regarding vessel design and construction, equipment, and effluent discharge standards. For oil-pollution abatement, the more important provisions include segregated ballasting for new tankers over 70,000 deadweight tons, and an oil-discharge limit of no more than 60 liters per nautical mile, and no more than 1/30,000 of ships cargo in total (1/15,000 for existing tankers).[17] Because of the specific nature of the Convention provisions, there will be little latitude given to national authorities in setting oil discharge limits. Instead, one must look to the agreement itself in evaluating the question of whether optimal abatement levels were selected.

The question cannot be definitely answered. Prior to the negotiation of the agreement, considerable study was devoted to the benefits and particularly the costs of marine source oil abatement. Studies had been commissioned to examine the cost and effectiveness of alternative control measures—segregated ballasting, load on top, onshore reception facilities, flexible membranes. The International Maritime Consultative Organizations (IMCO), under whose auspices the Convention was negotiated, also commissioned the United Kingdom as the lead country in studying the environmental and financial consequences of oil pollution at sea in an effort to develop data for damage (benefit) functions for pollution abatement. By and large the effort was a failure. Although useful information was accumulated for projecting oil reaching the oceans under alternative assumptions, it was not possible to translate this into economic damage functions.

Accordingly, when negotiating the Convention it was apparent that oil pollution of the oceans was considered an important problem, that measures should be undertaken, but that on the basis of gross judgment, some measures were too costly to contemplate. Specifically, with cost consideration in mind, the negotiations:

- Set a lower limit of 70,000 D.W.T. for requiring segregated ballasting facilities on tankers;
- Limited segregated ballasting to new tankers contracted for after December 31, 1975 or delivered after December 31, 1979, and did not require retrofitting of the existing tanker fleet (220 million D.W.T. at end of 1973);
- Did not accept the United States proposal for requiring double bottoms for new tankers.[18]

With regard to double bottoms it is not clear that the decision was made entirely on cost grounds. Some experts pointed out that refloating a grounded tanker with double bottom can be more difficult, and thus permit more oil to escape. Also the space between the cargo and hull may collect volatile gases and increase the danger of explosion.

Nor is there any evidence that the narrower self interest of countries highly dependent on imported oil, and presumably wishing to minimize transport costs, led the conference to adopt less than globally optimum abatement levels. The Prevention of Pollution from Ships Convention is inconclusive with respect to the issue of securing globally optimum abatement levels by negotiation among sovereign states without compensation mechanisms.

INSTRUMENTS

The now thoroughly argued merits of control instruments that work through the price system (taxes, subsidies) versus more direct controls (design and equipment standards, effluent/emission limits) have interesting sidelights in an international context.

First, an effluent/emission tax system on ocean dumping or on oil discharged can be defended not only on the traditional grounds that it automatically distinguishes between high and low alternative cost pollution sources, and provides a continuing incentive for pollution abatement, but also that the rental value of the assimilative capacity of the oceans can be captured by the putative owners. The conceptual underpinning for this contention is the "common heritage of mankind," a somewhat murky assertion that the oceans beyond territorial jurisdiction (yet to be agreed to) belong to mankind in common. This assertion has been pushed most forcefully with respect to ocean mineral resources, and especially the famous manganese nodules, in anticipation of some revenue from their exploitation. In principle there is no difference between extracting rent for mankind from mineral resources, or from assimilative capacity. Restricting ocean pollution by the more direct instruments now in use, such as permits for ocean dumping, design and equipment and effluent limits for vessel-source oil pollution, yields this rent to ocean waste disposers.

The more compelling criterion in choosing control instruments is attaining maximum compliance at least-enforcement cost. The enforcement question is critical in the international context and plays a large role in the selection of control instruments. For ocean dumping, the international convention and relevant United States legislation rely on permits by national authorities for controlling dumping of all but blacklisted, or prohibited substances. In the United States, the EPA establishes permit criteria and issues the permit, while the Coast Guard undertakes enforcement activities. The exception to this is dredge spoils, for which the Army Corps of Engineers is both the potential polluter and is given initial authority to issue itself dumping permits.

United States legislation is written in a fashion that allows, but does not guarantee, an economically efficient permit policy. In drawing up dumping-permits criteria, the EPA must consider the availability and cost of alternative disposal sites and mediums. Certainly this is essential to a rational waste-disposal policy—shunting the wastes from one site to another at higher social (environmental and financial) costs would be foolish. Moreover, the case-by-case approach taken by the EPA also allows, but does not guarantee, decisions that take into account differential disposal alternatives faced by potential ocean dumpers. Finally, EPA regulations require the permit applicant to supply information demonstrating that alternatives are not available, and will require ocean dumpers to pick up the cost of surveillance of the dump site. While it has been reported that the quality of the data supplied by permit applicants is inadequate, this source of information should be pressed.

Ocean dumping is a deliberate activity; routine oil pollution from tankers is an incidental result of ocean transport; accidental oil spills are just that, accidental.[19] In theory one could have strengthened the legal regime that makes ocean shippers responsible for damages and leaves to their discretion whether and how to take preventative measures, or whether to make damage payments. While attractive on the theoretical grounds that this would free shippers to seek the least-cost solution, the enforcement costs make this option unreasonable. Specifically, the assignment of responsibility between tanker owner, cargo owner, charterer, flag state, and so forth, the interests of port and coastal states, and the aggregation and valuation of the interest of damaged parties makes the transactions costs, including enforcement, prohibitive.

Rejecting this option, the next choice might have been simple discharge limits, giving tanker owners and operators their choice of abatement techniques. Again, as a practical matter, enforcement costs would have been too high. The technology of oil-discharge monitoring devices is not sufficiently perfected to employ them.[20] Rejecting discharge limits alone, the choice was one of differing design and operating techniques, and in particular Load on Top (LOT)[21] and segregated ballasting. Both were eventually required, although there is some evidence that the incremental benefit from requiring segregated ballasting in addition to LOT is very small compared to its cost. In any event, LOT is subject to the good intentions and skill of the tanker crew. In contrast, the design requirement of segregated ballasting automatically assures enforcement. The very delicate international problem of inspection becomes trivial—it is not necessary to post an inspector on each tanker voyage. A tanker can be certified at launching as having been provided with segregated ballast facilities, and no further inspection on this matter is required. Enforcement is assured, and international incidents over authority to inspect are avoided.[22]

FURTHER CONSIDERATIONS

In addition to the questions raised in the preceding section regarding the feasibility of negotiating optimal-abatement levels, and selecting instruments that take into account the special enforcement problems in ocean space, two further considerations should be raised. The first involves the character and areal extent of coastal state environmental jurisdiction. The second concerns land-based sources of marine pollution.

The question of coastal state jurisdiction for environmental control is especially complicated as it touches the center of Law of the Sea controversies—the breadth of the territorial sea claimed by coastal states. Indeed, the negotiations leading up to both the Ocean Dumping Convention and the Prevention of Pollution from Ships Convention almost foundered on the territoriality issue. They were only saved by the compromise of deferring to the then upcoming Law of the Sea Conference any resolution to the breadth of the territorial sea dispute.

The basic and unresolved environmental issue is whether coastal states should be accorded broad or narrow environmental zones in which they can exercise environmental jurisdiction. Some states have proposed coastal state environmental control up to the limit of the proposed "economic zone" of 200 miles. A superficial argument supporting broad zones can be made on the grounds that ocean environment deterioration can be traced to its common property resource status not under effective national control, and that coastal states, which stand in most immediate danger from offshore pollution, require jurisdictional authority to limit pollution and protect their interests. Somewhat in the fashion of Demsetz's proposition that property rights arise when external diseconomies become increasingly costly,[23] this argument would say that the first (although not sufficient) step in controlling ocean pollution is to extend national jurisdiction over what are now the high seas.

The argument is deficient on several counts. First, the alternative to broad coastal environmental zones is not necessarily a lack of environmental controls. Second, national governments have compiled a rather dismal record of conserving their environmental patrimony, and to award them additional territory in ocean space, while relying on their enlightened self-interest, seems needlessly reckless. Third, the extension of jurisdiction over broad zones does not internalize to the coastal state all externalities, and, in particular, those that are of a more global nature, such as heavy metals and petroleum pollution. Instead, pollution-generating activities in the broad zone would be cloaked in an extended national authority, and their external cost-creating activities would be as difficult to control as is now true for land-based sources of ocean pollution.

Fourth, the position taken by some states at the Caracas conference (summer 1974) that coastal states should have authority to regulate vessel-source pollution within the economic zone of 200 miles, could result in a chaotic patchwork of differing standards with respect to vessel construction and operation. At a minimum such a patchwork of standards could significantly increase marine transport costs. At the extreme, it would be an open invitation for unwarranted harrassment and interference with navigation for reasons quite unrelated to legitimate environmental objectives. The problem is most acute for states bordering on straits. Whether legitimate or not, some strait states have already asserted that supertankers and nuclear powered vessels do not conform to the doctrine of innocent passage.

While these points weigh against the blanket use of broad environmental zones, strait and other coastal states cannot rely on the beneficence of international law or on an, as yet uncreated, international environmental authority to protect their interests.

In my opinion it will be necessary to continue the somewhat fragmented approach to marine environment control already underway, with policies tailored to the nature of the pollutant and its sources. The current approach to vessel-source pollution, which involves international, uniform standards, and heavy reliance on design criteria, has certain disadvantages alluded to earlier. First the process of setting standards by negotiation may fall short of optimal levels; second, internationally uniform standards fail to account for local differences in benefit functions; and third, design criteria may overlook less costly abatement techniques. Nevertheless coastal state standards on vessels could be highly disruptive to marine transport, and as noted earlier, design standards certainly ease the inspection and enforcement problem.

With regard to activities in the economic zone, other than marine transport, and in particular offshore oil production beyond traditional territorial waters, some minimum international standards should be established, with primary enforcement responsibility given to the coastal state. Higher standards set by the coastal set would of course be permitted.

It is with regard to land-based sources of marine pollution that the most difficult problems remain.[24] A first step (that has apparently been resisted thus far) might be to construct an accurate registry of dirty river discharges, so the magnitude of the problem becomes better known.[25] A second step might be to provide a pool of technical expertise for evaluating the damages associated with land-based discharges, so that adequate local cost–benefit analysis can be done.

Although perhaps unrealistic, a third step might involve setting a system of fees or charges on the pollution content of river discharges. Such a system would have the advantages of providing a continuing incentive to curtail pollution and provide a source of funds for subventing pollution abatement among countries in the process of industrialization. While the industrialized countries would no doubt be assessed the heaviest charges, the distributional consequences could be supported on equity grounds, and give some substance to the concept of the oceans as the common heritage of mankind. Moreover, if we wish to persuade the developing countries to burden themselves with abatement costs that we ourselves were unwilling to bear, some burden sharing might be appropriate. If seriously considered, such a scheme might best be applied regionally to bodies of water that are jointly shared by industrial and developing countries. Examples would be the Caribbean and the Mediterranean. Barring these steps, we rely on the incidental benefits to the oceans of domestic environmental controls.

ACKNOWLEDGMENT

I would like to thank Wendy Takacs and Tracy Murray for several helpful suggestions.

NOTES

1. Ocean currents may in some instances bring the situation closer to unidirectional external diseconomies of an upstream–downstream character.

2. Some of the issues discussed here are elaborated in more detail in C. Pearson, *International Marine Environment Policy: The Economic Dimension* (Johns Hopkins Press, 1975); and in Pearson, "Extracting Rent from Ocean Resources," *Ocean Development and International Law Journal, 1* (3) 1973. See also, R. Shinn, *The International Politics of Marine Pollution Control,* New York: Praeger, 1974.

3. *The Convention on the Prevention of Marine Pollution by Dumping of Wastes and Other Matter,* 1972, and the related United States legislation, the *Marine Research and Sanctuaries Act of 1972,* and the 1973 IMCO Conference result, the *International Convention for the Prevention of Pollution from Ships.*

4. Ocean EC measures are also fragmented by spatial application (territorial waters, contiguous zone, high seas) and by authority for enforcement (coastal state, flag state, port state and so forth).

5. Nor are the groupings consistently employed in the literature. For example, Hardy groups pollutants such as: halogenated hydrocarbons, petroleum hydrocarbons, other organic and inorganic chemicals, nutrient chemicals, suspended solids and turbidity, radioactive materials, thermal energy. See M. Hardy, "International Control of Marine Pollution," *Natural Resources Journal,* Vol. II, April 1971.

6. Also certain important domestic EC measures designed to control air and water pollution within the U.S. have the incidental result of improving the ocean environment.

7. The Prevention of Pollution from Ships Convention is not yet in force.

8. For what it is worth, the EPA estimates total hydrocarbon emissions for the United States at 27.3 million tons for 1970. Council on Environmental Quality, *5th Annual Report,* Table 16, p. 276. The proportion and form of these emissions that reach the sea is not known.

9. Finally we emphasize that tonnage is a poor guide to relative damages, as the spatial location is unspecified. Coastal zones are of course much more economically productive and, hence, vulnerable to oil pollution damages.

10. Control of ocean fisheries is a second example of the intertwining of resource allocative efficiency and wealth appropriation motives for changing the legal regime.

11. Even the regional North Sea Ocean Dumping Convention involved 12 states.

12. One could easily position these curves, however, so that there would be a net welfare loss to one country at optimal abatement levels.

13. See for example the models constructed in *Problems in Transnational Pollution,* Paris: OECD, 1972.

14. R. Coase, "The Problem of Social Cost," *The Journal of Law and Economics,* October 1960.

15. Quite beyond the probably more important question of accurately estimating damage functions.

16.   The more serious problem is the difficulty of estimating benefit (damage) functions given the uncertainty surrounding biological and ultimately economic damages associated with dumping.

17.   Segregated ballasting is the provision of separate ballast tanks for sea water which is carried for stabilization purposes on return voyages. This prevents the use of cargo tanks for ballasting activities, and the consequent contamination of ballast water with oily residues. Deballasted oily sea water has been a major source of routine ocean oil pollution.

18.   Single-skin tankers use the vessel hull as the cargo container; double bottoms have a separated ship's hull and cargo container.

19.   Although of course routine oil discharge is intentional in deballasting operations, and accidental spills are, in a sense, anticipated.

20.   The convention does call for an oil effluent discharge record book to be kept.

21.   LOT is a method of pumping dirty ballast into slop tanks, letting the heavier sea water settle and be decanted, and taking a fresh load "on top."

22.   Burrows et al. have properly stressed the need to include the social costs of enforcement when estimating the cost-effectiveness of various control measures. They conclude that in-port cleaning of oil tanker tanks is the least social cost alternative, but for some unclear reason they did not consider segregated ballasting in their analysis. See P. Burrows, C. Rowley, D. Owen, "Operational Dumping and the Pollution of the Sea by Oil: An Evaluation of Preventive Measures," *Journal of Environmental Economics and Management, 1,* November 1974.

23.   H. Demsetz, "Toward a Theory of Property Rights," *American Economic Association Papers and Proceedings 57,* May, 1967.

24.   Despite the initial efforts found in the Baltic Sea Convention and the regional Conventional for the Prevention of Pollution from Land-Based Sources, Paris, 1974.

25.   Perhaps this is too pessimistic. The Intergovernmental Oceanographic Commission (IOC) is preparing to study dirty river discharge, and the U.N. Environmental Programme (UNEP) is supporting the joint working group on River Inputs to Ocean Systems (RIOS) in gathering data on river-borne pollutants.

Transfrontier Pollution and Institutional Choice

Anthony Scott

This chapter pursues topics that have come up in symposia on transfrontier pollution (TFP) at the OECD in Paris, and in semi-official meetings elsewhere. Its main theme is that economists who now spend time on the welfare-economic analysis of the optimum amount of TFP might be better employed investigating criteria for selecting among such alternative approaches to abatement as the levying of a common international tax, the institutionalizing of "trade" in abatement, or the appointment of an all-powerful abatement agency.

I first define a set of five alternative institutional approaches. I then discuss and reject the economists' traditional analytical approach, in which they ignore international power and distribution of wealth, and proceed to design the optimum-abatement program as though the frontier were not there. Next, I turn back to the choice of institutions, arguing that only two of the original five are worth discussing. Finally, I conclude with the opinion that economists should be devoting themselves to the search for the optimum international agency for the provision and monitoring of TFP abatement services.

THE CHOICE OF INSTITUTIONAL APPROACHES

The purpose of this section is to survey the institutional possibilities for dealing with TFP. To constrain the choice, we rule out the problem of global pollution of the atmosphere, and confine the survey to the problems of managing one river, lake, watershed, or airshed that forms, or crosses, the boundary.[1] Many suggestions have been made, and a number of institutions are actually in use. The approaches are set out here in order, ranging from those that involve least modification of conventional national institutions and diplomatic procedures, to those that involve a major change in the concept of national sovereignty.

Option 1: Diplomatic Channels

This traditional approach works best if a citizen in one country is harmed by the discharges of an identifiable plant or establishment in another country. Then the diplomats of the two countries, acting on behalf of their nationals, may be able to arrange a settlement, involving abatement, compensation, or bribe. The diplomat is a medium linking two points. He can also assist in situations in which the two parties are whole districts, or cities, but here both the capacity to accept wastes and the enjoyment of abatement become common property or public goods, and the interests on each side of the boundary, and their willingness to pay for changes, become confused. The diplomat finds it difficult to learn what his nation's interests are.

Option 2: Trade in Public Goods

Economists have found it useful to postulate a second category, where one or both of the two parties is a collectivity, so that there is a market like exchange in public goods. The actual institutions are not described—or even advocated—but it is implied that one "country" sells pollution abatement to the other. Presumably this could be modified to include one province, or city, selling to another, across a national border.[2] However, the economic analysis of offers is built up to synthesize both international-trade theory and public-goods theory, while the institutional forms are better described in still another literature, that on state-trading.

Option 3: Common Agency

A third step in the range of institutions is the setting-up of a commission or agency to undertake pollution-abatement activities for two or more countries. Its duties may range from merely collecting accepted and agreed information, through conducting hearings, making plans, and recommending solutions to the parent governments, to assuming some of the authority of its parents by coordinating national activities, actually supplanting them with an international body that can deal with private citizens to enforce its own rules, or even conducting its own taxing and spending arrangements.[3] There are few examples of such extreme delegated sovereignty, but military-alliance high commands and fishery commissions may approximate what is being described.

Option 4: International Property Rights

It is possible to keep national authority and sovereignty intact yet allocate pollution rights internationally by adopting a system of marketable licenses or warrants, and by making them enforceable in both countries. This approach was suggested to the OECD, and is a natural extension of the Dales idea to an international problem.[4] If discharge rights, or abatement, are public goods, such licenses could appropriately be acquired or held by national or local governments.

Option 5: Internationalization of Domestic Procedures

This approach includes providing access of nationals from one state to the courts or proceedings in another, and the enforcement of each country's money judgements in the other.[5]

One thing that the first and the last of these five approaches have in common is that they are extremely individualistic, depending in both cases on initiative taken by citizens, yet differing radically in the role for the governments. In both of them, the activity of governments is much less than in the intervening cases, which find much scope for government controls and provision of abatement services.

What has economics to say about the choice among these alternative approaches?

USING ECONOMICS TO CHOOSE THE LEVEL OF TRANSFRONTIER
POLLUTION

The point of this section is to argue that economists have not yet made a
helpful contribution to the problem of international pollution. Certain useful lessons do arise from their analyses, which are institutionally based on
some "agency" solution to a question about the optimum amount of TFP in
which the two or more nations involved *ignore* the international frontier;
with the help of some common body or agency they search for that international project that would maximize net benefits. Then the two countries
would divide the benefits (or the net benefits) on the basis of some previously accepted equitable principles—such as 50–50. The chief characteristic of this approach is that it segregates and attempts to suppress the
distributional question, and stresses the application of benefit–cost analysis
to the search for an efficiency goal.

The advantages of doing this are clear enough. In the first place, it cor-
rects the natural bias of diplomats and politicians that international
endeavour is typically a zero-sum game. Until an economist has worked on
international fisheries or international-project issues, he cannot appreciate
how valuable this correction is.

A second advantage, following from the first, is that it does tend to lead
inquiry into alternatives, into the search for the optimum project. The
natural bias of engineers and designers is to search for an abatement-system
design that will be merely "feasible" in the physical circumstances, given
both financial and distributional[6] constraints. The quest for an economically
optimum project, on the other hand, opens the eyes of those involved in
other designs, locations, services, costs, and time sequences. All such alternatives are, of course, worth scrutinizing; and a couple of them, location
and regional specialization, are especially worthy of note. By location, I
refer to the opportunity, when the efficiency of a joint project is under
consideration, to locate most of the works in one country, even if many or
most of the benefits are ultimately located in another. Regional specialization has a similar meaning: the opportunity to locate many activities that
would otherwise be damaged in one country, upstream of (or sheltered from)
a pollution source.

These are, of course, the common concerns of benefit–cost analysis
within one country, and the participants in TFP negotiations should be
grateful when economists insist on their relevance to several countries'
problems. When all is said and done, the instinctive approach of most nations to international proposals is not only nationalistic, but blindly mer-
cantilist and, therefore, ripe to benefit from the rather pallid interna-
tionalism that any economist tends to bring to the arena. To have a whole

profession as a conscience is no small advantage.

Furthermore, this approach does provide scope for needed empirical investigation. Once the border can be ignored, engineers, environmentalists, and statisticians can move in to balance the scarcity, and asymmetry, of information that is a natural condition in any frontier region. These can provide for the nations' peripheries the same careful consideration and fine tuning as is usually reserved for projects in their centers.[7] But is this all? Is the economist's contribution limited to the scanty list of results he has obtained from studying domestic pollution problems? What are these results?

First, an identification of first- and second-order conditions of economic efficiency. Second, some good warnings about second-best situations. Third, study of economic incentives, such as charges and subsidies, with warnings not to use the wrong bases for these. Fourth, realization that, because pollution abatement is a public good, it is no accident that its benefits are never well measured. Fifth, warning that the transaction costs of antipollution institutions may exceed their net benefits. Sixth, advocacy of a system of transferable, marketable, pollution rights. Seventh, warning that because pollution takes place over space, so that marginal shadow prices of abatement may differ over a single basin or airshed, a comprehensive, internalized, or systems-analysis approach may be preferable to a uniform price, subsidy or regulation approach.

As good as the analysis underlying all this work has been, its product has been essentially destructive, consisting of disclaimers and warnings. So little of this has been constructive that it is not surprising that in Anglo-Saxon countries, most pollution legislation and administration systems are the extension of the truly pioneering 19th-century work of medical experts and sanitary engineers on public-health policies. Placed at first in a municipal framework, they have recently moved up a level to their present scope in national governments, alongside water-resource technologists, meteorologists, and career public administrators, lawyers, and publicists. The contribution of most economists to all this has been merely to provide the "economic aspects" of whatever these other professionals advocate. Otherwise, the grim warnings that most academic economists can produce from their familiarity with Malthusian literature has been far more influential than anything they can say about direction of current policy, measurement techniques, or organization. I would even go so far as to say that most economists writing on pollution address themselves primarily to their colleagues, because they recognize their goal as one of plugging the market-failure gap in economic analysis. That is, most pollution economists seek merely to battle with Coase and Arrow. Pursuit of this laudable ambition, of course, does very little to advance an economic approach to pollution policy.

With this introduction, I now owe you more specific criticisms of the ignore-the-border and full-steam-ahead school of TFP economics. I list them here.

The first, having to do with competence and relevance, has already been sketched. Economists' contributions to domestic pollution policy have not been impressive enough to suggest that treating an international abatement project as though it were domestic can help us much. Indeed, the powerful tools of analysis of international economics have been largely ignored so far. They may be ripe for adaptation to a context in which sovereignties, different preferences, endowments, and price structures are the rule.

Second are public goods and bads. The abatement that brings them relief is to pollution victims more often than not a public good; exclusion is expensive if not impossible and a waste of resources anyway. Economists treat this characteristic of our subject as a *problem*—private demand for abatement cannot accurately be measured because of nondisclosure. So the problem is outside the market, and good economists throw up their hands, and turn to other domestic questions. My criticism is that in an international context, the demand for pollution abatement is not undisclosed. Governments do exist whose business it is to distill an impression of their citizens' demands and costs. These could not be considered as isolated individuals who indulge in strategic behavior to become free riders. Governments set tariffs and devalue currencies, and can represent their demand for abatement of TFP.

Of course, this recognition will not enable us to treat pollution abatement as a private good traded between governments. TFP and its abatement is not private; the economic analysis of bilateral monopoly and of alliances is just as tricky as that of public goods, but it presents different challenges to the economist.[8] For example, it is well-known to practitioners in international negotiation on environmental matters that a useful procedure is to invest in the presentation of reliable, verifiable information, for it is an arguable position that whatever success has been reached in joint pollution-abatement programs stems from mutual acceptance by neighboring countries of the same body of data about the extent of pollution, the costs of abatement, and the damage or suffering it is causing. The implications of this line of thought indicate how misleading is the analogy with domestic public goods. While public-goods theory is preoccupied with nondisclosure of preferences, and the costs of exclusion, the real world shows negotiating pairs of nations that are urging information on each other about the injuries they are suffering, and even downstream nations making offers to bribe upstream polluters. Why the difference?

As suggested, my explanation turns on the facts of sovereignty. Public-choice and finance economists commonly explain the nondisclosure of citizen demand for public goods as a species of strategic behavior (stemming from the fear that a full statement of willingness-to-pay will be met by others' understatement of their demand). As between nations between which communications are easy, misrepresentation is not serious. Facts are ultimately revealed, and a country cannot afford to have a reputation for false dealing with its neighbors. Suspicion, rather than misrepresentation, is the main barrier to agreement. A government's citizens must be convinced both that they will gain (in some sense), and that the other nation will not gain unduly.

The role of the sovereignty concept is this. Where all parties are under a higher government, it is obvious that the community will cohere, whether or not a party supports a particular abatement project. It pays each party to misrepresent its support for a project somewhat, because it has little to lose and much to gain. At worst it can be forced to pay for an unduly large part of the costs; at best it can be a free rider. However, when the sovereign parties are not subject to a higher government, they have much more to lose. If they object too much, by misrepresenting the facts, they will prevent any agreement. Hence bargaining between sovereign nations already implies not only a willingness to bargain, but an understanding that each party will contribute something. Misrepresentation of demand, such as characterizes private behavior about public goods, will simply prevent anything from taking place. Hence it is no exaggeration to say that, paradoxically, when negotiations are taking place, a lack of supreme sovereignty implies that all parties intend that some cooperative action or agreement should emerge. When such attitudes exist, the barrier to hard and fast agreement is not misrepresentation, which would imperil agreement, but suspicion.

An alternative explanation has to do with the size of the group. May it not be that the observation that suspicion is the main barrier to be overcome is due to the *smallness* of the number of parties in TFP problems? I have consulted industrial-organization literature on this point, to learn what makes for successful collusion between rivals. The difficulty of comparing explanations is that there are so few instances of international agreement to use for verification. Applied to international fisheries, both explanations seem to work. In small coastal fisheries, all authorities labor to produce agreed information, to overcome domestic suspicion that could endanger all cooperation, but at the UN Law-of-the-Sea Conferences at which scores of nations are represented, no nation has the power of veto. Those who wish to obtain agreement must labor to overcome dissimulation and misrepresentation. Thus two explanations of the difference seem equally correct: nondisclosure may be due either to the presence of a supreme government (the Law-of-the-Sea Conference as a whole) or to large numbers.

Third, the optimum amount of abatement may not be independent of distribution[9] because of the effect of the original distribution of rights to pollute. For example, the amount of pollution that a nation might choose to suffer when it is being compensated for its damages might be quite different from the amount it would choose, at the same "price," if it were forced to bribe the polluter. This would be an income effect on personal preferences. Similarly, if the production processes of damaged industries and pollution-creating industries were not characterized by homogeneous production functions, the original distribution of rights might have a scale effect on the optimum. Furthermore, the optimum amount of pollution may, as between nations, be affected by the different personal or functional distributions of incomes stemming from the original distribution of rights. For example, a country that receives payments for enduring pollution will, *ceteris paribus,* have a smaller export sector than one that must pay; the resulting difference in location of national production, or its capital intensity will affect wages, rentals, and so incomes, and finally the optimum amount of TFP.

I conclude from all this that, although there is much to be said for applying optimization techniques to a TFP situation rather than do nothing at all, as though the border could be ignored, one would not predict that economists who did so would get any farther than they have with domestic pollution problems.

In the next section I suggest a different application for economics.

ELIMINATING THE INDIVIDUALISTIC APPROACHES

In this section I return to the five types of approaches listed earlier, and weed out those numbered 1, 2, and 5.

I deal first, briefly, with Option 2, the trade-in-abatement between two or more countries. As already suggested, this is an artificial case, suggested by a number of economists chiefly to show their colleagues that there is something to be gained from specialization,[10] that is, that unless two or more nations are identical, there will be a gain if the abatement that some or all of them want is undertaken in whichever locations have a comparative advantage in selling this service. This is an important conclusion (also suggesting that a uniform tax on discharges that is uniform over all nations is likely to produce more costly abatement than a differentiated tax). However, the "trade" that it tends to justify is strictly a deal between two or more governments, having no resemblance to international trade in private goods in the usual sense. Hence Option 2 can be neglected as a suggested institutional approach to the TFP problem.

Numbers 1 and 5 refer to approaches to handling TFP problems that may be termed "point-to-point." The victim is located at one point and knows from which point in the other nation the pollution from which he suffers is emanating. He can, therefore, initiate proceedings. In Option 1 he uses government diplomatic channels to attempt to bring about some mitigation in the injury he suffers; in Option 5 he uses the courts of his own or the other nation. (In both procedures he can attempt either to assert his right to enjoy an abatement of the pollution, or to bribe the polluter to abate. Symmetrically, in both procedures the polluter can take the initiative to assert his right to pollute or to bribe the victim to acquiesce).

These two approaches will not be very important, in the years to come, for the following reasons.

First, because all but a very few TRP abatement proposals provide public goods, depending on individual citizens to take action through diplomatic or legal channels is likely to have extremely high transactions costs. This can be illustrated by a highly simplified and stylized reference to the well-known *Trail Smelter* case of the 1920s. The victims (in the United States) of fumes originating from a known source (a smelter) in Canada persuaded their government to demand that Canada indemnify the victims. The various subsequent diplomatic and arbitral proceedings showed, among other things, that the victims would probably have been able to sue the smelter for nuisance had it been within their own jurisdiction. Indemnity was eventually paid. Thus, as with Option 1, diplomatic procedures succeeded in duplicating for the victims what would have been possible domestically. The proceedings were costly in that they stretched over nearly 20 years. In finding the company liable they did provide a means by which the company could decide upon the "optimal" amount of pollution, à la Coase. The decision in the case went further, and asserted that no state has the right to permit the use of its territory in such a manner as to cause injury in another territory, when injury is serious and is established by clear and convincing evidence. The final clause is important. It suggests that if the damage were widespread but small, or if it could not be shown that all the damage came from a particular source, it would be even more costly than in the *Trail Smelter* case to attain abatement.

This would, of course, be true also in a domestic suit. That is why, when abatement would be a public good, economists have little faith in legal, or diplomatic, routes in the allocation of resources to abatement. The argument against the legal remedy is even stronger if the victims are tourists, sportsmen, or other transients whose abandoning of the region for greener fields elsewhere makes it impossible to find complainants whose injury is established by clear and convincing evidence.

Second, approaches 1 and 5, even if successful in bringing about abatement, will not necessarily bring about a low-cost solution. For example, in the *Trail Smelter* case, the best outcome might have been to move the victims (farmers) into Canada, upwind of the smelter; or to move the smelter downwind of the victims. Other solutions may be suggested: the smelter's customers might have been supplied by a United States smelter subsidized by the victims; or the victims' customers might have been supplied by Canadian farmers. Most of these types of solutions were ruled out completely by the nature of the proceedings, and would be by any action using routes 1 or 5.

Third, routes 1 and 5, in appealing to the courts or to general law, abandon other social objectives than those involved in the dispute. Both countries have distributional, developmental, and stabilization aims, (and other allocative aims) that are independent of the direct costs or damages of the two parties. This consideration suggests a role for governments and their agencies that cannot be filled by courts, or by diplomats acting for principals, or by arbitrators.

Fourth, routes 1 and 5 require that there already be agreement about where the rights to pollute reside; there must already be one body of law on the matter. I would suggest that to adopt this approach is to ignore the serious problems of TFP, where rights have not yet been established. On some point-to-point situations, adjoining nations may have sufficiently similar laws already (on nuisance concerned with noise or emissions) that each is willing to expose its citizens to the same responsibility toward foreigners that they have to their own fellow-nationals. There are already a few cases in Europe, and will be more under the proposed Nordic Treaty, in which this approach works.

However, where a common law does not yet exist, or where the two countries have not the same legal procedures, courts, or concepts of justice, how is this point-to-point solution between citizens to be achieved? What institutions are to get things started? The problem now regresses back to some earlier stage. While it is true that a single brilliant act of diplomacy, or a single show of force, might bring about agreement on pollution rights, it will be argued below that such agreement will be more effective if accepted information is first available to both parties.

THE NEED FOR SPECIAL INSTITUTIONS

In this section it is assumed that the rejection of Options 1, 2, and 5, urged in the previous section, has been accepted. We turn, therefore, to the special institutions or agencies that are suggested in routes 3 and 4. I have already suggested that such agencies cannot successfully become mini-governments taking over the affected watershed as a region with its own endowment and location for which to define an optimal program of abatement independent of the nation's preferences, laws, technologies, and initial endowments in the rest of their areas.

Furthermore, it cannot make its own expenditures and directly collect its own revenues. John Cumberland (and others) writing for the OECD conferences, has, in his surveys of the uniform regulations or changes for the whole TFP basin, made what amounts to the best possible case, for a mini-government. For me, the potential attractiveness of this idea is augmented by two further aspects. The first is that setting up a visible binational government works against the indifference symbolized in the saying that "everyone's resource is no-one's problem." The second advantage is that the administration of a multicountry policy for a single environment is made easier, because it appears to be more equitable, if citizens in different riparian nations are subject (and know they are subject) to the same regulations or charges. Even more, they seem to enjoy knowing that they are eligible for the same subsidies.

Thus it is possible to put forward a good case for delegating not only a little sovereignty, but also powers to tax, enforce, and spend, to a TFP mini-government. However, this version of Options 3 and 4, utopian in its promise of good management of TFP, is unacceptable in its implications for the nation-state. Prolonged defense of this statement can be avoided by simply reflecting on the following problems. A special TFP jurisdictional government would need decision rules, a system of representation that would be typical of neither nation. It is worth pondering that the most likely reason for the nations remaining independent of each other is that they have different attitudes or traditions. If it were possible for them to abandon these differences and join in a common governmental authority at the frontier (the frontier being the region where the difference between their religions, languages, laws, or other traditions is most insisted upon) it would already have been possible for them to contemplate some more sweeping union or confederation. Furthermore, because the effects of antipollution policy are allocational or distributional effects, they must be not merely fitted in to, but be consistent with, national policies for accepting or assisting similar adjustments.[11] That is, a special TFP jurisdiction's government would, when it took strong measures, find that one part of its "citizens" were differently affected by its decisions than the other part. It might even be forced, by a majority who could rely on social assistance from its own central government, to act as its agent in imposing costly abatement policies on a minority whose central government did not provide such a buffer or cushion.

My point is less that such problems would spoil the implementation of such a special TFP mini-government, than that the recognition of their likelihood would prevent the nations from ever setting it up. No politicians are ever happy about giving up the welfare of their citizens to other politicians, and citizens are rarely happy when their welfare depends on officials or politicians drawn from another country.[12]

Thus we may move on to suggest institutions that are less radically different from those already in existence. What are the minimum functions for such an agency starting from today in 1975?

We can deduce some of its characteristics from what has already been said. For example, it will not be representative of frontier citizens, but of their governments, for reasons implied in the foregoing discussion. The governments may be the national governments only, or they may include provincial, state, country, or municipal bodies.

Its form will be that of an agency similar to those found in some international fisheries' management commissions, possessing such strong powers of recommendation that their parent governments are reduced mainly to exercising a veto, rather than to making positive policies or even suggestions. Its members will be laymen, respected for their statesmanlike experiences rather than for their expertise in TFP-abatement economics, engineering, or ecology.

Like the fisheries' commissions, the main test of their success will be their assistance in obtaining information that is accepted by both nations in sufficient volume to make the negotiation of the agreement underlying, their eventual operations comprehensive rather than minimal. The *acceptability* of information about damages and alternatives for mitigating the damage, and about abatement costs and alternatives for reducing actual pollution is the key to success. The fisheries' commissions (and the existing international river commissions) have approached acceptability in two ways. On the one hand, they have set up their own "research" or fact-finding bodies, or retained their own consultants, and, on the other, they have attempted to use the specialists and experts already in the national bureaucracies in a constructive way that gives each person an incentive to willingly "wear two hats"; not only loyally to serve their own nations' public services as usual, but also to put their objective professional, scientific, or artistic talents at the disposal of the international agency. Capacity to use this second way of obtaining information is the test that distinguishes an agency that is a mere binational debating forum (as with some fisheries' commissions) from a commission or agency that is trusted in both countries to put forth plans that are widely accepted as based on indisputable facts and assumptions. Two devices help here. One is the use of hearings to obtain information and experience from riparian citizens in order to confirm or cast doubt on the reports of specialist experts. The other is the employment of expert boards made up of public servants from both countries who are instructed to produce a *unanimous* report on technology, environment, damages, and costs.

It may surprise the reader that I have given the agency the task of providing the information for an *initial* treaty or agreement. Today, this is essential. There are no generally accepted global principles to be implemented. Every river or airshed is different. Furthermore, most pairs of countries have a long history of both friction and cooperation along their boundaries (in the siting of customs posts and bridges and highways; in local fire prevention or public-health measures; in daily migration to hospitals, jobs, or schools across the frontier; in keeping navigation safe; and so on). Thus TFP abatement negotiation does not start between two or more uninformed and isolated nations, but in a situation that has, economically and politically, evolved over many years. The task of the TFP agency is, thus, to move coordination further, not to act as the first-ever instance of hands-across-the-border. To do this, the nations would be well advised to entrust it, first of all, with the job of building a foundation of data and understanding on which later operations can be based.

The other tasks of the agency flow easily once this basis has been established. They must recommend and monitor. They must see that the nations have proposals for cooperative contingency plans to deal with spills and other unexpected pollution episodes. They must keep abreast of new information about sources of TFP and of new methods of abating it. They must help both their parents by carefully considering complaints and suggestions from citizens. As long as they are seen to be struggling against being dependent on partisan sources of information, and to be striving to make recommendations that are not mere "judgments of Solomon", the work will flow to them.

The distributional task will be particularly difficult. Because every abatement project has distributional consequences, seeming to prefer citizens or firms on one side of the border as against those on the other, the agency will inevitably be faced with suspicion of bias or partisanship. However, it is not without defenses against this weakness. It can adopt a modification of a Pareto-optimal strategy, assuring that, with compensation payments and other costs included, its final recommendations will make both (or *all*) countries better off.[13] It can also protect itself if it is given the power to refuse to make recommendations on subjects that will make it appear to be the instrument of the power-politics of only one country. Such matters should be left for summit diplomacy. Finally, it can reduce the number of its sensitive activities by presiding over the semiautomatic operation of the pollution-certificates scheme already mentioned here as Option 4. The transferability, and retirement, of pollution certificates by market means can take the agency out of many situations that would otherwise enmesh it in recurring, divisive bickering. Such a scheme will not relieve the agency of all its responsibilities, but it will given it a base for intervening only when Pareto-optimal outcomes are likely not to be yielded by a certificate market. The success of a certificates' scheme is heavily dependent, of course, on the justice of initial endowment of certificates to individual citizens, or to the two countries. In any case some agency must participate usefully in the preliminary discussions of alternative endowments by providing information and forcing citizens and governments to confront the original distributional (initial "property rights") question.

Thus Options 3 and 4 can be used together. Any scheme like Option 4, in a world with new technologies, new tastes, new pollutants, and new knowledge about the dangers of old pollutants, has too few dimensions to be useful for meeting all goals. It must merely be part of the package of tools available to an international agency. This agency, I think is indispensable both to get started on, and to operate, a joint TFP-abatement policy. It is not a public-goods jurisdiction whose individual members try to mislead about their demand for abatement, but an agency of several governments whose information is otherwise inadequate and unreliable. Its members having been chosen to obtain and select relevant information; they can then be charged with additional duties of recommending and monitoring the policies and performances of the member nations.[14]

NOTES

1. For the possible types of TFP situation, see the map in Annex III of Anthony Scott and Christopher B. Bramsen. "Draft Guiding Principles Concerning Transfrontier Pollution," in *Problems of Transfrontier Pollution*, OECD, Paris, 1974, p. 313.

2. For examples, see Anthony Koo, "Environmental Repercussions and Trade Theory," *Review of Economics and Statistics*, 1974, pp. 235–244; Herbert J. Kiesling, "Public Goods and Possibilities for Trade," *CJE 7*, 402–417, 1974; Estelle James, "Optimal Pollution Control and Trade in Public Goods," *Journal of Public Economics 3*, 203–216, 1974; and for another approach, see the Eowville-Plympton problem discussed by Dorfman and Jacoby and summarized in "A Public-Decision Model Applied to a Local Pollution Problem," in R. & N. S. Dorfman, eds. *Economics of the Environment*, New York, Norton, 1972, pp. 205–215. Much of the extensive literature originates in the pioneering essay, Alan Williams, "The Optimal Provision of Public Goods in a System of Local Governments," *Journal of Public Economics 74*, 18–33. 1966.

3. For examination of a proposal that taxes and bribes be international, see J. H. Cumberland, "Establishment of International Environmental Standards," in *Problems of Transfrontier Pollution*, CECD, Paris 1974, pp. 213–229.

4. See the Scott-Bramsen paper, op. cit., Annex II, pp. 311–312.

5. There is now an extensive literature on "standing" in foreign courts, but that on pollution procedures is not yet widely published. See Robert E. Stein, "Legal and Institutional Aspects. . . ." In *Problems of Transfrontier Pollution,* OECD, 1974, p. 296.

6. For examle, that the countries must share equally in the employment created by the project.

7. The lack of careful planning for frontier projects is frequently mentioned by writers dealing with the development of international river basins. See John V. Krutilla, *The Columbia River Treaty,* Baltimore, Johns Hopkins, 1967, later articles by W. R. D. Sewell, and a series of articles in the *Natural Resources Journal.* The same approach is to be found in international fisheries' management.

8. The work of Ralph D'Arge and others already points to a recognition of the bargaining, game-theoretic, and bilateral monopoly aspects of TFP agreements, but this has not prevented others from transplanting all aspects of domestic pollution policy, including those of public goods, to the TFP problem.

9. That is, in diagrammatic terms, the contract line in the analyses developed by Dolbear, Shibata, Murarc, or myself is not a vertical line. See F. T. Dolbear, "On the Theory of Optimum Externality," *AER, 57,* 90–103, 1967. Hirofumi Shibata, "A Bargaining Model of the Pure Theory of Public Expenditure," *JPE, 79,* 1–29, 1971. Gilberto Muraro," "Economics of Unidirectional Transfrontier Pollution," *Problems in Transfrontier Pollution.* OECD, Paris, 1974. Anthony Scott, "Transfrontier Pollution: Are New Institutions Necessary?" OECD, forthcoming.

10. For example Estelle James writes of two communities that have different tastes and production functions. Goods, factors, and pollution can move across frontiers. She concludes that when TFP exists "local control produces the indeterminacy associated with bilateral monopoly, bargaining, blackmail and free riders. The outcome, will not, in general, be Pareto-optimal." (op. cit., P. 215).

11. For example, an abatement policy may imply that factories in two countries should close down. But one country's policies toward crop failures, market shifts, tariff alterations, and floods suggests that these factories should be helped to keep in business somehow, while the other is more ruthless in all these matters. Are the nationals of the first country to be deprived of their traditional rights to be helped in economic adversity? If not, what about the citizens of the second country—are they to be treated differently from their fellow-riparians?

12. Many observations support this assertion, ranging from the unpopularity of colonial administrators and the bitter battle for self-determination in many regions during the negotiation of the Treaty of Versailles to the unwillingness of "environmental" or "ecological" witnesses at IJC hearings to go so far as to advocate that a special body, drawn from both countries, replace their own municipal, provincial, or state institutions in controlling TFP.

13. The IJC's *Columbia River* and *Pembina* recommendations are particularly worthy of note in this connection, however successful they have been. Pearse, Jones, and Scott in a forthcoming paper attempt to formulize this strategy.

14. Enforcement, like taxing and regulating, should remain a national responsibility.

Environmental Protection, Recycling, and the International Materials Economy

David Pearce

It is difficult to tell whether modern environmental economics has been witnessing "paradigm shift" in recognizing the constraints that a "spaceship earth" imposes on economic activity. On the one hand, we might accept that economics has become "ecologized."[1] It now recognizes the finite nature of materials and energy resources, albeit with dispute over what the exact limits of resource availability are, and how technology may extend those limits. To a lesser extent there has been recognition that the environment will not degrade all and any wastes so that due care and attention must be taken to tailor the generation of wastes to the receiving capacity of the environment. Finally, the long-argued point that consumption is *not* the final act in the economic process, but merely an intermediary step in between resource extraction and residuals disposal, has entered into the conventional wisdom.[2]

On the other hand, little seems to have happened by way of altering the technique that economists use in approaching social issues. Environmental problems are treated at the conceptual level in the same way as any other economic problem: it is a matter of weighing the costs and benefits of taking action, whether that action is the "inert" one of leaving resources alone in order to conserve them, or whether it involve exploiting a resource or the environment for so-called material ends.

THE CASE FOR MORE MATERIALS RECYCLING

The suspicion must be that the shift is more apparent than real, and that, while this is not the place to discuss the validity of the competing paradigms, the somewhat unbending attitudes of economists on resource and pollution problems goes some way toward explaining the incompatibility of conservationists' demands and the economists' prescriptions.[3] The reuse of materials provides an excellent example of the two competing ideologies. As far as the economist is concerned, the problem is one of minimizing the total social costs associated with any program of resource-use and disposal. These aggregate social costs include all the costs borne by firms and private individuals (so-called "private" costs), the costs of disposal or reclamation (transportation, reprocessing costs, and the like), and the costs that tend not to be reflected in markets (pollution costs). In each case, the costing procedure relates back to some valuation of individuals' preferences.

A formal presentation of the economist's cost-minimization approach is presented in Appendix 1, which also shows that—if we ignore the non-market costs associated with recycling—there is an a priori case for supposing that existing rates of recycling are too low from the standpoint of what is socially desirable. Essentially this is because existing recycling effort is the product of purely private decisions that ignore the social costs of residuals disposal. Such a result is taken directly from welfare economics: an activity (recycling) generating social benefits (pollution reduction) will not take place on an optimal scale if those benefits are not appropriated via the charging of a price. As such, the "optimum" level of recycling is greater than the actual level. This conclusion is modified to the extent that a recycling process itself generates pollution. If, as is often the case, the pollution from recycling is less than the pollution from disposal, the previous conclusion remains, but the "optimum" level of recycling diverges less from the existing level. Of course, the existing recovery effort may be too low because of other market imperfections, particularly ignorance of opportunity, lack of market knowledge, and so on. However, these serve to strengthen our basic conclusion that economic analysis alone will *tend* to dictate the result that current recycling rates are too low.[4]

The issue on which the economist diverges from the conservationist—or, rather, from the caricature of a conservationist that is necessary to facilitate discussion—is in his insistence that the socially optimal degree of recycling is less than the maximum amount technically possible. To this end, the "total recycling society" called for by some environmental pressure groups, offends the economic paradigm and, in any event, is a technical myth. Quite simply, the maximization of recycling activity would almost certainly take us beyond the point at which the extra gains of recycling outweigh the extra costs. We shall in fact be using up resources that have a higher social value than those we save. It might appear that such an argument should appeal to the conservationist: There is little point in injecting more resources into a recycling program than can be saved by it. However, the crucial difference of opinion centers on the "value" of resources. What the conservationist believes is that the money values attached to resources by economists are not the socially correct prices. In the economist's language, there is a dispute about what constitutes the true "shadow price" of resources. If the value of reduced pollution is afforded a very high price relative to, say, the value of labor, then this will bias an analysis of recycling in favor of recovery rates higher than those recommended by the economist. Equally, if the value of resources in the ground is thought to be higher than their value in use ascertained by the economist, higher recycling rates will again be implemented.

If we adopt the conservationist standpoint, we can see that a recycling effort greater than that recommended by economic analysis will be justified. Yet, is the conservationist's case a good one? The dispute about values will, on many occasions, reflect a dispute about *whose* values are to count. This is the familiar debate about environmental elitism: the economist argues that his cost–benefit calculus is constructed so as to reflect the preferences of everyone affected by the recycling decision, and that the conservationist wishes to substitute for this "democratic process" an elitist imposition of values by those who are somehow more informed or more qualified to judge.[5] However, the conservationist's ideology also reflects a concern that the economist has not captured all that is important in his cost–benefit calculus.[6] The effects of economic activity on the stability of ecological systems are (arguably) always negative, reducing stability and, hence, reducing the capability of the system to withstand further shocks, such as pollution. In short, there may well be something in the conventional economic approach that leads us to ignore reductions in the system's ability to survive simply because those reductions tend to be unperceived and, hence, unrelated to human preferences. In this respect, the existence of an informed "elite" capable of issuing warning signals is important.

If this argument has substance, then in the field of recycling we have a stronger case for increased effort than that provided by the economist in his conventional guise. What we do not have are any clear guidelines as to how we could quantify the "ecologically desirable" level of recycling, but it seems possible to develop such rules.[7] What does seem certain is that the ecologically optimal level of recycling will be greater than the Pareto-optimal level that, in turn, will exceed the privately optimal level.

We have thus argued that current recycling effort is likely to be below the socially desirable level (1) for the familiar economic reason that the reduction in social costs by having more recycling is generally significant, and (2) because economic criteria may also understate the wider gains from recycling.

EXISTING RECYCLING EFFORT: THE PROBLEM

Any attempt to find out exactly how much recycling currently takes place is beset by problems of definition and measurement as well as limited and inconsistent data. These problems cumulate to the point at which the prospective researcher must wonder if the effort is worthwhile. There can be no *real* substitute for the detailed study of individual commodities, with research inputs from those who are active within the relevant industries. One notable document in this respect is the 1972 American report of the Battelle Institute,[8] and we can expect similar assessments to result from the commodity working groups of the U.K. Waste Management Advisory Council.[9]

However, it remains true that few investigations have attempted to compare recycling efforts over time within any one country, or to compare recycling efforts between countries.[10] Why for example, does the trend rate of recycling efforts (below) in aluminum appear to rise in Italy between 1963 and 1973, but remain virtually constant, though falling in the last few years, in the United Kingdom in the same period? Why is the same index of recycling effort negligible in Belgium and Luxembourg (combined) when compared to the United Kingdom and the United States, and significantly lower in France than in the United Kingdom and United States? The answers to such questions are complex, but may have important implications for policy designed to increase recycling effort if such policies are deemed desirable.

To take just one example, the *maximum attainable* ratio of recycled material to annual consumption for lead has been estimated to be below 60% for the United States, while the *actual* rate is estimated to be above 60% for the United Kingdom. If we can show that the level of consumption does not affect the ratio, and if end-users are not significantly different (so that dissipative and nonrecoverable use is higher in the United States than in the

United Kingdom), we need to explain how one country feels it cannot, even with wholesale effort, achieve a ratio already exceeded by another country. If it is the maximum attainable ratio for a given country that has been wrongly computed, then there are clear implications for policy in that country.

What follows is an attempt to look at some data on the "recycling effort" of a country over time with the foregoing questions in mind. It should be clear at the outset that the approach is an exercise in "applied heroics" in the level of generality it seeks. The data used and the problems encountered simply do not permit much faith to be placed in the figures. Only a major research program lasting some years can overcome these problems. However, with these conventional caveats and prior apologies made, it seems useful to offer an analysis (1) to raise questions that perhaps do not get raised otherwise, and (2) as an exercise in speculative analysis that may perhaps uncover some policy-relevant conclusions.

By looking at some of the determinants of recycling effort we can attempt to assess the relative importance of the explanatory factors. Where domestic policy is biased in favor of or against use of secondary materials it should be possible to see how far that policy is affecting recycling effort compared to other countries. Where price factors vary, perhaps because of variations in factor endowments, it should be possible to assess the effects of price policy measures (e.g., taxes or subsidies) on recycling effort. Most important, however, will be the relative importance of any "residual" factor that can be taken as a catch-all for variations in "recycling consciousness" between countries. If such a factor is important it will have clear indications for domestic policies towards recycling publicity.

CALCULATING RECYCLING EFFORT

While many commentators on recycling problems seem reduced to apoplexy when considering the definition of recycling, we propose to regard as recycled material all of the following: (1) Any material not directly embodied in the end-product of the producer, regardless of whether that material is re-used "in house" or whether it is forwarded to the secondary industry. In the nonferrous metals industries these two categories would be "home" scrap and "prompt" scrap, respectively; (2) Any material embodied in an end-product and which is re-used after being discarded. The critical word here is "discarded." For our purposes, it means that the end-use product is reclaimed and used again as an input, with or without reprocessing, for a *different* product item even if the product is of the same type. In this way, the lead from a discarded battery can be reclaimed, remelted, and re-used to make another battery. This is recycling. A discarded product that is reclaimed by someone, and is re-used without any such process taking place is not recycled in the same sense—it merely enters into the secondhand market. Although definitions vary, this general category of recycled material is often known as "old scrap," because it tends to be a flow from the consumption sector to the secondary production sector. Whereas the time lag between the generation of home and prompt scrap and its re-use can be negligible, the time lag for old scrap is a function of the end-product's economic life.

Figure 14-1 presents the general picture described above. Alternative definitions abound, but we argue that the difficulties raised with the approach adopted here are not likely, in practice, to significantly affect our use of recycling ratios. Indeed, much of the dispute about what is and what is not recycling occurs at a level of theoretical nicety for our purposes, although we would not wish in any way to deny that different definitions can give rise to different bases for measurement, and, hence, for possibly inconsistent policy measures.

Figure 14-1 simplifies the picture somewhat, since what is referred to as the "manufacturing" sector will, for example in the case of aluminum, consist of two subsectors: producers of mill and casting products, both of

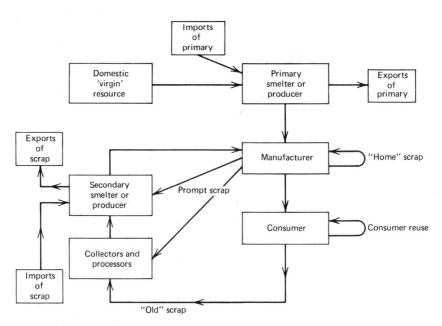

Figure 14-1   Materials flows.

whom receive their inputs from the primary and secondary smelters; and manufacturers of end-products who receive their inputs from the first manufacturing subsector. It is customary for the term "home" scrap to be reserved for the scrap generated and reused by the mill and casting products manufacturers, and for the term "prompt" scrap to be reserved for the scrap generated during the end-product manufacturing stage. For simplicity, these two subsectors of the manufacturing sector have been combined in Fig. 14-1.

One other issue of definition is perhaps worth mentioning, although it is not directly relevant to our empirical work. The "secondary producer" in Fig. 14-1 can in fact be a plant that uses scrap products as an input, but produces a product that is transformed beyond all recognition, through chemical and physical processes. Thus a pyrolysis plant becomes a "secondary producer" by this definition, using as its inputs refuse and other waste, but producing as an output metals, tars, oils, methyl alcohol, or whatever. Obviously, some of these products are part of the scrap inputs in identifiable form, but others are chemical transformations of these same products.

Armed with a working definition of recycling, scrap inputs to the secondary industry reflect imported scrap. The danger is that if we construct an index that responds in the suggested fashion to exports and imports of scrap, the index can be raised by the direct use of policy to reduce imports, say by prohibiting them. There is less of a problem with exports of scrap, because these disappear from the cycle shown in Fig. 14-1 at the "collection and processing" stage. They are not inputs to the secondary industry, but they do reflect recovery effort.

Now, if the ultimate aim is to use the index for policy purposes, there is a real danger in adopting a measure that in any way implies that reducing scrap imports is a "good thing." Quite simply, trade in scrap is one way in which the global effort to increase recycling can be bettered.[11] On the other hand, a secondary industry based on imported scrap does not reflect *domestic* recovery effort. An index that omits scrap imports altogether, or that includes them in a positive fashion would, we argue, be a measure of secondary activity in that country rather than an index of recovery effort. Accordingly, we propose to deal with imported scrap by treating it as a negative item in a recovery effort index. At the same time it must be borne in mind that this procedure will bias the index against those countries that base their secondary industry on imported scrap (e.g., Italy with aluminum).

Inspection of Fig. 14-1 shows that we require some measure of the flow of "old" scrap plus scrap directly re-used in industry ("home" plus "runaround" scrap) as a proportion of total consumption of primary and secondary material. This is the basic form of the "recovery effort index." Ideally, we should calculate the flow of old scrap before it reaches the secondary production sector. We might call this the "waste arisings" approach. Unfortunately, this is a complex approach, because of informational difficulties. Basically, data exist only for the United States for some materials. Hence, it becomes necessary to adopt a somewhat more roundabout route of measuring the flow of old scrap. This approach uses data on the *output* of secondary producers on which information is more readily available. However, output will not equal the input of old scrap, but will instead be some proportion of it, the proportion reflecting the technical efficiency with which the secondary industry converts inputs to outputs. The index we shall obtain will, therefore, systematically understate recovery *effort* per se, but for cross-sectional and time-series comparisons, it is not evident that the problem affects the qualitative nature of our results.

We propose that the numerator of the recovery index be calculated as

$$N = SC + X_s - M_s + DUS \tag{1}$$

where

SC = secondary material consumption
X_s = exports of scrap
M_s = imports of scrap
DUS = direct use of scrap (= home plus prompt scrap).

Now, we can also write

$$SP = M_s + OLD_s \tag{2}$$

where

SP = secondary production
OLD_s = old scrap

Equation 2 does of course ignore the efficiency factor in secondary production, as noted above, by implicitly assuming that materials inputs are identical to materials outputs (in weight terms). Further,

$$SC = SP - X_s \tag{3}$$

Substituting Eqs. 2 and 3 in Eq. 1 we have

$$N = OLD_s + DUS$$

which is what we require. We propose then to use data on the components of Eq. 1 to achieve a measure of old scrap and direct use of scrap.

The denominator of the index will be a measure of consumption of materials. For this we propose

$$D = PP + M_p - X_p + SP - X_s + DUS \tag{4}$$

where PP = primary production exclusive of imported primary
   SP = secondary production inclusive of scrap imports
Equation 4 reduces to

$$D = PC + SC + DUS \tag{5}$$

where PC = primary consumption
 since $PC = PP + M_P - X_P$
   and $SC = SP - X_s$
The recovery effort index (REI) is then calculated as

$$REI = N/D \frac{OLD_s + DUS}{PC + SC + DUS} \tag{6}$$

Even in this form, however, the index proposed gives rise to further problems. The component DUS is, as we saw, roughly equivalent to what is generally called prompt plus home scrap. However, the statistics on direct use of scrap appear to be somewhat more hazardous to use even than those for "old" scrap. Although data is frequently given (e.g., in Metallgesellschaft's *Metal Statistics* and in Battelle Institute, op. cit.) it appears to be the case that the collection of data has not been made on a systematic basis. In addition, these categories of scrap are highly sensitive to simple production decisions, such as varying the width of trimmings on products. Second, some countries secure prompt scrap by importing intermediate products—products that, when converted to their final end-use, yield a scrap flow.[12] In line with our previous argument it would seem appropriate to deduct this flow from the DUS figure. On the other hand, we could argue that reclaiming this scrap flow does reflect domestic effort even though the semimanufactures giving rise to the flow originate elsewhere. What seems appropriate, then, is to calculate the REI in two separate ways. First, we can calculate Eq. 6 above by calculating Eq. 1 and dividing by Eq. 4. Second we can calculate a modified REI as

$$REI^* = \frac{OLD_s}{PC + SC} \tag{7}$$

thus omitting direct use of scrap altogether.

One other issue of definition is perhaps worth mention, although it is not directly relevant to this essay. The "secondary producer" in Fig. 14-1 can in fact be a processing plant that uses scrap products as an input, but produces a product that is transformed out of all recognition, through chemical and physical processes. Thus a pyrolysis plant becomes a "secondary producer" by this definition, using as its inputs refuse and other waste, but producing as an output, metals, tars, oils, methyl alcohol, or whatever. Obviously, some of these products are "in" the scrap inputs in identifiable form, but others are chemical transformations of the inputs. This form of re-use is often called "open loop" recycling.

EMPIRICAL ESTIMATES OF RESOURCE RECOVERY EFFORT

Table 14-1 shows the values of REI for aluminum for six industrialized countries for the period 1963–1973. Data limitations precluded the estimation of $REI*$, which, it will be recalled, excludes the influence of direct use of scrap by manufacturers.

Aluminum

Italy apart, there is one distinct feature of the measured REI ıor these selected countries: it is fairly constant over time. If we place a regression line through the data, we find the following: (1) an average United Kingdom REI of approximately 34%, with a noticeable fall from 1971 to 1973; (2) the average REI in Italy has risen two and one-half times since 1963. Secondary aluminum production has tripled in this period, but with imports of scrap accounting for most of this in the early years. These imports have been held roughly at the same level over the period, however, so that a dramatically increased REI reflects domestic recovery effort; (3) the average Japanese REI of some 28% has been virtually unchanged since 1967; and (4) the average REI centers, approximately, around 22% in the United States, 25% in West Germany, and 21% in France.

The range of REI thus appears to vary from 21–22% in France and the United States to 34% in the United Kingdom. This is a magnitude of difference that cannot be explained by the data limitations.

Table 14-1   Recovery Effort Indices 1963–1973: Aluminum[a]

	1963	1964	1965	1966	1967	1968	1969	1970	1971	1972	1973
U.K.	32.4	31.8	32.6	35.6	34.1	33.4	35.7	34.4	38.2	33.6	28.5
Italy	6.4	18.4	17.0	12.6	13.1	18.3	19.1	21.6	24.0	22.5	24.0
Japan	24.9	27.5	30.0	30.1	28.4	27.8	27.3	27.4	27.8	27.0	28.0
U.S.A.	22.2	22.4	21.8	22.2	21.7	21.1	24.1	21.7	19.8	20.1	23.8
W. Germany	26.6	25.5	25.8	26.7	27.1	24.4	23.2	24.0	27.2	24.7	25.6
France	20.7	19.1	19.5	18.9	19.6	21.8	19.3	19.9	22.8	22.0	20.0

[a] Source: Metallgesellschaft, *Metal Statistics* 1963–1973, 61st ed., Frankfurt am Main, 1974.

One immediate factor that must be considered is that, while the *absolute level* of consumption of material does not affect the recycling rate (*REI*), the *rate of growth* of consumption does.

Let the amount of recovered material be *M*, and the level of consumption be *C*, so that M/C represents the recovery effort index. Now assume that the material in question has a "life" of one time period, and let the rate of recovery of past waste be *r*. We have

$$M_t = r \cdot C_{t-1}$$

t refers to the time period. If *C* grows at a constant rate, *g*, then

$$C_t = (1 + g)C_{t-1}$$

and the recovery effort index becomes

$$M_t/C_t = \frac{r \cdot C_{t-1}}{(1 + g) \cdot C_{t-1}} = r/(1 + g)$$

It can be seen that this index is independent of the level of consumption, but, if the life of materials remains the same and *r* does not change, we can see that an increase in *g* will *lower* the *REI*. Quite simply, when the rate of consumption proceeds faster than the rate of recovery, a declining proportion of consumption is capable of being met with recycled materials.

The relevance for the current study is that our cross-section comparisons are not affected by different levels of consumption, but in analyzing the change, if any, in *REI* over time for one country, we need to look at the growth rate of consumption as an explanatory variable.

However, in the case of aluminum the effect of changing growth rates is not significant. In the first place, growth rates of consumption in the countries selected for study fluctuate, sometimes wildly (as with West Germany), and there is no discernible upward or downward trend. Secondly, changing growth rates can only affect the *REI* if product life is short in relation to the time period studied, in this case 10 years. For aluminum the "life" of products appears to average some 10–15 years. Of course, this raises the issue of whether changes in *REI* in 1963–1973 are significantly affected by consumption variations in 1948–1963. A preliminary overview of consumption rates in this period suggests that variations in *REI* over time are not explained in this way.

Copper

Table 14-2 shows the *REI* for copper for the selected countries. Data limitations are more serious for copper than for aluminum, perhaps surprisingly so. In addition, copper alloys are an important source of scrap, but no attempt has been made here to allow for the copper content of these alloys.

Table 14-2 shows similar *patterns* of recycling effort over time in the various countries. Interestingly, effort falls in the last years of the 1960s with a trough in every country in 1971–1972 with the exception of West Germany, where the 1973 figure is even lower. Inspection of the data shows this to be due to comparative slump conditions in total consumption in these years. In the United States, for example, total consumption actually fell from 1969–1970; it was stagnant in Japan from 1969 to 1970 and fell from 1970 to 1971; it fell in Italy and West Germany from 1970 to 1971; fell in the United Kingdom from 1969 to 1971; and fell in France from 1969 to 1970. As we would expect, this affects secondary output and direct use of scrap. The latter tends to be a direct function of current output, whereas reductions in consumption will tend to depress primary prices making the incentive to use a secondary output less attractive. In Japan, for example, direct use of scrap fell from 1970 to 1971, the period in which total consumption falls, but secondary output stays roughly constant. In the United States the 1969–1970 slump is also accompanied by a stagnant secondary output, but direct use of scrap falls dramatically.

As we would expect, then, the *REI* will reveal cyclical movement reflecting cyclical change in the industry as a whole. Nonetheless, interesting intercountry comparisons remain. If we take 1968 ratios we find that the United States has the highest effort index (48.5%), followed by the United Kingdom (42.3%), Japan (37.5%), West Germany (36.9%), Italy (34.8%), and France (32.1%). Unlike aluminum, the *REI* fluctuates and comparative positions change over the period. However, throughout the period, the United States ranks consistently first, or, less often, second; the United Kingdom rises from fourth place up to the mid-1960s to second place

Table 14-2 Recovery Effort Indices 1963–1973 Copper[a]

	1963	1964	1965	1966	1967	1968	1969	1970	1971	1972	1973
U.K.	36.3	35.1	36.8	41.1	41.9	42.3	42.0	40.8	39.6	36.2	37.9
Italy	28.5	32.5	28.5	33.9	34.2	34.8	33.6	30.7	26.4	27.3	29.4
Japan	42.0	42.1	45.8	42.6	36.1	37.5	38.2	38.6	36.8	32.7	35.5
U.S.A.	43.3	46.4	47.1	43.9	45.0	48.5	47.2	47.0	44.4	43.2	44.7
W. Germany	37.9	35.5	40.4	47.3	38.0	36.9	37.6	36.3	37.6	32.7	27.0
France	34.8	31.5	32.4	32.5	34.9	32.1	34.9	31.0	29.2	23.9	26.9

[a] Source: Metallgesellschaft, *Metal Statistics* 1963–1973, 61st ed., Frankfurt am Main, 1974.

Table 14-3   Adjusted Recovery Effort Indices 1963–1973: Copper[a]

	1963	1964	1965	1966	1967	1968	1969	1970	1971	1972	1973
U.K.	20.6	18.2	20.6	26.0	26.1	27.0	26.6	28.0	25.6	21.0	20.2
Italy	neg	0	neg	neg	neg	neg	neg	neg	neg	neg	neg
Japan	7.4	6.6	13.8	15.8	8.8	9.2	12.4	11.6	11.2	7.3	11.9
U.S.A.	17.0	25.8	22.2	20.5	20.7	22.6	22.0	24.0	18.6	17.2	19.0
W. Germany	20.2	15.3	17.2	24.2	17.0	20.6	19.2	21.8	20.4	18.0	7.5
France	4.4	5.0	5.5	7.0	6.9	5.1	4.6	4.2	3.6	3.2	5.3

[a] Source: Metallgesellschaft, *Metal Statistics*, 1963–1973, 61st ed., Frankfurt am Main, 1974.

thereafter; Japan maintains a fairly constant third; West Germany loses its high ranking after 1966, dropping to fourth and then fifth; and Italy and France systematically occupy the lowest positions. This suggests a ranking of United States, United Kingdom, Japan, West Germany, Italy, France.

Table 14-3 shows the magnitudes of REI^*, the index that excludes direct use of scrap.

It will be seen that the effect of excluding direct use of scrap is to alter the rankings slightly to United Kingdom, United States, West Germany, Japan, France, Italy. Significantly, however, the basic groupings are the same as for the unadjusted REI measures. It remains somewhat unclear as to why the adjusted REI for Italy is negative. It will be found that the same effect occurs for lead. Essentially, refined copper from scrap in Italy tends to be insignificant when compared to the figures for direct use of scrap, and their positive nature is outweighed by imports of copper scrap. The problem arises because these imports are neither re-exported nor do they appear to enter the secondary production sector. Conceivably they are an input to secondary production, but are recorded as direct use of scrap, in which case the data on the latter would exaggerate the use of domestically generated prompt and home scrap. It has not proved possible to disentangle the problem here.

Lead

Table 14-4 shows the REIs for lead in the six selected countries. The disparity between countries is seen to be substantial. However, there are some serious doubts as to whether the West German figures are representative (Clay, op. cit.), and no scrap trade figures were found for that country. The

Table 14-4 Recovery Effort Indices 1963–1973: Lead

	1963	1964	1965	1966	1967	1968	1969	1970	1971	1972	1973
U.K.	52.1	55.7	56.0	55.7	61.1	65.4	63.2	66.2	60.6	63.0	61.6
Italy	3.9	10.1	neg	0	neg	2.1	neg	neg	10.2	11.6	19.7
Japan	32.2	26.2	29.8	30.4	23.8	23.6	27.1	22.4	21.6	22.4	22.1
U.S.A.	41.3	46.0	46.4	43.6	43.3	41.2	43.2	44.0	42.1	43.8	48.1
W. Germany	14.2	13.7	13.0	13.1	11.8	13.2	15.3	16.3	18.3	18.2	18.0
France	19.8	22.2	34.1	22.3	28.5	23.1	18.7	24.0	24.1	20.2	23.0

[a] Source: Metallgesellschaft, *Metal Statistics*, 1963–1973, 61st ed., Frankfurt am Main, 1974.

negative figures for Italy require some explanation. The data available suggests that Italy imported lead scrap in amounts *greater* than secondary output in 1965, 1967, and 1969–1970, and in an amount equal to secondary output in 1966. Unless the scrap finds a direct use that does not require re-refining or remelting, this suggests that the data is highly inaccurate for those years. It will be recalled that the *REI* measures domestic effort, so that positive secondary output can be offset by scrap imports.

If the figures are taken at face value it is fairly clear that countries are ranked in terms of *REI* in the order United Kingdom, United States, Japan, and France (equal over the period), West Germany, and Italy.

Overall Ranking

Drawing together the evidence on *REI*s as it stands, we obtain the rankings shown in Table 14-5. The bottom row of Table 14-5 shows the overall ranking if countries are awarded inverse points for their position.

If the adjusted *REI* for copper is substituted for the unadjusted one, the rankings in Table 14-5 are altered slightly in that West Germany secures an overall ranking of fourth and Italy moves to fifth.

Bearing in mind the important caveat that these rankings cannot be used for normative purposes until some explanation is given for variations between countries—difference that may be due to some purely technical factor—it would nonetheless appear that the United Kingdom and the United States have a better recycling record than the other countries studied. Little significance can be attached to the "distance" between the final overall ranking scores, but again France and Italy appear to be systematically low recoverers of waste, with the exception of zinc in Italy. Serious doubts surround the zinc and lead figures for West Germany, although it is perhaps surprising to see this country faring significantly less well than the United States and the United Kingdom.

EXPLAINING RECYCLING EFFORT VARIATIONS: OVER TIME

The preceding section has shown that recycling effort varies over time within a single country, and perhaps more interestingly, varies significantly between countries. We now seek to explain these variations. We observed that the *REI* for aluminum has been fairly constant for all countries selected, with the exception of Italy. In Italy's case a secondary industry based on domestic recovery has clearly become important. Compared to 1963, when secondary production was based almost entirely on scrap imports, the ratio of secondary production to scrap imports in 1973 was 3:1, with secondary production increasing 200% in the 10-year period and with scrap imports staying fairly constant. In contrast, secondary production in the United Kingdom has risen by less than 30% and total consumption by about 50%. Secondary production in Japan has increased by 400% and total consumption by 500%; the relevant United States figures are 100% and 100%; West Germany 100% and 150%; France 150% and 100%, respec-

Table 14-5   Recovery Effort Indices: Rankings

	U.K.	U.S.A.	Italy	France	Japan	W. Germany
Aluminum	1	4	5	6	2	3
Copper	2	1	5	6	3	4
Lead	1	2	6	3	3	5(?)
Zinc[b]	2	3	1	4	5	6(?)
Overall Score	6	10	17	19	13	18
Overall Ranking	1	2	4	6	3	5

[a] Source: Metallgesellschaft, *Metal Statistics*, 1963–1973, 61st ed., Frankfurt am Main, 1974.
[b] Calculations not shown here. As with lead, there are some doubts about the validity of West German data on zinc, and this probably results in an underestimate).

tively. In other words, secondary production in each country has increased significantly along with total consumption, making for relatively small changes in the *REI* once direct use of scrap is allowed for.

Since the availability of secondary materials inputs is determined by total consumption in current and past periods, there is clearly a problem of disentangling the extent to which *REI* variations reflect changes in *availability* and changes in "true effort." That is, we know that direct use of scrap and some secondary production is determined, in the main, by the flow of total consumption, but we also know that much potentially recyclable material is not recycled. A better measure of "effort" would, therefore, by an index relating actual recovery to potential recovery. However, there are numerous problems in calculating such an index. First, potential recovery depends on the entire past stock of waste and on the extent to which recovery of that stock is technically feasible. Second, even if we knew this, we would not be able to present such information in the form of an annual index, as is the case with our measure of *REI*, because how recovery of this past stock is distributed over future time is purely arbitrary. For example, if we have X tons of past stock deemed recoverable, we could add X to the current period's recovery figure if a large instant effort is made, or we could say that we shall recover one-tenth of X for each of the next 10 years, and so on. On the other hand, we could develop some index of past effort if we knew this stock, and if we knew past total consumption. Such an index would supplement the measure of *REI* used in this paper.

It is perhaps better, then, to consider an index of effort based on the *flow* of potentially recoverable material that is in fact recovered, ignoring the past stock. This will permit future recovery potential to be estimated and compared to the measure of *REI* used here. In case these various ratios appear confusing when not presented formally, we can write them as: (1) Index of past effort = cumulated recovered past flows/cumulated past consumption. This may then be compared to cumulated recoverable past flows/cumulated past consumption. The ratio of the two ratios is obviously recovered stock/recoverable stock. (2) *REI* = actual use of recovered material/consumption. (3) Potential *REI* = potential use of recovered material/consumption. The ratio of (2) to (3) will then be an index of current effort.

One exercise that reports calculations of ratios (2) and (3) is that if Fischman and Landsberg.[13] The authors assume that the potential for increased recycling must lie mainly in "old" scrap, the use of immediately generated scrap ("prompt" or "home" scrap) being by and large already a maximum.[14] By making assumptions about product life-times, the authors secure for the United States the results presented in Table 14-6.

How does all this assist in explaining variations in *REI* over time? We

can see the relevance by considering two propositions. First, if the *actual REI* for, say, aluminum is actually close to the *maximum REI,* we could argue that the constancy of the *REI* (or, at least, its nonincreasing nature) reflects that country's maximum. It simply cannot achieve more. However, the consideration of potential *REI* suggests that this is not the case, at least for aluminum and copper. Hence our second proposition, the existence of a gap between actual and potential rates, must indicate producer (and, perhaps, consumer) preference for the primary product over the secondary product, a preference that may well, in turn, reflect high recovery costs, differences in the productivity of secondary as opposed to primary materials, or technological factors that limit market opportunities.

This suggest two lines of enquiry. First, are the market opportunities the same for products made of secondary material as they are for primary material products? If not, have those markets changed over time so as to limit or encourage the use of secondary materials? Second, is there some price differential between primary and secondary material that varies so as to explain variations in secondary material use? In this preliminary analysis it has not been possible to test these hypotheses systematically a far greater research effort is required. Nonetheless, some information can be brought to bear on the questions.

If the rate of growth of secondary production of a material in a country exceeds the rate of growth of primary production of that material, then recycled material is taking a more than proportionate "share" of the expan-

Table 14-6 Fischman–Landsberg: United States REIs[a]

Metal	Year		
	1970 *REI*	2000 Potential *REI*	$\dfrac{REI}{Potential\ REI}$
Iron	47.3	48.9	0.97
Aluminum	17.3	42.6	0.40
Copper	44.0	54.4	0.81
Lead	43.9	47.2	0.93
Zinc	16.5	34.6	0.48

[a] Source: Fischman and Landsberg, op. cit. p. 98.

Table 14-7 Growth Rates of Secondary and Primary Output

	$G_s > G_p$	$G_s \simeq G_p$	$G_s < G_p$
Aluminum	Italy	U.S.A. France	U.K. Japan W. Germany
Copper	Japan U.S.A.	U.K.	France W. Germany Italy

sion. If we look at aluminum and copper in this light we get the results presented in Table 14-7.[15]

The table suggests that the secondary industries have failed to make any real inroad into market shares in 8 of the 12 cases considered. The remaining 4 cases are of interest. We have already discussed the Italian experience, and the French case is not one of a really significant difference in relative rates of G_s and G_P. Japan and the United States are the heaviest users of copper, and it is significant that copper rose in price by nearly 200% in the period in question. Nonetheless, even these cases where $G_s > G_P$ are scarcely dramatic.

If we consider the United States, we find that something like 85% of the market for old aluminum scrap is made up of castings, so that the fortunes of the recycling rate, as far as old scrap is concerned, are heavily dependent on the rate of growth of this market. Shipments of aluminum die castings grew at just over 11% per annum for 1960–1969, with the primary aluminum industry shipments growing at just under 10% per annum for the same period.[16] Forecasts of demand for old aluminum scrap suggest a rate of growth of about 6% per annum to 1979, a situation that, for the United States, is likely to mean a surplus supply of old scrap even at present recovery rates. The gap between actual demand and *potential* recovery is expected to be very large indeed, with potential exceeding actual demand by a factor of 9.[17] Since primary and secondary aluminum compete in virtually one market only—casting alloys—the indications are very strong that the failure of *REI* in aluminum to rise in the United States in the period in question is due to the highly limited market for secondary aluminum. In the absence of technological change that enables greater substitution between primary and secondary aluminum, there is every reason to expect the *REI* for aluminum to at least stay constant, and, quite possibly, fall.

What are the factors explaining the relative downward trend of copper

*REI*s for the period in question? The principal markets for secondary copper are wire and cable, brass mill products (the main one), and cast and bronze products. In this respect, and unlike aluminum, primary and secondary copper are very much in competition. In addition, whereas the real price of aluminum has fallen during the period in question, the real price of copper showed an upturn in the early 1960s.[18] Consequently, the climate should have been more favorable to increased recycling and to increased *REI*s than is the case for aluminum. Interestingly, however, this does not appear to have been the case, regardless of whether we use *REI* or *REI** as our measure of recovery effort. One suggested reason is that the primary industry, being mainly oligopolistic, favors price stickiness of primary prices, with producers waiting to determine the performance of market changes before changing market prices. Secondary producers, on the other hand, tend to be organized on a more decentralized and competitive basic, so that price volatility characterizes their market. Since, for many end-uses, primary and secondary producers are in direct competition, price rigidity in the primary sector is translated into inventory fluctuations in the secondary sector as demand changes are not met by primary price changes. The result is considerable variation in secondary prices and wide fluctuations in stocks. The importance of this volatility is that it induces an uncertainty of supply, thus making secondary materials recovery a somewhat hazardous occupation and, more important, placing reliance on it from a customer point of view even more doubtful.

Page[19] has also stressed the importance of marginal additions to supply having a more than proportionate affect on secondary prices. The general result is to reduce the incentive to recovery.

However, secondary materials' price volatility should not be exaggerated. Banks[20] has argued that secondary copper prices are in fact *less* volatile than primary prices, and that the competition nature of secondary production is what keeps price fluctuations down, contrary to the argument advanced above. Inspection of price data for the United States does seem to support the former proposition, although published prices are always hazardous to use, there being various discounts on announced prices. However, in so far as price series can be constructed, primary prices for copper rose at a fairly steady rate from 1961 to 1970,[21] while buying prices for scrap copper rose somewhat faster but in a more erratic fashion. Interestingly, at one point, from mid-1965 to 1967, scrap prices were *above* primary prices, and this does coincide with a fall in *REI** for that period. This would seem to suggest that supply has failed to increase sufficiently to meet demand increases for secondary copper, perhaps because of the fractionalized nature of secondary industry.

Clearly, it is impossible to derive any general conclusions about variations in *REI*s over time. Copper apart, however, declining real materials prices have surely played a substantial part in depressing recovery effort. In addition, labor costs have risen, and this adversely affects the labor-intensive secondary industries. The situation for copper does appear to be at odds with a rising real price. Recycling appears not to have kept pace with market opportunities with the result that scrap prices have risen with primary prices, but in a more volatile fashion.

What of the future? We have suggested that the relative constancy of *REI*s in individual countries in 1963–1973 is something that will change unless technical advance in primary production really does reverse the present hints of rising real costs. Also, there are other important factors that will determine the secondary–primary balance. In general, the energy costs of secondary production are significantly lower than those for primary production. Given the recent enforced price rises in energy, we must expect the new situation at the margin to favor secondary production. (Energy price rises may not affect aluminum, as is often argued, if hydroelectric power continues to be a major source of energy for primary production of this metal). And if other OPEC-style cartels succeed in the minerals markets, we can expect recycling to have a further boost.[22] To all of this we can add the extra costs of operating lower grade ores, and the probable relative bias of the polluter-pays principle against primary production. The future must surely favor the secondary producers.

EXPLAINING INTERCOUNTRY VARIATIONS IN RECYCLING EFFORT

Whereas variations in *REI* over time in any one country appear to be largely explained by variations in industrial activity rates and by relative price variations between primary and secondary materials sources, explaining variations *between* countries is more problematic. It is important to note several features of these intercountry variations as revealed in Tables 14-1 to 14-5. First, the variations are substantial. Taking 1973 figures alone, the variations are 18.0–61.6% (lead); 26.9–44.7% (copper); 20.0–28.5% (aluminum); and 12.1–29.1% (zinc). Second, other investigations suggest equally diverse results for nonmetallic commodities.[23] There would appear, then, to be nothing peculiar to nonferrous metal production to explain the variations. Third, although *REI* behaves erratically for some countries (notably lead), the intercountry variations are *sustained* variations over time. Fourth, while the data admittedly leave a great deal to be desired, it appears very unlikely that informational error can account for intercountry variation. We conclude that there *is* a phenomenon worth investigating. Lastly, we have already discussed the possibility that variations in *rates of growth* of consumption explain variations in *REI*. We concluded that, while such variations might explain *REI* trend differences over very long periods of time, they have little explanatory significance in the current investigation.

Numerous factors are likely to account for the differences in *REI*s between countries. Technologies may vary such that scrap re-use is less of an option in one country compared to another. No detailed analysis of this factor has been made here, but it seems unlikely to be a major explanatory item. Some secondary products appear to be jointly produced with other products such that "recovery" is almost a side-line. Perhaps the three most likely explanations are as follows.

Variations in the Structure of End-Use

If country A has, say, a small market outlet for aluminum castings, its secondary industry will be correspondingly small and the incentive to recover will be small. If country B has a large castings market, we might expect its *REI* to be higher than that of country A. This hypothesis is complicated by the fact of export possibilities for scrap, but, as we showed above, this part of the incentive should be picked up by the *REI* measure.

Variations in Primary-Secondary Price Differentials

If primary material is cheap in country A relative to secondary material, but expensive in B relative to B's secondary source, we might expect A to recycle less. What these price differences should reflect, of course, are variations in factor endowments. The list is a long one. First, countries may possess indigenous deposits of primary raw material. If recovery costs for secondary material are high, perhaps because of widely dispersed sources of waste, the bias in favor of using primary material will be high. Second, capital endowments will affect *REI*s since primary production tends to be capital intensive. If capital is cheap relative to labor, we can expect the balance to favor primary production, secondary production being labor intensive.

Residual Explanation

Where the first two hypotheses are found not to hold, variations in *REI*s will have to be credited to a "residual" factor. This is a catch-all for everything omitted by the earlier explanations. It might, for example, take account of the vertical integration of primary and extractive industries in some countries, which lends a monopolistic bias to primary production. On the other hand, it might be composed more generally of an attitudinal factor that we might best describe as "materials thriftiness."

Obviously, each of the above hypotheses, particularly the last two, subsumes many factors. For example, under the second we might consider the structure of secondary industries in the various countries. If the industry is poorly organized—perhaps including poor collection facilities—recycling ratios are likely to be low. However, if this is the appropriate explanation, we must be able to explain why secondary industries are more developed in some countries than in others. That is, a poorly structured secondary industry would seem to reflect either (1) the poor price competitiveness of that industry relative to primary industry, or (2), if price differentials exist, the failure to take up opportunities for profit. Proposition 2 brings us back to the third hypothesis above, that is, some statement about national characteristics. Proposition 1 can be tested by looking at intercountry price variations. Three popular suggestions in connection with the third hypothesis have been made.

First, certain societies have been labeled "post-affluent" and one of the features of post-affluence may be wastefulness. Although all six countries studied here are advanced industrial nations, we might expect this to show up in low rates of recycling in the United States compared, say, to Italy. However, the opposite is the case: the "throwaway" society also appears to be better at recycling than those less frequently tainted with this label.[25] Second, it is often argued that those most affected by war have developed a "recycling mentality." If this is true, we might expect countries that were besieged, or which expected isolation, to fare better than others. This might explain the apparently preeminent position of the United Kingdom. It does little to explain the record of the United States. Equally, it appears somewhat unlikely that any impetus given by war should continue to explain variations 20 and 30 years later at a time when countries not achieving high recycling rates could, in any event, have established secondary industries.

Third, and perhaps a subsidiary explanation allied to the war-participation factor, is the degree of dependence of countries on imports of primary material. That is, if a country has to import primary material, balance of payments considerations might lead it to encourage secondary production. Of course, producers, acting individually, will not have this objective in mind when deciding on materials sources, unless of course there are differing degree of certainty of supply. While such explanations may well bear on the future, they are not very pertinent to the period of our study. Accordingly, we would expect any concern for the balance of payments to be reflected in national legislation to encourage secondary production. However, there appears to be little validity in this explanation for the period under consideration. Indeed, as we have discussed elsewhere,[26] some national policies designed to stimulate recovery effort appear to result in *REI*s no greater, and sometimes less, than those of countries in which no such legislation exists—and in which positive disincentives to recovery exist.

Variations in End-Use

Space forbids a detailed assessment of end-uses in relation to recovery effort. However, we can illustrate the general finding—that variations in end-use often do *not* explain variations in *REI*—by considering the cases of lead and aluminum. One of the basic uses for lead is as a petroleum additive. Obviously, such a use is totally dissipative with zero probability of recovery. On the other hand, lead used in batteries is easily recoverable and re-enters the production system in less than 3 years (on the average). The two uses combined account for about 65% of lead in the United States, and 45% in the United Kingdom. Accordingly, variations in dissipative use could easily affect the *REI*. The respective rates are shown in Table 14-8:

Table 14-8 shows that the United States has had a systema-

Table 14-8   Lead End-Uses, United Kingdom and United States[a]

	U.S.A.		U.K.	
	Lead in Petroleum	Lead in Batteries	Lead in Petroleum	Lead in Batteries
	% Total Consumption		% Total Consumption	
1963	17.2	38.0	7.7	20.0
1973	18.4	47.0	15.0	30.0

[a] Figures computed by author. Data hazards arise again, however. *Annual Mining Review* quotes lead in petrol as being 29% of United States consumption, but only 5% of European consumption. It has not been possible to substantiate these figures, and the data used above is taken from figures for absolute usage by end-product. It is also worth noting that petrol additive lead is always primary lead.

tically *higher* proportion of lead consumption taken by battery use, the easiest source for recovery. Similarly, while the proportion going into petroleum additives was significantly higher in 1963 in the United States than in the United Kingdom, this differential has been reduced considerably in the current period. Further, this differential at no time outweighs the differential in battery use. In other words, the United States should have had, throughout the period in question, a distinct technical advantage in recovering lead compared to the United Kingdom. However, this advantage does not appear to have been exploited.[27]

Consideration of the outlets for secondary aluminum suggests a similar story.[28] By and large, secondary aluminum smelters supply their output to foundries for castings. If the market for castings differs between countries, and varies over time, we can expect these differences in market opportunities to go some way toward explaining differences in *REI*s. Table 14-9 shows the *REI*s for the six collected countries against the proportion of total castings to total consumption for each country. It is evident that there is no correlation. It is also the case that the "castings ratio" has fallen in West Germany (from 30 to 22%), in Japan (from 28 to 22%), and in the United States (from 19 to 14.5%) over the period 1963–1973, but that, in each case, the *REI* has remained virtually static, suggesting that these market changes do not have much explanatory power for variations in *REI* over time either.

Variations in Price-Differentials

The second hypothesis was that variations in resource prices between countries explain variations in *REI*s. Strictly we need to test this hypothesis by

Table 14-9   Aluminum *REI*s and Castings Ratios[a]

Country	*REI* (1973) (%)	Castings Ratio (1973) (%)
W. Germany	25.6	22.0
France	20.0	31.0
U.K.	28.5	21.5
Italy	24.0	41.0
Japan	28.0	22.0
U.S.A.	23.8	14.5

[a] Figures computed by author.

looking at the price differential between primary and secondary resources serving the same product use, that is, at price variations for alternative sources of supply with the same end-use. In a textbook world, of course, we would expect these prices to be identical since their "marginal product" is the same. In practice, all kinds of institutional and market factors generate differentials between primary and secondary prices. For any pairwise comparison of countries, then, we would want to test the hypothesis that

$$REI_i - REI_j = f((P_{p,i} - P_{s,i}) - (P_{p,j} - P_{s,j}))$$

where

$$P_p = \text{price of primary source}$$
$$P_s = \text{price of secondary source}$$
$$i, j = \text{country } i \text{ and country } j$$

In this preliminary analysis it has not proved possible to secure secondary prices for each country. Indeed, there is a severe problem of assessing *which* secondary price is relevant. Accordingly, the preliminary test was reduced to

$$REI_i - REI_j = f(P_{p,i} - P_{p,j/e})$$

Unfortunately, severe complexities concerning information availability have prevented this hypothesis from being tested in this fashion. The problem lies not so much in the multiplicity of secondary metal price series, but in finding out what the "true" primary price is. Published prices tend not to be the prices at which actual transactions take place.[29] While some spirited efforts have been made to derive market clearing prices by collecting evidence on the various discounts offered on list prices, it remains the case that primary price data is unreliable in the extreme. A more indirect approach would be to look at the relative capital and labor intensities of primary and secondary production, and then to compare capital/labor price ratios. Even these comparative studies are known to have numerous pitfalls, however, and are beyond the scope of this chapter.[30]

An analysis of domestic availability of raw materials does tend to support the view that factor endowments are important. For aluminum, only the United States and France have significant outputs of bauxite and in each case very little is exported. Italy has some production, but remaining countries in our sample have none, or, at most, negligible amounts. Japan, United Kingdom, West Germany, and Italy are dependent on imports. France has some import of bauxite, and the United States imported some 13 million tons in 1973 compared to domestic production of just under 2 million tons. With the exception of the United States, *REI*s vary with domestic availability roughly as one might expect if the price hypothesis were correct. Again, the only real test is to translate these factors into price variations.

CONCLUSION

This chapter has been entirely exploratory. Its aim has been to suggest a line of approach to an interesting question, the answers to which can have policy implications. Essentially, recycling rates do vary substantially between countries. Those countries that have comparatively low rates may, therefore, have much to learn from those that have comparatively high rates, although it must not be concluded that countries that appear to do well at recycling are as doing as well as they could, or even as well as they should. However, to be sure of this potential for "learning by observing," it has to be determined whether the variations in recycling effort are due to institutional factors (which, in any event, could be the subject of direct policy), to factor endowments, to differing market opportunities (again, still subject to policy), to purely technological factors, or to some national characteristic that shows up in differing attitudes towards recycling.

In such a preliminary attempt we have not been able to say whether the "positive" factors such as factor endowments are the main sources of explanation, or whether there genuinely exists a residual factor that can best be treated by publicity and persuasion. At most we have some indication that, in the case of lead, some countries are recycling at what would appear to be an unwarranted low rate. Until the hypothesis put forward in this paper are placed in the context of a formal econometric model, however, there can be no firm conclusion. In the meantime, we argue that comparative analysis of this kind can be fruitful and illuminating.

APPENDIX 1

Recycling and Cost Minimization

From the private cost standpoint the optimization problem can be stated in terms of the cost minimization corollary of profit maximization.[31] That is, the resource user's objective is to minimize

$$C = V(\bar{q}) + R(\bar{q})$$

where C is cost, V is cost of virgin materials, R is the cost of secondary materials, and $\bar{q}$ is a given level of output. From the social standpoint, however, the objective is to minimize a social cost function, S, which includes $V(q)$ and $R(q)$ together with:

$E_v(q)$ = any external costs associated with the use of virgin materials, including the external costs of extraction, but excluding disposal costs;

$E_r(q)$ = external costs associated with the use of recycled material;

$D(q)$ = disposal costs associated with the nonrecycling option *less* disposal costs associated with the recycling option. D is in turn set by the least-cost disposal option;

$G(q)$ = present value of gains from extending the "life" of an extractive resource;

such that

$$S = V(\bar{q}) + R(\bar{q}) + E_v(\bar{q}) + E_r(\bar{q}) + D(\bar{q}) - G(\bar{q}).$$

ACKNOWLEDGMENTS

I am deeply indebted to the following for providing helpful comments on the first draft of this chapter: Don Fink of the United States Environmental Protection Agency, Toby Page of Resources for the Future, Samprit Chatterjee of New York University, Michael Henstock of Nottingham University, Roger Betts of Imperial College, London, and Ray Tron of the Warren Spring Laboratory at Stevenage, Herts. Maurice Farmer of the Public Sector Economic Research Centre at Leicester University assisted with some of the calculations. None of these, however, bears any responsibility for the findings and arguments of this chapter.

N O T E S

1. Garret Hardin, "To Trouble a Star: The Cost of Intervention in Nature," *Bulletin of the Atomic Scientists,* 1970. Reprinted by R. T. Roelofs et al., *Environment and Society*, Englewood Cliffs: Prentice-Hall, 1974.

2. The best known essay is Kenneth Boulding, "The Economics of the Coming Spaceship Earth," in H. Jarrett, Ed., *Environmental Quality in a Growing Economy,* New York: Macmillan, 1968. However, Boulding had been making the same point very much earlier. See his "The Consumption Concept in Economic Theory," *American Economic Review,* May 1945.

3. See D. W. Pearce, "Are Environmental Problems a Challenge to Economic Science?," PSERC Discussion Paper 75-03, University of Leicester, 1975.

4. "Tend" is the operative word. Only detailed case studies will show how far this generalization holds. In addition, some current recycling effort is aided, often substantially, by government so that a divergence between actual and socially desirable recycling rates may not exist.

5. To call the economic calculus a "democratic process" is somewhat misleading since the distribution of voting power is weighted by the distribution of economic power, that is, by relative wealth and income. However, in principle, there are no problems of correcting cost–benefit studies for this bias. See C. A. Nash, D. W. Pearce, and J. Stanley, "The Evaluation of Cost–Benefit Analysis Criteria," *Scottish Journal of Political Economy,* June 1975.

6. D. W. Pearce, "Economics and Ecology," *Surrey Papers in Economics,* No. 10, 1974.

7. D. W. Pearce, "Economics and Ecology," *Survey Papers in Economics,* No. 10, 1974.

8. Battelle Memorial Institute Columbus Laboratories: *A Study to Identify Opportunities for Increased Solid Waste Utilization,* 9 volumes, distributed by National Technical Information Service, U.S. Department of Commerce, Springfield, Virginia, 1972.

9. The Waste Management Advisory Council was established in 1973 after the United Kingdom Government's "Green Paper" *War on Waste* was published. (Cmnd 5727). Subgroups of the Council are looking at recycling effort and waste disposal problems in paper, ferrous metals, nonferrous metals, rubber, and so on. The French situation for nonferrous metals is detailed in the French Ministry of Industry's report "Le Cycle des Déchets de Metaux non ferreus," 1975.

10. For an interesting preliminary paper that prompted this one, see H. A. Clay, "Future Developments—A Primary View of the Secondary Non-Ferrous Scrap Industry," unpublished, Rio Tinto Zinc, London.

11. For a pioneering effort that looks at some aspects of trade in recovered materials see I. Walter, *Environment, International Trade and Secondary Materials Recovery,* New York University Graduate School of Business Administration, Working Paper No. 75-73, October 1975.

12. I am very much indebted to Don Fink of the United States Environmental Protection Agency for drawing my attention to this point, which was totally overlooked in the initial draft.

13. L. Fischman and H. Landsberg, "Adequacy of Nonfuel Minerals and Forest Reserves," Chapter 4 of U.S. Commission on Population and Growth and the American Future, *Research Reports,* Vol. III (U.S., 6PO), Washington 1972.

14. It is not altogether clear from their paper how past stock was treated. The text and notes read as if this stock was not allowed for—our ratio (1)—so that potential is measured with respect to the future flow of "old" scrap.

15. Data problems intrude again. The *F-L REI* index of 17.3% for aluminum is well below our estimate of 21.7%; their index for copper is 44% compared to ours of 47%. Far more pertinent, however, is the fact that their *potential* index for lead is below the *actual* index for the United Kingdom in 1960. This issue is discussed below.

16. G_s = rate of growth of secondary production *excluding,* as far as possible, direct use of scrap; G_p = rate of growth of primary production.

17. Battelle Memorial Institute, op. cit.

18. Battelle Memorial Institute, op. cit.

19. The standard reference on declining real price of commodities is H. J. Barnett and C. Morse, *Scarcity and Growth,* Johns Hopkins Press, Baltimore, 1963. Their estimates end in 1957, however. A similar real price series extended to 1970 is reported in W. D. Nordhaus, "Resources as a Constraint on Growth," *American Economic Review, 64,* 2, 1974.

20. T. Page, *Economics of a Throwaway Society,* Resources for the Future, Washington, 1975.

21. F. Banks, *The World Copper Market: An Economic Analysis,* Ballinger, Cambridge, Mass., 1974.

22. The data used were producers' copper prices, Atlantic Seaboard, and buying prices for No. 2 scrap copper. See Battelle Memorial Institute, op. cit., p. 142.

23.   I am not, and never have been, convinced that OPEC is an example that cannot be replicated for other commodities. For the view that OPEC is unique, however, see H. Landsberg, "Policy Elements of U.S. Resources/Supply Problems," in *Resources Policy,* 1 (2), 1974.

24.   Walter is of the opinion that "the variance is probably even greater for nonmetallic wastes." See I. Walter "Environment, International Trade, and Secondary Materials Recovery," New York University, Graduate School of Business Administration Working Paper Series, No. 75–73, October 1975, p. 18. I have also shown elsewhere that the variation in recovery of waste lubrication oil is high. See D. W. Pearce, "The Recovery of Waste Lubrication Oil: A Comparative National Analysis," *Resources Policy,* June 1975.

25.   Spain has a 17% recycling rate in aluminum, and Austria has a 9% rate. If the data can be believed, African countries as a whole recycle less than 10% of aluminum. In the latter respect however, recycling is quite distinct from re-use, since waste containers, for example, simply tend to get used for receptacles and so on.

26.   While the data are even more hazardous to use, this appears to be the case with waste lubrication oil. See Pearce op. cit. Again, the United States fares well in such an international comparison, and it will be recalled that secondary production is scarcely encouraged in the United States by differential freight rates and by resource depletion allowances.

27.   Casual empiricism suggest that the United States simply doesn't bother. The recycling loop in the United Kingdom for batteries is a very tight one—hardly any batteries appear to be dumped. In the United States the sight of a dumped battery is not an uncommon one. Of course, if the recovery value is low relative to average incomes (or, perhaps, more important, relative to average incomes at the lower end of the income distribution) it will not pay to collect the dumped product. Again, however, it isn't obvious that *REI*s vary systematically with income levels.

28.   I am indebted to Roger Betts of Imperial College, London for drawing this example to my attention. However, my conclusion differs from that secured by Betts's own research. The explanation for the disparity of result is that Betts uses a different measure of *REI*—one that does not incorporate scrap exports and imports in the fashion chosen here. It was emphasized earlier that the form of index used here is not the only legitimate one. For very much more detail on aluminum recycling see R. J. Betts, *Recycling Aluminium,* Mimeo, Imperial College of Science and Technology, London, 1975.

29.   See page, op. cit., Chapter 3.

30.   It is hoped to test for this explanation in an extended research program on recycling to be carried out at Leicester University.

31.   For a diagrammatic exposition see W. O. Spofford, "Solid Residuals Management: Some Economic Considerations," *Natural Resources Journal,* Vol. 11, 1971; and D. W. Pearce, "Fiscal Incentives and the Economics of Waste Recycling: Problems and Limitations," in Institute of Fiscal Studies, *Fiscal Policy and the Environment,* London, 1974.

Chapter

15

The Transnational Dimension: Discussion

The discussion of transfrontier and resource issues relating to environment is necessarily a varied one. Some of its dimensions reduce to problems of bilateral bargaining between countries whose cost–benefit profiles differ. Others involve broader issues of global concern in which the costs and benefits are largely bi-directional in nature. Still others center around comparisons that can be drawn between policies implemented at the national level with possibly beneficial learning functions. In this chapter, the foregoing essays focusing on these issues are discussed and elaborated upon.

PROBLEMS OF INTERGOVERNMENTAL NEGOTIATIONS AND POLLUTION CONTROL

John A. Butlin

The foregoing chapters present a rather different perspective on the problems of international environmental control. After the discussion on theoretical aspects and empirical investigations into particular international effects of environmental policy, which occupy the first part of this volume, the chapters in this section have a much wider vision. The state of disarray at the third Law of the Sea Conference, which reconvened in Geneva early in 1975, was evidence of the timeliness of the topic. The dearth of material either in the economic, legal, or political science literature (the contributions of the three authors on this topic representing major exceptions) was a measure of the task that had been set.

The problems of managing international common-property resources should, in theory, provide no extra problem to the analytical economist. In theory, the use of the oceans or the atmosphere as a dump into which industrial waste is deposited is little different from the use of national rivers for the same purpose. As no right of ownership is defined over the resource, it will be exploited beyond the point at which the marginal deterioration in absorptive capacity is equal to the marginal gain to global society of the extra output produced jointly with the marginal unit of waste. Such an inefficient factor allocation can, in theory, be rectified by the appropriate Pigovian tax.

The words "in theory" intentionally convey an increasing note of scepticism in the above passage. The problems associated with negotiating a fishing treaty, an ocean-dumping treaty, a treaty to regulate the use of the stratosphere, or any other international effort to regulate the use of a global common-property resource, are many, and cannot simply be relegated to a class of "institutional" problems. The negotiations do not falter due to diplomatic ignorance of the appropriate Pigovian tax. There are very real problems in establishing the appropriate objective function, or "terms of reference," on the basis of which any international agreement ought to be negotiated, and, even more important, implemented. The problems in establishing terms of reference arise because negotiations will inevitably be undertaken in a *mutatis mutandis* framework. All governments have vector-valued objective functions, of which environmental quality is only one argument. Amongst the better established policy objectives the trades-off may be fairly well established, but the trade-off between environmental quality and balance-of-payments, or between environmental quality and the rate of unemployment, is not likely to be well-understood by national politicians or by international negotiators. Another apparent problem in defining objective functions for international negotiations is that equity may take precedence over efficiency. Whilst economic theory is strong on global optimality rules for allocative efficiency, it is remarkably weak on the problems of the personal and international distribution of income and wealth. Add to this the explicitly spatial nature of problems that are negotiated internationally, and it is seen that the problem is not so much one of failure to apply received theory as lack of appropriate theory.

Would all be well if we had a better theory that would, conceptually, provide some appropriate optimizing rule for global common-property management, with the objective functions and constraint sets appropriately specified? One cannot feel confident that the answer would be in the affirmative. Even in Pigou's simple laundry–steam-train case, if the laundry was in one country and the railway company in another, how would global allocative efficiency be restored? How would the appropriate tax be levied? By whom would it be administered? Would these solutions work if the countries were not contiguous, or did not trade?

Thus specified, problems of international pollution control appear insuperable. However, Professors d'Arge, Pearson, and Scott approach the problem constructively from three different angles, using different particular international pollution problems for illustration. d'Arge argues strongly for the victim-pays principle, both explicitly in terms of allocative efficiency and implicitly in terms of information requirements (vis-à-vis other global rules such as the polluter-pays principle). The case of supersonic flight in the stratosphere appears to bear out the Pareto-superiority of the victim-pays principle. Pearson's concern is more with the environment as a public good, and the more pragmatic problem of establishing workable rather than optimal controls to reduce the despoilation of the oceanic environment resulting in oil spills from tankers. Scott addresses himself to the problem of the optimality of approach to international negotiations and regulation on the issues of environmental quality, drawing on the example of transfrontier river-borne pollution.

Although the three contributors have different approaches, at least three characteristics of international pollution-control problems are common to the papers. Firstly, the issue of sovereignty is emphasized, particularly by Scott and d'Arge. The optimizing problem discussed conceptually above cannot ignore all the problems of aggregating national welfare functions into a grand, global welfare function that is to be optimized by international agencies of one kind or another. The problem of international pollution control has to be discussed with full weight given to the many national sovereignties involved. Conceptually, aggregating all nations' social welfare functions means that any particular nation's social welfare function can no longer be identified. This is what appears to be meant by "loss of sovereignty."

Secondly, problems of allocative efficiency are not the sole concern of negotiations. d'Arge and Pearson both argue that issues pertaining to the use and production of wealth in global common-property management must be considered together with the particular global allocation of wealth implied by any particular management scheme. The latter may dominate the former in negotiations.

The importance of the numbers of parties involved in international negotiations on pollution control for all but the simplest (two-party, one-source, uni-directional) class of problems is emphasized by all three authors. Why is it that treaties on uses of nuclear power are ratified more quickly than those on environmental control? Is it because, in the former case, the risks are more immediately catastrophic? Or is it because sources of nuclear power generation are more easily identified and monitored, and because the numbers of parties involved is limited? In the case of international environmental spillovers, the polluters, the victims, and their respective governmental advocates are more numerous, the sources of pollution are more numerous, and the damage more likely to be insidious. Problems of identification and measurement increase geometrically with the numbers of parties involved.

It should be no surprise that this set of papers carefully elaborates on approaches to particular sets of problems, rather than advocating global panacea. Indeed, it *is* surprising that anyone expects success out of massive international negotiations such as the third Law of the Sea Conference. In a world characterized by many nations with many resources, at most one would expect either deals between small numbers of countries or deals on particular issues. It is only when there are few negotiating parties, or the negotiations can be constrained to a small subset of issues, or both, that any outcome at all can reasonably be expected.

TRANSFRONTIER POLLUTION AND REGULATION

Larry E. Ruff

The discussion on transfrontier environmental issues by Professor Ralph C. d'Arge (Chapter 11) consists of two, tenuously related, parts. The second of these is a report on an attempt to estimate the costs and benefits involved in certain human activities, especially use of a fleet of supersonic transports (SSTs), which might affect global climate. I have little comment on this part of the paper, beyond the totally gratuitous observation that this excercise strikes me as a major step forward in the *reductio ad absurdum* of cost–benefit analysis. This is not a direct criticism of Professor d'Arge, who presumably is reporting on some competent, professionally done, state-of-the-art work commissioned by the Department of Transportation (DOT). The fault lies more with those in DOT who conceived the project and defined its scope. One can only hope that the effort does not stop at a discounted-present-value comparison between the SST with "good" engines and the SST with "bad" engines, but gets into comparison of other alternatives—including, even, no SST—and adopts more of a sequential decision-making approach to this problem involving great uncertainities, long time scales, and potentially huge consequences; this is precisely the kind of situation in which traditional cost–benefit analysis of the type d'Arge describes has the least to offer.

The first, and perhaps more relevant part of d'Arge's paper, deals with the theoretical aspects of economic solutions to transfrontier pollution (TFP) problems. Professor d'Arge teases us a bit by suggesting that a useful taxonomy of TFP problems is about to be revealed, on the basis of either "three central questions" or "certain characteristics," six in number. In fact, he only means to convince us that the real world contains TFP problems of many kinds, which are unlikely to yield to "an overriding general guiding principle." The bulk of the rest of this part of the paper is devoted to reminding us of all the little (or big) difficulties that can arise in real-world situations to thwart any attempt to universally apply a single-solution principle.

I have no real quarrel with this conclusion, either as an impossible-to-deny logical statement, or as an empirical generalization. Logically, we all know what economic theory tells us about how to solve TFP problems: we simply set the marginal *whatchamacallit* equal to the marginal *somethingorother*. Once one gets beyond this general role into more specific suggestions, it is easy enough to demonstrate that there may exist situations in which the specific suggestions lead to violations of the general optimality conditions. Even for domestic pollution problems, the bulk of current economic literature on the subject is devoted to such demonstrations—perhaps one of the reasons that *economists* have had so little impact on pollution control policy, even though *economics* has some simple and sensible things to say on the subject.

Professor d'Arge's point, however, is more empirical than logical. He is reminding us that the real world offers us no single dominant model of the TFP problem, making it very difficult to go from the general efficiency properties to broadly applicable policy suggestions. Even more than for domestic pollution, important TFP problems exist of all sizes and shapes; in virtually every cell of any useful taxonomy one could construct, there are real problems that are regarded, in some parts of the world, as the typical TFP problem.

This is an important and valid point, I think. As the representative of the U.S. Government in the OECD Committee that worried about TFP for more than a year, I was regarded as being rather unconstructive because I resisted every attempt to establish a "General Principle" for TFP, analogous to the OECD's polluter-pays principle (PPP) for internal pollution problems.

In fact, I was not all that enthusiastic about attempts to define the PPP very precisely for internal pollution, especially if it was to apply only to control and not damage costs. Those phenomena we like to call "pollution," and those actors we like to call "polluters" or whatever, are in reality a pretty diverse lot of things, especially where TFP is involved, and one wants to be careful about trying to force them all into the same mold. The closest I have ever been able to come to a universal generalization about solving TFP problems is to suggest that economic efficiency is too important to be ignored, that market like control strategies can usually be devised that are "better" than purely regulatory strategies, and that everyone involved—from political officials to economic theorists—should be flexible. Since I have left the OECD Committee, they have obtained agreement on some general TFP principles, which Professor d'Arge shows to be less than optimal in some conceivably important situations.

So I think d'Arge's conclusion is about right. If I were inclined to pick away at his argument, I might take exception to his implication that "the classical economic solution to pollution problems"—namely, to somehow internalize external costs—does not apply to TFP problems; neither he nor anyone else has suggested or could suggest any way to solve a TFP problem that does not, in fact, amount to some form of cost internalization, consistent with the general statement of this "classical economic solution." I would also, if I were inclined to pick nits, argue that d'Arge tends to dismiss some possible general-solution principles on the basis of his own individualistic interpretation of them, when a more sympathetic interpretation might allow them to work; for example, he says that the full cost PPP leads to inefficiencies when marginal and average damages diverge, which is not true for a single polluter (or a group of polluters somehow managed as an efficient collective polluter) that pays *total* damages and, hence, makes decisions on the basis of marginal costs and revenues.

However, I am not inclined to pick nits with d'Arge, because I basically agree with his negative conclusion about the possibility of a universal principle for dealing with TFP problems. So perhaps the best use of my remaining space is to offer some thoughts on the basic reasons for this negative conclusion, and what it means for the future contribution economists might hope to make to the resolution of TFP problems.

The classical "externality" line of economic thought orginating in Pigou concentrated its analytic attention on problems involving a few actors in more-or-less direct interactions, and ignored long-term, general-equilibrium considerations as often as not. Thus, this line led directly to the Coase conclusion that, if property rights were defined clearly, it made no difference to whom they were initially allocated or what sort of institutional arrangements existed for trading them: trades would be made until a Pareto-efficient allocation was accomplished. The recent wave of concern over environmental pollution, however, has focused on a rather different class of problems, in which many economic agents are making or could make destructive use of a common-property resource that also has valuable nondestructive uses to many (often the same) economic agents. Considerations of information and negotiating costs and "free rider" problems quickly led economists to the conclusion that a collective organization was needed to exchange rights, and the fact that it was the destructive uses that needed rationing soon led them to the conclusion that those who wanted to make destructive use of the resource should have to pay for it, *even if* some initial lump-sum payments to them were suggested on equity grounds. Thus, economists have had little difficulty agreeing on the desirability of the polluter-pays principle for this empirically important class of pollution problems, and the OECD, for the same economic reasons but with some politically expedient qualifications, was able to get acceptance of the PPP with relative ease.

With the internal pollution problems thus neatly solved, economists and the OECD turned to TFP problems. Two lines of analysis have developed. In one, the existence of national borders and governments is unimportant and can be ignored, leading to the so-far-nonoperational conclusion that the international resource should be managed as a single unit by some supernational group, presumably on the basis of the PPP. The other line of analysis sees the most important feature of TFP problems in the fact that negotiations among a few sovereign nations are required, bringing us full-circle back to the original problem discussed by Pigou and Coase: smoke from Britain's chimney is soiling Sweden's laundry, and any definite allocation of rights between Britain and Sweden will lead to an efficient solution; recognizing information and negotiating costs, and the absence of a single dominant model of "the" TFP problem, leads one rather directly to d'Arge's negative conclusion about the possibility of discovering a universal solution principle.

That is about where economic theorists have now brought us. National governments either should disappear or should act as individual *homo economicus*. It seems obvious that the direction we should now pursue is to develop a synthesis or middle ground, in which the real nature of national governments is recognized—as jealous protectors of their rights and the perceived interests of their citizens, but with imperfect knowledge about the ability to control their citizens. This synthesis requires careful distinctions to be made between, for example, the flow of payments and information between governments, and between citizens and their governments. It requires both theorists and political negotiators to recognize that successful international negotiation on TFP problems requires more than solemn (and too often hollow) agreement on high principle among governments, but requires careful consideration of, and eventual agreement on, information generation and exchange, and development of institutional forms adapted to the specifics of such situation. Economists can help by keeping economic efficiency and the advantages of market-type arrangements on the minds of the negotiators and institution designers, and by providing good journeyman economic analysis where needed. However, there is little point in my elaborating on this further because Anthony Scott does it better in Chapter 13.

ON INTERNATIONAL OCEAN DUMPING

Robert E. Stein

In considering the various ways to comment both on Professor Pearson's paper and the subject, I was immediately struck by the huge differences in approach to marine pollution taken by individuals in different disciplines. This certainly includes differences in approaches taken by economists and lawyers. For some reason, I was reminded of the "Nose Speech" and Rostand's Cyrano de Bergerac. In that speech, Cyrano with great eloquence, defines his nose—like the present subject, his is also a discussion of an externality—from a number of different "disciplines" or perspectives. He states what is this portent, this "phenomenon." One can certainly do the same with the phenomenon and the portent of marine pollution.

To continue a moment further with the analogy: some consider the oceans the most immediately threatened part of the biosphere; others, a place to legitimately dispose of the by-products or waste from the land; others, a place for transportation with all its attendant effects; still further, the body from which a new bed of riches can be found on the sea and the subsoil beneath the sea. For economists, the oceans and marine pollution are considered "reciprocal external diseconomies, of an environmental nature, that affect an international common-property resource, the oceans."[1] A legal definition that has found its way into a number of conventions (in more or less this form) is taken from the Paris Convention on Land Based Sources that states that pollution of the sea is "the introduction by man, directly or indirectly, of substances or energy into the marine environment (including estuaries) resulting in such deleterious effects as hazard to human health, harm to living resources and to marine ecosystems, damage to amenities, or interference with other legitimate uses of the sea."[2]

So there are differences. However, despite these differences, economists, and to a lesser extent lawyers, approach problems in a similar way. They predicate their analyses on sets of assumptions that exist in a rational system—inhabited at least in part by the proverbial "resonable man." This is my first general comment on the paper by Professor Pearson. It is premised on a rational system and certainly any observer of the way the international community has conducted itself in the context of the Law of the Sea negotiations, especially in the area of consideration of zones of national jurisdiction, indicates that rationality is not high on a list of values.

It would make sense, to look back to the 1972 period at the time the United Nations Conference on the Human Environment was held in Stockholm. From that time on, states have looked toward the Law of the Sea Conference for solution to a number of environmental problems. Yet with 140 countries, over 100 agenda items, three main committees, and even more subcommittees, I can only conclude that most of the individuals charged with developing a new law of the sea, and consequently a control to marine pollution, would not understand the kinds of analyses presented in this paper.[3]

One of the difficulties is that the decision to put into Committee Three the questions of pollution, scientific information, and transfer of technology was made early in the considerations of the Conference. This had resulted in little discussion of the environmental impact of those activities that are under discussion in Committees One and Two. Committee One deals with the important seabed regime, with potential environmental hazards, and Committee Two with the range of issues including the rules applying to the 200-mile economic zone in which the exploitation of resources—living and subsurface—are high on the priority list for coastal states. Moreover, it is in this area that pollution from ships is likely to have the most harmful effect on coastal areas.

Going into Geneva, Committee Three had not reached a consensus on a broad range of the issues before it. At Geneva a few things were worked out, but the single text was in need of considerable work.[4]

To return to Professor Pearson's chapter, the two conferences to which he refers may have been saved referring questions to the Law of the Sea Conference, but the inability of the Law of the Sea Conference to agree leaves the earlier dumping and marine pollution from ships conventions with gaps still waiting to be filled.[5]

Another area discussed in the chapter that deserves comment is the relationship between domestic legislation and international agreements dealing with marine pollution. I would maintain that international measures and international environmental-control policy are in many instances direct outgrowths of national measures. For example, pages 294 to 299 do not, in my view, capture the close relationship between the negotiation of U.S. legislation (the 1972 Marine Protection Research and Sanctuaries Act) and the 1972 London Convention. The legislation predated the convention, as did a regional agreement concluded by countries from the North East Atlantic area (the Oslo Convention). All adopted a similar approach, but there were some requirements that were not in the U.S. legislation that had to be modified in a few respects to meet the terms of the convention and permit its ratification by the United States. In the United States' case then, the domestic activity provided impetus to international regulation, but for many countries the reverse is true, so that there is no attempt to legislate domestically or adopt local strategies until the international instruments are in place. This force, though it introduces an "intervening layer,"[6] may well be the most effective way to develop environmental controls for a broad number of countries.

Where are we left? The discontinuities in developing a rational policy for management of ocean resources have thus far carried the day. States have, at the Law of the Sea Conference, not only opted for broad bands of national jurisdiction, but also have refused to grapple with the questions of which rules apply within the broad bands. I concur with Professor Pearson that the trend will be to continue this "fragmented approach."[7] Yet it is to be hoped that the regulation by the international community in conjunction with the States will be adequate to the problem and effective in implementation[8] since, in the end, it will be the environment that will suffer.

There is much work remaining since land-based sources of pollution have not been even marginally dealt with. The use of economic instruments will obviously be of value in this respect as well, but we should all remember that in the search for efficiency and optimum levels, the interest of the great watery mass covering two-thirds of the earth's surface be kept firmly in mind.

NOTES

1. Pearson, p. 375.

2. Convention for the Prevention of Marine Pollution from Land Based Sources, February 21, 1974.

3. The failure of the 1975 session at Geneva to agree on a treaty, indeed the failure to agree on even a basis for dealing with the range of problems on the deep seabed, is an indication of this.

4. At the Geneva session it was agreed that the chairman of each committee would prepare a single negotiating text for subjects under discussion in each committee. It was emphasized that the texts were to provide a basis for negotiations and would not prejudice any other proposals that might be made. The texts are found in U.N. Doc. A/CONF.62/WP.8. May 7, 1975. Another session of the Conference is scheduled for New York in March, 1976.

5. The 1972 Ocean Dumping Convention and the 1973 IMCO Convention of Pollution from Ships.

6. See Pearson, p. 296.

7. Pearson, p. 298.

8. I prefer "adequate and effective" to "minimum" since this latter concept implies a compromise that, though satisfactory to the parties, may not be sufficient to effectively deal with the particular environmental problem at hand.

INSTITUTIONAL PROBLEMS

Stanley P. Johnson

In his excellent chapter in this volume, Anthony Scott tended to opt for the common agency approach to the problems of transfrontier pollution (TFP). I would like to amplify further on the possibilities of this approach in the light of European experience. We can use several models that may be useful in this regard.

The first is the bilateral or multilateral agency (or "commission") that provides a forum for the discussion of TFP problems among the states concerned. This is likely to remain not much more than a "talking place" in the absence of more specific commitments to particular treaties and pollution-abatement programs. We can see how, over the last decade or so of its existence, the Commission on the Pollution of the Rhine, for example, has—in view of the relative lack of progress at the diplomatic level—moved towards the elaboration of a detailed Draft Convention on the Prevention of the Chemical Pollution of the Rhine, with the now customary approach of "black lists," "grey lists," and the like.

Second, there is the multilateral agency or institution that already exists for other purposes, such as the Council of Europe, but that decides to work out in cooperation with some or all of its members a draft convention in the environment area, for example, pollution abatement, and that then hopes that some of its members will be impressed enough by what has been achieved to want to sign such a convention.

Third is the ad hoc organization. The Oslo Convention of Ocean Dumping was worked out in a diplomatic conference of the states of the Northeast Atlantic who were specially concerned with the problem. Because the participants in the original conference were those most concerned with the problem, there is some chance that these ad hoc conventions will in fact prove effective. Another, rather similar, example is the Paris Convention for the Prevention of Land-Based Sources of Pollution.

A composite approach that contains some elements of each of the foregoing is the Framework Convention, and its associated protocols that are now
being elaborated for the Protection of the Mediterranean Against Pollution
(Barcelona, February 1976). Here we find the United Nations Environment
Programme (UNEP) inviting the riparian states of the Mediterranean
(including both the Arab countries and Israel) to draw up a general treaty
covering the principle sources of sea pollution. There will be special protocols on dumping and on cooperation in emergencies, possibly also on
land-based pollution and pollution that results from the exploration and exploitation of the sea-bed. The idea is that one or more of these protocols
will be mandatory, in the sense that a state that wishes to become party to
the framework convention will have to become party to at least one protocol.

The problems with all four approaches to TFP, or variations of them,
are: (1) difficulties in bringing them into force, and (2) difficulties in enforcing them when they are enacted. We note that, of all the examples cited
above, only the Oslo Convention is actually in force. As for the problems of
enforcement at national level of obligations entered into internationally, this
is hardly unique to environmental issues.

Let me make a few additional comments from the perspective of the European Communities. The EEC can play a useful role in counteracting the
aforementioned inadequacies. The institutions of the EEC, the Commission,
the Council, the Parliament, and the Court of Justice, can be brought into
play to give these treaties and conventions and pollution-abatement programs "teeth" that they might not otherwise have.

First, the EEC can prepare Community legislation to give effect, on a
Community level, to the provisions of the relevant conventions, and it can
of course do this even before the convention has entered into force.

Second, by creating a Community obligation in addition to the international obligation a state may assume bilaterally in the framework of a
particular convention, the Community may reinforce the processes of sanc-
tion and enforcement for any infraction of the convention. For it is only the
convention itself that is breached in such a case, but also obligations entered
into by a member state of the Community under the Treaty of Rome. In
this context the Community is seeking, wherever possible, to become party
to the relevant conventions in its own right, and alongside the member
states. This has already been admitted in the case of the Paris Convention.

Finally, within the context of the Community's Action Program on the
Environment that was adopted by the Council of Ministers in November
1973, the Community is now involved in creating in effect a body of TFP
legislation specific to the nine member states of the European Community.
Common programs of pollution abatement are being proposed for dis-

charges into the aquatic environment of the Community, including emission norms. Common quality objectives have, in certain cases, already been adopted by the Council. There is a general obligation on one member state to ensure that actions or inactions in respect of pollution do not make it impossible for another member state to attain or maintain environmental quality objectives laid down and approved at the Community level.

It might be said, therefore, that by bringing into play the whole range of mechanisms and institutions provided for under the Treaty of Rome, the EEC is in a particularly favorable position to deal with the TFP issue. One aspect still to be worked out in detail and embodied in the appropriate Community instrument is the extension of the polluter-pays principle to TFP. Here too, the particular nature of the EEC offers some scope for applications of the PPP to TFP, which have real meaning and which can be implemented through courts of law.

COMPARATIVE ASPECTS OF MATERIALS RECYCLING

Samprit Chatterjee

I agree essentially with Professor Pearce when he says that the level or recycling effort should be viewed in the entire context of all economic activities. As he clearly points out, there is often a disagreement on the question of the "value" of a resource. This difference I feel sometimes arises not merely due to a difference in "imputed" value, but due to the use of different discounting rates. In analysis of economic problems that deal with decisions regarding the optimality of present consumption to future consumption, one of the crucial variables is the discounting rate. In attempting to determine the optimum level of recycling effort, attention I feel should be paid to this crucial variable.

Let me make a few comments on the Recovery Effort Index (*REI*). I have some reservations on the index as it is presently constituted. I will try to make my point by sketching a brief scenario. Think of a small country that has developed the technology, and has an industry that almost entirely runs on scrap. Since it has a small consumption of the material, it does not generate a sufficient amount of domestic scrap to supply its industries and consequently imports it. In Dr. Pearce's *REI* scale this country will show up rather poorly, because import of scrap enters negatively in the index, although the structure of this particular industry in the said country is highly efficient with regards to recycling. Consequently, it gets a poor grade when it deserves a very good grade! I think this shows up in some of Dr. Pearce's calculations in which for some countries he gets a negative value of *REI*. I feel the recovery effort index should be positive ranging from 0 to 100, and if the index is low then it should not be due to the source of the material it recovers. The conversion of imported scrap also constitutes a recovery operation, and should augment the index rather than detract from it. It may be interesting to calculate an index on the lines of Dr. Pearce, but slightly modified, as follows:

$$(REI)_2 = \frac{SP + DUS + X_s + M_s}{C}$$

using the same notation as in the original paper. The only difference between *REI* and $(REI)_2$ being that imports enter positively in the latter while negatively in the former.

After talking of *REI* and $(REI)_2$, and without wanting to cloud the picture further, I would like to propose a third index to measure recycling effort which I feel may have some merit. The index which I call Recovery Index (*RI*) for year *i* is defined as follows:

$$RI = \frac{\text{Material Recovered from Scrap for Year } i}{\text{Total Consumption of the Material for Year } i}$$

The scrap used in the definition consists of old scrap as well as new scrap, a distinction already made by Dr. Pearce. There may be problems of time lag, but when these quantities are considered over a number of time periods, material balance questions will even out. The index focuses on the consumption side for a country, and indicates what fraction of the material consumed comes from recycled sources; consequently, the complement of the index indicates what fraction of the material used comes from virgin sources.

To illustrate the new index, I have calculated it for aluminum and lead. The source of the data for the analysis is the same as Dr. Pearce's *Metal Statistics,* published by Metallgesellschaft, 61st edition.

Table 15-1 shows for 1963–1973, the aluminum Recovery Index for the six countries under study. Table 15-2 ranks the recovery efforts for aluminum for these countries for the same period. The last two columns in this table shows the overall ranking for the entire period by the index I have proposed, and the overall ranking as obtained by Dr. Pearce. Without getting into details, the major difference arises in the case of Italy, which is 5 on *REI* and 1 on the *RI* scale. Other rankings remain relatively the same except for Japan, which goes from 2 to 4. The most dramatic change is in the case of Italy, which I feel was given the short end of the stick as it were, by REI, because it imports a lot of scrap and then recycles it.

Table 15-1   Recovery Index for Aluminum 1963–1973

	63	64	65	66	67	68	69	70	71	72	73
U.K.	31.7	32.1	33.7	34.1	33.6	32.5	35.1	33.4	35.4	30.3	27.5
Italy	34.6	32.6	31.2	33.7	36.3	31.6	33.5	36.7	37.3	35.8	36.1
Japan	28.7	29.5	30.6	27.9	28.8	27.8	27.2	27.1	27.8	27.2	28.1
U.S.A.	20.4	21.1	21.4	20.3	20.8	20.6	23.5	21.2	20.3	19.8	20.4
W. Germany	35.9	35.2	36.3	33.0	31.6	31.0	30.9	18.0	30.0	30.3	28.8
France	17.2	16.3	16.2	16.7	16.7	19.0	19.4	17.8	20.6	21.9	21.5

Table 15-3 ranks the six countries considered in the study for the years 1963–1973 with respect to their recycling efforts in lead. There are no major changes in the rankings here, although some change in relative standings take place. The countries that are ranked in the top half on their recycling efforts in lead by *REI* continues to be ranked in the top half by the *RI* scale.

Before much is made of these relative standings, I must enter the same caveat as Dr. Pearce, namely some of the published data is highly suspicious, and any calculations based on them must be interpreted with caution. I present these alternative sets of calculations, in order to raise issues, stimulate discussion, and certainly not as final answers.

Table 15-2   Ranking on the Basis of Recovery Index for Aluminum[a,b]

	63	64	65	66	67	68	69	70	71	72	73	A[c]	B[d]
U.K.	3	3	2	1	2	1	1	2	2	2	4	2	1
Italy	2	2	3	2	1	2	2	1	1	1	1	1	5
Japan	4	4	4	4	4	4	4	3	4	4	3	4	2
U.S.A.	5	5	5	5	5	5	5	4	5	6	6	5	4
W. Germany	1	1	1	3	3	3	3	5	3	2	2	3	3
France	6	6	6	6	6	6	6	6	6	5	5	6	6

[a] Recovery Index $= \dfrac{\text{Material Recovered from Scrap for Year } i}{\text{Total Consumption of the Material for Year } i}$

[b] Source: Metallgesgesellschaft, *Metal Statistics* 1963–1973, 61st ed., Frankfurt am Main, 1974.

[c] A Overall ranking on the basis of recovery index.

[d] B Pearce's ranking.

Table 15-3   Ranking on the Basis of Recovery Index for Lead[a,b]

	63	64	65	66	67	68	69	70	71	72	73	A[c]	B[d]
U.K.	4	4	5	3	2	3	3	3	6	4	4	3	1
Italy	3	3	4	4	5	5	6	6	3	3	2	4	6
Japan	1	2	2	2	3	2	2	2	2	2	3	2	3
U.S.A.	2	1	1	1	1	1	1	1	1	1	1	1	2
W. Germany	6	6	6	6	6	6	4	5	5	6	6	6	5
France	5	5	3	5	4	4	5	4	4	5	5	5	3

[a] See Table 15-2[a].
[b] See Table 15-2[b].
[c] See Table 15-2[c].
[d] See Table 15-2[d].

Let me now move on to another topic that is raised in the paper, namely the intercountry variations in the recycling effort. Dr. Pearce cautions us that the analysis he has presented is only preliminary. I would like to add a few more cautions. Attempts to explain the intercountry variation must be made in the context of a larger econometric model or in the framework of the country's industrial structure. The attempt to explain the variation by examining the effect of one factor while the other factors vary can as is well known, lead to very misleading conclusions. The recovery effort may not be related simply to the price of the primary source of the material, but the level of technology present in the country. So the analysis of factors taken one at a time without allowing for the variation in the other factors is highly dubious, and I am not quite sure whether we can say, from the analysis presented, that the amount of recycling effort in a country is a function of the national attitude to waste. Is the national attitude to waste a function of the Puritan ethic, Calvinism, Shintoism, or Maoism? From reports I have read, China is the world's most recycled economy. Did Max Weber have the last word? Is the attitude to waste a function of the structure of a country's economy, its level of technology, its balance of payments, and other economic factors? I think this is still an open question.